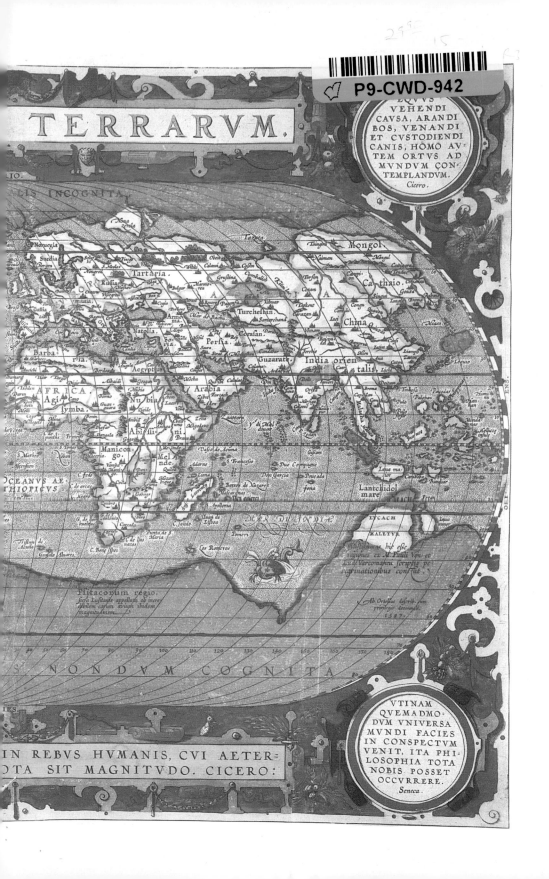

Marco Polo and the Discovery of the World

Marco Polo

and the
Discovery of the World

John Larner

Yale University Press
New Haven and London

Designed by Adam Freudenheim

Set in Ehrhardt by Best-set Typesetter Ltd., Hong Kong
Printed and bound in Hong Kong through World Print Ltd

Library of Congress Cataloging-in-Publication Data

Larner, John, 1930–
    Marco Polo and the discovery of the world / by John Larner.
      p. cm.
    Includes bibliographical references and index.
    ISBN 0–300–07971–0 (cloth: alk. paper)
     1. Polo, Marco, 1254-1323? Travels of Marco Polo.   2. Voyages and travels.
3. Travel, Medieval.   4. Asia – Description and travel
Early works to 1800.   I. Title.
G370.P9L27   1999
915.04′2 – dc21

                                                    99-24887
                                                     CIP

A catalogue record from this book is available from the British Library.

10 9 8 7 6 5 4 3 2 1

For Jane

Contents

Illustrations

Maps

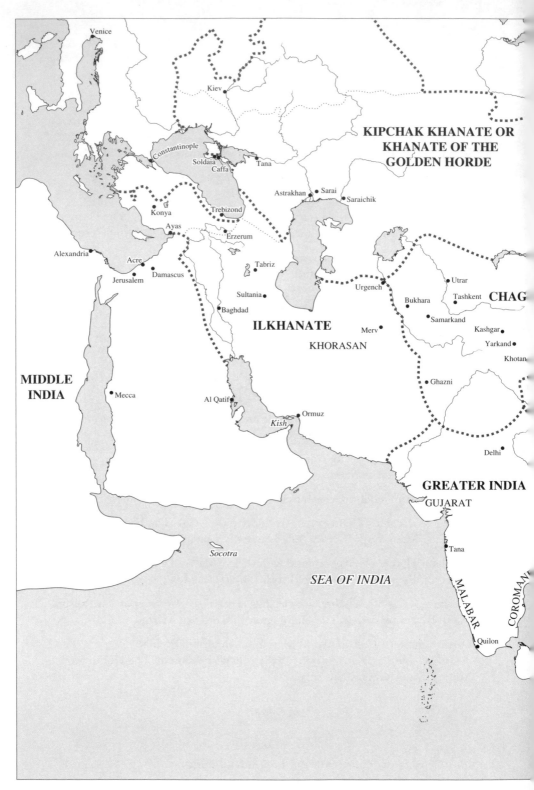

Marco Polo's Asia

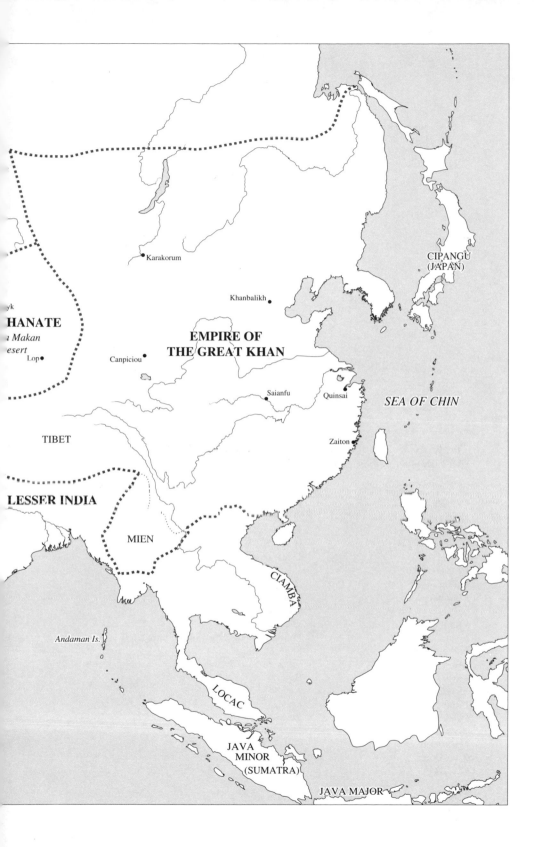

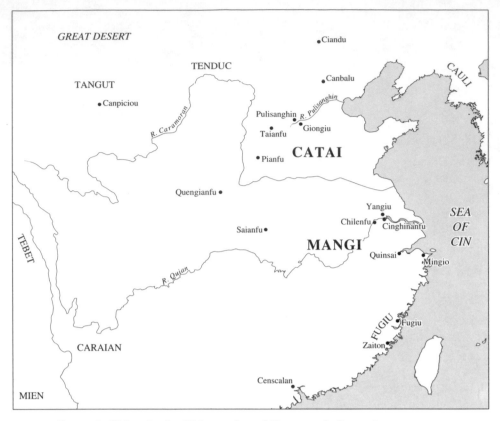

Europe's China in the Thirteenth and Fourteenth Centuries
(All European names, apart from Censcalan, from F text of Marco Polo)

European Name	Chinese and/or other names
Canbalu	Beijing, Peking, (Mongol – Khanbalikh)
Canpiciou	Zhangye
Caraian	Yunnan province
River Caramoran	Huang He, Yellow River
Catai	Cathay, northern China
Cauli	Korea
Censcalan	Guangzhou, Canton
Chilenfu	Nanjing
Ciandu	Shandu, Xanadu
Cinghinanfu	Zhenjiang
Fugiu	Fujian (province), Fuzhou in Fujian (city)
Giongiu	Shijiazhuang
Mangi	the southern provinces
Mien	Burma
Mingio	Ningbo
Pianfu	Linfen
Pulisanghin	Zhengdin
River Pulisanghin	Hong He
Quengianfu	Xian
River Quian	Jiang, Yanji, Yangtze
Quinsai	Hangzhou
Saianfu	Xiangyang
Taianfu	Taiyuan
Yangiu	Yangzhou
Zaiton	Quanzhou

Preface

Although I have not always followed their recommendations and must, of course, exempt them from any responsibility for errors in the text, I am particularly indebted to the advice offered by two Oxford scholars who have read this book in typescript: George Holmes, formerly Chichele Professor in History, and John R. Woodhouse, Fiat-Serena Professor of Italian. In particular I must thank John Woodhouse who, with unstinting generosity of time and energy, has commented on it in detail, offering literally hundreds of points for further thought.

I must also thank Adam Freudenheim, my editor at Yale University Press, for helpful suggestions, and Tu Zheung Hua who has conveyed the substance of some Chinese studies to me. My friend and former pupil, Aziz Boukenna, has introduced me to many insights of Arabic geographers of the Middle Ages which have served for comparative purposes. Michael Clanchy and John Davey have both given good advice; Mrs Pam Nye, most efficient of secretaries, has been an ever-dependable support.

In rendering place names from Asian languages I normally give Chinese names in Pinyin; for other tongues I use, with the omission of some accents, those transliterations most commonly employed today by English-speaking scholars. But, quite often, when a common form has long been established, and it might have been confusing to the reader to abandon it, I have stayed with that.

Introduction

Marco Polo is one of those comparatively few people from the thirteenth and fourteenth centuries of whom everyone today has heard. Yet his popular fame mirrors very little of his importance in history. His name has come to stand above all for prosperous East-West contact and sophisticated travel, giving rise to such curious phenomena as 'Marco Polo Class' (i.e. luxury class) on one Asian airline, the 'Marco Polo Leisure Suitcase' (made in Taiwan) which I once came across in Woolworths, or the 'Polo' car marketed by Volkswagen. It is not simply that for anyone who has looked at the first pages of his Book, the idea of luxury travel, leisure, or an easy ride strikes at once an incongruous note, it is rather that this image significantly ignores his true achievement. For what is most important about Marco Polo is not that he visited the Far East; many merchants and missionaries of the later Middle Ages did that. It is that, in writing about what he had found there, he produced one of the most influential books of the Middle Ages.

That this plays little part in the common perception of its author, however, is not altogether surprising. The originality of his Book in its own day is not in question. What it offered to readers of the time was a portrait of a world which south of the Pamir, east of Badakhshan and Karakorum, was wholly new. Above all it told of the amazing empire of the Great Khan, of the provinces of China, of an urban civilisation of dazzling riches and prosperity, and then again of the countries surrounding the Indian Ocean, the source of those 'spices' and other precious goods sought so avidly in that period by western merchants. It is no exaggeration to say that never before or since has one man given such an immense body of new geographical knowledge to the West. For this he could justly be thought of as foremost in creating that intellectual climate in which European exploration of the non-European world developed. Yet, against this, very many scholars have discounted any importance which the Book may have had. This on the supposed grounds that in the Middle Ages and Renaissance it was never believed; that it was held to be a romance or fable, and so never enjoyed any general credence. Typically, Leonardo Olschki, one of the most learned and persuasive Polo scholars of the twentieth century, writes of 'the small influence of his book on geographical and cosmo-graphical authors of the late Middle Ages', while S. E. Morison, the great historian of Columbus, in his round dismissive way, asserts that 'most learned men at that era regarded The Book of Ser Marco Polo as pure fiction'. Similar verdicts abound: its 'contents seemed incredible'; its material 'was long frozen in the limbo of fables'; it was a work 'downgraded to the genre of literary marvels'; it was 'chimerical in the eyes of the prudent geographers of Lisbon'; it 'never gained credibility among its readers'. These, it is true, are not the only judgments, but they are those of the clear majority of commentators on the Book and they could easily be replicated at some length. Having cited several examples of medieval and sixteenth-century writers who ignored Marco, the Swedish historian, A. E. Nordenskiöld, very erudite in this field, remarked that he could have given 'innumerable' other examples testifying to the slight value the learned attached to his work. (However, he added an unfamiliar twist: 'But with the unlearned public the case was different. It accepted Marco Polo's descriptions, and in most cases quite justly as revelations from a new world'.)[1]

It was a series of doubts, growing from a long time back, about that com-monplace – in particular queries prompted by my reading of historians of cartography, who did not normally go along with it – which first persuaded me that there was room for a further study of Marco Polo. It is this theme – what was generally believed about the geography of the world and the changes that Marco's Book brought to those beliefs – that is a principal object of my enquiries here. In order to mark a base-line from which Marco's own contribution might be assessed, I have first presented a sketch (a brief epitome of material which others could easily expand to book-length) of what was known or believed about Asia in western Europe before Marco's birth. To this is joined a short account of the creation of the Mongol Empire, the Empire which made possible the first journey of the Polos to China, and a consideration of the European travel literature to which that gave rise. Chapters 3–5 discuss Marco and the composition of the Book. After which chapters 6–10 address the issue of the reception of the Book. Here are reviewed the manuscript forms and translations in which it appeared, and learned and unlearned reactions to it. These are examined, as they appeared, first in Marco's lifetime, and then during the course of the rest of the fourteenth century, at a time, that is, when there was quite extensive western missionary and merchant penetration into Asia, and when some other Europeans were drawn to write of the East. The story is continued into the fifteenth century when western penetration had almost wholly ceased but when the current intellectual vogue of Humanism brought a new and particularly valuable stimulus to the study of geography and map-making. I have then looked at the use of the Book in the age of Columbus, and finally in the centuries which followed when it came to be seen in a new guise, as an exotic curiosity or an object of historical scholarship rather than an inspiration to the traveller or geographer.

In the course of my reading I was struck over and over again by the way in which in recent years scholars' attempts to depict Marco had ended in a whole series of questions, such as: Who is the man? What is his book? Is it *his* book? What is its title? What is it about? How was it written? Is it a fraud? On these themes many interesting and important publications have recently appeared. I think particularly of those by Li Tse-fen, Jacques Heers, Umberto Tucci, John Critchley, Christiane Deluz, Syed Manzurul Islam, Frances Wood, Barbara Wehr, Folker Reichert, John W. Haeger and Juan Gil. From all of these authors, even on those occasions when I have presumed to disagree with them, I have learnt a lot. Yet many of their writings have been published in monographs directed exclusively to specialists, many were not yet available in English, and several of their conclusions (which from time to time were in marked conflict with each other) seemed to deserve reconsideration. Accordingly it seemed to me that there was a place today for a study which would re-examine those issues which they have addressed in order to present a general portrait of Marco Polo and his Book.

That so many basic questions have been asked about the Book is in part related to certain key aspects to be considered in any examination of it. Though I write of these from time to time in the body of this work, and discuss them again in Appendix I, it may be helpful to the reader to say something briefly about them at this juncture. As virtually all scholars, and I myself, believe, the Book was first composed in prison in Genoa, the fruit of a cooperation between Marco and a fellow-prisoner, a man who had experience of writing chivalric-epic prose stories, called Rustichello da Pisa. Inevitably, then, we are faced with such speculations as: What was the nature of their partnership? What compromises have gone into their joint work? How much of what we have from them represents Marco's thought, how much Rustichello's attempts to adapt what was for the thirteenth century very strange material for the benefit of a European readership? In addition to the problems raised by this relationship, there are others, often present when studying other types of medieval writing but noticeably prominent here. In particular that one is sometimes uncertain whether to speak of 'the Book' or 'the Books'. The autograph begun in Genoa does not survive, and of the texts of some hundred-and-fifty manuscripts that remain it has been said that no two are exactly the same. Quite apart from any of the normal, involuntary mistakes made in copying, the differences between them are sometimes to be explained by the privilege claimed now and again by clerks in a manuscript culture of making their own improvements (additions and omissions) to what they transcribed. This urge to correct and improve the text, often of course wildly mistaken, is most noticeable and leads to very sharp differences between versions where translations are concerned. In the case of Marco's Book there are two notable examples: when a friar translates from a Romance language into Latin for the benefit of a mainly clerical and learned audience; and when an Irishman decides that his translation into Gaelic from this very same Latin text requires an immense amount of jazzing-up to reach a wide readership.[2]

But the differences go beyond that. For aside from any disparities which came about through this sort of thing, the surviving manuscripts fall into two main groups. Those in the first (A) ultimately all go back to a text known as 'F' which seems to be the earliest and closest to that which was composed in prison. The second (B) is composed of very few pieces, though among them there is often much fuller material than in the A group. Some scholars try to reconstitute the substance of Marco and Rustichello's original lost manuscript simply by putting together the material found in the two groups. For others there are virtually two versions of the Book. The first, 'A', is that begun in prison in 1298. The second, 'B', is a rewriting of the A text which includes many additions, clarifications, sometimes omissions, which was produced some time after Marco's return from Genoa to Venice. In this view 'B' is a restatement which is directed perhaps to a more private and restricted readership. Whatever may be concluded about this, it will be seen that in discussion of the Book it is quite often necessary to know which manuscript is being referred to. Throughout this work I normally cite the F text, the closest to the prison-original (what in modern terms one might think of as the first edition). I have rendered this in a very literal translation in an attempt to give the true flavour of the original. But I frequently allude to other manuscripts; I have set out the most common editions of these, and the short forms in which I refer to them, in the note following this introduction.

In all of this my purpose is first (in chapters 2–3) to review what can be known about Marco and his family, seen within the context of Venetian merchant culture, and then to examine the controversies surrounding his life in the East – notably here the argument, first advanced in the eighteenth century but recently revived, that the Book is a fake and its author a liar, that neither Marco nor his relatives ever visited China. I go on to examine the circumstances in which the Book was composed and the nature of the cooperation between Marco and Rustichello. I look, in particular, at the contention lately advanced that the whole story of Marco's imprisonment in Genoa and cooperation with Rustichello is a myth. After which chapters 4–5 are devoted to considering interpretations of the nature of the Book. Is it basically a merchant's handbook? Or directed by a religious purpose? Or a book of wonders (and here we have to examine what created a sense of wonder in the Middle Ages)? Or simply a work of geography? In what tradition was it written, and on what sources, apart from personal experience, is it dependent? Is it an early example of a profoundly hostile and distorting European 'Orientalism' in its treatment of eastern peoples and non-Christian religions?

This study, it will be seen, is not a work about Asia as such. I am not qualified to write, in the manner, for example, of those brilliant scholars, Henry Yule and Leonardo Olschki, any commentary offering specialised knowledge on the history, flora, fauna, local practices or ethnography of the lands which Marco's Book discusses. My primary aims are simply to portray the way in which the Book came into being, the author's purpose in writing it, and its fortunes in succeeding years. At the same time the personality of Marco Polo has always been at the back of my mind, and I wish to convey something of that too, if only indirectly. One writes this conscious of the doubts it will arouse. Coming from a city which, at least in its early days, notoriously discouraged any cults of personality, Marco, as it happened, found as coadjutor an author who specialised in an epic-prose literature which was also marked by a profound absence of any individualisation. Yet Marco's very silences about himself are eloquent and, between those silences and what he does say, something of his character, his sympathies, integrity and generosity of mind, do, I believe, appear.

Note on Citation of Texts

For an introduction to the texts, see Appendix I, 'A Note on Manuscripts of the Book'. Unless otherwise stated I cite passages in Marco's Book by the chapter and, where appropriate, line numbers within chapters of the F text, as published in *Milione. Le Divisament dou monde*, ed. G. Ronchi (Milan, 1982). This brings some corrections to the text of *Il Milione*, ed. L. Foscolo Benedetto (Florence, 1928), whose valuable introduction (reprinted as *La tradizione manoscritta del 'Milione' di Marco Polo* [Turin, 1962]) I cite as 'Foscolo Benedetto'. The F text forms part of the A group of manuscripts. The other principal editions referred to are:

IN THE A GROUP

Bertolucci Pizzorusso

Milione. Versione toscana del Trecento, ed. V. Bertolucci Pizzorusso (Milan, 1975).

Pauthier

Le Livre de Marco Polo citoyen de Venise, conseiller privé et commissaire impérial de Khoubilai-Khaân, ed. M. G. Pauthier (Paris, 1865), an edition of a manuscript in Northern French, B4. Notes valuable for use of Chinese sources.

Pipino

I refer to Fra Pipino's early fourteenth-century Latin version by book and chapter. A manuscript of this version was published as *Marka Pavlova z Benátek, Milion*, ed. J. V. Prásek (Prague, 1902).

Yule-Cordier

The Book of Ser Marco Polo the Venetian, ed. H. Yule, 3rd edn., revised by H. Cordier (London, 1903). Reprinted in two volumes (New York, 1993). A translation into English of Pauthier's text, with some additions from Ramusio (see below). Still vital for its commentary.

IN THE B GROUP

Moule-Pelliot, vol. 2

The Description of the World, ed. A. C. Moule and P. Pelliot (London, 1938), vol. 2. An edition of the Z text.

Ramusio

G. B. Ramusio, *Navigazioni e viaggi*, ed. M. Milanesi, vol. 3 (Turin, 1980). This contains a sixteenth-century translation into Italian, based on the Z text or some manuscript close to it, together with other materials. The first edition of Venice, 1559, has been reprinted in facsimile (Amsterdam, 1968). I give my own translations.

UNITING THE A AND B GROUPS

Moule–Pelliot, vol. 1   *The Description of the World*, ed. A. C. Moule and P. Pelliot (London, 1938), vol. 1, an English translation of the F text and of passages which are not in the F text but which are found in one or more of another seventeen texts.

Chapter 1

Images of Asia and the Coming of the Mongols

I

In the century in which Marco Polo was born the peoples of western Europe had a vision of the East which was formed from theological learning, classical memories and their own vivid dreams.[1] In order to assess those changes to knowledge which his book was to bring we must begin by summarising the elements of that image of the Orient: the curious miscellany of information where biblical knowledge and stories of the mission of St Thomas the Apostle to India mingled with legends of Alexander's conquests and tales of the stupendously powerful Prester John. Then we must turn to the first transformation of those elements which came with the creation of the Mongol Empire. We must consider the tales told by European legates and missionaries who first visited the Mongols in their heartland and the later development of relations between the Mongols and the West, that development which created the conditions in which the Polos were able to travel to the Far East.

In its simplest form, early medieval understanding of the geography of the earth is found in the so-called TO maps (see Illustration 2). Within the O or circle representing the world, Asia, largest of the three continents, fills the upper semicircle. Below is a T whose arms are formed by schematic representations of the Don and the Nile, and whose upright is the Mediterranean, dividing Africa to the right from Europe to the left. In the *mappaemundi* or world-maps of the age that basic pattern is amplified. At the very centre of the O (following the Book of Ezekiel 5:5: 'I have set her in the midst of the nations') is Jerusalem (as in the world map of Pietro Visconte, see Illustration 6). At the top, in the Far East (see Illustration 3), is the Earthly Paradise, ringed by fire, within which Adam and Eve eat the apple. Following Genesis (2: 10–14), this was the source of four great rivers, sometimes visible, but sometimes meandering underground for many hundreds of miles before re-emerging: the Pishon (identified with the Indus, the Ganges and at times even the Danube), the Gihon or Nile, the Hiddeckel or Tigris, and finally the Euphrates. As in the map in Hereford

Cathedral, the image of the East might also take in such scenes as Abraham at Ur of the Chaldees, the resting place of Noah's Ark, the Tower of Babel, Lot's Wife, Joseph's Granary and the track of the Israelites from Egypt to the Holy Land. Here too might be seen the Magi, following a star to the new-born Christ (only slowly was the western Church transforming them into three kings, representing the three known continents).

Asia, itself very often called simply 'India', was frequently subdivided into three parts, sometimes 'Lower', 'Middle' and 'Upper India', sometimes 'Lesser', 'First', 'Greater India', and so on. These terms signified different things to different authors, but normally comprised first Egypt with the Ethiopian Kingdom, second lands to the east including today's subcontinent of India, imagined then as projecting hardly at all into the Indian Ocean but with the vast island of 'Taprabona' lying off it, and finally 'the lands beyond the Ganges' (in which from the fourteenth century China came to be included).[2] Each of these had its apostle: St Matthew in Ethiopia, St Bartholomew in 'the third India',[3] and, most celebrated, St Thomas in India proper. Towards the end of the ninth century King Alfred from distant England had dispatched alms to the supposed shrines of Bartholomew and Thomas,[4] while the apocryphal Latin versions of Thomas's *Acts* and *Passion*, telling of how, before his martyrdom, the architect-saint had built a palace for the Indian King Gundoforus, enjoyed great popularity (surviving in over a hundred manuscripts from before 1200).[5]

Secular literature too played its part in this geography. From the classics men remembered the Seres or Chinese making silk garments, while of particular importance were the legends which proliferated around Alexander's conquest of India in the fourth century BC.[6] These told of his wars against Darius of Persia and Porus of India, and 'the mightiest mountains in the world' he had found there. They describe how he had enclosed Gog and Magog behind Iron Gates set in a great wall of bronze across the Caucasus. This pair were sometimes portrayed as two great giants, sometimes identified with the Ten Lost Tribes of Israel, who would, it was said, at the coming of the Last Days, break from their confinement to bring destruction to the world.[7] Other stories spoke of Alexander's visit to the frontiers of the Terrestrial Paradise, of his correspondence with Didimus the Brahmin,[8] where the conquered Indian is made to draw a contrast between on the one side, riches and power, on the other, naked asceticism, community of goods and pacifism. Immensely popular were stories of the Amazons and all the progeny of the monstrous races that Alexander had encountered – Cynocephali or dog-headed men; the Blemmyae with faces on their breasts; Sciopods, with only one leg, yet running with amazing swiftness, and who, at rest, used their vast foot as a sunshade; 'The Anthropophagi, and men whose heads / Do grow beneath their shoulders', and so on.[9] Together with the monstrous races were found strange beasts: camels and elephants (these occasionally found in western royal menageries), unicorns, griffins, the rhinoceros, mantikhoras with the body of a lion and the face of a man, crocodiles, dragons, serpents with two feet.

This material was copied in hundreds of manuscripts in languages from all over (and from outside) Europe. In the twelfth century the West's vision of Asia as a land of glorious otherness was enlarged first by 'the visit of the Patriarch John' and then by the legend of Prester John. In 1122 a man claiming to be the Patriarch John of India arrived at Rome, seeking papal confirmation of his office. We are faced here perhaps with no more than some confidence-trickster, skilfully playing upon papal hopes with an imaginative and enterprising imposture. Both Odo, abbot of St Rémi of Rheims, and an anonymous independent account (surviving in eleven manuscripts) describe with reverential awe the lecture on India he gave before the papal curia in which he describes the huge city of Hulna, built on the river Phison and inhabited by devout Christians, and outside the city the twelve monasteries erected in honour of the twelve apostles and the Great Church of St Thomas, visited by all the Christians of Asia on his feast-day.[10] This tale of powerful Christian communities in the East was echoed and reinforced some twenty-three years later. In 1145 Otto of Freising wrote of how, at the court of Pope Eugenius III, he had met a bishop from Syria who had told him that recently a certain John, king and priest, a Nestorian Christian, descended from the line of the Magi ruling beyond Persia, had defeated the Medes and Persians in battle. He had been prevented from advancing further to bring aid to the Christians of the Holy Land only due to the difficulties of ferrying his army across the Tigris.[11] On the basis of tales such as these, combined with the romances of Alexander and the stories about St Thomas, a talented anonymous writer, some time before 1180, concocted the richly imaginative *Letter of Prester John*.[12] Ostensibly directed to the Emperor Manuel Comnenus, it is a work that survives in over one hundred and twenty manuscripts in many languages, and was to enjoy an immense success in the late Middle Ages.

In the letter John announces that he is a Christian king and priest who proposes to visit the Sepulchre of Christ. He rules over the three Indias and has under his authority sixty-two Christian and many other kings, together with a patriarch archbishop, and many bishops. He describes the magnificence of his palace, 'built in the style of the one which St Thomas designed for King Gundoforus', and of the solemn feasts with which he entertains his peoples. He writes of the prosperity of his realm, where milk and honey flow, of the river Phison in which, since it comes from Paradise, all manner of precious stones are found. He tells of its salamanders, of the fountains of youth which abound, and how no serpent or reptile can live there. In his city there is no perjurer, no counterfeiter, no fornicator or adulterer. Thousands of people at court, together with all pilgrims are fed and accommodated at his expense. He can put into the field 10,000 knights, the same number of sergeants and a 1,000 cross-bow men. The land abounds in gold and silver, corn, wine, myrrh, incense and silk. Doctors are unnecessary, since the region's precious stones, fountains and trees possess all the virtues necessary against wounds and poison. So it goes on. 'There is no king as powerful in this world as am I.' The original text was progressively expanded by copyists anxious to enliven the material still further. English manuscripts tell of how 11,000 Englishmen were to be found at his court, all knighted by him on arrival, while French versions tell of the presence of 11,000 French knights. Others add all the traditional material of Asian lore: Amazons, Brahmins, Gog and Magog, the Ten Lost Tribes and others.

Without reaching any generally accepted conclusions, historians have asked how the letter should be read. Leonardo Olschki has interpreted it as the representation of an ideal theocratic Utopia.[13] Bernard Hamilton takes it to be a forgery produced at the court of the Emperor Frederick I, designed to show the splendours of a world in which clerics are in just subordination to righteous rulers.[14] It may be so; or it may be simply a poetic wish-fulfilling dream which enticed contemporaries through its rich exotic surfaces, the concoction of some goliard scholar amusing his friends with a vision of the Land of Cockaigne. Whatever the answer – beyond all the details which might be doubted – the popularity of the letter left in most people's minds the quite false conviction that somewhere in the East there was indeed a most powerful Christian ruler who could be seen as an ally in the struggle against the Muslim world. Tales of Prester John, of 'many Christian kings living in the Orient', of John's son, King David, were still to be rousing illusory hopes at the time of Columbus and beyond.

II

While in the twelfth century the West's understanding of Asia was expressed in these fantasies, the religion and commerce of Islam were flour-ishing as realities throughout that continent. In which circumstances, it may be briefly enquired first what geographical knowledge of the continent was to be found at the time in the writings of Arab scholars in lands close to Christian realms, that is to say in the Middle East, the Maghreb and

Spain. Second, to what extent was any such information transmitted to the West to check or modify current beliefs. In neither case can one give any very positive responses. Among Arab geographers of the ninth century can be found some notices of India, the East Indies and even China (it was a time when there were, though briefly, regular direct sailings to Canton from the Persian Gulf).[15] Notably, in his *Amusement for Him who Desires to Travel Round the World*, completed in 1153–4, the celebrated North-African scholar, al-Idrisi, gives some information on India and South-East Asia.[16] Yet what he writes is confused and confusing, for the work is structured not on countries but on the various *climates* of Ptolemaic theory. Looking forward to the turn of the thirteenth and fourteenth centuries, the work of Abulfeda contains material from earlier geographers, together with a rather small amount of contemporary knowledge. This was a time when the so-called Karimi merchants of Cairo were conducting an extensive trade with, in particular, India and the Spice Islands.[17] Yet their knowledge seems to be very slightly drawn upon in his account. And of China, where Egyptian merchants were to be found, though not in great numbers, Abulfeda offers very little:

> Writers on the customs and kingdoms of the world have in their works mentioned many provinces and places and rivers as existing in China under the different climates, but the names have not reached us with any exactness, nor have we any certain information as to their circumstances. Thus they are as good as unknown to us; there being few travellers who arrive from these parts, such as might furnish us with intelligence, and for this reason we forbear to detail them.[18]

He continues by offering twelve place names, with a grudging, perhaps sceptical, reference to his source as 'the accounts of merchants who have travelled in those parts'. One is tempted to conclude that this is one of those scholastic works – we shall find examples later in the West – which drew upon and trusted books rather than experience.

As it was, Europe learnt nothing of this Arabic knowledge. During the twelfth century western scholars acquired a large measure of Arabic scientific learning but, for reasons which have not yet been fully clarified, they largely ignored what related to geography. From Ptolemy's works in Arab translation, they turned into Latin the *Almagest* on the shape of the heavens and the *Quadripartitum* on astrology. But though it was a work which had been read in the Islamic world from the eighth century, they showed no interest either in the *Geography*, or in any other Greek or Arabic geographical studies. Exceptionally, al-Sharif al-Idrisi had written his *Amusement* at the court of Roger II, King of Sicily. But it seems likely that he had been called to Palermo rather for the political importance of his high blood (*al-Sharif*) than for his learning.[19] Certainly his book remained untranslated until the seventeenth century (and even then was published in abbreviated form and anonymously). It was never to have any influence on European geography during the Middle Ages. In the same way, though European Jews were sometimes aware of their co-religionists in Islamic lands who traded occasionally with India and beyond,[20] their information gained no general currency. In particular Christian Europe ignored the work of the Spanish Jew, Benjamin of Tudela. Between 1166 and 1171 Benjamin had travelled from Tudela (on the Ebro in Aragon) through Italy, Greece and Palestine, to Damascus, Baghdad and Egypt. From the island of Kish (Jazireh-ye-Qeys) in the Persian Gulf, at that time a great staging point for trade into the Indian Ocean – and probably the furthest east to which he travelled – Benjamin sailed to Al Qatif in Bahrain. From here, he was told, it took seven days to sail to the port of Quilon on the Malabar coast (in the Middle Ages a very important point of encounter between the Arabian Sea and the Bay of Bengal), from Quilon a twenty-three day journey to 'Ibrig' (Ceylon? . . . but if so, it seems far too long), and from Ibrig to Zin (China) a voyage of forty days. These observations are not easy to interpret, but they give the book which he wrote on his travels the distinction of being the first work of the Middle Ages, written in Europe, to mention either China or a route by which it might be visited.[21]

III

Yet it was a book not read by Christians. For the moment all that was generally known in the West of the East were such myths and hopes as were aroused by Prester John. Behind these hopes lay in fact, however blurred and grossly magnified, a reality. In the early Christian centuries subtle enquiries into the nature of the Godhead had produced in the East two particular interpretations of the person of Christ which were condemned as heretical by the Greek and Latin Churches. The first of these was the doctrine of the Monophysites who held that in Christ there was one person, one hypostasis (a word variously interpreted but perhaps meaning 'reality') and – in this lay its difference from Catholicism – one, wholly divine, nature. Adherents of this view were gathered in the three 'Jacobite' Churches, that is to say the Churches of the Copts, the Abyssinians and the Armenians.

In much greater numbers were the Dyophysites or Nestorians. In the fifth century, Nestorius, the Greek Patriarch of Constantinople, had been anathematised and condemned because he preached the doctrine that within Christ there was one person, two natures, but *two* hypostases. Theologians today still debate whether this might imply an 'heretical' overemphasis upon the Divinity's two natures rather than his one person. For our purposes it is sufficient to note that in the Middle East the unrepentant followers of St Nestorius – as he was known to them – followed doctrines at variance with those of the Greek and Latin Churches, and employed a liturgy in the Syriac tongue.[22] With their patriarchate established at Baghdad, Nestorian churches were prominent in Syria, Asia Minor, Iraq and Persia. In the early medieval centuries, in competition with Manichees, Buddhists and then Muslims, they pursued an intense activity of proselytism within Asia. It was the Nestorians in reality, and not St Thomas, who had first brought Christianity to India. By the eighth century there were Nestorian Christians in Turkestan and China while, among the nomadic tribesmen of Mongolia, the Kerait and Ongut could, had they wished, enjoy Christological debates with the Jacobite Uighurs, each denouncing their opponents as heretics doomed to be excluded from salvation.[23] Along the caravan routes of Asia news of the fortunes of their brothers in Christ no doubt circulated back to the Nestorian churches of the Middle East. It was perhaps the victories in 1141 of one Yeh-la Ta-shih, ruler of the partially Christianised Khitans, over the Muslim sovereign of Khwarezm and the Seljuk Sultan Sanjar that had first given rise to those rumours of 'John, King and Priest' which Otto of Freising was to hear at the Roman court five years later.

However this may be, in the course of the next century the existence of the Nestorian and other Christian Churches in the East were to provoke great, illusory, expectations.[24] These are to be seen in the context of a period in which the Roman Popes had entered on a policy of actively seeking some form of overlordship over the known world. In the north crusades were launched which by fire, sword and compulsory baptism were ultimately to bring Livs, Letts, Estonians, Prussians and Finns under their spiritual authority. In the Mediterranean the Crusade of 1202–4, originally designed to attack Muslim Egypt, was diverted against the Byzantine Empire which professed the Greek Orthodox faith. Although the Papacy was not directly responsible for the attack, it welcomed the result: the establishment of a Latin empire controlling most of the European provinces formerly under Greek authority. Only in the Holy Land had the cause suffered a setback. Here, from the failure of the Third Crusade in 1192, Jerusalem was (save for the brief period 1229–44) lost, and Latin control was confined to the Principality of Antioch, the County of Tripoli and a narrow coastal strip of the former Kingdom of Jerusalem. Yet even here the effects of Muslim successes were to throw the Latin settlers, more than in the past, into dependence upon the Papacy.

In the same period the spiritual climate which had both fostered and was fostered by the expansion of the Papacy had brought about the foundation of new religious orders which, under the influence of St Dominic (d.1221) and St Francis (d.1226), sought the promulgation of Latin Christianity through a closer involvement in everyday life. Among their followers the missionary spirit burnt strongly. The Latin occupation of Constantinople allowed both Latin merchants and missionaries to penetrate into the Black Sea, to the Crimea in the north and to Trebizond in the south. In the vicinity of 'the Great Sea', as they spoke of it, and between Syria and Khorassan, they discovered more Christians, principally followers of the Orthodox Church: Russians, Georgians, the Goths of the Crimea, the Alans of the Caucasus. At the same time Dominican missionaries from the Latin Christian kingdom of Hungary began to proselytise the pagan nomadic Comans or 'Polovtsy' of the steppe-lands of southern Russia. In the 1230s, in their search for 'Greater Hungary', the heartlands from which, many centuries before, had come the peoples who had created the Hungarian Kingdom, the friars reached some 750 miles north of the Caspian.[25]

Yet it was less pagans than eastern Christians who caught the attention of the West. Their numbers, it was asserted, were enormous. The Nestorians and Jacobites alone, claimed Jacques de Vitry, Bishop of Tyre, exceeded the numbers of Latins and Greeks taken together, and within Muslim lands, apart from Egypt and Syria, far exceeded the number of Mohammedan believers.[26] Hence the rise of a great hope: if these people could be brought to acknowledge the supremacy of the Roman See, what vistas of Latin–Christian advance opened up, what spiritual, what worldly gains! Yet as it fell out, by the 1240s these hopes of new triumphs were to give way to new fears, and the first tentative Latin–Christian penetration into Asia beyond Palestine was overtaken by the creation of the Mongol Empire and the Mongol discovery of Europe. Some consideration of that discovery – which like most discoveries in history was extremely painful for the discovered – is a necessary preliminary to any consideration of the Book of Marco Polo. For it was that discovery which made possible the first visit of Marco's father and uncle to China and Marco's subsequent career as a servant of the Great Khan.

IV

At the end of the twelfth century, the Mongols were merely one among a variety of Turco–Mongolic nomadic tribes on the high plateau beyond the Altai Mountains.[27] In the years before 1209 these groups, till then continually at war with each other, were united by Temüchin, a minor princeling, henceforth to be known as Genghis Khan ('Very-mighty Lord'). Once established as leader, he directed his followers to the conquest of the outer world: to the east over the Tanguts of Gansu, and then those territories north of the Yellow River which were subject to the northern Chinese empire of Chin. After which, turning to the west, he gained the Kingdom of Kara-Khitai in eastern Turkestan and, with amazing impetus, the vast Khwarizmian Empire, which included Persia, Khorassan, Transoxonia, Samarkand and much of Afghanistan.

Genghis died in 1227. His successor Ögedei completed the conquest of the Chin Empire and of Korea and in the west established protector-ates over Georgia and the Turkish sultanate of Anatolia. In 1240 his army compelled the Russian principalities to submit to overlordship and occu-pied the steppe plains bordering the Black Sea. Other forces turned on eastern Europe, advanced through Poland and Silesia, and defeated the King of Hungary. Isolated detachments pushed forward to reach Dubrovnik and the Adriatic. At this point, for a variety of reasons but in particular as a result of the death of Ögedei in the spring of 1241, the leaders of the invasion withdrew to the Kipchak steppe. Both Ögedei's death and then that of his successor Güyük provoked severe internal conflicts, and it was only ten years later, with the emergence in 1251 of Möngke as the fourth Great Khan, that the Mongols turned again to expan-sion. In the meanwhile a rudimentary administrative system was estab-lished by the Uighur Turks (often touched by Buddhist and Nestorian Christian beliefs, and thus literate) and the Khitans (among whom was some Chinese influence) who had become part of the empire, and an impe-rial communication system was established – the *Yam* – whose relay posts allowed messengers of the Khans to travel at great speed from the Yellow Sea to the Black Sea.

In the West the first news of the Mongols reawakened hopeful fantasies. In November 1219, Jacques de Vitry, Bishop of Acre, was preaching that David, 'King of the two Indies', was leading ferocious peoples to assist the Christian warriors and 'eat up' the Saracen peoples.[28] When, in 1237, the Mongols first invaded Europe such illusions soon dissolved.[29] Thanks to the name of the 'Tatar' tribe among them (which had, in fact, been virtu-ally destroyed by Genghis Khan), they were, almost from the start, given the name of 'Tartars', as if they had arisen from *Tartarus*, the infernal regions. Whatever their origin, warned Fra Julian, a Dominican friar of Hungary, these peoples are seeking nothing less than the conquest of Rome and world dominion.[30]

Matthew Paris, monk of Saint Albans in England, gave his own account. Here were men with heads grossly disproportionate to their bodies, feeding on raw, even human, flesh, impious and inexorable.[31] From his chronicle one gains a picture of letters being dispatched all over Europe, scanned, copied, and passed on, for the fearful news they bear. Calling for a crusade against them, the Emperor Frederick II expresses the hope that they are not destined to destroy Christianity. But other letters say that it is Frederick who has called them into Europe. Where have these people, so long hidden, lain so long concealed? Are the Jews, seeing the Mongols as being of their own race, aiding them? Are they the descendants of the Magi Kings, seeking to recover the bones of their ancestors buried in Cologne?[32] The Tartar chief has asked the Prince of Antioch for a tribute which includes 3,000 virgins. A letter has been received by the Archbishop of Paris which says that they are the tribes of Gog and Magog, once imprisoned by Alexander the Great behind the Caspian Mountains, now, in the Last Days, due to devastate mankind.[33] Meanwhile at Palestrina, south of Rome, Ruggiero delle Puglie, who had recently served as Archdeacon in the cathedral chapter of Nagy-Várad was giving literary form to his experiences with a *Carmen miserabile* or *Letter Upon the Destruction of the Kingdom of Hungary Effected by the Tartars.*[34]

Pope Gregory IX's attempt to raise a crusade against the Mongols in 1241 petered out almost at once.[35] Two years before he had embarked on a war against the Emperor, and the divisions within Latin Christianity paralysed any attempts at a united front before the invaders. None the less, shortly before the meeting of the First General Council of Lyons the Papacy made a determined attempt to discover something about the dangers which threatened.[36] In March 1245 Pope Innocent IV wrote two letters to 'the King and people of the Tartars'. The first contained a resumé of Christian doctrine, the second an expression of astonishment at the attack upon Christian peoples. Copies of these were given for delivery to groups of friars, together with (in pursuance of the old dream) a papal bull (*Cum simus super*) asserting the primacy of the Roman Church which was to be presented to any Christian but non-Latin prelate whom they might meet. It was planned that two parties of friars should seek out Mongol commanders in the Near East to whom the letters should be consigned. Another was to go west through Poland and Russia and deliver the papal messages to the east of these territories.

All these envoys enjoyed some measure of success. Crossing the Holy Land, the Dominican André of Longjumeau reached Tabriz, from where the Mongol leader, Baiju, ruled Greater Armenia, north-west Persia and the former Seljuk Sultanate of Konya. The second mission, consisting of the Dominicans Ascelino of Cremona, with Simon of Saint Quentin and two other friars of the order, came upon Baiju's summer camp in the Armenian highlands at Sisian. By nature impolitic, perhaps even seeking the glory of martyrdom, Fra Ascelino succeeded remarkably well, at least, in antagonising his hosts. But he ensured that the papal letters, translated into Persian, were dispatched by the Mongol posts to the Great Khan at Karakorum in Central Asia, the Mongol capital. When the reply came he returned to Lyons accompanied by two Mongol envoys with whom the Pope had a series of unfruitful discussions.[37] These Dominican embassies, as we shall see, were to give rise to written accounts of the Mongols which were in many ways both remarkably original and destined to be of considerable influence in western Europe.

The third legation was led by the Italian Franciscan Giovanni di Pian di Carpine. Born near Perugia, now in his late fifties or early sixties and considerably overweight, Giovanni had had an important career as an administrator in his order, and was a man who found it easy to speak with kings and princes. His party set out from Lyons on Easter Sunday 1245, was joined in Silesia by a Polish Franciscan, Brother Benedict, who acted as interpreter in Slav lands, and after an exciting journey which he describes with great vividness, reached the Volga and the camp of Batu, Khan of the Golden Horde, at the beginning of April 1246.[38] He handed over the letters and presumed that his mission had been accomplished. But at this point, Batu told the two friars that he required them to attend the assembly in Outer Mongolia which was shortly to elect the new Great Khan Güyük. Perforce, on Easter Sunday, with two Mongol guides, they set out again, hard riding, changing horses five or seven times a day, through the Cumanian steppes, the former Empire of Khwarezm with its 'many devastated cities, destroyed castles, deserted villages', Otrar, Kara-Khitai, the land of the Naimans where, despite the season, 'the snow fell heavily and we suffered intense cold'. Finally on 22 July they reached Güyük's Syra Orda or 'Yellow Camp', half a day's journey from Karakorum. Representatives from many lands were present for the ceremonies. After the election and enthronement, they were summoned to the presence of the Great Khan. The 'Emperor', Giovanni writes, was very intelligent, and the Christians in his household were convinced that he was about to become a Christian. But negotiations did not go well. The friars delivered verbally the sense of the papal letters that Batu had already forwarded, and with the help of an interpreter of one of the Russian princes they made a Latin version of Güyük's reply – an uncompromising rebuttal of Innocent IV's arguments and a demand for his personal appearance and submission. They returned in winter, reaching Kiev on 9 June 1247. Their journey of well over 3,000 miles to Karakorum had taken five and a half months, they had stayed four months at the court of the great Khan; they had spent six months in returning to Kiev.

However unsatisfactory as an exercise in diplomacy, Fra Giovanni's mission gave rise to sober and informative accounts of the peoples through which he had passed. His companion Benedict left a very brief narrative which survives in two manuscripts and a somewhat longer version dictated by him to a 'Friar C. de Bridia' (*sic*, the very unusual absence of a Christian name has given rise to suspicions that this is a forgery).[39] Giovanni's work, the so-called *Historia Mongolorum*, of greater length and written with much greater skill, uses the same body of notes on which Benedict's account was based. This too is found in a shorter and in a longer edition (of about 20,000 words).[40] These reveal a strong practical sense, a genuine intellectual interest in the peoples among whom he had passed, and striking powers of observation. It is written in a typical early Franciscan style, that is to say one which avoided all rhetoric and cultivated an assured simplicity and directness. It avoids almost all learned reference (there is a passing mention of Isidore) and even (what is otherwise common in Franciscan style) biblical quotation. Yet this apparent simplicity is in some ways deceptive, for at the beginning of the work, Fra Giovanni lays out the plan of what will follow, which in its schematic form clearly derives from scholasticism, the methods used in teaching in the cathedral schools[41] and from carefully structured lecture notes:

> Wishing to write an account of the Tartars in which readers will be able to find their way about, we will divide it by chapters in this way. In the first we will speak of the country, in the second of their peoples, in the third of their religion, in the fourth of their customs, in the fifth of their empire, in the sixth of their wars, in the seventh of the lands which they have subjected to their rule, in the eighth of how war should be waged against them, and in the last of the journey we made, of the court of the Emperor, and of the witnesses we came across in the land of the Tartars.[42]

Each chapter is prefaced by a similar spelling out of the matters which are going to be treated. So the first, on 'the country':

> We propose treating of the country in this way: we will say something first of its position, secondly of its character, and third of its climate.

Within this framework, Giovanni offers a remarkable description of an alien world. In the first eight chapters, he considers the Mongols' methods of warfare (organisation of armies, weapons, armour, river-crossing, battle lines, siege-tactics), and peace-making (only on terms of complete submission). Then again, offering what he believes is a history of the

Mongols, he gives an interesting resumé of the abundant folklore which had grown up around Genghis Khan. Stories of the great hero had already fused with traditional eastern stories about Alexander (of which there was a contemporary Mongol version[43]) and the Monstrous Races (sciopods, the country of female monsters and male dogs and those who feed on the smell of food) and this material he gives his readers, without any expression of doubt. At the same time he essays a useful genealogy of the Mongol princes and gives a sound account of the Great Khan's power.

In addition Giovanni has a strong interest in ethnography: the Mongols' beliefs, marriage customs, food and drink, clothes, divination, burial practices and purification by fire. His schematism becomes very marked when he tries to distinguish their good qualities – obedience, avoidance of brawling, honesty (at least among themselves), hardiness, chastity – and their bad – arrogance, impatience, filthy eating habits and drunkenness. This is much more than a simple diplomat's report on the dangers posed by these people. It reveals genuine interest in details which he himself probably felt went beyond what was required of his mission. (So, for instance, having described the physical appearance of the Mongols, Giovanni in a later chapter excuses himself, as it were, by saying that this will enable Christian commanders to distinguish between captives who are genuine Mongols and those who have been pressed into their armies.)

Yet, at the same time, in the first eight chapters there is little that can be translated to a map. Giovanni's painting of the landscape of the Mongolian heartland is instantly recognisable. Here are mountain and infertile plain, both overwhelmingly of sandy gravel, largely treeless (with fires built from animal dung). Here is the irregular weather: the snow which comes in the summers, when there are sudden alternations of great heat and extreme cold. Here is a land of flocks of sheep, cattle, goats; felt-tents taken around on carts drawn by one to four oxen; the whole territory 'large, but otherwise . . . much more wretched than we can say'. But his attempt to situate it within its boundaries is vague and over-succinct: 'To the east is placed the land of the Kitayoi and also the Solangi; to the south the land of the Sarraceni; to the south-west the land of the Huyrii; to the west the province of the Naimani; to the north it is bounded by the Ocean'.[44] By the Kitayoi he means the Chinese. Their neighbours, it is to be presumed, are the Solangqas, dwelling in Manchuria and Korea. The Huyrii will be the Uighurs, and the province to the west was indeed the province of the Naimans. Yet the Sarraceni, who must be the Muslims of Central Asia, are also (as is clear from other references in the text) the Persians, who both lived a long way to the south-west rather than the south. So too Giovanni's account (the first European description) of the Kitayoi/Cathayans/Chinese ('friendly and most humane . . . they have no beard and the shape of their face is very like that of the Mongols, though they are not so broad in the face . . . their land is very rich in corn, wine, gold, silver and silk.'), is marred by seeming to identify them, perhaps following over-optimistic information from Nestorians, as Christians.[45] And, apart from a list of the peoples whom the Mongols have conquered which can only have confused a contemporary reader,[46] that is all we are given of the relation of peoples to peoples until we arrive at the final chapter.

This final chapter describes the itinerary taken by the friars, gives an account of their negotiations with the Mongol leaders and enumerates the witnesses who can testify that they have actually visited the East. Apart from being our principal source for the business of the embassy, this section offers a great deal on the geographical character of the Mongol world. Though no distances are given it would have been possible for a reader of the time to deduce that it took Giovanni two months to travel from Kiev to the Volga, and, riding at very great speed, another three and a half months to go from the Volga to the Great Khan's *orda* near Karakorum. It would also have been possible for him to mark in more detail the times of Giovanni's journey from the Volga, across 'Comania', to the kingdom of the Kangits (the Kangli Turks), the kingdoms of Khwarezm, of Kara Khitai, the land of the Naimans, and so to the Great Khan's *orda*. Then again, on the return journey a contemporary geographer could have noted that, journeying in winter, Giovanni reached the Volga almost five months after leaving the Great Khan, and took a month to pass from the Volga back to Kiev. (The work would also have reinforced the time-honoured European error that the Volga and the Ural both flowed into the Black Sea rather than the Caspian.)

Yet such knowledge never became general. This final chapter was written, it could be said, only as an afterthought, when doubts had come to be expressed about the truth of the report. (Already in the prologue Giovanni remarks how hard it is to be called a liar.) It was an attempt to validate the truth of what had been told by elaborating on the journey, and providing names of witnesses to it. Yet only three manuscripts which contain this section survive. In other words, despite its brilliance and the astounding journey it records, the strictly geographical elements in the book had a very limited circulation. These were perhaps more widely diffused through the lectures Giovanni gave about his experiences when he returned. His fellow Franciscan, Fra Salimbene, has described these sessions, when Giovanni's book would be read aloud, after which he would answer questions from his auditors.[47]

V

The central message that Giovanni di Pian di Carpine delivered to the Pope was advice against treating with the Khans and a call to resistance. The Great Khan Güyük and his princes have raised his banner against the West; within three to four years, Giovanni claims, their armies will again be attacking Hungary and Poland. But they must be resisted: 'because of the harsh, indeed intolerable, and hitherto unheard-of slavery, seen with our own eyes, to which they reduce all peoples who have submitted to them.' Moreover resistance is possible: 'They are fewer in numbers than the Christian peoples and weaker in body', and many in their armies would be happy to fight against rather than for them. Some of this advice seemed to be borne out by Güyük's letter to the Pope:

> This is an order sent to the great Pope that he may know and understand it. You have said: 'Become Christian, it will be good'. Thou hast been presumptuous: thou has sent a petition. This petition of thine We have not understood. How dost thou know whom God forgives, to whom He shows mercy? By the power of God from the going up of the sun to his going down He has delivered all the lands to Us; We hold them. Except by the command of God, how can anyone do [anything]? Now you must say with a sincere heart: 'We shall become your subject; we shall give [our] strength'. Thou in person, at the head of the kings, must all together at once come to do homage to Us. We shall then recognise your submission. And if you do not accept God's command, and act contrary to Our command We shall regard you as enemies.[48]

Like the popes themselves the Mongols claimed a divinely ordered 'plenitude of power' ('I have set thee over the nations and the kingdoms'). Yet the idea that negotiations were possible still lingered on. In December 1248, less than a year after Giovanni di Pian di Carpine's return, two Nestorian Christians, representing Eljigidei, the commander of the Mongol army of western Asia, arrived in Cyprus where King Louis IX of France was assembling his army for a crusade against Egypt. These envoys claimed that both Eljigidei and the Great Khan Güyük had been converted to Christianity. To which encouraging news they added that Güyük's mother was the daughter of Prester John. In which circumstances they urged an alliance against Islam. This news seemed to be borne out by a letter written at Samarkand by Sempad, Constable of Armenia, telling the King of Cyprus of the Great Khan's conversion.[49] Louis responded by sending an embassy under André of Longjumeau, the Dominican who had already penetrated to Greater Armenia on behalf of Innocent IV, furnished with rich gifts including an elaborate portable chapel. However, on reaching Tabriz Longjumeau's party learnt that Güyük had died, that his widow had become regent, and that the question of the succession made everything uncertain. Eljigidei sent Louis' emissaries on to Karakorum. Here, planning the succession of her son to the Great Khanate, the regent found it opportune to represent the King's gifts as implying the formal submission not alone of the King of France but of all 'the Franks' i.e. of all Latin Europe to him. She sent a letter which reached Louis in the summer of 1251, commanding his personal appearance at her court and demanding tribute of gold and silver. No word appeared in it of conversion to Christianity or alliance.[50]

At which point Louis decided to have no more to do with the Mongols. Nevertheless a Franciscan in his entourage, the Fleming William of Rubruck, hearing a rumour that Sartaq, son of Batu, had become a Christian, obtained the King's permission to set out, not as his envoy but simply as a missionary, to the Mongols of the Golden Horde.[51] William was at the time between his mid-thirties and mid-forties, 'a very heavy man', who knew Paris well, and may already have visited Egypt. With him went an Italian from his order, Bartolomeo of Cremona. Setting off in May 1253 they travelled from Constantinople by sea to the port of Soldaia (today's Sudak), at that time a great emporium on the Crimean peninsula. The officials of the port, perhaps seeing advantage from being associated with envoys to the Mongols, gave them four covered and two uncovered ox-wagons. The friars, themselves riding horseback, were accompanied by 'the clerk' Gosset, an interpreter Homodei, a slave called Nicholas bought at Constantinople, and two waggoners. Setting off from Soldaia, 'on the third day we came across the Tartars; when I came among them it seemed to me as if I were entering some other world'. Two months later they arrived at the camp of Sartaq, three-days' ride to the west of the Volga. By no means the Christian which rumour had made him out to be, and believing that the friars, whatever their protestations, were ambassadors of King Louis, he sent them on to the camp of his father Batu beyond the Volga. Batu in turn, around mid-September, ordered the two friars with their interpreter to be escorted by a Mongol troop of some thirty horses on to the new Great Khan Möngke at Karakorum. It was bitterly cold, but the officer appointed as escort wrapped them in furs from head to foot and placed their baggage on two other horses. Like Giovanni di Pian di Carpine before them, they took three and a half months to travel the 3,000 miles between Sarai and Karakorum. Here they were interviewed by Möngke who, though displeased that they were not ambassadors, allowed Rubruck and Bartolomeo to stay for six months.

In that time William discovered much, and he gives a most vivid description of the barbarian capital, the Mongols and the cosmopolitan groups of adventurers, fanatics, officials, tricksters and ambassadors which he found there. Here were many Europeans, as well as all the peoples of the East. He tells of the paper money of Cathay, of scribes writing Chinese characters with a brush ('with a single character they make several letters which form one word'), and of Buddhist monks in saffron robes repeating their mantra (though he mishears it), 'Om mani padme hum'. He tells of taking supper on Palm Sunday with Guillaume Boucher, master goldsmith of Paris (whose brother Roger lived on the Grand Pont), his wife, daughter of a Hungarian born in Lorraine, and one Basil born to an English father in Hungary.[52] In the Khan's palace Master Guillaume had built a large ingenious silver tree, with four silver lions at the foot dispensing mare's milk, and a mechanical angel at whose blast on the trumpet, four different types of wine poured out.

There were twelve pagan temples, two mosques and a Nestorian church. At Easter, Hungarians, Alans, Russians, Georgians and Armenians were among those receiving communion in the church of the Nestorians, where Rubruck was uncertain whether to take the sacrament from their hands. Some of the Khan's family and some of the administrative heads of the empire were Nestorians, but the friar's disgust at their 'heresies' forbad any useful cooperation. When the Great Khan asked for a disputation, Rubruck found himself debating with Nestorians as well as Mohammedans and 'Tuins' (Taoists?). He claims a victory; asserting that 'the Saracens' admitted that he had had the better of the argument: 'And they confessed that in all their prayers they ask God to allow them to die as Christians die'. (This curious motif continually recurs in missionary accounts, suggesting that in order to sustain the morale of the faithful back home, the orders had made it obligatory to include some such form of words in accounts of disputations.) Yet, finally disillusioned, William decided to return. In a last interview, the Great Khan spoke to him of his own belief. 'As God has given different fingers to the hand, so he has given different ways to men.' Rubruck tells us frankly of his frustrated reaction, a sobering insight into the missionary instinct: 'If I had had the power to work miracles like Moses, he might have humbled himself.'

His companion, Bartolomeo, worn out, we are told, by the journey to Mongolia and unable to face the return voyage, remained. Rubruck left Karakorum in July 1254, reached Batu's camp in just over two months, and then in more leisurely fashion made his way across the Caucasus, into Asia Minor, and so to the Holy Land. From Acre he sent a report of what he had seen to Louis IX, by then back in France, which can without exaggeration be described as one of the great works of travel literature. It is written by a learned man, one who had been educated in dialectic, probably at Paris,[53] and who was later to be a teacher of theology. Before setting out, he had read the accounts of Brother Julian, Giovanni di Pian di Carpine, André de Longjumeau, as well as the old authorities, Solinus and Isidore. But he never allows his learning or prior knowledge to stand in the way of acute personal observation. Unlike Pian di Carpine he structures his account along a narrative, the story of his going to and returning from the court of the Great Khan, and in this he gives a clear picture of the position of the lands through which he passes. So, for instance, the mention of his setting out from Constantinople to Soldaia draws him to a description of the Black Sea area and its surrounding territories, its trade and its rulers. Thenceforth at each stage of the journey he attempts a similar portrait. Again, on reaching the Volga 'a very great river, four times wider than the Seine and very deep', he is the first author of the Middle Ages to point out that Isidore of Seville was wrong to see the Caspian (into which the Volga flows) as a gulf of the ocean, that it is in reality a vast inland sea. As for the monstrous races, people told him that they had never seen them, 'which made us wonder whether what Isidore and Solinus say is true'.

But in addition to this type of notice he gives an extraordinary picture of the Mongols in their territories, which is much longer and more detailed than that of Pian di Carpine's. He tells of the *gers* or tents, being drawn along on carts by – as he counted on one occasion – as many as twenty-two oxen; of the chests in which they kept their possessions on wagons pulled by camels; of the interior of their tents, their dances, the women's head-dresses, food and drink; how they made *koumiss* out of fermented mares' milk. Behind very many of these passages there is little attempt to give information useful to the western missionary or warrior, but sheer fascination with the new and the visually strange: 'I would have liked to have painted everything for you if I'd known how to paint.' At the same time the people repel him. The considerable privations, hunger and thirst ('It seems to me I have never had anything to eat', remarks Fra Bartolomeo at one point) of the journey through lonely deserts was acceptable. 'But not the wretchedness I endured when we came to inhabited places. I can't find the words to tell you of the misery we suffered when we came to the encampments.' Here were ignoble savages, churlish, arrogant, intimidating, with filthy habits. Nor for Rubruck do they represent a military threat. If the Pope were to declare a crusade against them, they would all run off; a Christian army would find it 'very easy' to conquer all their territories.

VI

By the mid-1250s many, like King Louis' emissary, Baldwin of Hainault, had visited Mongol territories without writing about them, and a substantial amount of information about the Mongols could be found in manuscript in western Europe.[54] Altogether this represented a large increase in knowledge from that available thirty years previously when Genghis Khan had been seen as Prester John and the East as the world of the Monstrous Races. Yet it is apparent that written accounts were not particularly well-known or much studied. Matthew Paris' *Chronicle*, with its interesting reports of the invasion of Europe and its material taken from André de Longjumeau was never to be read during the Middle Ages outside the monastery in which it was written.[55] On the work provoked by the attack upon Hungary, the Dominican Julian of Hungary's letter survives in only four manuscripts, and Ruggiero of Puglia's *Carmen miserabile* in one. Of the friars sent by Innocent IV to the Mongols, Giovanni di Pian di Carpine's account can be found in a substantial sixteen manuscripts and Benedetto's in three, yet as we have seen the most valuable chapter in Giovanni's work was found in only three manuscripts and is unlikely to have been widely read.[56]

The report of Ascelino's legation to Baiju was written up by Simon de Saint-Quentin, who had accompanied him to Greater Armenia, in a work called (like Giovanni di Pian di Carpine's) *Historia Mongolorum*. This contained valuable information on the customs and way of waging war among the Mongols and on the general situation, particularly affecting the Georgians, Armenians and Seljuks in the Near East. The original is now lost, though much material from it was incorporated in the last books of Vincent de Beauvais' *Speculum Historiale*, the historical section of his vast encyclopaedia, the *Speculum Maius*. This was a work which enjoyed great popularity in the later Middle Ages, surviving in over fifty complete manuscripts, and in translations into French, Catalan, Spanish, Dutch and German. In the *Speculum*, Vincent also took over material from the report of Giovanni di Pian di Carpine. Yet where we can compare what he chose to include with what was in the original work, it can be seen that he was in fact largely indifferent to geography, which he subordinated or suppressed in favour of chronology. In fact he takes no passages at all from chapter 1, which gave Giovanni's account of 'the position, character and climate' of Mongolia or from chapter 9 which describes his itinerary.[57] Yet it was Vincent's work which in the Middle Ages became the standard source for information about the early Mongols and as such it was drawn upon by many other popular encyclopaedias and chronicles.[58] One effect of this was to drive out demand for the briefer, physically less-substantial, works on which it was

based. Completed in 1253, its solid authoritative mass may well have con-
tributed in particular to the small circulation of William of Rubruck's own
treatise written two years later. William had returned to Paris some time
afterwards, meeting there the English Franciscan Roger Bacon, who men
tions a few, in fact rather unimportant, details from it in his *Opus Maius*.[59]
It may be that it was this encounter which explains the fact that out of the
five manuscripts of William's work which we possess, four come from
English sources.[60]

VII

Further knowledge of Asia was to come through the profound changes
which came to the Empire of the Great Khans from the 1250s. For a time
their conquests continued. With the emergence of Möngke as fourth Great
Khan, the Mongols turned again to expansion. Möngke himself, with his
brother Khubilai, began to take over China. In the west their younger
brother Hülegü was assigned Persia and its neighbours. After destroying
the Assassins, the military order of the Ismaili sect which had long ter-
rorised the Middle East, Hülegü invaded Iraq, conquered Baghdad, and
took to himself the political power of the Abbassid Caliphate. In 1260 he
advanced on Syria, conquered Aleppo and Damascus, and received the
suzerainty of the Christian crusader-states of Antioch and Tripoli. When,
however, news of the death of Möngke arrived, Hülegü withdrew most
of his troops to Azerbadjan, leaving only skeleton forces behind. At this
point, seizing the advantage, the army of Baybars, Mamluk Sultan of
Egypt, marched out to inflict a decisive defeat on the remainder of Hülegü's
forces at the battle of Ayn Jalut in Galilee (3 September 1260). It has
been taken as a turning point; certainly the myth of the Mongols' invinci-
bility was shattered and, though contemporaries did not come to realise
it immediately, the limits of their permanent conquest in the West had
been reached.

Those limits were still of enormous extent. As a result of some fifty years
of conflict four Mongol Khanates now dominated huge areas of Asia. The
Great Khan held the heartland of Mongolia and China north of the Yellow
River. From 1279 he was to take over southern China as well. Central Asia
was commanded by the Chaghadai Khanate, centred on Balasaghun and
extending south to the Hindu Kush. To the west, with its capital at Sarai
on the Lower Volga, the Kipchak Khanate, or 'Khanate of the Golden
Horde' controlled the steppe lands and exercised suzerainty over the
Russian principalities. In the south-west the Ilkhanate (i.e. the 'subject'
khanate, subordinate in name at least to the Great Khan) reigned over

Persia, Mosul and Baghdad. After years of war and immense destruction, a predatory barbarian upper-class moved towards a more sedentary exploitation of the peoples they had conquered, and everywhere a system of perhaps not so much taxation as systematic spoliation was put into operation. At the same time, if any *Pax Mongolica* had ever existed, by the 1260s it had ceased. On Möngke's death there followed four years of war between Khubilai and his brother Ariq-böke. Thenceforward the Chaghadai Khanate, notably under Qaidu (d.1301), was in constant conflict with Khubilai, while from 1261 there were many wars between the Golden Horde and the Ilkhanate of Persia.

As these divisions intensified, individual Mongol leaders began more and more to establish genuine *ententes* with Latin Christians, alliances which were greatly to expand the range of geographical knowledge in the West. For some time already Latin merchants had begun to seek their fortunes in Mongol lands. Giovanni di Pian di Carpine mentions five of 'the most important merchants' he had met at Kiev in 1247: 'Michael the Genoese and Bartholomew, Manuel the Venetian, James Reverius of Acre, Niccolò Pisani'. In May 1253 Rubruck met 'certain merchants from Constantinople' at Soldaia. Particularly impressive was the growth of trade with Mongol Persia, some of which flowed southwards via Sinope from the Black Sea port of Trebizond. Some again went through the Kingdom of Little Armenia, which dominated the coastal strip of Cilicia in the shade of the Taurus Mountains. In 1246 its king, Hetoum I, had acknowledged the suzerainty of the Mongols, and his territories served thenceforth as a natural bridge between the West and the Ilkhanate of Persia. From its port of Layas (otherwise Ayas, Lajazzo) in the Gulf of Alexandretta, caravan routes passed to Baghdad, and, through Erzerum, to Tabriz.[61] By 1263 Latin merchants were already established at Tabriz, then the leading commercial centre of Persia. In that year Pietro Vilione (otherwise Vioni) from Venice, trading in linen, cloth from northern Europe and Venetian crystals, drew up his will in the city, calling as witnesses two Pisans and a Frenchman.[62] Three years later we learn of Arnaud Marinier of Marseilles securing a safe-conduct from Prince Charles of Anjou to travel to the Black Sea port of Trebizond 'and the land of the Tartars'.[63]

If trade brought cooperation between the West and the Ilkhanate of Persia, so too did external politics. From 1260 Baybars, the Mamluk Sultan of Egypt, forged what was to be a long-standing alliance with the Golden Horde or Kipchak Khanate against their cousins, the Mongols of Persia.[64] To counter this threat the Ilkhans were drawn to seek out the alliance of the Latin Christian powers. Particularly enthusiastic was the Ilkhan Hülegü's son and successor, Abaqa (1265–82). Though a Buddhist of sorts, he had a Christian mother, and one of his wives, Mina, was the natural daughter of the Byzantine Emperor Michael VIII Palaeologus. Hence from the 1260s Christian diplomats and missionaries were prominent in Persia. A leading figure here was the English Dominican, David Ashby, who having spent some ten years at the court of Hülegü and Abaqa, was sent as Abaqa's ambassador to the Second Council of Lyons in 1274, and who wrote an account, now lost, of the Mongols.[65] Not all that much, it may be granted, came of these flurries of diplomacy. The failure of the attempt to coordinate military action between Abaqa and the crusade of Prince Edward of England between 1270 and 1272 was just one example of the great difficulties facing successful cooperation. None the less a certain generalised friendship between the West and the Mongols of Persia continued to prevail.

One illustration of the new situation is to be found in the remarkable story of the Nestorian monks Rabban Sauma and Rabban Mark. Rabban Sauma was born in Beijing; Rabban Mark was the son of an archdeacon in Shanxi province.[66] Both were men of Turkish, Uighur or Ongut race. In the 1270s, no doubt as agents of the Great Khan's religious policy – for they were given money for the journey by the two governors of Tungchuan, who happened to be the sons of Güyüg and Khubilai Khan respectively – they set out on a pilgrimage to Jerusalem. Their route can be traced along the Silk Road: Khotan, Kashgar, Tus (capital of Khorassan), and then in the territories of the Ilkhan, to Azerbadjan, to Marageh, and, in 1280, Baghdad. Here, though they found the road to Jerusalem closed through war, the Metropolitan Nestorian Patriarch consecrated Mark as Metropolitan of Cathay and Ong (Shanxi) and Sauma as his Vicar General. In the following year the Patriarch died and Mark (who though ignorant of Syriac was the only metropolitan who could speak Mongolian) was elected – possibly by command of the Khan – in his place. As for Rabban Sauma, his travels had not yet ended. In 1287 the fourth Ilkhan, Arghun (1284–91), sent him as his emissary to Europe. He was accompanied by two Italians, Tommaso of the Genoese banking family of the Anfossi, and a certain Ughetto 'the Interpreter'. Reaching Rome they found that they were unable to negotiate, since the Pope had died. Accordingly they travelled on to Genoa, to an interview with King Philip IV at Paris, and then to Bordeaux, where, in an extraordinary transcontinental encounter, Edward I of England received communion from Rabban Sauma's hands. In February 1288 Sauma was back in Rome to be received by the newly elected Nicholas IV. He returned to Arghun with offers of assistance, and also, as he believed, with a grant of patriarchal authority from the Roman See over all the peoples of the East. At Rome, meanwhile, the account he had given of the fortunes of Christianity in China prompted Nicholas to dispatch there the first Latin missionary.[67]

Later Arghun sent the Genoese merchants, Buscarello, Percivalle and Corrado Ghisulfi, as his envoys to Paris and London. From London they brought back Sir Geoffrey de Langley, representative of Edward I, who – since Arghun had died in the interval – negotiated with his successor at the end of 1292.[68] Although from the reign of Ghazan (1295–1304) the Ilkhans came to adhere formally to Islam, this brought no conclusion to their rivalry with the Mamluks of Egypt, and the Mongols still sought alliance with European powers against the threat they posed. Ghazan's brief invasion of Syria in 1300, indeed, persuaded Boniface VIII and the Latin world that the papacy was about to receive Jerusalem as a gift from his hands.[69] Though any such ambitious hopes were of course unfulfilled, the imperatives of Persian foreign policy meant that, up to the end of the Ilkhanate in 1335, Christian merchants and missionaries were allowed residence. Meanwhile the Kipchak Tartars, based on the steppes at Sarai, were also pleased to welcome traders. It is in this period that the Italian cities began to colonise and develop what was to be the great commercial centre of Tana where the Don flows into the head of the Sea of Azov. It is within the context of these developments that the first voyages of the Polos must be placed.

Chapter 2

The Polos

I

As we have seen, by 1260 Latin missionaries and Italian merchants had already penetrated into western Asia. It was Marco's father and uncle who pioneered the journey to China. No authentic records of these men (nor of Marco himself) have been found in Chinese sources.[1] There are a few surviving Venetian documents which speak of them, but for their travels we are almost wholly dependent upon the very thin introductory chapters which form the prologue to Marco Polo's Book. These chapters were written within a medieval and Renaissance tradition of biography which is alien to modern conceptions of what constitutes biographical information,[2] in this case being designed to justify the text that followed rather than to present an invariably literal account of the family's deeds. Their purpose was to persuade the reader that the witnesses to what is to follow, Marco's father and uncle, were 'unfailingly noble, wise and provident' and that Marco himself was 'wise and provident without measure' and admired by the Great Khan. Other information is ignored, indeed throughout the Book it is on occasion ignored, as it were, ostentatiously. In chapter LXII, for instance, we are teased with the information that the Polos stayed at 'Canpiciou', the principal city of Tangut, 'for a year on business of theirs which is not worth mentioning'. The purpose of any biographical assertions was simply to try to authenticate, however artificially, the truth of the body of the work.[3] Paradoxically, it is for this very reason that they have to be read with considerable caution. Our caution will grow when we recognise that these chapters are cast in the literary form of thirteenth-century chivalric prose romance. The only other biographical information we have is that provided by the sixteenth-century editor Raumusio's preface to the Book, which has all the appearance of being no more than conjectures and unverified popular gossip.[4]

Within these limitations we may offer the following account, though some of it is controversial and will have to be returned to later. In the 1250s, there were three brothers, Venetian merchants: Marco, the eldest, Niccolò (father of the author of the Book), and Maffeo (the earliest Franco-Italian manuscript calls him, 'Mafeu'; the Tuscan version 'Matteo'). Their family house was in the parish of San Severo, between the back of San Marco and Campo San Lorenzo, a district of narrow lanes and unpaved footpaths, lined by ditches which sometimes broadened out into canals, sometimes ended in marshland. To the south its alleys led to the basin of Saint Mark whose waters opened out through the port of San Niccolò del Lido – patron saint of seamen, after whom Marco's father was named. To the west was the Doge's palace and the state-basilica of St Mark's with their spoils of war and commerce, the four horses from Constantinople, the porphyry statues, the body of the saint himself.

These brothers were united in a *fraterna compagnia*, a family partnership. Merchants, they were born in that period when Venetian trade was expanding at a rate which was never again to be equalled. These were the years which were to culminate in the first minting of the Venetian gold ducat, the international currency of the Middle Ages. Much of the city's commerce was with the East, with Alexandria and with Acre ('St John of Acre') which from 1187, when Jerusalem had fallen to the Muslims, had become the capital of the Christian Kingdom of the Holy Land. Acre had its own Venetian quarter – with churches (S. Marco and S. Maria) and a *funduk* or *fondaco*, a combined warehouse, inn and expatriate club, set round a courtyard – and to this centre the caravans from Damascus brought vases, precious cloths, carpets, fruits and sweets.[5]

But more than this the Venetians of the day were the heirs of their fathers who had fought in the crusade of 1204, a 'crusade' of sorts, which had ended with the Latin conquest of the Byzantine Empire. In the division of the spoils the Doge had been acknowledged as 'Lord of a fourth part and a half of a fourth part of the Empire of Romania [i.e. the Byzantine Empire]'. Venice, which already had its own quarter on the western bank of the Golden Horn, was now confirmed in its possession of three-eighths of the city of Constantinople, including the port facilities. In this area stood their six jetties, their two great *fondachi*, and the churches for their use: St Akyndinos (with its mill, its oven, its inns and its weights and measures) now rededicated to Saint Mark, San Niccolò and Santa Maria Latina.[6] To this new colony came thousands of Venetians, among them the Polos. (In 1280 the elder Marco, back at Venice, describes himself in his will as 'formerly of Constantinople', just as some English Nabob of the eighteenth century might, at Bath, declare himself to be 'formerly of Bengal'.)

From Constantinople two annual convoys bore silk, dyes, furs, pepper, ginger, cotton, peacock-feathers, slaves and timber to Venice for re-export throughout Europe. Other Venetian settlers in the city made their fortunes through import and export to Egypt, and still others through the carrying trade in the Black Sea.[7] Among these were the Polos, who owned a house in the Crimean port of Soldaia which at that time was the main emporium for all Italian merchants in the region. Here in May 1253, it will be recalled, Friar William of Rubruck had met 'certain merchants [among whom, no doubt Italians] from Constantinople' who had advised him about setting out into the 'other world' of the Mongolian steppe lands. For some of these there were great fortunes to be made. Here the Russians brought amber from the Baltic, honey, wax and furs – marten, sables, ermine and black fox. And from here Venetians exported Tartar, Bulgar and Caucasian slaves to the Muslim rulers of Alexandria. Yet the great days of the Black Sea trade lay in the future. Most of the port's merchants – Greeks, Armenians, Turks, Jews, Genoese, Venetians – were engaged in small-time commerce along the coasts, directed to provisioning Trebizond and Constantinople with salt, fish (barrels of salted or smoked sturgeon and caviar) and corn. Bulk cargo loomed large; in the 1260s in time of famine in Italy Venice itself was dependent upon corn from these regions. The principal means of exchange was still *bocharame* (called by Marco *bougrans*), pieces of very fine cloth made in the central-Asian city of Bukhara.

At some point – all the main texts of the Book say in 1250, though the most probable date is around 1260[8] – Niccolò and Maffeo Polo left their base here at Soldaia and set out to trade in jewels within the Mongol Khanate of the Golden Horde. At Sarai, near the present-day Volgagrad, across the Lower Volga, they met the Khan Berke. According to the Book, they made him a present of their jewels and received in return gifts 'of at least twice their value'. It has been argued that these words are to be seen as an attempt to play down the fact that they were 'in trade' (as if Venetians saw this as a social stigma!). The truth is that this was a normal way of doing business with eastern potentates: in 1338 we find six merchants, also from Venice, who had travelled by way of Astrakhan to Delhi, dealing with its Sultan – and extremely profitably – in just the same way.[9] The brothers then had achieved a notable coup. Yet this triumph – though the Book says nothing of it – must have been marred by frightening news from the West. In July 1261 the most powerful enemy of the Venetians, Michael Palaeologus, the Greek ruler of Nicaea, acting in alliance with the Genoese, reconquered Constantinople and restored the Byzantine Empire. An orgy of vengeance was unleashed against any Venetian merchants who fell into their hands; some fifty were captured and blinded or mutilated.

It was probably news of this that persuaded the Polos to seek some way back to the Mediterranean other than through the newly restored Byzantine lands. It could well be that they thought first to travel south, through Georgia and Armenia, to the Venetian merchant colony at Tabriz within the Ilkhanate of Persia – through the lands of what Marco calls 'the

Tartars of the Levant' – and to work their way to the Mediterranean by this route.[10] Yet, precisely at that point, in the winter of 1261–2,[11] war broke out between Berke Khan of the Golden Horde and Hülegü, Ilkhan of Persia. Hence with this escape route blocked, they had to resign themselves to a longer stay in Mongol lands. After lingering at Berke's court for twelve months, they went north to Ukek, a town on the right bank of the Volga. Then they struck east; 'across a desert which extended for seventeen days' journey; there they found neither towns nor villages, but only many Tartars with their tents, living with their animals'. This can have been only the first stage of what must have been at least a sixty-day journey, travelling within the Chaghadai Khanate of Central Asia to the great commercial city of Bukhara in Transoxonia.[12] Once they arrived, they found that the war still prevented them from going back.

After three years at Bukhara, an embassy coming from the Ilkhan Hülegü and bound for the court of the Great Khan passed through the city. Seeing the two brothers, the envoys suggested that they accompany their mission to the Great Khan who, they said, had never seen any Latins and would be pleased to speak with them. (The truth of this has been impugned on the grounds that the Chinese annals record the visit of *Falang* [foreigners] to the Great Khan in 1260–1.[13] Yet since these people are said to be blond and white, and to have come across two seas to make their visit, it seems rash to insist that they were 'Latins' which, I take it, is being used here in the sense of 'Southern Europeans'.) The brothers accepted – it would have been an invitation difficult to refuse – and, according to the Book, travelled, 'for a whole year [this seems too long] northward and north-eastward before they reached the court of the prince' (though where this was at the time is not said). The early Latin translation says that at this point they were accompanied by 'Christian servants whom they had brought from Venice'.[14]

The Great Khan Khubilai (reigned 1260–94), 'Lord of the Tartars over all the earth, and of all the kingdoms and provinces and territories of that vast quarter of the world', received them well. By then it is possible that, after their three year stay in Bukhara, they had learnt to speak Mongolian. (In 1323 the Franciscans of Caffa believed that Hungarians, Germans and Englishmen could manage to learn Mongolian while Frenchmen and Italians could rarely do so. But it seems an exceptionally dubious generalisation.[15]) If not, then through interpreters the Great Khan questioned them about the political situation in Europe, and about the Papacy and the Latin Catholic religion. Finally he asked them to return with one of his 'barons' to Europe on an embassy to the Pope. He gave them letters in Mongolian which asked the Pope to send him a hundred men skilled in the seven liberal arts (the standard educational curriculum of the learned at that time in the West) capable of acting as missionaries within his domains, together with some oil from the lamp which burnt in the Church of the Sepulchre of Christ in Jerusalem. This request seems hardly likely to be the result of the Polos' skills in Christian apologia. It has been more convincingly suggested that, ruling over a north-Chinese people resentful of alien government Khubilai hoped to acquire educated foreigners who could be employed as his administrators both there and in southern China which he hoped soon to conquer. Or perhaps he was looking for skilled magicians from the West to conquer the magic of his enemies. The request for the holy oil, again, it has been plausibly inferred, was owed to either those of Khubilai's wives who were Christian, or to hopes of using it, as Rubruck tells of other Christian relics being used, for magical purposes.[16]

The Polos were given a *paiza*, one of the gold tablets which served as safe-conducts and which entitled its possessor to use of the Yam or relay-posts and provision of escorts and supplies throughout the Mongol domains. After setting out, the Mongol 'baron' who was to accompany them fell ill and was unable to continue, but the two brothers carried on for three years until they reached Layas, the Mediterranean port in the Kingdom of Little Armenia. In this case the length of time given again seems extraordinary, especially if they were able to use the Mongol postal system, and the explanation offered does not sound at all convincing: 'it took them so long because they could not always advance, being stopped sometimes by snow or by heavy rains falling or by great torrents which they found in an impassable state.' Throughout the introduction to the Book, the authors seem to be exaggerating the time taken to go to and from China, possibly in order to emphasise the immense distances they had traversed.[17]

At Layas they must have learnt that the Pope had died and that no successor had yet been elected. They went on to the port of Acre in the Holy Land. Here the Book offers us one of its rare dates – April 1260 – though one which must be a mistake. Pope Clement IV died in November 1268 so the year must have been 1269. Moreover, the Book claims that at Acre on this occasion they conferred with the Archdeacon Tedaldo Visconti. Yet Visconti first set eyes on the Holy Land in 1271 (while he never held, as is claimed here, the title of 'Legate for the whole kingdom of Egypt').[18] It seems probable enough, however, that, as the Book says, the brothers decided to return to Venice to wait until a new pope was elected. At Venice Niccolò was reunited with his son, Marco, who, according to the Book, was then fifteen years old (hence born in 1254). In fact the papal interregnum was to be the longest on record, and for the Polos this must have been a time of ever-increasing frustration. After two years, still no pope had been elected. In order, it could be assumed, to maintain contact, they decided to return and report the situation to the Great Khan. With them they took Niccolò's son, Marco, then aged seventeen.

II

Can anything be known of the culture in which the young Marco had grown up? Can anything be said of the forming of his mind? Some influences can at least be assumed. First of all Venice itself, whose uniqueness was already a commonplace of contemporary description. A few years before Marco's birth, a central–Italian had written of it as 'incomparable . . . its floor is the sea, its roof is the sky, and its walls are the flow of its waters; this singular city takes away the power of speech because you cannot nor will ever be able to find a realm such as this'.[19] Yet 'beauty' for these men was very often particularly commingled and almost identified with power. Above all here were the great central symbols of the Venetian state in St Mark's Square. Within this setting, the boy would have absorbed all the spirit of those great quasi-religious ceremonies and processions which the Serenissima employed to attract the reverence of its subjects, the great rituals of state. Each year, on the eve of Candlemas, the Doge solemnly processed to vespers in the parish church of Santa Maria Formosa, neighbouring Marco's own parish of San Severo, returning next morning to mass. The following day six large ships, draped with cloth of gold and tapestries, sailed through the city from the Palace to the Cathedral in the Castello district where the Doge received the Bishop's blessing, then returning through 'waters covered with craft laden with men and women', and 'great numbers of ladies and damsels splendidly dressed, at the windows of the palaces and on the banks on both sides'. Then there were the coronations, with homage given to the Doge and his Dogaressa; the celebrations of the Annunciation on 25 March, when, so it was said, Venice had been founded; the feasts on Saint Mark's Day; the marriage to the sea on Ascension Sunday; the masquerades and all the chivalric pageants, the knights jousting in the Piazza di San Marco, which grew up under government patronage. And at the central moment of all the ceremonies, the great cry:

> Christ conquers! Christ reigns! Christ rules! To our noble lord Lorenzo Tiepolo, by grace of God, Doge of Venice, Dalmatia and Croatia, and ruler of a fourth part and a half of the whole Empire of Romania, health, honour, life and victory! Aid him, St Mark![20]

If Christ conquered, reigned and ruled, so too, would Venice.

All this would have given the young Marco a taste and feeling for those rituals of power he would find later at the court of Khubilai Khan. Yet though such ceremonies played an important part in the life of the city, the essence of its existence was business. The area of San Marco was notable not simply for pageantry but for its moneychangers and food sellers. And at the Rialto, where Armenian, Slav, Albanian, German and Italian merchants came together to buy and sell, even the concerns of government were temporarily transcended. 'Merchandise', wrote a chronicler of the day, 'flows through this noble city as water through fountains.'[21] And it was this trade which dictated the character of Marco's upbringing. In Venice merchants' sons, destined to follow in their fathers' footsteps, normally had only the most superficial contact with the Latin learning of the grammar schools. Their education was almost wholly devoted to their future vocation.

A prime exhibit here is the fourteenth-century miscellany known as the *Zibaldone da Canal.*[22] This is a merchant's commonplace book, which was elaborated from a student's workbook of mathematical problems. It is clear that a large part of the material has a didactic rôle, and we can gain from it a good impression of the education of the Polos as of all but a very few of the city's merchants before the coming of humanism. In the first place the *Zibaldone* (meaning 'Miscellany' or 'Ragbag') places the strongest emphasis on practical arithmetic, inculcated by many problems together with their solutions. These occupy the greater part of the work and are closely geared to the student's future career. As for example (here I cite the admirable translation of J. E. Dotson):

Make me this calculation: 2 merchants have their wool on a ship. One of them put 13 sacks and the other of them put 17 sacks [on board]. And when they had arrived in Venice the captain demanded his freight charges from the merchants and they said to him, 'Take one of our sacks from each of us and sell it and pay our freight costs and return the remainder.' And the captain took 2 of these sacks and sold them and gave 10s. from the proceeds to him who had 13 sacks after the freight had been paid. And he returned 3s. to the man who had 17 sacks and his freight was entirely paid. And the merchants said to the captain, 'We want to know how much you sold the sacks for, and how you calculated what you took from it for freight charges.' [Follows the explanation of how the sum is done][23]

With these go tips on business, taxes and fees and on securing value in goods bought: 'The characteristics of ginger are that it should appear long, and that it not be rough, and it be firm and big. And one wants to cut it open to see that it is firm and white; and white is better than dark.'

Here too are found extensive notes on the conversion of foreign weights, measures and money, the sort of material found in merchants' manuals of the time, which, with the mathematical problems, occupies between half and three-quarters of the book. The accounts of the exchanges into

Venetian measures and money seem almost to serve as an introduction to the geography of commerce, to all the merchant's future ports of call throughout the Mediterranean and the Black Sea. So of Soldaia or Suduk from which Niccolò and Maffeo had set out on their memorable journey to Berke Khan:

> A *soma* of silver from Sudak weighs 45 *pesi*, which *soma* is reckoned for payment at 120 aspers, and an asper is worth 2s. of *piccoli*. The *soma* comes to 7½ *solidi grossi* of Venice. And the *peso* is worth 2 *grossi*, and this is sterling silver.
>
> A mark of Venice becomes 53 *pesi* in Sudak.
>
> 100 marks of Venice become 117 *some* and 35 *pesi* at Sudak.
>
> A gross pound of Sudak is 23 pounds and 3 ounces of light weight of Venice, and one *occhia* is 2 light pounds.
>
> A gross thousand weight of Venice becomes 68 pounds at Sudak.
>
> 4 *bracchia* of Venice becomes 3 *picchi* in Sudak.

One senses that these conversions of money, weights and measures are here not simply for reference, but, like the long tables of division ('$\frac{9}{40}$ of a £ is 6d. $\frac{5}{48}$ of a £ is 5d.' etc.), are designed to prepare the mind and spirit of the boy who reads them for a lifetime of mental arithmetic. This is how money is counted; this is how it is made.

To this material the *Zibaldone* adds simple astrological information ('Know that in the first hour of Friday Venus reigns, and in the second Mercury reigns'), and hints on weather prognostication ('know that if the Sun will be very pale in the morning, that is, lifeless in colour, as if bleached, or yellowish, it means that there will be storms that day, or other bad weather'). There is a miscellany of religious matter: in the first place charms, such as 'when you want to go on board a ship, recommend yourself to Saint Oriele and Tobias. + Christ conquers + Christ reigns + Christ rules + Christ conquers + Christ reigns + Christ in heaven + Christ on earth' (an interesting adaptation of the acclamation of the Doge). There follows a list of the Ten Commandments; the so-called Precepts of Solomon ('Do not beat your wife without reason . . .' etc.); the days on which when bled you need have no fear from sorcery; and so on. There is a four-page chronicle: from 'Adam was 2857 years before the coming of Christ' to 8 August 1303, 'a great earthquake on the island of Crete'. Then there are worldly-wise saws ('Courtesy from the mouth is very valuable and costs little'), and just occasionally some extracts which might (were they not so crude) be called Venetian literature. Some poems from the tradition of the Provençal or northern French troubadours and a story deriving from French oral epic, as chance has it, a story about King 'Milliadus', the father of Tristan. (It was, we shall see, to an author who had written on this same 'Milliadus' or Mèliadus that Marco Polo would turn when he came to writing up his knowledge of the East.)

In all, the *Zibaldone* can be thought of as giving a fair sample of the mind of the Venetian merchant class and of Marco himself, as he prepared to follow his father and uncle to the court of the Great Khan. It is worth spelling out that there is nothing there which might be called 'high culture'. The city of the lagoon stood adjacent to the mainland of the 'March of Treviso', the *Marca Amorosa*, the *Marca Gioiosa*, celebrated in Italy for its chivalric courts, troubadours and cultivation of verse, particularly in Provençal. (Some 90 per cent of medieval Provençal poetry, whether written in Italy or France, is known to us only through a manuscript tradition originating from Treviso.) Yet very little of this seems to have touched Venice itself. And certainly no Venetian – at that time or for some time in the future – who wished to make a literary impression wrote in his own language. One, Bartolomeo Zorzi, wrote verse in Provençal. But he was an isolated figure who probably took to the pen only during his seven years in a Genoese prison (1266–73). (In Genoa, normally as mercantile and unliterary a place as Venice, there were, however, some circles where Provençal poetry was cultivated.) One Martin da Canal (perhaps of the same family as the author of the *Zibaldone*) wrote a dazzling, quasi-chivalric chronicle detailing *Les estoires de Venise*. Yet as its title shows he chose to do so in French. There was some chronicle writing at a quite low level in Latin, though outside the ranks of priests and clerks attached to the office of the Doge, there is little evidence for anything but the most basic knowledge of Latin. (It is perhaps significant that in Venice, almost uniquely in Italy, the art of the notary, drawing up his documents in Latin, was carried out by ecclesiastics and not laymen – it could be because so few laymen there knew Latin.) And when in the fourteenth century some patricians, like Zanin and Niccolò Querini (*ca.*1310), began to attempt serious verse composition, they already accepted the inadequacy of their own tongue and wrote in Tuscan.[24] But in the thirteenth century hardly any Venetians strove to write for literary effect in any language; to try to do so, one feels, was an un-Venetian activity. All of which is to have its relevance when we come to look at the composition of Marco's Book.

III

This was the sort of cultural baggage which the seventeen-year-old Marco took with him, when with his father and uncle he set off from Venice to the court of the Great Khan. The Polos began their journey by returning to Acre where they consulted with the prominent ecclesiastical politician, Archdeacon Tedaldo Visconti. What Visconti was doing in the East at this juncture is not clear. But the expeditionary force of the Lord Edward of England (the future King Edward I) had arrived there on crusade towards the end of April 1271[25] and possibly the Archdeacon was acting with some sort of quasi-legatine authority in liaison with Edward's forces. Having conferred with him, the Polos went on to Jerusalem and secured some oil from the lamp of the Sepulchre. (This may have been dangerous, for the Muslims who controlled the town must have felt menaced by the crusade and would have been at this moment particularly hostile to infidels.) Then, fortified with letters from Visconti which sought to explain the situation in the papal Curia, they set out for the Kingdom of Little Armenia on the first stage of the journey back to Khubilai's court. From the port of Layas, which had recently become the most important point of access from the Mediterranean to the lands of the Middle East, they planned to strike inland on routes which were already becoming familiar to Italian merchants journeying either north to Trebizond or east to Tabriz.

Shortly after their arrival at Layas, however, they learnt that the papal election had finally been made and that the choice had fallen upon none other than Archdeacon Tedaldo Visconti. This was a striking coincidence, news 'for which the two brothers had great joy'.[26] Soon they received a message ordering them to return to him for further consultation. The King of Little Armenia (this must have been Leo III) put a galley at their disposal to take them back to Acre. Here Visconti – who had decided to take the title of Pope Gregory X – gave them new credentials and appointed – as a substitute, as it were, for the hundred men trained in the liberal arts – two Dominicans to accompany them, Fra Niccolò of Vicenza and Fra William of Tripoli.[27] After receiving the papal blessing, the party probably left Acre in November 1271 but in the course of the journey north the friars lost heart. The Book says that 'Bendoquedar', that is to say Baybars, the Sultan of Egypt, invaded Armenia and laid it waste: 'so that our envoys ran a great peril of being taken or slain', and that, terrified by this, they abandoned the expedition. In fact, there is some confusion here, for Armenia was not devastated at that time. There seem to have been skirmishes between the Mongols and Mamluks in November and early December 1271, though the effect of these did not prove so alarming as, apparently, was rumoured at the time, and it may be that it was news of these that brought about the friars' defection.[28] Yet at the same time one cannot entirely resist the reflection of Bertolucci Pizzorusso that in the Book the weakness of the friars – as earlier the failure of the Mongol 'baron' to continue to Europe – may be no more than an authorial device designed to draw a contrast with the firmness of the Polos.[29] However this may be, the Polos, of course, continued, and the Book tells us, after a three-and-a-half-year journey, reached 'Clemeinfu' (Shangdu, Xanadu), the summer palace of the Great Khan in northern China.

If it be true that the Polos took three-and-a-half years (though even accepting the explanation of the Book – 'owing to the bad weather and severe cold they encountered' – this seems inordinately long), they must have arrived in 1275. They were to spend the next seventeen years in China. In August 1280 when Marco's uncle, the elder Marco, drew up his will at Venice, he seemed to assume that his brothers were still alive, since he appointed two other relatives (Giordano Trevisan and Fiordilige Trevisan, the stepmother of *our* Marco, wife of Niccolò) as his executors 'until my brothers, Niccolò and Maffeo shall be at Venice'. Perhaps a letter, carried by some now forgotten visitor to China, had reached him, telling him what they were doing in the East. We are less fortunate. No Chinese source can be used to gain evidence of them. (They might well, of course, have adopted Mongol names when living among the Mongols of China.) No evidence exists, except what we may deduce from the Book. In general terms this tells us that Khubilai, who seems to have abandoned at this stage the idea of further negotiations with the West – or at least of using the Polos as his negotiators – employed Marco in some administrative rôle. In 1273 Khubilai had conquered the last remaining stronghold of southern China; after three centuries the north and south of China were now reunited. In asserting his authority in this empire he sought to free his administration from reliance upon the native mandarin class and to secure as many foreigners, whose loyalties lay solely with his person, as officials in his government. Indeed it has been suggested that the use of foreigners, whether Muslims, Khitans, Uighurs or Europeans, particularly in tax-collection, was aimed to provide a non-Mongol focus for Chinese resentment against Mongol government.[30]

Against this background, the Book portrays Marco as one who was high in the counsels of the Great Khan. He was, we are told, very quick to learn the customs of the Mongols, their language and their practice in war, and he came to speak several languages and to master four written alphabets. What these languages might be is debatable. On the evidence of the text, Cordier argued that in fact Marco knew only Persian. However this may be, what is certain is that – here all commentators agree – Chinese was not among them.[31] Nonetheless, we are told, he made a good legate and many missions were entrusted to him (xvi), on one occasion at least, as far away as India. We are told that Khubilai's emissaries – just like Venetian ambassadors with their *Relazioni* – were expected to produce some general account of what they had seen:

[Marco] had seen and heard many times that the Great Khan, when he sent messengers through the various parts of the world, and when they returned to him and told of the embassy which they had undertaken and yet could not tell of other novelties of the countries to which they had gone, that then he would tell them that they were fools and ignoramuses and would say that he would rather hear of the novelties and customs and the usages of these strange countries than hear of that for which they had been sent. And Marco that well knew all this, when he goes on his embassy made it his purpose to know all the novelties and the strange things in order to tell of them to the Great Khan.[32]

Marco, the Book continues (XVII), particularly excelled in providing this sort of information for the Khan, so that he flourished at the court: 'And the Great Khan was so pleased with the work of messer Marco that much did he favour him and made him such honour and held him so near to him that the other barons had great envy of him.' All this, of course, must lie under suspicion of being written simply to provide an explanation for, to give authority to, what the Book tells us about the East. Indeed, given that Khubilai's court was 'rich in human resources', with many Chinese-speaking Central Asians – members of the Khitan and multilingual Uighur Turks – within it,[33] the Book's account of Marco's eminent rôle here must be treated with some scepticism.

After being in China for some time the three men, we are told, several times sought permission to return to Europe but were always refused. Their opportunity came when the Great Khan decided to dispatch a Mongol princess as bride to the Ilkhan Arghun of Persia (ruled 1284–91). Three Mongol nobles, appointed to escort the lady to her groom, requested, it is said, that the Polos accompany them, and the Great Khan reluctantly agreed. According to one version of the work (the Ramusio text), they set off by land, but after eight months found the roads closed through war between the Mongol Khanates, and returned to make the journey by sea. Another version (the F text) declares that from the beginning it had been decided that the princess should go by sea because this was less fatiguing than the land route. Before departure Khubilai gave them, 'two tablets with commandment that they should be free through all his lands and wherever they went they should have provisions for themselves and their following', together with messages to be delivered to the King of France, the (as a later text has it) King of England, the King of Spain (since no King of Spain existed at this period, this is perhaps the King of Castile), 'and the other kings of Christendom'. The expedition was provided with thirteen four-masted ships, provisioned for a two-year journey. After three months they reached Sumatra; after another eighteen months of navigation in 'the

Sea of India' they reached Persia. According to the Book the voyage was racked by disaster. Following one text, of the six hundred people, not counting the crews who had originally embarked, all but eight died. Both Chinese and Persian sources mention the marriage and embassy, though without referring either to the Polos or the supposed disasters upon their voyage.[34]

On arrival in Persia the ambassadors found that Arghun had died (12 March 1291) and that his brother Geikhatu (ruled 1291–5) was now Ilkhan in his place. Geikhatu instructed the Polos to escort the lady to Arghun's son, Ghazan, who (according to the Ramusio version) was at that time in the province of Khorassan so that, following Mongol custom in such circumstances, he himself could wed her. Having done so (still following the Ramusio text), they rejoined Geikhatu and stayed in his court for nine months (this would be in 1294). On leaving him, they were given four gold *paiza*, and travelled to Trebizond on the Black Sea, where, though the Book is silent on this, they found themselves in new difficulties. The Comneni Emperor, who ruled from this capital a territory carved out of the old Byzantine state, was, at this moment, in dispute with Venice. As a result goods of great value – the Polos were to claim that they were worth 4,000 *hyperpera* (which might be about 2,000 Venetian gold ducats) – were taken from them.[35] They passed from there to Constantinople, and from there via Negroponte to Venice which they reached in 1295. They had been away for twenty-four years; Marco was 41 or 42 years old.

Whether they ever imparted the messages which, as the Book has it, had been entrusted to them by the Great Khan for the King of France 'and the other kings of Christendom' is passed over in silence. No evidence for their delivery has survived. Perhaps 'the message' is the Book itself. The next that we are told – though, as we shall see, all this has been contested – comes from the beginning of the Book, where Marco is 'in the prison of Genoa' in the year 1298, telling his story to one 'Rusticiaus' of Pisa. How Marco had arrived there is unknown. In his *Imago Mundi seu Chronica*, written, it would seem, in the first half of the fourteenth century, the Dominican, Jacopo d'Acqui, mentions a sea battle between Genoese and Venetian merchants at Layas in 1296 in the pontificate of Boniface VI (*sic* for Boniface VIII), in which Marco was captured and how then, in prison, he wrote his Book on the wonders of the world. This cannot be true since the battle of Layas was fought in 1294, the year before Marco returned to Venice. The sixteenth-century editor, Ramusio, whose account of Marco seems to depend largely upon either the doubtful testimony of oral history or upon his own imagination, asserted that, serving on a galley as *Sopracomito* (Gentleman-commander), Marco was captured by the Genoese in the sea battle of Curzola. This was the greatest Venetian defeat of the thirteenth century which took place in the 'Gulf of Venice' or Adriatic itself, in September 1298. Since, however, this leaves precious little more of 1298 for Marco to make the acquaintance of Rusticiaus and to write his Book, Moule-Pelliot, doubtful of all this, offered the formula that Marco was 'taken prisoner at some obscure and otherwise unrecorded engagement of armed merchantmen in 1296'.[36]

Marco was released, probably in July 1299 when the Genoese-Venetian peace treaty was ratified,[37] and returned to Venice. Here the family had bought a palace called *Il Milione* in the quarter of S. Giovanni Crisostomo. Roberto Gallo argued that the name 'Milione' is a corruption of 'Vilione' and that it was the palace of the Vilione family (from which we have already met Pietro Vilione in Tabriz in 1264)[38] which the Polos bought. Though not all that large, it was built around a courtyard and had a tower.[39] Marco's uncle, the elder Marco, and his descendants took the name 'Milion' as a surname; and in the course of time the word came to be applied to Marco himself as a nickname. Jacopo d'Acqui writes of him as 'Marco who is called "Milono" [sic] which is how the Venetians say "riches of a thousand thousand pounds"'.[40] Eventually the word 'Milione' was used in some manuscripts as a title for his Book. Great riches, in fact, are not at all in evidence. Marco ended his days in modest patrician style. He married Donata Badoer by whom he had three daughters who in their turn married into various minor patrician families.

He enjoyed considerable contemporary fame. During the next twenty-five years, his Book came to be current in French, Franco-Italian, Tuscan, Venetian, Latin and, probably, German – an unparalleled record in the Middle Ages for translations effected during the life of the author. The learned consulted him, as we know from the words of Pietro d'Abano, the brilliant and unorthodox professor of the University of Padua, who sought his opinion on that hoary old question in academic geography, whether the equatorial regions were habitable. In his *Conciliator differentiarum philosophorum*, which was published 1310, d'Abano remarked: 'I have been told of this and other matters by Marco the Venetian, the most extensive traveller and the most diligent inquirer whom I have ever known'.[41] This reputation also attracted the attention of at least one prospective crusader in the East. In 1307 Thibaud de Chépoix, Vicar General to the titular Latin Emperor, Charles de Valois, obtained a copy of the Book from Marco himself at Venice.[42]

Yet despite such moments his life gives off an air of the humdrum. He passed his time in money-lending (to his uncle Maffeo and other relatives) and in other modest business deals, engaging for instance as a commission agent to sell musk. He is found litigating against relatives and others. (Some commentators, who presumably have stronger family feelings than were felt in the fourteenth century, have been scandalised that he should have sued and obtained a judgment against a cousin who had not repaid money owed to him.) Only in his possessions comes the note of the exotic. As inventoried after his death, they include bedding of Tartar workmanship, sendal from Cathay, brocades from Tenduc, a Buddhist rosary, the silver girdle of a Tartar knight, the head dress, adorned with gold and pearls, of a Tartar lady, and a *paiza*, a gold tablet 'di comandamento' from the Great Khan.[43] He drew up his will in January 1324, making donations of some 2,000 *lire dei piccoli* (a respectable amount, say about 45 ducats, the annual wage of a skilled artisan) to priests and for pious purposes, and the rest, including his share of the family palace, to his wife and daughters. (That Marco cut out his *male* cousins in their favour was ascribed by Moule, not without some expressions of indignation, to the probable wiles and machinations of these ladies while he lay *in extremis*.[44]) At the same time he released his Mongol slave, Pietro, from slavery. He died, aged sixty-nine, on Sunday 8 January 1324, between sunset and midnight, and was buried, as his father had been, in San Lorenzo. It was the Dominican, Jacopo d'Acqui who, some time later, first gives us the famous story that 'because there are many great and strange things in his book, which are reckoned past all credence, he was asked by his friends on his deathbed to correct it by removing everything that went beyond the facts. To which his reply was that he had not told one half of what he had actually seen!'[45]

Chapter 3

Marco Polo and Rustichello

I

What we are left with is the Book. Yet this is not without a certain opacity, and to understand it more fully we must look at Marco Polo's cooperation with his co-author, Rustichello da Pisa, the style which Rustichello brought to it and how far this style has fulfilled or betrayed Marco's original purpose. More than this, we have to assess the (as I believe mistaken) claim recently advanced that the supposed cooperation is a myth, that the two men never were in prison together in Genoa, that Rustichello has simply taken over for his own purposes, and translated into his own speech, a (now lost) original manuscript written by Marco alone. And having considered the likelihood of that deception, we must go on to review the possibility of a still more radical fraud, to examine the contention, first advanced in the eighteenth century but now strongly reiterated by a contemporary scholar, that neither Marco nor his father and uncle ever were in China, the thesis that brands them as liars and charlatans. That view too I hold to be false, and so finally we have to review what can be known about where Marco resided in China in the seventeen years of his stay, and what he was doing there.

The original manuscript has not survived. Most scholars believe that it was written either in French or in a variant of French, an artificial literary language popular in Italy at the time, called Franco-Italian or Franco-Venetian.[1] The earliest manuscript which does survive is written in this Franco-Italian – though, to complicate matters, its language is so strongly marked by Tuscan and Venetian as to make it different from any other work in that language.[2] All the French and Franco-Italian texts which survive open with a declaration that it was a cooperative work, written in prison: 'He [Marco], residing in the prison of Genoa, caused messer Rusticiaus of Pisa who was in the same prison to recount all these things in the year 1298 from the birth of Jesus Christ.'[3] It is not necessary to think here in terms of a prison cell. In Genoa, it seems, prisoners of war were often entrusted to families who took them into their own house, perhaps holding them as hostages for members of their own family in enemy hands. It was in these conditions, less rigorous than close confinement, that the two men, it has been suggested,[4] could have come together to write.

Who was this 'Rusticiaus' of Pisa? His name in Italian was either Rusticiano (though no Pisan of the time has been found with that name) or Rusticello or – as we shall call him here, being the form used by most Italians near to the time – Rustichello.[5] The doubts about the form of the name reflect how little is known about the man who bore it. Most scholars assume that he was captured by the Genoese at the devastating Pisan naval defeat at Meloria in 1284, and that he was not released until the general release of Pisan prisoners in the summer of 1299. If so, he had plenty of time on his hands to develop literary skills, and it is not necessary to assume, as is often done, that he was in any way 'a professional writer' rather than someone for whom writing was in large part a means of killing time. As to whether he can be pinned down more closely, various suggestions have been made. As for instance that he was – though no trace of legal or academic culture appears in his work – the Rustichello, son of Guido Rustichelli, found as a judge and notary at Pisa in January 1277; or another judge with the same name found in Pisa in the early fourteenth century; or again one 'Rustik' who was in imperial service as a treasury clerk at the time of the Emperor Henry VII's expedition to Italy (between December 1310 and May 1313). But the name in its various forms is quite common at the time in Pisa and elsewhere; one finds in this period, for instance, a Rustighello, a Dominican friar, making his will at Venice.[6]

The one thing we can be certain about him is that he was the author of *Méliadus*, an abridgement of prose stories written in French or Franco-Italian concerning Arthur's father, and other Arthurian heroes. This is established by the many verbal parallels between the two works. It has been pointed out many times how the first words of the *Méliadus* echo, at times word for word, the opening of the Book, a form of opening otherwise unknown in the literature of the age. The *Méliadus* starts with the words:

Lords, emperors and princes, dukes and counts, and barons and knights and vavassours and townsfolk and all the worthy men of this world who are accustomed to taking pleasure in romances, if you take this book and have it read from end to end, you will hear all the great adventures which befell the knight errants of the time of King Uther Pendragon . . .

Compare the beginning of the Book of Marco Polo:

Lords, emperors and kings, dukes and marquesses, counts, knights and townsfolk and all people who wish to know of the various generations of

men and the diversities of diverse regions of the world, take this book
and have it read to you. And here you will find all the great marvels and
the great diversities of [the provinces of the East] . . .

In other words, the author of the *Méliadus* is also the co–author of
Marco's Book.[7] This *Méliadus* forms part of a genre of chivalric literature
particularly popular in Italy in those years. Throughout the thirteenth and
fourteenth centuries Italy produced many stories in both prose and verse
which took as their theme either the paladins, the great heroes who served
with Charlemagne, or the knights and ladies of King Arthur's court. The
cantastorie sang these tales in the marketplace and many signorial libraries
contained versions which were often finely bound and illuminated. They
were sometimes written in Italian, sometimes in Franco-Italian, and sometimes in French. In the 1280s and 1290s – those years in which Dante, by
precept and example, was preparing his attack against 'those wicked men
of Italy who prefer the languages of others to their own' – many Italian
authors wrote in French and were prepared to claim that it was the French
language which was '*la plus delitable a lire et a oire que nule autre*'; the most
delightful to read and hear than any other.[8] It was within this tradition that
Rustichello wrote.

In the *Méliadus* he claimed to have received the material on which its
stories are based from 'a book of my lord Edward, the King of England,
at that time that he passed the sea in service of Our Lord God to conquer
the Holy Sepulchre'. If true, this would have been about twenty-five
years before the meeting with Marco, sometime between 1271 and 1273.
At that time Rustichello might indeed have met the King, perhaps in
Palestine, or perhaps later, either at the court of Charles d'Anjou at Naples,
or on Edward's return to England through Italy. But how likely is it that he
did? Is it simply another example of that fiction by which writers of the age
sought to enhance the interest of the work by associating it with a great man?
On the strength of being willing to go along with the forgeries of the monks
of Glastonbury the King has in the past been described in fulsome terms as
an 'Arthurian enthusiast'. Yet given his lack of patronage to any writer at all
(other than that which Rustichello, by implication rather than direct statement, claims), and given that he was essentially someone with little enthusiasm for anything other than war and conquest, my own suspicion is that
Edward has no place in this story.[9] If I am correct in this, it would follow that
the common belief that the *Méliadus* was written in 1272 has no foundation.
In which case one would guess that it was another work compiled to wile
away the boredom of the Genoese prison.

However that may be, the *Méliadus*, it is clear, and the tradition in which
it was found, played an important part in producing the style of Marco's

Book. Throughout the introduction, in Rustichello's version, we have the continuous sense that we are reading a tale of knight errants. Much of this is lost in most English translations because in them almost all the oral-epic verbal style is eliminated. This is because modern translators are embarrassed in particular by two of its characteristic features: first, the very frequent use of the historic-present tense and second the simple and repetitious vocabulary whose monotony they seek to avoid by elegant variation. As a result they destroy the patina of the original. But if we translate without paraphrase the tone comes through. So, in chapter III, we read, of the brothers:

> And when they had stayed somewhat at Soldaia, they decide that they shall go still further on. And what shall I tell you about it? [*Et que voç en diroie?*] They part from Soldaia and they take to the road and ride without meeting any adventure worthy of mention until they were come to the Khan Berke.

Just like Arthurian heroes on a *queste*. Again, when they return with Marco to the court of Khubilai Khan (chapter xv):

> *Et que voç en diroie?* When Messer Niccolò and Messer Maffeo and Marco were come to that great city they go to the principal palace where they find the Great Khan with a very great company of barons. They kneel before him and prostrate themselves as low as possible. The Great Khan has them rise to their feet and receives them honourably and with great joy and great welcome, and asks them many questions as to their life and how they have sped. The two brothers reply that they have sped very well, since they find him well and strong. Then they present the credentials and letters that the Pope sends, from which he has great happiness. Then they present the oil from the Sepulchre, from which he has great joy and holds it most dear. The Great Khan, when he sees Marco who was then a young gallant, he asks who he is. 'Sire,' says Messer Niccolò, 'This is my son and your man'. 'Welcome be he,' says the Great Khan. And why should I make a long tale of it for you? Know in very truth that much was the joy and great welcome that the Great Khan makes and all his court at the coming of these messengers. And much were they served and honoured by all. They stay in the court and had honour above the other barons.

Even in this attempt to keep to the style of the original, there have entered several elements of paraphrase. The word which I have translated as 'gallant' is '*bachaler*'. In reality this word has the same sense that is intended by Chaucer when, writing of the Squire in The *Canterbury Tales*, he describes him as 'a lovyerc and a lusty bacheler', meaning not, as English readers today expect, 'an unmarried man' but (as in 'Bachelor of Arts') 'a probationer', in this case a probationer hoping to be dubbed a knight. So too I have paraphrased the word '*apostoille*', which means strictly 'Apostolicus' or 'Apostle', as 'Pope', this being the word which Rustichello, as was customary in prose-epic style, constantly uses for that dignitary. Again the modern reader may not realise that when Niccolò introduces his son as '*vestre home*', 'your man', he means the *home* who gives him *homage*, acknowledgement as his feudal lord.

The whole passage might serve as an exemplar of the style of the French prose courtly epic. The first two sentences illustrate the two most common ways in which that style carries its argument further, first the omnipresent question: *Et que voç en diroie?*; second a temporal preposition (normally *quant*). (And this *quant* comes shortly again – 'The Great Khan *when* he sees. . . .') Later we come to a third way: the sentence that asks us to *know* something: *sachiés tout voirement* . . . . At the same time we note another characteristic feature, what philologists are pleased to call 'synonymous dittology' (i.e. virtually repeating yourself in different words). As for instance when the Khan asks the brothers 'as to their life and how they have sped' and receives their 'credentials and letters' honourably and 'with joy and welcome'. But the Polos are not received simply in those terms but, in accordance with the customary hyperbolic expression of chivalric rhetoric, with '*grant* joie *et grant* feste' and through the whole of the passage that hyperbole is maintained. The Polos find the Khan surrounded by *mout gran* company of barons. They bow before him *tant com il plus puent*, and are *mout* enquired of by him; to which they reply that they have *moult bien fait* . . . . Then the Khan has *grant* joy of the holy oil and holds it *mout* dear. After all this, predictably enough, *mout* was the *grant* joy and welcome and *molt* were the Polos *servi et honorés* by all. All this is in a narrative present tense.[10] (Notice, incidentally, the three spellings, *mout*, *moult* and *molt*, in the course of seven sentences. The orthography of the manuscript is extremely labile.)

Et por coi voç firoie lonc cont? Today school-teachers could take this paragraph as an illustration of how not to write. Yet for the audience of the time this style, with its repetitions, was designed to produce a lulling, undemanding, hypnotic rhythm which carried them forward effortlessly in the story. Indeed the whole scene, as has frequently been pointed out, in its language and in the exemplary *courtoisie* of the brothers' response to the Khan's enquiry, mirrors, often word for word, the description Rustichello paints in the *Méliadus* of the reception of Tristan at the court of Camelot. It is as if Cathay is simply the stuff of Arthurian legend. After the introductory chapters, moving to the geographical description, this chivalric tone becomes less emphatic. But it re-emerges strongly in the last section of the Book where the great battles of the Khans are described. Here the Mongol ambassadors bear a striking resemblance to, and speak in the same manner as the heralds of the Arthurian world. The battles themselves, all six of them, are described in much the same way as the single combat between the knights of Ireland and Cornwall found in the *Méliadus*.[11]

The text of this work is sometimes referred to as 'our book', sometimes as 'my book'. The protagonist is sometimes 'I' and sometimes 'he'.[12] For some scholars the cooperation implied here is a question of simple dictation, which Rustichello simultaneously translates into chivalric rhetoric; for others it is a more general cooperation based on joint consideration of Marco's memories and his notes. In many ways the Book gives the impression of having been dictated. There are jumps backwards and forwards, the taking up and then dropping of subjects, the decisions not to go forward with a subject which has been begun, phrases such as 'but I forgot to say that . . .', and so on. A notable example is found in chapters CCXIX–CCXX:

> CCXIX There is nothing else worth mentioning; so let us leave Rosia, and I will tell you about the Great Sea, and what provinces and nations lie round about it, all in detail; and we will begin with Constantinople. First, however, I should tell you of a province that lies between north and north-west . . . a province called Lac. . . . There is nothing more worth mentioning, so I will speak of other subjects; but there is one thing more about Rosia that I had forgotten . . . Now let us speak of the Great Sea, as I was about to do. To be sure many merchants and others have been there, but still there are many again who know nothing about it, so it will be well to include it in our book. We will do so then and let us begin first with the Strait of Constantinople.
>
> CCXX At the straits leading into the Great Sea, on the west side, there is a hill called the Faro. But since beginning on this matter I have changed my mind, because so many people know all about it, so we will not put it in our description, but go on to something else. And so I will tell you about the Tartars of the Ponent. . . .

Yet the convention, the deliberate artifice designed to give the impression that one is reading a book that has been dictated (with declarations of forgetfulness, suggesting spontaneity and freshness) is as common and as misleading in medieval prose epic as the eternal convention that a poet *sings* his verse. It follows in that same oral tradition in which in the opening paragraph of his work the author urges his audience – quite anachronistically if we were to take the words literally – to 'have the book read to you' (*'le feites lire'*). I have a suspicion that that rhetoric comes out most strongly when Rustichello feels embarrassed, as for instance in chapters CCXIX–CCXX, which we have quoted: at that precise moment, Rustichello, who has promised in the prologue that he will tell his readers of 'the divers regions of the world', breaks it to them that in fact a lot of the world is going to be left out.

Rustichello's text, I take it, was not simply dictated from Marco's memories but relies on his notes as well. The immense amount of detailed and precise information in the Book cannot have been given without the aid of extensive written notes taken by Marco in the East. In the Ramusio version (of which more later) Marco, in his description of the city of Quinsai, refers to making these notes.[13] In fact any belief that the work was simply dictated from memory implies a belief that people in (that perhaps over-handy generalisation) 'pre-print societies' had a prodigious capacity to retain in their minds an amazing mass of detailed information. Some people do indeed believe this. Yet there are many points where, when Marco is relying on his memory, he gets things wrong, as for instance in references to his own family and himself in the early chapters of the Book. (We have seen, for example, how in chapter X Marco is nine years out in dating his father and uncle's return to Acre in 1269; and how he has them conferring with a papal legate two years before that man ever arrived in Syria.) It seems certain, that is, that whenever he speaks accurately and in great detail on places and districts, he is doing so not on the basis of memory but with documents – we shall examine later of what sort they were – before him.

II

So far I have written as if it may be taken for granted that the Book was the result of a cooperation between Marco Polo and Rustichello undertaken in prison at Genoa. That cooperation, after all, is clearly asserted at the opening of the F text and in most of the A group of manuscripts which derive from it. Quite recently, however, the learned German scholar, Dr Barbara Wehr, in lectures delivered in Italy and Britain, and in an article which has gained some considerable fame,[14] has argued with some emphasis against that traditional position. Hers is, I believe, very much a minority stance. Yet the implications of her thesis are so revolutionary that it is necessary at this juncture to consider the substance of her arguments. In Dr Wehr's view, in fact, Marco was never in a Genoese prison. Rustichello's text, she believes, is a translation into French and into chivalric rhetoric of a pre-existing text written in Venetian, probably by Marco Polo himself. The text closest to this is (for reasons which she does not explain) not some ancestor of the surviving group of manuscripts in Venetian (VA), but the extremely well-ordered Latin translation of Fra Francesco Pipino, made from a Venetian original between 1310 and 1317. This text – precisely because it has no elements of Rustichello in it, no incoherence, no chivalric rhetoric – is to be thought of as corresponding most closely to Marco's original. Rustichello, Dr Wehr maintains, has claimed that Marco dictated the work to him, has inserted passages seeming to give the impression of dictation, because this is something which would be likely to give the flavour of authenticity to his own text. He has said that this took place in the prison of Genoa because this was a place where a Pisan and a Venetian might plausibly be supposed to meet. He has written in French because he aims at an audience in the northern world, perhaps in particular the patronage of King Edward of England. Since Dr Wehr believes that Edward I was the patron of Rustichello's *Méliadus*, she considers that Rustichello might well have believed that the King would be eager for another work from him. As one interested in crusade – indeed negotiating with the Ilkhans on this in the 1290s – Edward I, she points out, would have been particularly interested in knowledge of the East. (Dr Wehr might have referred to Edward's emissary, Sir Geoffrey of Langley, who returned through Genoa in January 1293 with the leopard that the Ilkhan had gifted to his King, something which must have caused a considerable stir.)[15] Accordingly, Wehr continues, Rustichello has produced, with Edward in mind, a distorted version of Marco's true text, adding to it in particular those last chapters (CXCIX–CCXXXIII) detailing the wars of the Mongols, so out of key with the rest of the Book.

Considering these claims one must first ask which is the more likely: that Rustichello has deliberately imposed incoherence on a coherent text, or that Pipino, with the education in logic of a learned Dominican, has transformed a primarily disordered work into the sort of book that the learned could read without contempt, the sort of book written by Giovanni di Pian di Carpine? There is, after all, no reason at all to think that Marco himself, who had no education in, or experience of, the liberal arts, so culturally specific to the West, would have been able to produce a text anything like Pipino's. Then again Rustichello does not say, as Dr Wehr claims, that the Book was 'dictated', but that Marco '*fist retraire*', caused Rustichello to 'recount' it, to cooperate with him in producing the Book. It is true, as we have seen, that his rhetoric makes some of the text sound like dictation. The style of oral-epic, the very frequent use of such phrases as 'but now I forgot to say that . . .' etc., do indeed lend themselves to that idea. That said, the only imposture we are faced with here is the imposture of a form of rhetoric. As I would see it a literary cooperation was almost essential. On the one hand there is a practised writer. On the other a man who, from the age of seventeen has lived in the East, has returned home after twenty-four years, and who must have been frequently very bewildered by what he found there. During his absence he would have been ignorant of all western literary tradition. He knew no Latin, may also have found it difficult to express himself with any facility even in Venetian (not considered a literary language in Italy), and may very well have had many doubts about how to present his material to a strange and very largely unknown audience. Nothing, in these circumstances, would be more normal than that he should welcome an opportunity to acquire help in giving literary form to his notes.

One has still to enquire whether this all took place in a Genoese prison. If the Book was not dictated, Dr Wehr observes, it must have been taken from notes, and how could these have been available to Marco in prison? Again, if Marco was imprisoned would this not have been mentioned in contemporary chronicles? (It is, of course, mentioned by Jacopo d'Acqui, but his account, as we have seen, is in a couple of respects garbled.) Then again, if he had been in prison, surely he would have described in his Book how this had come about? More than this would he, in Genoa, the arch-enemy of Venice, have written a book which gave 'precise indications' of how to arrive at the riches of distant regions? These arguments for me have no substance. As to the notes, Ramusio in the sixteenth century imagined that Marco wrote to his father asking that his 'writings and materials' should be sent to him. The assertion doubtless rests on no more than editorial intuition; but it shows at least what he and his readers could believe possible. Then again that Marco's imprisonment should not be mentioned with accuracy by any chronicler will strike any medieval historian as the most natural thing in the world: the number of interesting things that medieval chroniclers ignore about what was going on in their time would fill enough books to double the size of all the national libraries of the world. Again – and of importance for understanding the Book – one must add that Marco's silence on how he came to be in prison reflects one of its most salient features, namely its extraordinary impersonality. Let us suppose that, after sixteen years in pagan China, where the Polos had, it would seem, flourished – though once again Marco is quite tight-lipped on this – they had, on their way home, as it were on the last lap of their travels, passed through Christian Trebizond where the government had robbed them of goods to the value of 4,000 *hyperpyra*. Would not Marco have written at length on this ironic and interesting theme? But of course – as we know from a document which has survived from some fifteen years after the event – that did actually happen, and yet no word is said about it in the Book. Nor, to consider the final point, does the Book in fact give any 'precise indications' of how to arrive at the riches of distant regions. (And if the publication of the Book had indeed provided valuable information by which the Genoese might harm Venice, it would of course, if generally circulated, have done every bit as much damage whether written in Venice or Genoa.)

In addition, Dr Wehr argues that there are things in the Book of no interest to Marco which must have been written exclusively by Rustichello. She claims, for instance, that once Marco had returned to Venice, news of the accession of Ghazan to the Ilkhanate would have been of no interest to him. At which point, given that the Polos had escorted Ghazan's future wife from China and had delivered her to him in Persia, I can only wonder at my own and Dr Wehr's different understandings of human nature. Again, Wehr herself remarks that the Z text, which is in many ways independent of Rustichello, refers to the death of Prince Noqai in Central Asia in the autumn of 1299. Here is clear evidence that Marco retained an interest in the East and the fortunes of its rulers after his release from prison. And how could he not?[16] In fact there is good evidence that Marco fully approved the Rustichello text. The three manuscripts, B3, B4 and B5, which are basically copies of a translation of that work into northern French, end with the assertion that Thibaud de Chépoix, Vicar General to the titular Latin Emperor, Charles de Valois, procured a copy of the Book from Marco himself at Venice in 1307, and that this copy was presented by his son, Jean, to Charles. All three manuscripts add that Marco gave Thibaud 'the first copy' of the original, which cannot be true. Yet given that Chépoix is known from other sources to have been in Venice in 1307, it is difficult to think that the story of Marco's gift can be anything but the truth.[17]

None the less, setting aside the arguments we have already examined, could it be that Marco is simply agreeing to take part in a rhetorical fiction, that the idea of prison is simply a literary device? In the same way that Boethius' *Consolation of Philosophy*, another work written in prison, gains a resonance through the contrast between the body which is imprisoned and the soul which is free, could Rustichello have sought to create a powerful literary charge through having Marco's story of limitless distances told within enforced confinement? Yet this too, on reflection, must be rejected – just as on the same general grounds we must reject Dr Wehr's larger argument – because it would have been impossible for either Marco or Rustichello to have imperilled their credibility by beginning a narrative offered in deadly earnest as true with a lie which hundreds of witnesses could easily have contradicted. These city states were small worlds in which everybody made it their business to know everybody else's; if there had been a deception it would have been known, and, more particularly given the rapid early diffusion of the Book, it would rapidly have been noised abroad. This is not to say that the entire text was necessarily written in prison. It is not unlikely that the collaboration with Rustichello continued after Marco's release. It could have been then, for instance, that the last chapters treating of the battle at Aqsai between Noqa and Toghtogha in the Khanate of Kipchak, which took place while Marco was in prison in 1298, were inserted.[18] Yet, that granted, my own conclusion is that the first version of the work cannot have been begun in any other way than as a literary cooperation between Marco and Rustichello at Genoa in the year 1298.

III

I also conclude that Rustichello wrote in French or Franco-Italian, not because he was seeking the patronage of Edward I (whose name would otherwise surely be mentioned prominently in the preface and not passed over in absolute silence), but rather because this was a normal thing for a north-Italian writer to do, particularly when seeking to follow the tradition of Arthurian thirteenth-century prose narrative. That tradition has not been much admired in the past. It is only recently that literary critics have tried to come to terms with its quite remote conventions and aesthetic.[19] One thing, for instance, which strikes modern readers as strange about the Book is that Rustichello has given it a beginning and a middle, but no end. It just stops. This lack of any rounding off is quite at variance with our contemporary sense of form. But it was quite normal in prose epics of the period. Perhaps the intention was to suggest that the story did not end because the writer had stopped, but that the adventures were still going on. In fact, when one reads the Book in a modern translation, one always finds an ending. This is because an early Tuscan translator of the original, who had been reared in a different tradition, felt it needed one.[20] And modern versions have always seized on this ending and put it in. But it is clear that it was not there in Rustichello's original text.

The genre itself, then, has not been much admired, and within the genre Rustichello has always been treated as an inferior master. This is, in part, because of the character of the *Méliadus*, which is the only work, outside the Book of Marco Polo, which survives from his hand. In the form we have it, this is certainly a flawed work. Yet however jarring the style for readers today – prolix, repetitious, stereotyped – it had its contemporary admirers. It found readers, right up to the mid-sixteenth century, when it was first printed; and it enjoys the distinction of being the only romance work, of which a part was – around 1300 – actually translated into Greek iambic tetrameters.[21] Yet, beyond this, a more potent cause for the condescension with which Rustichello has been treated, comes perhaps from the fact that on innumerable occasions his version of Marco Polo does not give us what we would like to know. Why does he tell us so little of what Marco said, thought, or did? Instead he tells us a great deal of what we are not looking for. What the modern reader is not looking for, but what he gets, is a work of geography which Rustichello has tried very hard to place within the transitions, formulas, dialogue and general rhetorical traditions of chivalric literature. As we have seen, the *Méliadus* and the Book of Marco Polo have a great deal in common. As for instance, battles fought in chivalric splendour. It is on coming to the battles that the patience of most readers dissolves. With these, Colonel Yule, that most devoted editor of the Book, breaks out in tense irritation: 'A considerable number of the quasi-historical chapters in this section . . . are the merest verbiage and repetition of narrative formula again and again repeated. We shall not inflict these tiresome repetitions again on the reader.'[22] Given that these same battles, as has been said, resemble the single combats found in the *Méliadus*, it is easy to assume that these 'tiresome repetitions' are due to Rustichello's defective art, and by extension that everything we want to read comes from Marco, everything we do not want from Rustichello. All this has led to Rustichello being written off in terms of mild contempt: 'an industrious, simple man,' writes Colonel Yule, for example, 'without method or much judgment'.[23] That conclusion is too hasty. Given his audience, which consisted not of nineteenth- or twentieth-century historians but of readers of chivalric literature, Rustichello has, it may be argued, done quite a good job with the very difficult materials Marco has offered him.

That said, the meeting with Rustichello and the experience of imprisonment was not, I would think, the primary stimulus towards creation of the Book. It is common to read that but for this change, this happy misfortune, this enforced leisure, Marco would never have thought to share the story of his travels with the world. Or, as others have it, that Marco, who, after three years back in Italy, had still not committed himself to writing, would not have written at all without finding himself, not so much in prison, as in prison with Rustichello.[24] This, it seems to me, is untrue. It is contradicted in the words of the opening chapter:

No man . . . knows so much or has experienced so much of the various parts of the world and its great marvels as has this Messer Marco. And for this reason he said himself that it would be too great an evil if he did not have put in writing all the great marvels that he had seen, or heard of as true, so that other people who had not seen or known them might come to know of them through this book.

It seems to be contradicted still more forcefully by those materials which Marco, as we will see, brought back from China in order to be able to tell his story. The particular intervention of Rustichello, that is to say, rather than some other amanuensis was merely due to their chance meeting in prison.

Then again, though it is true that in 1307 Marco offered Thibaud de Chépoix a version of Rustichello's text, and seems on this account perfectly satisfied with what Rustichello had done, this is not to say that the 1307 text contained all that he had to say. Among the 150 surviving medieval manuscripts, there are two distinct traditions (see Appendix I.) The first (A) derives from a very early Franco-Italian version, probably a copy of the original text written in French or Franco-Italian while Marco was in prison. The second (B), which, despite the sparseness of its manuscript tradition is unquestionably authentic, is found, apart from two fragments, only in the Latin version written around 1470, now in the Chapter Library of Toledo, in an eighteenth-century copy of that work, and in the Italian translation from other manuscripts by the Venetian humanist Giambattista Ramusio, published in 1559. The modern Moule-Pelliot edition assumes that both the A and B traditions derive from a lost copy of the one original autograph.[25] This is conceivable, but it seems more probable to me that there were two original versions. The first (A), Rustichello's version begun in the prison of Genoa, was designed for general consumption. The second (B), containing expressions of openness to non-Christian religions and Mongol attitudes of religious tolerance – passages which it might well have been dangerous to make public at a time when the Roman Inquisition was flourishing[26] – represents a more personal authorial statement, and for that very reason enjoyed a much more limited circulation. Or perhaps there were several different versions, all equally 'authentic', the result of successive attempts, set down, left and then taken up again from time to time in an attempt to encompass the whole of Marco's experiences and his changing memories of and reactions to them. In this respect John Critchley has very convincingly suggested that the Z manuscript, the most important of the B group, emerged as the result of intelligent questioning of Marco by readers who had already gone through a text in the A group.[27]

IV

Yet to speak of the 'authenticity' of the various texts can only lead to questions about the authenticity of the material found within them. From the eighteenth century, as a result above all of Marco's silence about many things in the China of his own time, the suspicion has been roused in some readers that we are faced here with a fiction, the nagging doubt that the whole of Marco's story of having been to China is untrue. Why does he never mention the Great Wall? Why is there nothing about what, in the fourteenth century, Odoric da Pordenone was to notice: fishing with cormorants, or the binding up of young girls' feet? Why nothing on printing, Chinese script, acupuncture, tea or tea-houses? Why no mention of Confucianism or Taoism? Had he actually *seen* China with all its great Confucian temples with their splendid ceremonies?[28] It is not too difficult to offer answers to most of these points. The myth of the Great Wall, for instance, obscures (among lots of other things) the fact that much of it had fallen down by the thirteenth century. Almost everything the tourist is normally shown today was built in the sixteenth century.[29] (Neither Odoric nor Giovani Marignolli who both passed between China and Mongolia in the fourteenth century mentions it; indeed the first European reference doesn't come till the end of the sixteenth century.) Referred to as the 'sensi' or 'sensin', Taoist monks are in fact briefly mentioned in chapter LXXV. Footbinding was at this period limited to upperclass ladies who were confined to their houses, and would be rarely observed by anyone outside their family. Tea-culture at that time had not reached North and Central China, where Marco mostly resided.[30] Setting these individual rebuttals aside, it can also easily be thought that Marco identified himself so strongly with the Mongol rulers that he was indifferent to the mass of the population over whom they rule. (Just as writers in thirteenth-century Italy had little to say about peasants.) It is always difficult to deal with the negative evidence of silence.

Less negative, it might seem, is the argument from the strong presence of Persian names and forms in the Book. Place names normally appear, if not in Mongol, then in Persian dress[31] – as in Quengianfu, Pianfu, Taianfu, Sainfu, Ciorcia, Çardandan. On one occasion Marco uses the term 'facfur', an old Persian word for the Emperor of China, meaning 'Son of Heaven'.[32] He writes of southern China as 'Mangi', the Persian derivation from the Chinese Man-tseu, and never uses the Mongol name for the southern provinces, 'Nangias'. In his account (in the Ramusio text) of the Chinese and Mongol calendar, Marco writes of 'lion' for 'tiger', clearly thinking from a Persian word used in Central Asia which has both senses.[33]

In the twentieth century individual specialists in Chinese history have occasionally picked up on these issues. Herbert Franke, for instance, remarks that the question of whether the Polos were ever in China 'is not yet settled', but concludes, with a notable lack of enthusiasm, that until definite proof can be adduced that the material of the Book is not taken 'from some perhaps Persian source, we must give him the benefit of the doubt and assume that he was there after all'. More recently the learned Sinologist Dr Frances Wood has more emphatically dismissed his presence there out of hand.[34] If this were the case, the very large amount of verifiably accurate information that the Book contains about the Mongol Empire and China must be presumed to have been gathered in some other centre, perhaps Mongol Persia or, as one suggestion has it, the Chaghadai Khanate, or even within the Khanate of the Golden Horde, as Dr Wood has it, not 'much further than the family's trading posts on the Black Sea and in Constantinople'.

It is, of course, not absolutely impossible to imagine the Polos holed up for twenty-four years in Near or Central Asia, questioning travellers, listening to bazaar gossip, and reading and taking very elaborate notes on (now lost) Persian accounts, in order to accumulate an enormous mass of detailed information on the geography of countries which they have not visited. At the same time one has to recognise what an unusual thing this would have been for them to do, since, as we shall see later, there was no precedent for any European behaving in this way. And one very strong objection here is that the people they are said to have drawn on must also be supposed to have ignored those very things which Marco and Rustichello have been damned for not mentioning. It is equally necessary to criticise the authors of these sources for not having been to China, to ask what sources *they* were relying on, and so on in an infinite progression. Then again it can be argued very reasonably, as Yule and Cordier did, that Persian forms are common in the Book because Persian was a *lingua franca* in the court of the Great Khan.[35] And it could equally be suggested that – as I would guess – Marco derives the form of the place names in his Book from a map of the East which he brought back, executed by one of those Persian cosmologists, such as Nasir ud-Din,[36] who worked for the Mongol rulers.

In all, the claim that Marco Polo never went to China provokes three initial questions. Is there anything intrinsically improbable in the story that three Europeans reached China at the end of the thirteenth century? Were there any advantages to be gained by the Polos in absenting themselves from Venice for twenty-four years, and then returning to tell marvellous stories of places to which they themselves had not been and of which their contemporaries had not heard? And if the Polos were not in China in this period, where were they? To the first question, the answer must surely be that while the Marco–Rustichello narrative may provoke doubts through silence on what we today would find interesting in Chinese life, there is no evidence at all to suggest that the story of those first chapters in which the Polos are portrayed as reaching China, as many other westerners were shortly to do, is in itself either impossible or improbable.

As regards the second question, Marco's own experience on his return to Venice shows that – aside from any hopes of posthumous fame (not something of which the Book speaks) – no advantages were to be expected. It is the third question which clinches the matter for me. Above all the idea of the Polos skulking elsewhere meets an obvious obstacle. If they were not in China for seventeen years (away from Venice for twenty-four years), where were they? The thought that three Venetians would spend twenty-four years at Bukhara, without at intervals returning to Venice to visit their kinsmen, to hear all around them their native speech, and to receive the sacraments from their parish priest, beggars belief. And if they were in fact spending their time carrying on trade in any of the western Mongol khanates – the Ilkhanate of Persia would have been the best for picking up knowledge of China – there were, already by the 1280s, plenty of Italian merchants who would have resided there with them, and who could have denounced their claim to have been elsewhere.

To which might be added the difficulties one faces in explaining how Marco acquired the Great Khan's *paiza*, the gold tablet 'di comandamento' recorded as among his possessions. Dr Wood meets this by hinting that he stole it from his uncle Maffeo. She believes that Maffeo's will of 1310 shows that Marco had borrowed one from him and that it reveals 'some jiggery-pokery over one of these gold tablets' (my own reading of the document provides no evidence for these claims). Then again she holds that it demonstrates 'considerable family division' between them, a division, she tells us, deriving from the fact that Marco had written himself into what was in fact Maffeo and Niccolò's story. (This is not so. The truth is that in the will Maffeo appoints Marco to be the first of his two executors and then leaves him, together with his daughters, the lion's share of his estate.)[37] What is true is that in the course of the deed Maffeo enumerates, as is standard and customary in merchants' wills of the time (these people lived on extended chains of credit), the debts he has satisfied and those which he has yet to meet. Among these he records that he has repaid a loan by Marco to him of 500 pounds Venetian, in part by discounting money which Marco owed him from compensation paid for loss of goods in Trebizond, partly by handing over jewels, and partly with 'three tablets of gold that were of the magnificent Khan of the Tartars'. So it is possible that, the particular *paiza* inventoried among Marco's possessions could have come (though not at all as the result of any 'jiggery-pokery') from Maffeo. How, one asks, had Maffeo obtained it, together with the other two mentioned in the will? Dr Wood tells us that, though the story of the second journey in company with

Marco is fiction, Maffeo and Marco's father had indeed gone on a first journey into Asia which had taken them as far as Karakorum (but no further) where 'one of the Mongol leaders, though not necessarily Qubilai himself' had given them one or more of the tablets. My own reaction to this, apart from wondering how she knows all this, is to reflect that in the will these tablets are described as being 'magnifici chan tartarorum', and this, 'the magnificent Khan of the Tartars' cannot, to my ears, be this or that minor khan but only the Great Khan Khubilai himself.

How then could Maffeo have obtained these tablets of the Great Khan? Had he perhaps stolen or purchased them? Or had he persuaded some skilled goldsmith to forge them? And who might this goldsmith have been, and where did he operate? But any thought along these lines, brief or prolonged, will lead most of us to the conclusion that Maffeo had acquired them through personal contact with the Great Khan (and not in Karakorum but in China, where from 1261 Khubilai was engaged in continuous war with the Song). And if the truth of Marco's Book is validated by Maffeo's contact with China, why should one go on to doubt Marco's association with the Khan? Closely allied to which is the evidence offered by Marco's contemporary Fra Pipino, first translator of the Book into Latin. As we shall see in chapter six,[38] Pipino did not make this translation as a result of any abstract intellectual curiosity or as *belles lettres*, he was, under the command of his ecclesiastical superiors, producing a practical work of deadly seriousness designed to serve the work of Christian missions. In which circumstances, given 'the many strange and unheard of things that are related in sundry passages of this Book', the reliance which could be placed on the word of Marco, Niccolò and Maffeo was of key importance. And here Pipino, after considering the trustworthiness of Marco and Niccolò, expressly remarks that uncle Maffeo, 'a man of ripe wisdom and piety', 'maintained unflinchingly' on his deathbed, shortly before, as he believed, he was about to meet his Maker, that the story told in the Book was true. What light does this oath throw on any assertions either that Maffeo and Marco were at odds because Marco had stolen 'his chance of glory' or that Marco's description of his and his father and uncle's voyages to China was a lie?

Yet beyond this, is it true, as Dr Wood assumes, that the Polos in fact could have obtained in Western Asia the knowledge of the Far East which is presented in the Book? How likely is it, for instance, that one would stumble on those long itinerary-like lists of Chinese city names (without the character of travellers' tales or bazaar gossip), apparently drawn, as we shall see, from Mongol administrative documents, in Tabriz or 'on the Black Sea and in Constantinople'? These remorseless bureaucratic enumerations have quite a different character from the sort of information dispensed about China by the Persian historian Rashid al-Din at the beginning of the fourteenth century.[39] Then again of key importance here is Marco's account, however absurd and misleading, of Japan, Cipangu (Jih-pên kuo). To my knowledge, outside Marco's Book there is, before the sixteenth century, no record at all of the existence of Japan to be found in Central Asia, Western Asia or Europe. How likely then is it that the existence of this 'Land of the Rising Sun' could be picked up on the Black Sea?

V

The truth is that if the Polos were to return to life with a writ for libel in their hands, there is not one shred of hard evidence, nothing outside fantasies of 'jiggery-pokery' and a wholly imaginary hostility between Maffeo and Marco, compounded in a mass of unbridled conjecture, which could justify the accusations so blithely brought against them. That said, it must be admitted that on two of the very rare occasions when Marco is spoken of within the main body of the Book the truth is not told. In chapter CXLIV we are told that Marco governed the city of Yangzhou, at the junction of the Grand Canal with the Yangtze, for three years. If this were so, Marco must have been a very important person indeed, since, as he tells us, this city had twenty-seven rich and powerful other cities under its rule, and was administered by one of the Great Khan's Twelve Barons or major counsellors. But in the local annals of the city which contain a list of all office-holders at the time of the Yuan dynasty, it is impossible to find any governor who can be identified with him or fitted into a three-year rule.[40] Two chapters later we are told that what he calls Saianfu (Xiangyang in Hubei, on the Han river), the last city of the southern-Chinese Song Empire, surrendered to Khubilai Khan after Niccolò, Maffeo and Marco had supervised the construction of three mangonels (siege-engines for launching missiles) for the siege. In fact, from both the Persian Rashid al-Din's *History of the Mongols* and the Chinese annals, the *Yuan shih*, it is known that the siege ended in 1273, that is to say, as it would seem from the Book, two years before Marco ever reached China. Both the Persian and Chinese historians agree that the construction of mangonels was decisive and both give the names of the foreigners, a small family group from the remote west, who built them. In the words of Rashid al-Din, they were 'Talib, the Mangonel-Maker from Ba'albek and Damascus, with his sons, Abu Bakr, Ibrahim and Muhammad'.[41]

It could be that Marco himself is responsible for these stories, that he wishes to exaggerate his importance in the East, perhaps, it has been suggested, because he wants some impressive job in the West.[42] Yet what job? As he must have very quickly realised, twenty-four years in the East qualified you for no post at all in Venice or the rest of Europe (certainly not, as has been surmised, in the kingdom of France, whose inhabitants hated and despised both jumped-up nobodies and Italians, indeed foreigners of all sorts). In these circumstances it seems more likely that we owe these claims to Rustichello. It is he, depressed by the sheer impersonality of the bulk of Marco's material and faced with the task of describing the cities of 'Mangi' (CXXXI–CLI), with their formulaic enunciation of city after city (Cayu, Pauchin, Tigiu, Cingiu, Yangiu, etc.), who is seeking to break up and put some personal interest into the text. Marco, indifferent, meanwhile shrugs his shoulders at a literary strategy. (Significantly enough, both stories are omitted from the Z version of the text which seems closer to Marco's own account.) That impersonality, that pronounced lack of interest which Marco has in telling us anything about himself, is one of the most obvious and remarkable characteristics of his Book. At the same time, it should be added, it presents a powerful argument against seeing him as a man who felt the need to make a false boast that he had been to China. But whether this is so or not, these two falsehoods do not at all of course affect the question of whether Marco ever reached China. All that they bear on is the issue of whether he was anxious in the West to exaggerate his status in the East. And as John Critchley puts it: 'even Polo's proven lies are of the sort which only someone who knew what he was talking about could have told'.[43]

On the question of Marco's supposed status (as opposed to his presence) in China, Li Tse-fen, author of an authoritative five-volume study of the Yuan dynasty, has offered a robust rebuttal of the claims of the Book.[44] Though he admits that Marco knew four languages and various scripts, he was (and all commentators accept this) ignorant of Chinese. (Professor Li Tse-fen tells us in this regard that backward peoples have simple tongues which are easy to master, but that to learn the languages of an advanced society such as that of China presents much greater difficulties.) On the evidence of the Book, however, Marco was also ignorant of the most basic Chinese customs and culture: the Five Fundamental Relations, the Battles of the Dragon on the fifth day of the fifth lunar month, the climbing of hills on the ninth day of the ninth lunar month, and so on. Hence, Professor Li Tse-fen argues, Marco would have been incapable of holding any civic office or making any useful reports on the Chinese domains of the Great Khan. The Book must be considered no more than a farrago of half-baked information based on conversations in taverns with similar low-ranking foreigners.

Considering these arguments, one reflects that in these years China was a subject Mongol colony. One wonders, by analogy, how many British officials in Hong Kong during the colonial era knew any Chinese or had much interest in the peoples over whom they ruled. Certainly it is clear from Chinese sources both that Khubilai himself required interpreters when being addressed by Chinese scholars,[45] and that in his reign several Nestorian Christians, Tibetan Buddhists, and above all Muslims, held very high office, men such as Saiyid Ajall Shams al-Din who was governor of the province of Yunnan, and Nasir al-Din who led the expedition against the Kingdom of Pagan in Burma.[46] Most noticeable in Marco's own Book (though only in Ramusio's version) is Achmad, the high functionary who is finally punished for his ill governance.[47] Though the Book seems to be exaggerating Marco's importance, yet precisely because he was an alien in this world, he might well have been a useful emissary at some level. Paul Pelliot, on the strength of the interest shown by the Book in salt, suggested that he worked in the salt administration. Yet, given that this office required a knowledge of the basic characters of Chinese, this seems improbable.[48] (Since a very prominent feature of Venetian power in Northern Italy and the Adriatic was the maintenance of a rigorous salt monopoly,[49] it would not be surprising that, even though not personally involved, the Polos should have taken an interest in the subject.) Li Tse-fen suggests that he might have had some form of commercial function within the Mongol state. It might, one hazards, be something on the level of the 'companion by name Çurificar, a Turk' whom he writes of (LX, 7) as administering for three years the state-mining of asbestos in a northern desert province. Certainly, I find it difficult to think of a Marco, who does not know Chinese, acting as the Great Khan's observer in Chinese regions, and would hazard that his claim to have done so is simply a device for giving authority to what he has to say about the Khan's realms.

Turning then to the need to explain, on the one hand, the mass of detailed and true information in the Book, together with those things which are ignored or ill-treated, the most satisfactory solution, it seems to me, is that provided by John W. Haeger.[50] Haeger points to the particular weakness of the Book in considering South and Central China, those passages distinguished by 'their formulaic character, their pallor and their shortage of descriptive detail', giving the impression of second-hand information. We might take as an illustration a passage from chapter CLIV:

> When one leaves Quinsai one goes a day to the south-east, finding very delightful houses and gardens, and all foodstuffs in great abundance. And at the end of the day one finds the city that I have named before

called Tanpigiu, which is very big and fair and is under Quinsai. They are subject to the Great Khan, and have paper money, and are idolaters, and burn their dead in the way I have described above. They live by trade and crafts, and have great abundance in all foodstuffs. There is no more to be said about it, and for this we part from there and tell you of Vuigiu.

And when one leaves this city of Tanpigiu, one goes three days to the south-east, finding always many towns and villages, most fair and large, where one finds all goods in great plenty and cheapness.

The people are idolaters, obey the Great Khan, and are in the lordship of Quinsai. There is no novelty to mention here. At the end of three days one finds a city which is called Vugiu [sic]; this Vugiu is a big city and they are idolaters, and they obey the great Khan, and live by trade and crafts, and they too are under the lordship of Quinsai. There is nothing there that we want to put in our book, and so we go forward and tell you of the city of Ghiugiu.

With passages of this character Haeger compares the descriptions of the Mongolian steppe and the north-China plain, the accounts of Khubilai himself, his palaces of Shang-tu and Khanbalikh, the vivid account of the great hunting parties and the solemn festivities at the Great Khan's court, such as that of the new year. Summarising chapter LXXXIX Haeger writes that

the Kaan and all his subjects dressed in white robes, gifts exchanged among themselves and made to the Kaan of silver and pearl and white cloth, the Kaan's barons and knights embracing and greeting each other as they exchange gifts, white camels and horses given to the Kaan ('if they are not altogether of white, they are at least white for the greater part, and very many white horses are found in those countries'); a parade of the Kaan's elephants and camels 'covered with beautiful white cloths worked artificially and richly in gold and silk, with many other beasts and with birds and lions embroidered.' And on the morning of the festival, 'all the kings and princes and all the dukes and marquesses and all the counts and barons and knights and astrologers, and philosophers and physicians and falconers, and many other officials of the king, captains and rulers of lands and of armies come into the great hall before the lord, and those who by reason of the multitude do not achieve this stay outside the palace in the halls at the side, in such place that the great lord who sits on a throne can see them all well'. And then the text describes the protocol of seating and how 'a great wise ancient man, as one might say, a great prelate stands up in the middle' and intones the liturgy of the feast. And the ceremony is described step by step, through the feast itself to the 'musicians and jugglers and buffoons' who come to amuse the court when the meal is done.[51]

On the one hand, there are the descriptions in north China – as, for instance, in the account of the new city built at Peking where 'the main streets from one side to the other of the town are drawn out straight as a thread and are so straight and so broad that if anyone mount on the wall at one gate and look straight, one sees from the one side to the other side opposite to that' – where one senses a genuine effort to reproduce an image.[52] To be contrasted with that is the schematic recital of places along imaginary itineraries that one finds in the matter relating to southern China. The form of these place names derived through Persian or Turko-Mongolian, suggests a knowledge of southern China gleaned from conversation with, or reading the reports of, court emissaries, writing or speaking in those languages (just such emissaries among whose ranks, according to the Book, Marco himself is said to have served the Great Khan). The result is a European's impressions of what he has learnt from Persian and Mongol servants of the khans, yet much more detailed and intimate than anything that could have been learnt from someone trying to draw the same picture, from, say, distant Persia.[53] With this theory, then, Marco, his father and his uncle, are men who have lived in the Great Khan's court, as it moved between its winter quarters at the new town of Daidu near Peking and the summer capital of Shangtu to the north. But, until their passage to Zaiton (Quanzhou) in order to depart by sea for Persia, they know of southern China only through hearsay.

Haeger's conclusion offers a convincing solution to the problems associated with Marco's knowledge of China. Yet in a sense, of course, for the historian of geography, none of this much matters. For his purposes one could say, after the manner of those who expound literary criticism, that the very idea of the author was a fiction, a mere function of discourse, that what was important was not the author but the Book.

Chapter 4

The Making of the Book

I

T he Book was a collaborative work, and like any collaborative work
was born of a whole series of compromises, the more particularly
because of the difficulty of translating the remoteness and strangeness of its material into terms acceptable to a western audience. It is for
this very reason that it has given rise to so many different interpretations.
It is these which are to be examined in the present chapter. The first of
these is that it is an adventure story and that its title is *The Travels of Marco
Polo*. This reading, it could be, ultimately derives from a misunderstanding of the text prepared by Ramusio in the sixteenth century, who to adapt
the work to his collection of what were basically travel narratives
(*Navigazioni e viaggi*), called it *I viaggi di Marco Polo*. Yet anyone who
approaches the work looking for a tale of heroic exploration is going to be
badly disappointed. Nothing is more striking here than Marco's silence
about the difficulties and dangers he must have faced or about the character of the journeys he made. This comes out very clearly when one compares the Book with the accounts of Giovanni di Pian di Carpine or William
of Rubruck, which contain, among other things, true adventure stories.
One remembers how Pian di Carpine tells of how he passed 'in continual
danger of death' within the Mongol realms; of how 'On the first Friday
after Ash Wednesday we were preparing camp as the sun was setting when
some armed Tartars rushed upon us in a threatening way, asking who we
were; we replied that we were envoys of the Pope, whereupon they went
off straightaway, taking some of our food'; of how at Karakorum 'beaker
after beaker' of fermented mare's milk was forced upon him and his com-
panions. Or one thinks of Rubruck: 'We would go for two days, sometimes
three, without any nourishment but mare's milk. Sometimes we were in
great danger, unable to find a living soul, short of food and our horses worn
out.' And so on, giving us many sharp vignettes of exciting, dangerous,
wearying moments. In Marco's Book there is nothing of this, no sudden
glimpses of friendly or hostile individuals or bands, no account of lame

horses, escorts, difficulties or dangers, no specific dates, no crises, no hunger or thirst. Any sense of awe we feel at this journey comes not from anything Marco tells us but from our own reflections on what must have been there but of which he himself says nothing.

A major difficulty for Rustichello must have lain in how little action, how little adventure Marco reported. But were there not, at least, the voyages to and from China? In fact it is remarkable how silent Marco is on incidents from them or on their specific routes. In every historical atlas one finds a map on which are traced 'The Voyages of the Polos'. These supposed itineraries, alas, are fantasies. After the first nineteen chapters, the Book is indeed written as if it described a series of routes. It is interspersed with passages such as (XLIX): 'Now we leave these provinces and these parts and do not go forward, for if we went further on we should enter India; and I do not want to enter there at this point. For on our return journey will be told to you all about India, in order. Let us go back therefore to Badakhshan, because we are not able to go by another route.'

Yet this is clearly not the route of the Polos through Asia; it is an organising device, the route along which Marco and Rustichello lead their readers from west to east and then back from east to west, the route through the Book: '*pour aler avant de nostre livre*'.[1] In fact the Book does not say in anything but the vaguest terms how the Polos went to China or returned from it. The routes which our historical atlases so confidently mark out have been constructed simply on the order in which Marco speaks of the various regions. Yet a large part of Polo scholarship has been devoted to attempts to define them in ever greater detail. This has led to the most improbable conclusions; for instance, that on their outward journey the Polos journeyed 400 miles south of the main Silk Road (which might be traced through Bukhara, Samarkand, Kashgar, Khotan and the southern edge of the Takla Makan), and quite perversely, if they were consciously seeking to deliver as rapidly as possible the Pope's letters to Khubilai, decided to ascend the remote high Pamir and the mountainous Hindu Kush: 'so high,' says the Book, 'that it is said to be the highest place in the world'.[2]

The Book then is not a story of adventure and it is not a description of travels. Those, for us, all too brief introductory chapters (II–XIX) which give the most summary account of how the Polos chanced to know of the East, are not at all the subject of the Book. They are merely a foreword intended (however unsatisfactorily, since they raise far more problems than they solve) to validate the truth of the material which follows. (They are comparable to the last chapter of Pian di Carpine's work which, in describing his journey, had the same purpose.) The Book, it is clear, does not describe travels or adventures. Another interpretation is that it is a work, written by a Venetian merchant, whose title is *Il Milione*, meaning

'Masses of Money', and that its essential character is that of a merchant's handbook. For Ugo Tucci, for example: 'the book is the most thought-provoking that has come to us on the mentality of a Venetian merchant in the thirteenth century'.[3] For Franco Borlandi, Rustichello has constructed the Book from a merchants' handbook which Marco had composed while in the East.[4] In a Florentine manuscript of the Book, dated 1431, there is a note which claims that in Venice Marco's work was available to all at the time for public consultation: 'Marco Polo is a book that treats of parts of the sea and land and of the great and miraculous things that are found in the world. And this book is at Venice on the Rialto, fastened with chains, that each man can read it.'[5] This chained book, Borlandi believes, was not Rustichello's version but the original merchants' handbook drawn up by Marco.

The arguments for all this derive from Marco's frequent reference to commercial goods, his description of paper money, markets and so on. These things are certainly omnipresent. One thinks of the Book's attention to gems, pearls and corals – 'rubies, sapphires, topazes, amethysts and many other precious stones' (just the goods the elder Polos first ventured into the East to trade), its notices of silk, cotton, salt, rice and scores of other commodities. Above all one is struck by its close concentration on 'spices' – that term which in the Middle Ages included, as well as seasonings, perfumes and substances used in medicine – the more particularly when the Polos travel to the China Sea, the East Indies and the Indian Ocean. Through Zaiton, we are told, valuable goods, precious stones and pearls come to the province of Mangi. For every shipload of pepper going to Christian lands through Alexandria in Egypt you can find a hundred in this port. The Great Khan takes a tenth of all imports; the shippers have freight charges of 30 per cent on small wares, 44 per cent on pepper, 40 per cent on lignaloes (the so-called eaglewood or 'sinking incense'), sandalwood and bulk goods. As a result merchants have to spend a half of their investment, yet they still make a profit. There follows the remarkable account of the junks which carry the trade: clinker-built (with overlapping planks) with iron nails, with four permanent and another two removable masts, single-decked but with fifty to sixty cabins, one for each merchant aboard, and with watertight compartments in the hull. Manned by 200 to 300 mariners, each vessel was capable of carrying 5,000 or 6,000 baskets of pepper and was accompanied by its own flotillas. First by two or three large tenders or barges 'large enough to carry 1,000 baskets of pepper' with their own complement of fifty to eighty seamen, then by ten small craft to fish, lay out anchors and bring supplies. (Ships are one of the few things which stimulate Marco to eloquence, whether here or in the description of the Arab dhows at Ormuz, or the thousands of decked, one-masted vessels on the Yangtze.)

Thereafter Marco turns to the China Sea where he describes the operation of the monsoons on trade and then the larger East Indian islands. Of Java (CLXIII) we learn:

The island is of very great wealth. They have pepper and nutmegs, musk and spikenard and galingale [an aromatic root] and cubebs [a form of pepper] and cloves, and all other spices one can find in the world. To the island come a great quantity of ships and merchants who buy much merchandise and make great profit and great gain. . . . And from this isle the merchants of Zaiton and of Mangi have drawn much great treasure and draw it every day.

In Sumatra ('Java the Less') he writes (CLXVI) of 'costly spices – lignaloes and spikenard and many others that never come to our parts' and in the Kingdom of Lambri in the north-west of the island (CLXIV) 'much camphor and other spices'.

Then in India he remarks on 'pepper and cinnamon and ginger', 'ginger and pepper and very fine indigo', and 'brown incense' near Bombay. At the then flourishing port of Quilon on the Malabar coast where Chinese merchants met those from Arabia, he mentions the local production of brazilwood, indigo and pepper, and explains how the pepper trees are cultivated and the indigo is prepared. In the Kingdom of Malabar (CLXXXIII):

There is great abundance of pepper and ginger and there is much cinnamon and other spices in great quantity and turbit [once used in medicine] and nuts of India. They also have many buckrams, the finest and most beautiful in the world. They have much precious merchandise. And again I wish to tell you what merchants from other parts bring to this country when they come in their ships to buy its goods. You should know that the merchants carry copper in their ships; they also bring here cloths of gold and silk, sendal, gold, silver, cloves and spikenard and other spices that are not here, and these things they change for the merchandise of this country. And you should know that ships come here from many parts but especially from the great province of Mangi. Their own goods go to Aden from where they are taken to Alexandria.

Yet from Malabar and the adjacent Kingdom of Gujerat piracy continually menaced trade. Marco describes how twenty to thirty pirate ships sailed in line at intervals, thus covering up to a hundred miles of sea in order to sweep up their prey. Further west in the ocean at Socotra, and then again in Madagascar and Zanzibar, he refers to ambergris, used in perfumes and extracted from the belly of the whale, 'for there whales are plentiful', while on the Arabian coast and at Dhofer there is 'white incense' (frankincense) and a vast trade between Aden and India.

All this certainly seems to show that from his education (in the tradition, we have seen, of the *Zibaldone da Canal*) and presumably at the prompting of his uncle and father, Marco acquired a professional knowledge of the most precious items of eastern commerce. What we have here is the first detailed account for the West of the provenance of the major spices and a mass of exact information about trade goods. Does this mean that the Book is Rustichello's expansion of a merchant's handbook? Another argument proffered for this thesis springs from some of Marco's silences which we have already considered. Why does he never write of the Great Wall of China, Confucianism, foot-binding, printing, etc.? Answer: these things are of no interest to someone writing a merchants' handbook. Why no mention of tea? Answer: in Italy, with its excellent wines, tea would have been unmarketable. But it is precisely at this point that one's first doubts arise, in that it then becomes necessary to explain the presence in the Book of all those things which do not refer to commerce. How many Italian merchant handbooks can you name which give an account of the Sakya-Muni Buddha? The improbability of the notion becomes obvious when one looks at a description of China in a genuine merchant's handbook. In the *Pratica della mercatura*, drawn up by the Florentine merchant, Francesco di Balduccio Pegolotti, one section, based, it would seem, on information from the period 1310–30, is devoted to 'Advice about the journey to Cathay by the road through Tana for those going and returning with wares'. Here Pegolotti explains step by step how to travel from the Black Sea port of Tana to Khanbalikh: what to wear, what servants are needed, what provisions should be taken, what the cost is in precise figures, how safe were the various stages of the journey, what goods should be offered for sale, what bought, what transport problems might arise, and so on.[6] Marco, by contrast, offers nothing on these matters, nothing, that is, on what a merchant would actually want to know. The Book lacks any specific notes on organisation of voyages, volume of business, conditions and problems of markets.[7] We have instead what one finds in the guide-books of the *Touring Club Italiano*, reference to trade goods, not as in a trade directory, but as indications of the wealth, activities and occupation of the local inhabitants, and in Marco's case, with a distinct preference for what is spectacular rather than mundane (nothing here, as Olschki points out, on alum, Indian iron-mines, bronze or lead-mining).

One commentator has remarked that Marco's interest in trade is more that of a tax-official than a merchant,[8] and that thought harmonises with one suggestion of what office the Polos may have filled under the Great

Khan. Gritting our teeth, let us look at another section of the imaginary itinerary through Mangi (CLI, 11–18):

> Now we will quit Suigiu and go to a city which is called Viugiu, and you should know that this Viugiu is a day from Sugiu [sic, labile spelling]. It is a very large city, and a good place and of great trade and with great manufacturers. But as there is no novelty to be called to mind there we will leave it and I will tell you of another city called Vughin.
>
> And this Vughin is also a very large and noble city. They are idolaters, obey the Great Khan and have paper money; there is much silk there and much other precious merchandise. They are skilled traders and skilled craftsmen.
>
> Now we will part from that city and tell you of the town of Ciangan. Now you should know that this city of Ciangan is very large and rich. The people are idolaters, obey the Great Khan, and have paper money. They live by manufactures and trade. Here they make quantities of sendal of many kinds and in great quantity. There is much game and hunting there. There is nothing else which comes to mind, so we shall go on. . . .

In these staccata-burst sentences there is some economic information, yet – since to this day it has been impossible to identify from Marco's information where Viugiu, Vughin, or Ciangan might be[9] – there seems nothing here likely to persuade a Venetian merchant to visit them. (Unless, perhaps, such a merchant were in quest of sendal, a particularly valuable type of cloth which Marco would have seen in the umbrella carried over the Doge's head.)

It might also be added that conspicuously absent from the Book is any information about the *ortoghi* or merchant associations and profitable partnerships maintained between Mongol princes and the Inner and Central Asian merchants[10] Nor is there anything here detailed enough to make a tax-inspector's heart beat faster. What we have is not at all any professional interest in the economy; Marco's purpose seems to reach beyond that. The cumulative effect of these, for us, tedious repetitions, would have been to give the medieval reader an extraordinary vision of a whole hitherto unknown world of cities engaged in trade and commerce set within the East. The sense of wonder with which such pages would be examined by someone of Marco's own day is incomparably greater than that which any reader today – fortified by and to a great extent dependent upon notes, maps and commentaries by learned Orientalists – can hope to experience. And it is that wonder, not any professional advice, which Marco offers here. Quite apart from which, the idea that an Italian merchant would *publish* a *Libro di mercatura* is utterly improbable. When these men drew up a

73

handbook, it was designed solely for the benefit of their own firm. It was not at all something to be exhibited at large, chained or unchained on the Rialto, for the benefit of their competitors.[11]

II

The Book, it may be concluded, is not a work by a Venetian merchant about commerce in the East. Another interpretation is latent, though not fully endorsed, in one of the most valuable works on the subject, Leonardo Olschki's *The Asia of Marco Polo*. For Olschki the Polos feel themselves to be (among other things) lay apostles of the faith, stand-ins, as it were, for the 100 Christians learned in the liberal arts whom Khubilai has requested of the Pope; Marco is seeking to give his Book 'the character of a religious mission'.[12] Its title is that of the Franco-Italian version: *Le divisament dou monde*: 'The description of the World'. It has a two-fold religious purpose: first as a guide to Western missionaries; second to reveal the magnificence of God's creation. In favour of this view it is certainly true that the departure of the three Polos was blessed in person by Pope Gregory X and that it was as emissaries of the Church that they returned to the Great Khan. Then again, from early on the Book was adapted to religious purposes, to serve as a contribution in that ancient tradition of Hexaemeric literature (reflections upon the *Hexaemeron* or the six days of creation) which has been seen as a principal source for early medieval interest in geography. Sometime before 1314, at least nine years, that is to say, before Marco's death, a Bolognese Dominican, Francesco Pipino, was commissioned by his order to translate the work into Latin, specifically to act as a spur to evangelisation and a handbook for mendicant missions. And in his preface Pipino introduces Marco, sure enough, as one who has given the world knowledge of 'the variety, beauty and immensity of creation'.[13]

Yet the idea of Marco as missionary seems impossible to sustain. Although he defines people by their religion, this is in a purely sectarian spirit. His comments on the various faiths always refer to externals, and he seems indifferent to and ignorant of the essential content of their beliefs. If he knows the Christian scriptures, he never quotes from them. Throughout the Book he frequently refers to the various Christian sects in the East without any reference to the way in which their beliefs differed from those of Rome, or between each other. He makes only three, extremely cursory references to the numerous Jewish communities in the East.[14] He makes no mention at all of Confucianism, and only one brief reference (LXXV) to Taoism, or rather to Taoist monks, 'men of great abstinence after their fashion'. Of 'idolatry' as he calls Buddhism, he has more to say. He is (though understandably) mistaken in ascribing its origins to Kashmir, but notes correctly that the 'eremites after their fashion' (i.e. their non-Christian fashion) were held in great reverence for their asceticism (XLIX). In Tangut (LVIII) and particularly in the city of Canpiciou (Zhangye in Gansu province), they have many abbeys and many monasteries. These are (LXXV) immense, sometimes as big as a small town, with over two thousand monks in one abbey. These are completely filled with idols of many fashions, 'some of wood, some of clay, some of stone and all covered with gold and highly polished'. He refers in particular to recumbent colossi with figures kneeling in reverence before them but gives no sign that he realises that they are representations of the Sakya Buddha entering Nirvana. He is very interested (LXXV) in the Bacsi, the enchanters called 'Tebet' and 'Quesmur [Kashmiri]' – 'which are the names of two nations of idolaters', whose spells divert clouds and storms from the Great Khan's palace, and who at his banquets serve goblets filled with drink through the air without touching them.

Yet even in externals truth is mingled with error. ('And know this, that all the idolaters of the world on death are burnt' is false.) And on occasion creeds other than Buddhism are lumped together under idolatry: in chapter LXXV the priests who scatter mare's milk to the spirits, and in chapter CLXXVII the Brahmins (mistakenly categorised as merchants) of the province of Lar, and the Ciugui or Hindu ascetics. (My own suspicion is that Confucianism has disappeared in the same way; that for Marco once you had seen one temple, whether Buddhist or Confucian, you'd seen them all.) This is not to say that there is not much of interest here, but that it is looked at uncertainly and from outside. Marco's account of the Hindu Ciugui – their nakedness, their drinking of sulphur and quicksilver, their prohibition of killing even a flea or a louse, the testing of their will by sexual abstinence – is immediately recognisable. And on coming to Ceylon and the mountain of Adam's Peak where the Sakya-Muni or Gautama Buddha had his sepulchre (CLXXVIII), Marco gives a quite vivid account of how the young, wealthy and powerful Prince perceives the hollowness of his happiness after chancing upon first an aged man and then a corpse:

And when the King's son has fully understood death and old age he returns to his palace and says to himself that he will dwell no more in this evil world; but he says that he will go to find that which never dies, and so he did. And then he leaves his palace and his father; he goes to the great and trackless mountain and there remains all his life most worthily and chastely, and practises great abstinence. For certainly if he had been a Christian he would have been a great saint with our Lord Jesus Christ.

The zealous Dominican Fra Pipino omitted this observation from his translation (Pipino III, 22) and Marco has been praised by contrast for the supposed tolerance which the passage demonstrates. Yet though Pipino was clearly a man of many other excellent qualities, to be singled out as being more tolerant than him is not, as we shall see, any particularly striking compliment. And a closer consideration of the passage reveals the obvious, namely that the Buddha is being praised not as an exponent of the doctrines of Buddhism but because of his supposed adhesion to a Christian ideal of virtue. One is reminded of the remarkable way in which during the Middle Ages and Renaissance – as a result of the very widely diffused story of Barlaam and Josephat – the Buddha came to be canonised as a saint of the Catholic Church, transmuted into St Josephat.[15] Though earlier, at one point in Ramusio and the Z text, reincarnation is briefly mentioned,[16] here the reader learns nothing of it. The (from a twentieth-century perspective) superficiality of Marco's interest serves as a great contrast with the friar William of Rubruck who like some homing pigeon zooms in sharply on the mantra 'Om mani padme hum',[17] something which, however many times he may have heard it, means nothing to Marco.

Of Marco's attitudes to Islam I shall defer consideration until the next chapter in which we shall examine S. M. Islam's strictures upon him. For the moment I shall merely remark that though, like a football supporter, he seems normally to hope that his own team will win, and is quite happy to cheer up his western readers by asserting at one point that Khubilai was a closet Christian,[18] it is remarkable how his own loyalty to Christianity is not normally given any emphasis. When the admittedly Nestorian, but still Christian, Nayan, Khubilai's uncle, revolts against the Great Khan, Marco's sympathies (LXXVII–LXXX) are passionately given to Khubilai rather than to his co-religionist. Again, on one occasion, in those remarks on Mongol beliefs found in the much more private and less generally distributed Z version, Marco lets slip sentiments which might almost suggest that he had acquired that indifferent tolerance of all religions which the Mongols themselves professed:

These Tartars do not care what god is worshipped in their lands. If only all are faithful to the Lord Khan and quite obedient and give therefore the appointed tribute, and justice is well kept, thou mayest do what pleaseth thee with thy soul. And yet they will not that thou speak evil of their souls, nor interfere in their doings. And thou may do what thou wilt with God and thy soul whether thou art Jew or Pagan or Saracen or Christian who dwellest among the Tartars. They confess indeed in Tartary that Christ is Lord, but say that he is a proud Lord because he will not be with other gods but will be God above the others in the world. And so in some places they have Christs of gold or silver and keep them hidden in some chest, and say he is the great Lord supreme of the Christians.[19]

The insouciant tone of the passage, in no way balanced by any fervent protestations of Christian devotion, seems to me to point away from any deep attachment to missionary expectations.

III

If we are to reject these interpretations of the Book, what we are left with is simply and essentially a work of geography. This is not, to be sure, geography as defined by Ptolemy. One of the very few remarks Marco makes on that suggests a quite startling lack of knowledge or thought about basic cosmography. The island, he tells us (LXXI, 9), in the Northern Ocean where the Great Khan's gerfalcons are bred lies so far to the north that there you leave the North Star some way behind you to the south. Marco's interest is confined to chorographical and anthropological geography.[20] If this is so, in what traditions were Marco and Rustichello writing? One answer is that of the eloquent and learned Jacques Heers who remarks that the Book is 'an encyclopaedic treatise forming part of a long and living tradition. This tradition, solidly anchored, accords in the description of the world, a large place to fabulous legends.'[21] He refers at this point to works of a quasi-encyclopaedic character like the *Tresor* of Dante's master Brunetto Latini and Ristoro d'Arezzo's *Composizione del mondo*, written in 1282. Yet on consideration these works seem remote from the Book. In Brunetto's *Tresor* there is indeed, amidst discussions of philosophy, theology, historical facts, the books of the Old and New Testaments, the nature of animals and many other things, a chapter tersely elaborating a description of the three known continents. In Ristoro d'Arezzo's book, which is principally about astronomy, there is, again, a chapter of about three and a half pages, giving geographical names.[22] All this seems very different from the amplitude and detail of Marco Polo's Book. The truth is that in the geographical culture of the Middle Ages from Solinus, to Isidore, to Gossuin, there is to be found nothing like the Book of Marco Polo.

Are we then on firmer ground in seizing hold of Heers' 'fabulous legends'? Should its title be either *Il Milione*, meaning this time 'a thousand thousand marvels' or, as it is often called in early manuscripts, the

Livre des merveilles du monde. (Or again 'Hereafter begins the Book of Marco Polo of *the Marvels* of Asia the Great and India the Greater and Lesser and of the diverse regions of the world' or 'Here begins the Book of the Great Khan which speaks of Great Armenia, of Persia, and of the Tartars, and of India, and of *the great Marvels* which are in the world'.)[23] The Middle Ages of course had, like us today, a particular obsession with 'marvels'. (Thousands of people in the United States, it is said, believe today that many of their fellow citizens have been abducted by aliens into flying saucers and subjected there to degrading sexual experiences. Or at least hundreds of thousands of Europeans, equally in search of the marvellous, believe that that is what thousands of Americans believe.) In the fifth century, St Augustine, in his *City of God* (Book XXI, chapter 4), drew upon the marvellous to defend what Christians believed. So, for instance, in justifying the reality of an Eternal Fire which did not consume the wicked but allowed for their perpetual grilling, Augustine had referred to such *mirabilia* as that of the salamander which was burnt and yet survived within the flames or, again, of the volcanoes of Sicily which burnt unceasingly without being consumed themselves. In the following chapter Augustine urged unbelievers, who mocked 'our' miracles to explain equally strange things in the natural world, such as, for instance, 'the fact' that in Ceylon 'the trees never cast their leaves'. Do these passages indicate that in the Middle Ages people were fascinated with the idea of the marvellous because marvels could serve as an element in Christian *apologia*? It would be difficult to point to many passages in medieval literature which could justify this contention. Rather the enthusiasm for marvels seems simply to meet, then as now, a persistent human need.

We have already encountered many of them in our first chapter. One thinks of the tales about 'the monstrous races': Cynocephali, the Blemmyae, Sciopods, and so on. Throughout the later Middle Ages they maintained their hold on the imagination. They proliferate in John of Hildesheim's *History of the Magi Kings*, written in the second half of the fourteenth century, and surviving in over five hundred manuscripts;[24] in the numerous versions of the Alexander legends; and in the hundred or so extant manuscripts, in a variety of languages, containing the *Letter of Prester John*. They still riot in chapbooks, such as *The Travels of Prince Pedro*, printed some ten years after Vasco da Gama's epoch-making voyage.[25] Normally this kind of material was associated with the East. But not exclusively. In the dedication to his *History and Topography of Ireland* (*ca.*1188) Gerald of Wales remarks that among the matters to be discussed there are 'what new things, and what secret things not in accordance with her usual course had Nature hidden away in the farthest western lands'.[26] He goes on to explain that

Just as the countries of the East are remarkable and distinguished for certain prodigies peculiar and native to themselves, so the boundaries of the West are also made more remarkable by their own wonders of nature. For sometimes tired, as it were, of the true and the serious, she draws aside and goes away, and in these remote parts indulges herself in these secret and distant freaks.

In Book II, dedicated to 'The Wonders and Miracles of Ireland', Gerald – citing the Psalmist: 'Come and see the works of the Lord, the wonders that he has worked on the earth' – expresses the hope that he will come to be seen as one who revealed the wonders of the West as others had those of the East.[27]

Some twenty years later the Englishman, Gervase of Tilbury, dedicated to the Emperor Otto IV his *Otia Imperialia* or *Imperial Leisures*. Of this Book I dealt with 'the Creation of Heaven and Earth' and Book II with 'the three parts of the world in its regions and provinces'. These were, it is clear, merely considered as preliminaries to Book III 'the marvels'. Although Gervase may very well be the author of the Ebstorf map, in which, following Gerald's formulation, the marvels are to be found in 'remote places', those of the *Otia* are found closer to home; the majority of those discussed in his book came from France, England and Italy. At the same time, they are distinguished from those miracles – things which do not obey nature, works of divine omnipotence – with which Augustine had compared them. 'By marvels we understand what, though natural, has escaped our understanding: what makes the marvellous is our inability to understand its cause.' Taking up what he has read in Augustine about the salamander which lives in the fire, Gervase says that at Rome he has seen a leather salamander strap as wide as a sword belt which when thrown on the fire was not consumed. We tend, he says, to ignore familiar *mirabilia*:

If we were told the sort of thing about some stone from India without being able to verify it, we would certainly think of it as a lie or we would be quite amazed and marvel at it. But those marvels which are under our eyes all the time, though no less astonishing, lose their worth because we are accustomed to see them, to such a point that certain marvels of India itself [such as, he mentions later, the magnet which, he clearly believed, came from the East], which is a distant part of the world, have ceased to excite our wonder once their coming here has made them less remarkable.[28]

His book, he explains, will help its readers to distinguish true marvels from the false marvels of impostors. While a long way from the modern scientific method, Gervase's book is of interest for its attempt to think about the meaning of the marvellous and for its testimony to the existence of a medieval scepticism encompassing the marvellous.

None the less, the marvellous, it has been justly said, was an essential element in medieval geography.[29] From the time of Pliny and Solinus, geography itself might indeed be seen as merely providing a context for marvellous tales (as it still did in Gervase of Tilbury's work). And in a later chapter we shall meet Friar Jourdain's *Mirabilia descripta*, written in 1328, which describes 'the many and boundless marvels' of India and the way thither. So too, writing two years after Jourdain, the Franciscan Odorico da Pordenone told of the 'many great marvels which I did hear and see' in China. Turning to Marco's Book, it is not at all surprising that an idea of the marvellous looms with some prominence. Take this Book, Rustichello urges in the preface, and have it read to you and you will learn of 'the various generations of men and the diversities of the diverse regions of the world'. It continues: 'And here you will find *toutes les grandismes mervoilles* and the great diversities of Great Armenia and of Persia and of the Tartars of many other provinces. . . .' So too Pipino's preface: 'Let all know Messer Marco Polo, *horum mirabilium relatorem*, to be a most respectable character.'

What 'marvellous things' are at issue here?[30] Briefly I would isolate six broad types:

1. What we – with the benefit of hindsight – might call, thinking of Gervase of Tilbury's definition, 'rational' marvels. As examples one thinks of, in the Baku peninsula, 'a fountain which jets oil in great abundance, not good to eat but good to burn' (XXII) or 'a sort of black stone which burns like wood' (something which was to amaze Aeneas Sylvius Piccolomini when he came to Scotland).

2. Descriptions of towns of greatly exaggerated size and extent; claims such that the city of Quinsai was a hundred miles in circumference and had 12,000 stone bridges. (Odorico of Pordenone in the fourteenth century gives the same figures for a circuit of the city and its bridges; it has been suggested that he and Marco are repeating some popular saying.)[31]

3. Christian miracles: the '*grant mervoie*' of the Caliph and the Shoemaker, dated to 1275 (XXVI–XXIX); the Saracen stone in the Church of St John at Samarkand (LII); the provision of fish in Lent in a Georgian monastery (XXIII); the miracles at the tomb of St Thomas in India, in particular that of 1288 (CLXXVI); and the girdles of St Barsamo (in Ramusio).

4. Tales of men known already to medieval Europe. Among these are stories of Alexander, sometimes from a western source (*The Book of Alexander*) as Iron Gate (xxiii); sometimes apparently from eastern sources, as the *Arbre Sec* (xl); the marriage at Balkh (xlv); notice of his descendants (xlvii), and of the descendants of his horse Bucephalaus (in Ramusio). To which should be added eastern lore on the Magi (xxxi–xxxii) and the Old Man of the Mountains (xli–xliv).[32]

5. Stories of conjuring or of miracles carried out by those who are not of the Christian religion, like 'the wise astronomers and wise enchanters', the Bacsi, who, in chapter lxxv, preserve the Khan's palace from bad weather and who (this story will come to be told too by Odorico of Pordenone),[33] without any human touching them but by their enchantments, transport goblets through the air from the centre of his hall to his table.

6. Then there are what might be called the traveller's tales. Here the marvellous consists sometimes in the abundance of wealth, sometimes in the strangeness of things beyond nature. Both are found most notably in Cipangu, which Marco never visited but which he had perhaps learnt of through Khubilai's recruiting propaganda for its invasion. In the Book it has something of the character that the East in general had for the West; all that he writes here (clix, clx) is colourful. It is an island, 1,500 miles (*sic*) to the east, with measureless quantities of gold, where the ruler has a palace roofed in fine gold, with chambers paved with fine gold, over two fingers thick, with halls and windows decorated with gold.[34] Its value 'would pass the bound of the marvellous'. It has countless riches with pearls and precious stones in abundance, and it is a land of 'a great marvel'. Here Khubilai Khan's invasion force sought to behead eight prisoners. But they were unable to do so because each had a stone embedded under the flesh of his arm whose properties made its possessor invulnerable to steel. Only by beating with clubs could they be put to death; the stones then taken to India are much in demand.

These stories of the irrationally marvellous are to be found particularly in that area of the world which Marco defines as 'India' (Eastern Asia omitting China). Many of these stories were already in existence, often for many centuries, before Marco's own lifetime. As for instance, of the two islands called *Male* and *Female* (clxxxix) and of the Rukh, the great bird of Madagascar which pounces on elephants, draws them high into the air and then releases them to smash their frames (cxci). Or the description of hunting for diamonds in the Kingdom of Mutfili (clxxv). The diamonds lie in valleys guarded by venomous serpents. From the crags above, hunters throw down meat; thereupon white eagles swoop to retrieve it; as soon as the birds return to the heights, the hunters frighten them away and pick up the diamonds which have stuck to the meat. All these tales are found in many eastern sources as well as in Chinese sources available at the time.[35]

The same is true of stories of dog-headed men. J. Needham has pointed out that most of the monstrous races of Greek geography and medieval legend – dog-headed men, pygmies fighting with cranes, giants, Sciopods, tailed-men, centaurs, Cyclops or monocoli, Blemmyae etc. – are also found in the *Shan Hai Ching* or *Classic of Mountain and Seas*, a work, much of whose material can be dated from between the the late fourth century and second century B.C., destined to be read avidly in China for some two thousand years.[36] As it happens, though they are often said to do so, dog-headed men do not appear in Marco's Book. In chapter clxxii Marco speaks not of *cinocephali* but of men with faces *like* dogs; he is merely signalling a common reaction to what Colonel Yule called the 'allophylian' type of countenance found in the Andaman Islands.[37] In fact none of the monstrous races are to be found in the Book.

This is a staggering omission. At the turn of the fourteenth and fifteenth centuries, miniaturists commissioned to illustrate Marco's work, though not finding them in the text, decided none the less to include images of them (see illustration 4); a work about the East *must* have such things in it! Yet this was a betrayal of the author's text and of his intentions.[38] For Marco is always keen, whenever he can, to dispel the truth of legends dear to western readers. Take the salamander, immune to fire, a character, as we have seen, cosily familiar since the days of St Augustine. The salamander, Marco points out emphatically in chapter LX, is not at all an animal, 'as it's said to be'. 'And this is the truth of the Salamander that I have told you and anything else they say about it is lies and fables.' In chapter CLXVI again, he observes that the unicorn (which he identifies with the rhinoceros) is not at all like the creature which is said to be trapped by hunters through the chains of a virgin, and goes on to say that those who bring home 'pygmies from India' have in fact been cheated with the bodies of depilated monkeys. Other traditional marvels are given short shrift. As, for instance, Prester John. Instead of the infinitely powerful potentate ruling the three Indias in incomparable splendour, we find a Central Asian princeling who meets an ignominious death at the hands of Genghis Khan, and whose line, thenceforth, continues in humdrum vassalage to the Great Khan Khubilai (LXIV–LXVIII). At the same time Gog and Magog, the dreaded all-powerful harbingers of the ultimate apocalypse, are dismissed in two sentences (LXXIV): 'This is the place that we call in our country Gog and Magog; but they call it Ung and Mungul. And in each of these provinces there was a descent of people; in Ung were the Gog and in Mungul dwelt the Tartars.'

This has been written of as if Macro were simply supplying new marvels to replace the old ones. The truth is that the retailing of legendary marvels is secondary and subsidiary to the Book's main purpose. Compared with any earlier western description of the East the legends found in Marco's Book though certainly present, are by any comparison few and far between. That is to say that the 'marvels' in the Book are above all the marvels of a workaday geography and anthropology, of, as Caroline Bynum has put it, 'a world that encompasses such staggering diversity'.[39] The title to chapter CLVIII reads: 'Here begins the Book of India and it will describe *toutes les mervoilles* that are there and the manner of them'. And straightway he begins on that theme: 'Since we have told you of those many mainland provinces of which you have heard, now we will set aside all this material and begin to enter India to tell of all the *merveios couses* that are there; and we will begin first of all with the ships in which the merchants go and come to India.' At which there follows a quite unlegendary description of the Chinese junk. Here what is marvellous to the West, following Gervase of Tilbury's insight, is a normal and everyday part of life in the East. And it is these everyday things which form the bulk of Marco's marvels. For some readers it might have been, indeed, Marco's rejection of received wisdom, rather than any wholesale acceptance of it which would have been likely to induce scepticism. Yet for the early reader, belief must have trembled not before the absence or presence of accepted marvels, but before a quite different class of wholly new marvels that Marco offered. It was not difficult to believe what was said about India. Alexander's conquests and trade in the age of the Roman Empire had left behind, in the works of Solinus and Pomponius Mela, among others, some information, however slight, of the sub-continent. It was in what lay beyond, in the region known as 'Further India' or 'India beyond the Ganges', with its description of China, Indochina and the Indonesian archipelago, that scepticism would arise. Was it possible that far away – how far was not clear, but it seemed to be, under difficult circumstances, a journey of three and a half years – there existed a wholly new world of towns and cities, which looked – this is most difficult to credit – more flourishing and richer in goods, than those in the West?

IV

Marco's Book, then, was not written in the tradition of books of marvels as such. Turning to less general writings, we again draw a blank. There were descriptions of the Holy Land, but these were still, before the fourteenth century, confined to enumerations of sacred sites, their legends and the indulgences to be gained at them.[40] There were, from as early as the eighth century, some very occasional descriptions or 'praises' of cities.[41] But there were only two authors who had previously attempted any work of chorography. Around 1080 Adam of Bremen, in the fourth book (entitled 'A description of islands of the North') of his *History of the Archbishops of Hamburg-Bremen*, had sought to define the boundaries of the metropolitan church of Hamburg and had given a full account of the Baltic, the North Sea and (with some references to Iceland, Greenland and 'Vinland') the North Atlantic.[42] About a century later, Gerald of Wales, perhaps responding to the same curiosity provoked by border-regions – what he calls 'the last corners of the earth'[43] – wrote interesting descriptions of Wales and Ireland. Adam of Bremen's work survives in twenty-four medieval manuscripts; Gerald's *Description of Wales* in six, his *Itinerary of Wales* in seven, and his *Irish Topography* in some twenty-nine (including a translation into Provençal).[44] Then again, of course, there were those lively accounts of the Mongol world drawn up by the friars, Giovanni di Pian di Carpine (extant in sixteen medieval manuscripts, and incorporated in Vincent of Beauvais' encyclopaedia) and (though very little diffused) of William of Rubruck.[45] Yet I would hazard that it is extremely unlikely that any of these were known to Rustichello, let alone to Marco. To write the Book, that is to say, a new genre of western literature had to be created.

By contrast, a strong chorographical tradition already flourished in China. In Chinese literature there were accounts of travels, local topographies, geographical encyclopaedias and anthropological-geographical descriptions.[46] In the mid-thirteenth century, for instance, Chau Ju Kua, Inspector of Foreign Trade in Fu Kien province, wrote a *Description of Barbarous Peoples*, giving information on Burma, Java, Sumatra, India, Baghdad and even a few isolated notes on the Mediterranean. (Even Mount Etna appears: 'This country has a mountain with a cavern of great depth in it: when seen from afar it is smoke in the morning and fire in the evening, when seen at short distance, it is a madly roaring fire.'[47]) Again in the thirteenth century, come three city-descriptions of Hangzhou (Marco Polo's Quinsai) under the Song dynasty.[48] There was *The Wonder of the Capital*, written around 1235 by Chao, the Old Gentleman of the Water Garden Who Attained Successes Through Forbearance,[49] Wu Tzu-mu's *Dreaming of Splendours in the Midst of Deprivation* (whose preface is dated 16 September 1274) and Chou Mi's *Anecdotes* (before 1299).[50]

These works have nothing in common with the Book of Marco Polo. The descriptions of Hangzhou which range in detail across festivals, public buildings, offices, police, firemen, postmen, temples, pagodas, monasteries, shops, gardens, pleasure-grounds, clubs, the unemployed, prostitutes, theatres, professional story-tellers, restaurants and taverns have an immediacy and vividness wholly lacking in the Book. On the other hand it seems possible that Chinese civilisation had, at one remove, some influence on the Book. As we have seen, Marco never learnt to read Chinese or to speak a Chinese language. Like the majority of his Mongol masters in the early years of the Yuan dynasty, he remained aloof from or was unable to penetrate Chinese civilisation. Yet, it is also clear that something of native geographical culture rubbed off on to the new Mongol upperclass. It is known, for instance, that Khubilai who sent out many missions in search of strange birds and beasts, dispatched an expedition in 1280 to discover the origins of the Yellow River and that the results were then written up.[51] Again, under the Mongols, ambassadors to foreign powers continued, as they had done for several centuries, to produce reports on the places they had visited,[52] just as, in his Book Marco himself claimed to have done.

In addition to such reports there were road-guides and itineraries all along the Silk Road to Constantinople. The first that survive date from the Ming dynasty, but it seems most probable that they were in existence under the Yuan. Finally, from very early on, the Chinese had drawn maps, required tributaries to send them maps, and had themselves been forced on occasions to send maps as tribute to their enemies who had triumphed over them.[53] At times they produced maps based on a sophisticated rectangular grid system; there survives, for instance, from the early fourteenth century a map of this type, from a lost book called the *Institutes of the Mongol Dynasty*, which represents about a hundred towns to the north and west of China proper, up to and including Constantinople, Damascus and Damietta. From this lost book, too, one chapter survives, an enumeration of the post-roads in China and part of Mongolia.[54]

It is something of all this perhaps that is to be found in the Book of Marco Polo. Its true title is some variant of that of Pipino's Latin translation: *De condicionibus et consuetudinibus orientalium regionum*, 'Concerning the conditions and customs of eastern regions'. It is essentially a mediation to the West of such Chinese geographical culture as has been absorbed by its Mongol rulers. If this is so, who is Marco Polo? He is not an adventurer, a merchant, or a Christian missionary; he is rather a minor Mongolian civil servant who during his years in the East has been an observer or student of the topography and human geography of Asia, of its customs and folklore, of, above all, the authority and court of the Great Khan, all seen from a Mongol point of view. Then, having taken early retirement, he has sought an audience for his memories.

Marco left Venice in 1271 at the age of seventeen. He returned in 1295, twenty-four years later, aged forty-one. Take these facts, together with a truly remarkable feature of the Book: that in describing the eastern world there is no evidence of culture shock. In a famous phrase, Friar Rubruck declared that on entering the lands of the Tartars 'it really seemed to me that I was entering some other world'.[55] This response, of course, is the most natural in the world; it is the theme of most travel literature, surviving well into the age of mass tourism. Take the French friar, Jourdain of Severac, who returned from India in the 1330s. The final message of his report is: 'there's no place like home'. 'One general remark I will make in conclusion: to wit there is no better land or fairer, no people so honest, no victuals so good and savoury, dress so handsome, or manners so noble as here in our own Christendom.'[56] These attitudes are reversed with Marco Polo. The splendours of Khubilai's court, the magnificence of his autocratic rule (in such contrast to the spirit of Venetian republicanism), the great cities of Khanbalikh and 'the paradise'[57] of Quinsai, seem, as we read of them, to surpass anything in the western world. This is not simply because the cities of thirteenth-century China outshone Venice and Pisa, but because 'East-West, home's best', and for Marco home was China. Here is a Mongolian court-functionary who has returned to the Christian West and who must have often been bewildered by the strange world he finds there. In sixteenth-century Venice there was a legend of the Polos' return to Venice: 'Through the length and trials of their voyage and through the many fatigues and demands upon their spirits, these gentlemen were changed in aspect and had got a certain indescribable touch of the Tartar both in air and accent, having all but forgotten their Venetian tongue.'[58] In these circumstances, the story continues, their relatives refused to believe that they were indeed who they said they were. It is a legend; but one which surely must correspond to some part of the truth: namely, that these men who returned to Venice after more than two decades were not merely wearing Tartar clothes but were also men who were in many ways thinking like Tartars and looking through Tartar eyes.

Why did Marco want to return to Venice, to leave behind friends, perhaps even a family? Out of loyalty, it could be, to his father and uncle, perhaps through the tie to his birthplace created in the first years of his life. Or perhaps because he was afraid of what would happen if Khubilai should die. The Book refers to court factions: 'the Great Khan was so pleased at the bearing of messer Marco that much did he love him and made him such great honour and held him so near to him that the other barons greatly envied him.' This, it seems possible, is merely either his or Rustichello's boasting, yet Pegolotti, in his merchant's handbook, was to warn of the dangers to which foreigners were exposed at the death of the ruler.[59] As Khubilai grew older the Polos may have felt they had to go in order to survive. One of the great themes in Italian literature of this period is that of exile.[60] For Marco the pain of virtually enforced exile from

Mongolian China was perhaps ameliorated by the thought that when he returned to the West, he would bring with him, not simply the *paiza* of the magnificent Khan of the Tartars, the Buddhist rosary, the silver belt worn by Tartar knights, the woman's golden head-dress inset with stones and pearls, which we know to have been among his goods, not simply the Mongol slave, Pietro, whom he frees in his will,[61] not simply all these things, but the whole of the East where he had spent most of his life and which he would now attempt to recreate in words.

Chapter 5

The Description of the World

I

In his recreation of the East what materials, outside memory, did Marco Polo have to draw upon? What areas are covered in his depiction, and with what relative intensity and depth are they considered? And in what spirit does this westerner treat the various places and peoples of the East? Does he seek, by a distorting emphasis upon such things as their diet, sexuality and religions, to represent them as 'the Other' or has he achieved any harmony with them? In this chapter we shall examine these questions in order to consider more closely the character of 'The Description of the World'.

Turning, first, to the materials which he puts before Rustichello, it seems certain that whenever Marco speaks accurately and in great detail, he is doing so not on the basis of memory but with documents before him. It is the evidence for the existence of these documents which shows that the work was planned before leaving China and that it was not simply produced by any chance imprisonment. When, for instance, Marco comes to his great set-piece, his description of Quinsai, the City of Heaven, today's Hangzhou, he says this (CLII):

> In this we shall tell you of its nobility following what the Queen of this Kingdom sent in writing to Bayan who conquered this province, that he should send it on to the Great Khan, in order that he might know the great nobility of this city, so that he might not destroy or injure it. And what was contained in that writing was the truth, as I Marco Polo saw after clearly with my own eyes.

One version adds that Marco paid several visits to the city and made notes on what he observed.[1] Again, in chapter CLIII, he says that he knows about the revenues of the city because he was sent by the Great Khan to inspect them several times. And this suggests other likely sources which he uses, namely reports of those emissaries (of which, perhaps untruly, he is said to have been one) who went on Khubilai's missions.

I would think it probable too that Marco had before him itineraries of the type used in the Mongol relay-posts. This would explain the way in which the description of China is structured like an itinerary. Take these examples (CVI and CVII):

> And when one has left this town [Giongiu] and gone a mile you find there two routes, one of which goes west and the other south-east. That to the west is for Cathay, that of the south-east goes towards the great province of Mangi. And know in truth that one rides to the west through the province of Cathay for ten days and finds there at all times many beautiful cities and many beautiful fortified-towns. . . .
> When one has ridden for ten days after leaving Giongiu, then one finds a kingdom which is called Taianfu. And the head city of this province where we have come is also called Taianfu, it is very large and beautiful. . . . And when one has taken leave of Taianfu he [*sic*] rides a good seven days to the west through a very beautiful countryside. . . . Then he finds a city called Pianfu, which is very large and of great worth. . . .

According to the Book (CV, 1–2) this route was actually followed by Marco in a mission for the Great Khan. Yet more probably these formulas (which vary between '*Quant l'en s'en part . . .*' and '*Et quant il a alés . . .*') are to be seen as a rhetorical device designed to break up what would otherwise be an even balder enumeration of towns.[2]

In writing of China that concision is normal. Christiane Deluz has remarked that of the seventy Chinese towns which are recorded in the Book only two – Quinsai and Khanbalikh – receive any full description. The rest are recounted in stereotypes. First the town is allotted a status – 'noble', 'very noble', 'great', 'very large', 'huge', 'mistress'. Then, if appropriate, it is related to its subject hinterland, as above with Taianfu. Third, reference is frequently made to the religion of the inhabitants ('idolaters', 'Saracens', etc.), and their subjection to the Great Khan, as is shown particularly by their use of paper money. Finally comes reference to economic activity and, if appropriate, to any remarkable buildings or bridges. Dr Deluz follows Pauthier in his attempt to show that the enumeration of these cities follows the administrative divisions of Yuan China rather than any itinerary.[3] In either case it seems to me probable that this type of material is based on a document used in the Mongol administrative service.

Away from China, in his description of the Indian Ocean, Marco is using what he calls (CLXXIII, 2) 'the *mapemondi* of the mariners of those seas' and (CXCII, 25) 'the charts (*conpas*) and writings of experienced mariners'. In the

Ramusio version Marco makes this explicit, saying that he will describe the three Indias (i.e. the three parts of Asia) from what he saw personally, what he heard from good report, 'and things that were shown on the maps of the mariners of the Indies'.[4] But more than this, the overall construction of the Book, moving first from west to east, then discussing China, then moving back through the Indian Ocean to the west, seems to have been imposed on Marco's material by his having before him a map of Asia either prepared for the Mongols by one of their Persian cosmologists or, it could be, a Chinese map, translated into Persian, with some such title as 'China and the Barbarian Peoples'. (Which, one might hazard, could be taken as the true title of Marco's Book.)

In addition to the geographical materials and the myths (as we have seen, the Book is important for the transmission of eastern mythography),[5] there are the historical sections (particularly chapters LXV–LXIX, CXCIX–CCXVI and CCXXII–CCXXXIII), telling the story of the Mongol rulers. When checked against eastern sources they are found to be shot through with errors and imperfections. What these represent, I take it, is that body of folk-memory, ruler and dynasty-worship, current at the Mongol court. Discussing one incident within this material the Book says: 'Now the stories say' (*or dit le contes que . . .*),[6] which is a normal formula. But does it in this context actually refer to a specific body of material? Olschki has answered that behind this are Marco's memories of epic-verse sung by Mongolian folk-singers.[7] If this is true one returns to Rustichello's repetitive, cliché-ridden battles in this section of the Book with a new insight. Because in them Marco and Rustichello have found a western objective-correlative to Mongolian epic poetry which, like all oral literature, depended upon just such formulaic material for its delivery.

All this miscellaneous material Marco, on his return, perhaps began to translate into his childhood Venetian. As he did so the difficulty of giving it any acceptable literary form must have been sharply borne in on him. Then, in prison, he chanced upon Rustichello. That meeting was crucial, not, as so many have argued, in persuading Marco to decide to write his Book, but in giving him the ability to do so. For what is owed to Rustichello is the familiarity with the Franco-Italian literary traditions of his day which allowed the publication of the work. Much of the raw material which Marco brought back with him would have been immensely tedious to anyone but the academic geographer, and in the West at that time academic geographers did not exist. The information from the itineraries and maps, those records of town after town, characterised simply by a laconic sentence would, by themselves, have caused the Book to die. What preserved it was the skill with which Rustichello breaks up this simple information with other tales which Marco has brought back: stories of marvels which were sometimes true, sometimes false, and sometimes deliberately falsified by Rustichello in order to secure an audience for his collaborator. Western readers would come to brood over Marco's descriptions (LXXXIV) of the externals of Khubilai's palace at Peking – a description whose accuracy can be verified from Chinese sources – because Rustichello had clothed their walls in that gold and silver – not found in any Chinese source, and clearly fictitious – which were a commonplace of fantasy palaces in western romance.[8]

II

What geographical knowledge does Marco actually give in his book? Its depth and extent can best be considered by setting out its contents schematically. In order to give an idea of the space devoted to each area I shall refer to the number of pages in Gabriella Ronchi's printed edition of the earliest surviving F text. It must be remembered that, unlike today's readers, those of the thirteenth century would have no maps beyond the conventional *mappaemundi* to guide them, and no possibility of identifying places and distances where indications of these are not given. In all, the Book can be divided into ten parts:

Part I (chapters I–XIX), 19 pages. In this, the introductory matter telling of the Polos' journey and their supposed relation with the Great Khan, we receive an impression of distances travelled, however greatly exaggerated[9]: three years from Khubilai's court to Layas; three and a half years back from Acre to 'Kemenfu'. However inaccurate, these would at least correct the impressions likely to have been implanted by *mappae mundi*, where the placing of Jerusalem in the centre of the ecumene tended to suggest there was an equal distance west and east from Jerusalem to 'the Ocean Sea' (i.e. the Atlantic in one direction, and, in the other, the Sea of Japan).

Part II (chapters XX–XLV), 35 pages. These chapters consider the Middle East and the lands of the Ilkhans of Persia: Little Armenia, 'Turcomanie' (most of Asia Minor), Great Armenia, Georgia, the Caspian, Mosul, the city of Tabriz 'where merchants make great profits', Kerman to Otmuz, the desert of the Arbre Sec, and Balkh, 'the end of the empire of the Lord of the Levant [i.e. the Ilkhan]'. The geographical content is much diluted by other matter: anecdotes about the miraculous lake of St Leonard's convent in Georgia, the Caliph's gold, the miracle of the shoe-maker (XXVI–XXIX), the Magi (XXXI, XXXII – serving in place of a description of Persia), Alexander stories, stories of the Old

Man of the Mountains and his Assassins (XLI–XLIV). Again, without a map, it cannot always have been easy for the reader to relate the various parts to each other.

Part III (chapters XLVI–LXIII), 21 pages. Westward on an unusual itinerary to Cathay, the Book takes us through Badakhshan, the Pamir, Kashmir, then north-eastwards to Kashgar, Samarkand (another Christian miracle, with only the most perfunctory notice of the town), Khotan with its rivers of jade, Lop and the Great Desert, the cities of Tangut. Almost all of this area would be wholly new territory for any western reader.

Part IV (chapters LXIV–LXXIV), 21 pages. Karakorum and the heartland of the Mongols. Here there were already in existence the accounts of Giovanni di Pian di Carpine and William of Rubruck which, as so far as they go, are more telling and vivid than those of Marco's Book. But these were to enjoy a comparatively small circulation in the Middle Ages, while Vincent de Beauvais omitted what most pertained to geography in his choice of material from them. For most readers, that is to say, the matter here would be new, while even those few who had read the earlier accounts would find new material. There are interesting (though, as is known today, often very inaccurate accounts) of Tartar history: on Genghis Khan and his defeat of 'Prester John', and on Genghis' successors. There are chapters on Mongol customs, transhumance, gods, warfare and justice. The Book goes on to speak of the Province of Tenduc, ruled by the descendants of Prester John.

Part V (chapters LXXV–CIV), 50 pages. The world of the Great Khan and the provinces of Cathay.[10] In this section Marco writes with particular knowledge and enthusiasm, speaking of the summer palace of Shangdu; the revolt of Nayan against Khubilai, his defeat and execution; the person of the Khan, his wives, concubines and family; his guards, his rewards to his captains of 'the tablets of authority'. He goes on to describe the city of Khanbalikh, the Great Khan's palace there and his son's; the splendid feasts for his birthday and the New Year, his great hunting parties. Though saying little on administrative institutions in general, Marco gives good reports on paper money, taxes, the relay-posts, tax relief and corn-doles in time of famine and assistance to the poor. For the West this was wholly original material, sometimes highly coloured, but fundamentally true, and often vindicated in its essentials by modern studies.[11] On the other hand, among the northern neighbours and subjects of the Great Khan, Korea, only mentioned in passing, has a notably low profile.

Part VI (chapters CV–CXXX), 40 pages. Khanbalikh to Burma. This section is structured on an imaginary journey which Marco Polo is declared to have made, into 'the western provinces', taking the road from Peking to the town he calls Giongiu (Cho-Chiu or Cho-chau), then taking a western route to Shijiazhuang, across the Yellow River to Zhenghzou, and passing on, presumably through Shanxi, Shaanxi and Sichuan, to the south-west. There follow accounts of Tibet, Yunnan province and its cities, Mien, i.e. Burma (a battle with elephants between the King of Mien and the Mongols), a brief mention of Bengal (apparently thought of as part of Vietnam). Everything here would have been completely new to the West. On the other hand, it is a mixture of formulaic and ethnographic material, which shows many signs of being second-hand, and where, as for expert commentators today, it must have been very difficult for the reader to make an identification of the places named.

Part VII (chapters CXXXI–CLVII), 39 pages. Mangi or South China. ('The Book uses words derived from Persian to distinguish northern China – Cathay – and southern China or Mangi.) The reader is now returned to 'Giogiu', and proceeds southwards to the Yellow River, on crossing which he enters 'the great province of Mangi'. A chapter covers the conquest of Mangi by the Great Khan; then the Book refers to Yangzhou (a most laconic description for the city Marco is supposed to have governed for three years); then (very much off the route) Saianfu, today's Xiangyang (and its capture thanks, supposedly, to the mangonels built by the three Polos); 'the greatest river in the world, which is called Quian' (still today the Chinese call the Yangtze simply '*Jian*' – 'the River'); the Grand Canal; the Sugiu, Viugu, Vughin, Ciangan and others that we have already encountered; Quinsai or Hangzhou (a description of eight pages); Fugiu (Fuzhou in Fujian); Zaiton (Quanzhou), 'one of the two greatest harbours in the world for commerce' (though already, it has been suggested, in decline).[12] Apart from the description of Quinsai, a great deal of this is formulaic, and suggests only second-hand knowledge. Rustichello must have had great difficulties with this section, seeking, for instance, to offer moments of relief from the recital of names which would have, at the time (as still often today), meant nothing to the western reader by inserting the untrue stories about the Polos to add colour to colourless descriptions. In the end there seems an abdication, a recognition that all the material available to Marco, precisely because it is all going to sound the same, simply cannot be presented. Chapter CLVII announces that three 'kingdoms' of Mangi have been spoken of: Yangiu (Yangzhou), Quinsai (Hangzou), and Fugiu (Fujian). 'We could tell you of the other six, but since it would be a long business to go over, we will keep silence about them. . . .' (In fact it is difficult to understand what Marco meant by these Nine Kingdoms, and he is often mistaken in the number of subordinate cities that he ascribes to the larger cities that he mentions.[13])

In Marco's China there are, outside Xiangyang, no references to cities in the interior, while even Canton (Kuangchou, Pinyin Gaungzhou) is not mentioned. What the western reader would have gained from these sections is perhaps less any precise knowledge of the individual towns than a total picture of a hitherto utterly unknown, prosperous world, teeming with rich commercial cities, great rivers and trade. The author is, as we shall see, very little concerned with the native Chinese. He has no interest in rural life or the work of the peasantry. In describing China, as elsewhere, he offers his readers nothing on the physical appearance of men and women or what they wear. His main theme is Mongol rule (though little is made of the fact that the Mongols were foreign rulers). From republican Venice, Marco is above all else a champion of the glories of Khubilai Khan, and gives great importance to the history of his rule: the conquest of the south of China, the campaigns against Champa (1282–5); the projected conquest of Japan; the revolt of Qaidu (from 1286) and (though not in the F version[14]), the plot against Achmad. The Great Khan, wisest and most powerful of rulers, has about him something of Prester John, and with his 'face white and red as a rose, eyes black and beautiful, nose well-formed' seems to resemble more the stylised features of a king in western iconography than the features with the little beard and Mongol moustache which peer out at us from the actual Chinese portraits of the time (though these too, one fancies, are not naturalistic).[15] Yet when all the reservations of Chinese scholars have been taken into account, Marco's description can still be seen as 'an unsurpassed description of Khubilai's reign at its height'.[16]

Part VIII (chapters CLVIII–CLXXII), 20 pages. 'Here begins the book of India'. The chapters which follow were to exercise a particularly important influence on late medieval and Renaissance cartography. After the famous description of Chinese junks, Marco tells of 'Cipangu' (the Chinese 'Jin-pön-kuo', 'Land of the Rising Sun' or Japan). His two brief chapters on the country (see above page 81) can without exaggeration be described as nonsense, yet it was to be immensely fruitful nonsense, while they remain the only western reference to Japan before the sixteenth century. Here Marco, who of course never visited it, was probably, as Olschki has suggested, influenced by Khubilai Khan's recruitment propaganda for his attempted conquest (though Marco takes as one invasion the two of 1274 and 1281).[17]

This section continues with accounts of Champa (central Vietnam); a reference to the 7,448 islands in the 'Sea of Chin'; Java; 'Java the Less' or Sumatra, with its eight kingdoms, costly spices and cannibals; the Andaman Isles; with description of the 'idols' of Cathay, Mangi, and Cipangu, and the account of the Sakya-Muni Buddha. Here are chapters where Marco's misapprehensions were, at least indirectly, to stimulate Columbus; and where misinterpretations of what he had written were to allow sixteenth-century cartographers to postulate the existence of a vast southern continent below the East Indies.

Part IX (chapters CLXXIII–CXCVIII), 61 pages. India Part II: Ceylon, 'Greater India', the western Indian Ocean. Here is the description of a world previously known only in fable. Fables remain, but mingled with interesting information, partly from heresay, but partly too from direct knowledge: 'Maabar' (the Coromandel Coast); the shrine of St Thomas; Quilon; Malabar; Tana; Gujerat and Cambay; hunting diamonds with eagles. Thereafter the Book takes us through the Indian Ocean, though with information which is largely second-hand and unreliable, to the Isles of Men and Women; Socotra; the Rukh; Abyssinia, Zanzibar and the island of Madagascar (which he seems to confuse with the mainland of Mogadishu).[18]

Part X (chapters CCIX–CCXXXIII), 52 pages. The Ilkhanate and the Golden Horde. Here, apart from some pages on the northern world, the Book's main theme is the recent and contemporary history of the Mongol khanates: the wars of Qaidu with Khubilai; of the Khanate of the Golden Horde with the Ilkhan Abaqa. There follows an account of the succession to the Ilkhanate between 1282–95. After some remarks on the northern steppes, home of 'the proper Tartars', where are found dog sledges and the precious skins of the black fox, the Book speaks of the 'land of darkness' and Russia, where there is 'the greatest cold that is to be found anywhere'.

At this point, Rustichello begins a description of the Black Sea but rejects its relevance (CCXVII) on the grounds that 'so many people know all about it' – a rhetorical means perhaps of emphasising the profound originality of what has so far been written. The Book then turns more fully to the history of the Khanate of the Golden Horde or Kipchak Khanate: with the war of Berke against the Ilkhan Hülegü, and the succession of Khans within the Golden Horde. John Critchley has very convincingly interpreted this section as standing separate from the main body of the work, perhaps added later as 'an appendix tagged awkwardly on at the end', which is to be read in the context of a renewed interest among western Christian powers at the end of the fourteenth century in an alliance against Islam with the Mongols of Persia.[19]

One is struck above all by the work's comprehensiveness, in the sense of its endeavour to cover the whole of the East. We have already seen that this is not a book of 'travels' in the conventional sense. At the risk of restating the obvious it is not, as is sometimes said, a book about China. Gabriella Ronchi's edition of the F text fills 358 pages. Of these 19 form the Preface. Of the other 337 pages, 129 deal with China within its present boundaries, and 208 with other parts of Asia. It was, first of all, the geographical scope of Marco's enquiry that made it so ambitious an enterprise, and then, further to that, the variety of matters considered within that geographical coverage. At the end of Part VII ('Here begins the book of India') he gives us one version of what his Book is about (CLVII, 17–18):

> For well have we told you of Mangi and of Cathay and of many other provinces and of the people and of the beasts and the birds and of the gold and silver and of the stones and of the pearls and of the merchandise and of many other things, thus as you have heard. And yet our Book has not yet finished all that we wish to describe, for it lacks all the facts about the Indians which are indeed things to be made known to those who know them not. For here there are more marvellous things than there are in all other worlds and for this it is good and most fine and profitable to put it in writing in our Book. And it will all be put there clearly just as messer Marco Polo describes and says it.

'The merchandise' is there as we have seen, and artisan production. So too are (what the friars William of Rubruck and Giovanni di Pian di Carpine wholly ignored) the birds, fish, exotic vegetation and animals: lions, tigers, elephants, wild asses, the gazelles of Gansu, sheep – fat-tailed, four horned, and the long-horned 'wild sheep of great size' (*Ovis Poli*) of the Pamir – the five types of exotic crane, sakers, gerfalcons, peregrines, with the hairless chickens of Fujian.

And then so much else, names of provinces and cities, governments, religions, crops, customs. Complaints about the work's low level of cultural engagement or of what has been left out often neglect what it was possible to write about in medieval Europe. As for instance, there are no descriptions of landscapes in the Book because the Gothic thirteenth century had discovered nature but not yet the idea of landscape. It should be added that it is precisely both Marco's omissions, taken with his frequent mere grazing of the surfaces about what he does write, that permitted him to take on the whole of Asia. In that sense a modern history of early anthropology which discusses Marco in terms of 'What a chance missed!' is direly off the point.[20] If Marco had been passing his twenty-four years abroad in the equivalent of participant observation among the Nuer or Azande, the Book would never have been written or, if written, would never have been read in the Middle Ages. This Book has to be thought of, judged, as a geography and neither a work of anthropology nor a travelogue. In this respect, the fact that Marco had wide-angle-lens vision, that his close-ups generally lacked all the intensity found in the reports of the friars, were positive advantages. (No doubt it reflects their respective skills in description, but it also mirrors in a way the intensity of the friars' six-months' or a year's experience of the East as compared to his twenty-four years.) For the supreme strength of the Book lies in its organisation, its steady progress, people by people, province by province, town by town, each with its own political arrangements, religion, natural and manufactured products and other peculiarities, individually distinguished. Never before or since has one man given such an immense body of new geographical knowledge to the West.

III

In all this a principal interest relates to what he, born in Venice, writes of the people of the East among whom he lived for so many years. In our own time, Edward W. Said's influential studies of imperial and colonial literary and scholarly culture (above all in his *Orientalism*, first published in 1978) have drawn our attention to the figure of the western 'orientalist'. In Dr Said's studies the 'orientalist' is portrayed as one who seeks consciously or unconsciously to strip his subject of power, even of his own identity, by casting him in the rôle of 'the Other', and as one who by exoticising what he examines serves to represent it as more feeble, contemptible, and so ripe for domination or conquest. With the diffusion of such notions (though in Said's case these are directed to writings from the eighteenth century), it is not perhaps surprising that the Book of Marco Polo has recently been cast in precisely that rôle, as in the words of Syed Manzul Islam in his book *The Ethics of Travel from Marco Polo to Kafka* 'an exemplary instance of the Western discourse of othering', and as 'singularly obsessed with devising a discourse of othering'.

For Dr Islam – to summarise very briefly his complex arguments – Marco is guilty of postulating a total 'otherness between Christianity and non-Christianity and of 'one of the classic tropes of colonial discourse', namely the 'deterritorialisation' of the peoples of Asia. (By this word, as I understand it, is meant the displaying of other peoples in such a light as to imply that they are unworthy of the territory they hold, which can therefore be taken from them.) Marco, Dr Islam argues, does this, by holding up for inspection the 'disorders' of the East: things such as its supposed monsters – unicorns, dog-headed men, the Rukh – and those dietary differences (notably cannibalism) and sexual practices which offend western tabus:

> The making of relative difference, through the mediation of the 'common unit' of dietary and sexual manners and customs, not only dramatises the otherness of others but subjects this otherness to an evaluative judgment. Marco Polo gives his readers a panorama of transgressive topoi with their rude chaos and abomination which deterritorialises other habitudes . . . Marco Polo's representation of other habitudes, despite being shaped by the displaced underside of the normal of his own world, is troped as autochthonous, as if their appearance as abominable topoi were entirely due to their own organic resonance.[21]

I have great difficulties with this. The 'monsters', we have already seen are not common in the Book and all of them that do appear feature in eastern folklore. If both Chinese and Arabic sources speak of Rukhs (and indeed the great Arabic traveller, Ibn Battuta, describes a nasty encounter with, and narrow escape from, one on his return from China to India in the 1340s[22]), should Marco have kept silent about them? Monsters cannot be in themselves 'deterritorialising' since, as again we have seen, Gervase of Tilbury locates his almost exclusively in France, Italy and England itself.[23] As to diet, it is true that Marco reports unkindly on what was eaten in Quinsai (CLII, 20): 'They eat any flesh, that of dogs and any other brute beasts and animals that no Christian would eat for anything in the world'. Yet who reading that chapter can doubt but that Marco has the most profound admiration for the city and in many respects for its people? Marco's comment is of the order of those Englishmen (who have now for a long time abandoned any hope of 'deterritorialising' the French) who express disgust at the Parisians' taste for frogs' legs and snails, declarations distinctly insular in character but hardly either significant or malevolent. As to anthropophagy, Marco makes five references to it, all in distant parts. Of these one (CLXI, 8) does look as though it derives from imperialist propaganda. That the Japanese think that 'no meat is so good' as human flesh is a story which, it is likely, would have been concocted about the time of one of Khubilai Khan's invasions. Of the others, who knows? Marco writes (CLXVI, 8) that cannibalism is current in the hill-country of Sumatra. In the nineteenth century Colonel Yule, at this point, noted the comments of the German anthropologist Junghuhn who had lived among the Battas of Sumatra (and 'who could not abide Englishmen but was a great admirer of the Battas'), explaining the 'precise laws' under which it was practised.[24] Are there no authentic examples of cannibalism, and if so is, if not the practice, the very mention of the subject, to be condemned?

Nor will anyone who is inspired by Dr Islam's words to make a close study of the text find a great deal of illicit or unconventional sexual or marital practices. Dr Islam makes much of the references to prostitution. In fact there are only two. In Khanbalikh (XCV, 6–8) no public woman is allowed in the city. But in the suburbs there are some twenty thousand of them, which will give you an idea, Marco remarks, of the size of the total population. I doubt if there is any criticism in this. After all in the Italy of the day the communal governments tried in the same way to localise and control the trade so that they might profit from it, something Marco does not describe the Mongol lordship as doing. And in the second contribution (in Ramusio) there is positive enthusiasm for the marvellous courtesan-like creatures of Hangzhou, these *donne* or ladies (not women), magnificently dressed and perfumed, with their splendidly furnished houses, their allurements and caresses, their ready speech adapted to every sort of person: 'So that strangers who have tasted them just once seem beside themselves and are so greatly taken by their sweetness and charm that they can never forget them. And so it comes about that when they return home they say they have been to Quinsai, that is the City of Heaven, and they cannot wait for a chance to return there!'[25] Not, I would hazard, words born of a crafty colonialism but of altogether warmer sentiments.

As to eccentricity in sexual or marital practice, there is one occasion when this is described together with condemnation and another when it is spoken of with contempt. In chapter LXII (10–13), at Canpiciou (Zhangye in Gansu) the priests of 'the idolaters' keep themselves from lust though their followers may have up to thirty wives and may reject one wife and take another. 'They take their cousins in marriage and the wife [presumably widow] of their father. They do not hold as sinful what we hold as very great sins, for they live like beasts'. (This 'live like beasts' is Marco or Rustichello's phrase for breaking a tabu: so the cannibals of Sumatra – CLXVI, 8 '*sunt tiel como bestes*'.) In the province of Gaindu (western Tibet, CXVII, 5) a husband (described in pitying terms as '*le chetif*') will allow his wife to sleep with visitors. Otherwise these things are described neutrally. There is the *couvade* on the Tibet–China border (CXX, 6–8). Along the caravan routes of the extreme north-west of China husbands and wives who are separated for more than twenty days are free to marry again (LV, 7–9). The customs of the Tartars include marriage to fathers' widows and so on (this time with no condemnation, LXIX, 18) and the *merveliose usançe* that the parents of sons who die before marriage 'marry' them to daughters who die before marriage (LXX, 33). In the province of Caraian (CXVII, 9) it is a matter of indifference if a man lies with another's wife, provided she consent. As it happens the Muslim writer Rashid al-Din was, shortly after, to remark that the men of this region 'have no shame respecting their wives'.[26] I doubt very much whether these anecdotes, some perhaps true, others false, can be seen as a conscious or unconcious attempt to 'deterritorialise' anyone. What they represent is a natural human interest in, amusement at, and embroidery of, the strength and variety of human sexuality. The frequent playful subtext of such stories is uncovered at the end of the description of how in Tibet (CXV, 12–19) girls, though completely faithful after marriage, were expected to sleep with any strangers before marriage: 'Now have I told you of these marriages which makes a good story [*che bien fait a dir*]; and this country is a good place for a young chap of sixteen to twenty-four years.' (This being one of the only two jokes in the Book; it must be conceded that neither Marco nor Rustichello displays a powerful sense of humour.)

Further to which, portrayal of sexual gratification can be used – and is used by Marco – in wholly opposed senses in different contexts. So in his description of the palace and gardens of 'King Facfur', i.e. the last Song Emperor in Quinsai, and of the thousand young girls in his service, Marco writes of the delightful grounds, the preserves for animals and the pleasures the King would enjoy there:

> They would run with dogs and give chase to these animals, and when they were tired they would go to the groves that grew by the shores of the lakes, and they would leave their clothes there, come out naked, go to the water and swim about here and there, and the King stood watching them with the greatest pleasure and then they returned home. Sometimes he would have a picnic served by these damsels in the groves which were thick with very high trees.

A charming, extravagant variation of *déjeuner sur l'herbe*; but since the Song were destined to be losers, something which had to be paid for dearly: 'And with this continual sporting with the ladies he was brought up without knowledge of arms, and it was this which finally brought it about that through his cowardice and stupidity the Great Khan took over his state to his utter shame and contempt as you have heard above.'[27]

Which is not to say that the Great Khan lives like a monk. In addition to his four wives he has large numbers of concubines taken from the Qongrat tribe which was famed for the beauty of its women. Commissioners are sent out to recruit the fairest among them according to an agreed marking-system (so many points for hair, lips, eyebrows, and so on – Yule compared the process to the, in his day newly introduced, competitive examinations for entry to the British civil service). The successful candidates at this stage are then taken to court and committed to the care of elderly ladies who sleep with them to make sure that they do not snore or have bad breath or any bodily defects. Those who are finally approved then attend the emperor in turns, six (Ramusio, five) damsels serving for three days and nights, then being relieved by another six and so on throughout the year.[28] All this of course is seen in a different light to the *continuo trastullo delle donne* of poor King Facfur. This inexhaustible, if almost bureaucratised, sexuality is a symbol of majesty and power, and the men of the Qongrat, we are told, are deeply sad if their own daughters fail the exam and ascribe their misfortune to the malign influence of the stars. It is, as Dr Islam himself acknowledges, one of the symbols of the Great Khan's absolutism.

On the other hand these two anecdotes point to one area where I am tempted to agree with Dr Islam, namely that in one sense at least Marco's Book can certainly be seen as a 'colonialist' work. One must here contrast Marco's portrayal of, on the one hand the Mongols, on the other their subjects. On the one hand there is the constant idealisation of the Great Khan, his glory and power, and even of the primitive Mongols for whom at one point (LXX, 28) he produces an almost nostalgic regret; they have now, he says, become *mout enbatardi* – bastardised, degenerate – having taken on in the East the customs of the Buddhists, in the West of the Saracens. On the other hand are the conquered peoples of China, those peoples among whom Marco lived for seventeen years without learning their language or languages or anything of their culture. (In one striking passage he shows that he realises that there is one common written form of their language, but at the same time gives the very misleading impression that the various spoken languages are no more than dialects which are mutually intelligible to those who speak them.[29]) In fact, very little is said about them, and what is said is almost confined to the B group of manuscripts which seem to represent Marco's replies to questions put to him about his original text.

Here Marco distinguishes the Cathayans of northern China, and the men of Mangi in the south who until 1275 had lived under the Song Emperors. The Cathayans who have no beards (in their revolt against the evil rule of the minister Achmad they planned to murder 'the bearded ones' – Tartars, Saracens and Christians) hate the rule of the Great Khan, who for this reason employs foreigners to administer his government.[30] There are some very brief remarks on their religions (without reference to Confucianism), good manners, filial piety and fondness for gambling.[31] So far the Ramusio text. In the F version (CLIII) we meet the former subjects of the Song only in his elaborate description of Quinsai. The wives of their great men are 'delightful and angelic'; the people eat dogs (which as we have seen Islam thinks of as 'deterritorialising'); they go to the baths a lot, having 'the most beautiful and largest and greatest baths that there are in the world'; and they are much taken with astrology, being most careful to record the precise times of their childrens' nativities. (It is not easy to understand Marco's emphasis on this, since astrology also played a very prominent rôle in the West at the end of the thirteenth century – but perhaps this is the reason.) There are some fuller remarks in Ramusio at this point. We have already noted the praise of the *donne di partito* but then the people in general are 'white [*sic*] and beautiful', the women *bellissime*. The native citizens are peaceful, having been brought up in that way and following the style of their kings who had the same character. They know nothing of arms and do not keep them in their houses. One never hears of conflicts or disputes between them. They are excellent craftsmen, their trade and business dealings are conducted with great honesty, and they are very willing to give foreign merchants advice and help. They are without jealousy of their wives to whom they show great respect.[32] The elements of generalised idealisation represent one classic style of how rulers describe their subjects, with the emphasis on their unwarlike character (regarded as an ambiguous virtue) bringing a particular sense of contentment. But what is more telling is the brevity of all this, compared with what is said of the Mongols. As he has not bothered to learn their language, so Marco, like his masters, has not given them much more than a superficial glance. The description of Asia which Marco brings back with him to the West is undeniably that of the powerful among its rulers.

This is not to say that Marco, like most of us, does not have his occasional burst of prejudice and outbreak of irrational contempt.[33] Yet I cannot leave Dr Islam's thought-provoking arguments without some comment on his strictures upon Marco's religious tolerance and his supposed postulation of a total 'otherness' between Christianity and non-Christianity. I have already commented upon Marco's attitudes to Buddhism where I see none of this, and shall turn now to Dr Islam's description of the Book in which he believes 'anti-Islamic paranoia reaches the fever pitch of a Tafur on an apocalyptic crusade'.[34] (The Tafurs were, according to some Christian crusading epic poems, a fanatical offshoot of the peasantry on the First Crusade who practised cannibalism against their Muslim foes.) This extreme formulation, although mirroring in some way the judgment previously made by Leonardo Olschki,[35] seems to me unjust. Admittedly there are several hostile judgments upon Mohammedans in the Book. There are, for example, three stories telling of Muslims who are said to ill-treat Christians. The first (XXVI–XXIX) tells of a Caliph of Baghdad who plans to kill all the Christians in his territory – 'for it is true that all Saracens in the world wish great evil upon all Christians in the world' – but is frustrated by a Christian cobbler whose faith is able to move a mountain.[36] The second (LII), also a miracle story, is set amid the rivalries of the two faiths in Samarkand. The third (CXCIII) assigned to the year 1288 (though there seems to be no evidence that it is in any way historical) tells in very strong chivalric-rhetorical tones of how a Christian King of Abyssinia exacts revenge upon the Sultan of Aden for his forcible circumcision of an Abyssinian bishop. He ravages his land and kills many Saracens: 'nothing marvellous in this; for it is unworthy that Saracen dogs should rule over Christians'. Then again we are told that the Saracens of Tabriz (XXX, 8–9) 'are most wicked and untrustworthy, for the law their Prophet Mohammed has given them commands them to do all the evil they can against people who are not of their law; and nothing they do against them can be taken as sinful; and because of this they would do great harm were it not for the government [i.e. of the pagan Mongols].' In chapter XXXIII (7–9), Marco extends this judgment to all the subjects of the 'Tartars of the Levant'. In the Ramusio text again the account of the Great Khan's evil minister Achmad the Bailo goes a long way to suggest that he is evil precisely because he is a Muslim.

All this is, sure enough, evidence of a gross generalised hostility. Yet it must be considered against the background and the entrenched attitudes engendered both by the centuries of war between the two faiths and by the fact that Marco's hero, Khubilai Khan himself, having being led to misunderstand Sura 91 of the Koran (which at first sight seems to urge Muslims to kill all polytheists), had himself initiated in China a seven-year persecution of Muslim beliefs and practices. This taken into account, and considering the habitual ignorance and bigotry evoked by the Islamic religion and peoples in the writings even of the best educated propagandists of medieval Christianity,[37] it could be argued that Marco is at times remarkably open to 'Saracens'. It is not simply that on occasions he praises particular Muslims – those of Tonocain 'are a handsome race; the women are beautiful beyond measure', while those of Badakshan are 'valiant [*prodhommes*] in arms'. On two occasions he shows himself as resisting the whole influence of the culture in which he was raised. In chapter LX (7) he writes of how: 'I had a companion [*un conpagnons*] by name Çurificar, a Turk who was very wise', a servant of the Great Khan who tells him about the Salamander. This *conpagnons* (a word which, if not meaning 'friend', cannot mean 'enemy'), as is shown by his name (Zu'lfikár, the name for the edge of Ali's sword[38]), was certainly a Muslim. But more than this there is one passage in which Marco consciously pays tribute to the civilising force of the Islamic religion. In chapter CLXVI, 8, he remarks that in the Kingdom of Ferlec in the island of Sumatra Muslim merchants 'have converted the people to the law of Mohammed and these are they of the city only; for those in the mountains are just like beasts for I tell you in truth that they eat human flesh and all other flesh good and bad'. In translating that passage into Latin the Dominican friar Pipino, much more a child of western culture, shows his queasiness with his own rendering: 'those inhabitants of this kingdom who live near the sea accept the law of the *abominable* Mohammed'. And it is Pipino's constant preoccupation to add abuse to the very name of Muslims whenever they appear in Marco's text.[39] Here, seen in relation to men of the thirteenth century and not against the standards of a twentieth-century international sensibility, is surely the true measure against which Marco should be judged.

Chapter 6

Varieties of the Book

I

It is difficult to believe that Marco and Rustichello can have looked upon the completion of their work with anything but a profound sense of triumph. Drawn by a chance destiny, Marco's father and uncle had travelled further east than any westerners before. He himself had then been exiled, first from the Venice of his childhood and early manhood, and then again, all those years later, from whatever social world he had constructed in the realms of the Great Khan. Yet from that experience he had retrieved something which would guarantee his fame: he could bestow on Europe an amazing gift, a geographical treatise of a vast extent and complexity, an unparalleled opening of horizons. For his part Rustichello had taken the most diverse, unpromising collection of materials and turned it into a work which would be read. He had in the process transformed a *Divisament dou monde*, an austere chorography of a vast continent, with an intimidating extent of information and mass of detail, into a *Livre des merveilles du monde*, which tells of the strange, the marvellous, and offers a variety of edifying and amusing stories from foreign parts: in short a text which could find an audience. In this the two together had presented to the West, had, one could say, created, a new world, a myriad and unparalleled assemblage of new names, places, peoples, as well as their resources, customs, religions.

Yet how far was it read and believed? Marco's Book opens with an emphatic assertion of its truth. A wise and noble Venetian, drawing upon twenty-six years' experience (*sic*, for twenty-four), distinguishing carefully between what he has seen in person and learnt from hearsay, is offering an account in which all may place perfect faith. It is one thing to offer a vision of the world to one's readers; it is another to have them accept it, or part of it, as authentic. From the time of Ramusio scholars have frequently argued that in the Middle Ages it was never accorded any general credence, that it was considered a romance or fable. This view is supported by a variety of questions. Why does Dante never mention Marco Polo? Why is he ignored in the treatise on the strategy and tactics of crusading written by his fellow Venetian Marin Sanudo – when Sanudo does refer to the description of the East by Prince Hetoum? It is sometimes claimed that his Book inspired Columbus to seek out the East by sailing west, but more generally it is said that it had no influence, that its contents were seen as unbelievable, that it was treated as a collection of fables.[1] How far can we accept these verdicts?

The arguments *ex silentio*, it seems to me, can be given short shrift, or at least met with adequate counter-contentions. In the case of Dante, for instance, it has also been argued that Dante's impassioned query on the possibility of salvation for the guiltless pagan born on the banks of the Indus was triggered by a reading of the Book.[2] Or then again it could be said that Sanudo would consult Hetoum – on whom more later – as someone whose book offers much greater knowledge of the Middle East than does Marco's whose information on it is comparatively rather slim. And certainly the Book had a large readership on publication. Rustichello's version was written, we have seen, either in French or Franco-Italian. In the first twenty years of its existence it appeared in Franco-Italian, Tuscan, Venetian, German, Latin and in a remodelled French. There were few medieval works before this which, at so early a stage of their existence, were to be found in so many other languages. Later, from the 1370s, its popularity declined, and it came to be superseded, for most, by the much more readable tale of Sir John Mandeville. Marco's Book survives in only some hundred and fifty medieval manuscripts,[3] whereas Mandeville's, written some seventy years later, is found in over three hundred.[4] None the less, given that what we have here is not a great work of literature, not a tale of adventure, but, essentially, a quite flatly written compilation of ethnographic geography, it is possible to go along with Foscolo Benedetto, one of its three great editors, and to write of its 'rapid, vast and uninterrupted diffusion'.[5]

Yet, whether or not it was popular says nothing, of course, about how far it was believed. In 1312, Mahaut, Countess of Burgundy, is found paying for the copying, illumination and binding of the text which is described simply as *le romant du grant kan*.[6] Is she here acquiring a geography of the East, or indeed, a book of marvels: *The Romance of the Great Khan*? For readers of the day the prefatory assertions of truth may have been neither here nor there. For writers of Arthurian and Carolingian romance were accustomed to open their quite fictitious stories with precisely the same assertion.[7] The different titles which appear in different manuscripts suggest that either answer might be given. On the one hand: 'Here begin the rubrics of the book which is called *The Description of the World*, which I, Grégoire, rendered from the Book of Messer Marco Polo, the best citizen of Venice, believing in Christ [i.e. an honest man]'.[8] Alternatively, as we have seen: 'Hereafter begins the Book of Marco Polo of the Marvels of Asia the Great and India the Greater and Lesser and of the diverse regions of the world' or 'Here begins the Book of the Great Khan which speaks of Great Armenia, of Persia, and of the Tartars, and of India, and of the great Marvels which are in the world'.[9]

The title of a manuscript – as is shown by the very diversity of forms it could take – was of less importance or had less resonance than that of a printed book, and it would be misleading to make over-nice distinctions between these or other formulae. Instead, while not attempting to construct an imaginary *mentalité* or *Zeitgeist* in which everyone thought and believed much the same things,[10] it might be profitable to consider those aspects of the Book that would be most likely to provoke scepticism in the latter Middle Ages. These were, of course, not necessarily the same as those which would strike a modern reader. I am thinking here of Leonardo Olschki, who, believing that the Book had only a small influence on geographical and cosmographical thought, argued that this was due, above all, to the character of its opening chapters (XX–LII), describing the Middle East and western Asia. Here are found four of the Book's five Christian miracles, all its references to the Alexander stories, the tales of the Magi, news of the Assassin-leader, the Old Man of the Mountain, and the moralising story of the Caliph's gold. This section of the Book, certainly, has an anecdotal and ungeographic character. It is as though Rustichello is sweetening the pill, is introducing us gently to the more formidable and much more unfamiliar information to follow. Yet, for contemporaries, very little of this would necessarily provoke disbelief. Most of the stories were already familiar and the miracles fitted easily within a belief system where such things were, if not commonplace, not at all unlikely. Indeed, to have denied their possibility would have been dangerous. It was only when Marco produced tales of the Magi from eastern tradition at variance with those in the West that he was likely to be challenged. His Venetian and German translators become distinctly hostile when faced with the news that the Three Kings were buried in Saveh in Persia: '*zercha questa istoria dixeno molto buxie*' ('on this story they tell many lies') or '*das alles nit war ist!*'[11] They, after all, knew for a certainty that their last resting place lay not at all in the East but in Cologne, on the Rhine.

From the miraculous one turns to the creatures of myth, which as we have seen are not all that prominent in the Book. There are the islands of Male and Female, men with tails, the Rukh and wonders in Japan. Yet, in comparison with the time-hallowed portrait which for so long constituted the agreed popular and general knowledge of the subject, Marco's Asia is strikingly deprived of wonders. The real difficulty for the western reader was in believing in the revelation of a wholly new world of towns and cities, which looks – this the most difficult to credit – more flourishing and richer in goods than those in the West. Was it possible that there existed 'the great Lord of Lords whose name is Khubilai Khan', seemingly more powerful than any western ruler, one who was attended by 12,000 lords and knights, who employed 10,000 falconers and 20,000 dog-handlers, at whose banquets 40,000 guests assembled? Was it possible that from Khanbalikh, 'importing more precious and costly wares than any other city in the world' and with a palace, 'the largest that was ever seen', he ruled over Cathay and the nine kingdoms of Mangi with their 1,200 cities? Did there really exist a city called Quinsai with 12,000 stone bridges, 3,000 baths, with palace grounds 10 miles in circumference, and with 1,600,000 houses? Did there exist, 1,500 miles further a way, the island of Cipangu whose ruler had a palace roofed with fine gold? A French monk, little attuned to a highly numerate ethos, would, perhaps, be less startled than an Italian merchant by the numbers used, would take, say '40,000' simply to mean, as it meant in most non-Italian chronicles, 'a very large number'. Again, a Scotsman would be less surprised than Marco himself to learn (CII) of 'a kind of black stone existing in beds in the mountains which they dig out and burn like firewood'. But what must have caused doubts all over Europe was that this teeming world should exist without having ever previously been known to the West. Perhaps the stories of the marvellous lands of Prester John would have prepared European minds for these marvels? Yet could it be that the great ruler of these eminently civilised provinces was no Christian going back to ancestors converted by St Thomas but the grandson of that Genghis Khan, well-known in the West as an appalling mass-murderer, yet here portrayed as a chivalric hero?

To accept the truth of Marco's Book depended, that is to say, upon a very drastic revision of everything previously thought about the East. When, back in the 1250s, William of Rubruck had first entered the Mongol steppe-lands, he had written of himself 'as entering into some other world'.[12] The reports of that world which survived, though not, it would seem, widely diffused, were well known in missionary circles and at the papal court and presented no fundamental obstacles to belief. That world, strange and remote enough, was, none the less, the ultimately comprehensible world of a tribal barbarism. As we shall see when considering the reaction of Pope Pius II, it was much more difficult to believe that, out there, beyond Karakorum and Inner Mongolia, there existed, not more of the same nomad pastoralism, but a magnificent civilisation.

II

One speaks of whether 'the Book' was believed. Yet, in some ways it is easier to think of 'the Books' since the transmission and translation of the original text, even if we confine ourselves for the moment to the public 'A' version rather than the more private 'B', was to give rise to a whole range of 'Books', of different Marco Polos. (And often involving very remarkable retranslations of the original text; an interesting example is offered by the early sixteenth-century Vaglienti manuscript in the Riccardiana Library of Florence, which is a Tuscan translation of a Latin translation of a Tuscan translation of the original French or perhaps Franco-Italian text.[13]) While it is not at all unusual for medieval texts to display great variations from each other as they were successively copied and recopied – the scribes often related to their text by moulding it to their own vision of what they felt the author should be saying[14] – some of the Polo manuscripts were startlingly different from each other. The anonymous translator of the fifteenth-century Irish Gaelic text, for instance, presumably because he believed that the original matter was too tedious, tried to inject new interest into it. What he had before him was the Latin translation completed by Francesco Pipino. In his own translation he turns this man into 'a king's brother in the habit of St Francis, called Francesco', one skilled in many languages, who in the year 1255 had translated the Book from the Tartar language, in which, so he claims, it had originally been written, into Latin. On being first asked to work on the Book Francesco had refused: 'I am afraid to spend mental labour in the works of Jews and unbelievers.' Asked again, however, he agrees: '"It shall be done," says he. "For though tidings of non-Christians are here made known, there are marvels of the true God . . . I am not afraid of this book of Marco's for there is no lie in it. Mine eyes beheld him bringing with him the relics of the Holy Church."'

What follows has often, insofar as one can judge from its translation into English, a strong literary force. Take the passage (LXXIX) in which the army of the rebellious leader, Nayan, is set upon in an early morning attack by that of Khubilai: 'They saw the beautiful winged standards and the crimson bossy bucklers and the radiant hard-rigid helmets on the stalwart soldiers of Cambalu. And they recognised Khubilai's standard above the helmets. And this it is that wakened an army out of its sleep, the sounds of the trumpets and the pipes, and the warriors shouting their battle-cry.' The original Rustichello–Marco text had described that battle in an elaborate and highly formalised way, using the vocabulary and literary conventions employed to describe battles in Arthurian prose epics. Both the Italian versions and that of Pipino had trimmed and abbreviated that material. Here Pipino's Irish translator had wholly recreated it in a manner acceptable to its new audience. The winged standards, the crimson bossy bucklers, the radiant hard–rigid helmets, Khubilai's standard above the helmets, the sounds of the pipes, and the warrior's battle-cry are not found in his source. They derive, I would assume, from Celtic bardic traditions, and they reflect the translator's intention of transforming what he must have seen as one romantic fantasy into another, of domesticating thrilling experiences in Outer Mongolia to the familiar fields of Erin.[15]

No other manuscript so distorted the material of the original as this. Yet by the middle of the fifteenth century one can distinguish three principal forms which the Book assumed. The first was written in French and found most frequently in upperclass milieux. Their owners were men like King Charles V of France (who had no less than five copies in his library at the beginning of his reign), the Graville family, and Louis of Savoy; one copy was made for the poet-prisoner of the Tower of London, Duke Charles d'Orléans.[16] One thinks here of that manuscript (A1) executed in the second half of the fourteenth century and owned by Jean, Duke de Berry, or of the *Livre de Merveilles* (A2), most probably written for Duke John the Fearless with its eighty-four miniatures,[17] or the British Library manuscript (B1), with its thirty-eight miniatures,[18] or the stupendous volume in the Bodleian Library in Oxford, once the property of King Edward IV's brother-in-law Richard Woodville.[19] These splendid parchment books were works of art, and indeed the Duke de Berry is found commissioning not just the illuminations of the Book but at the same time six tapestries based on it.[20] Handling them, one does not feel at all that they were brought into existence in order that the matter contained in them should be given deep or thoughtful study. Certainly, the illuminators who worked on them gave the most summary regard to the text. Glancing rapidly over the rubrics, for instance, they would notice the word 'brothers' (referring to Marco's father, Niccolò, and uncle, Maffeo Polo), whereupon they would leap to the conclusion that the Polos were friars and would portray them as such. Going on to see the phrase 'gold table' – meaning the gold tablet, which the Great Khan gave as a mark of his protection – they then drew a large and splendid gold table to go with it (see illustration 5). When Marco tells us that the Kings of Georgia were born with the mark of an eagle on their shoulder, the hasty perusal of the text by the artist leads him to portray a King with a splendid eagle resting on his shoulder.[21] Or, having realised that this was a work concerned with the East, they would introduce here the well-known monstrous races from the West, even though these did not appear in Marco's Book (see illustration 4). The miniaturists were called upon to represent a reality wholly unknown to them and responded to an impossible demand either by not bothering too much or by such feats of imagination as the episcopal-type hats in which they painted the Great

Khan and the Old Man of the Mountain.[22] At the same time, the language and style of writing, very close to Rustichello's original version, modelled on Arthurian prose epic, may have allowed some readers to equate Marco's account with something they identified as romantic fiction. (And it has been observed that the probable effects of binding together books on 'marvels' from the Alexander stories, etc. with Marco Polo was not necessarily to allow comparison and sifting of falsehood from truth but rather an assimilation of truth and falsehood, and a dissolution of both into some vague picture of a never-never land.[23]) Yet with these lavish manuscripts, the question of credibility hardly arose; the books were not made to be believed or disbelieved; they were made to be lovingly, lingeringly, admired.

A second group of Marco Polos consists of Tuscan and Venetian translations from the French, and (from the second half of the fourteenth century) Tuscan translations from the Venetian.[24] (Foscolo Benedetto suggested that, since Marco was a Venetian, it was thought that the Venetian text would be more authentic than others. That could be; or it might be that the phenomenon of a Venetian text being translated into Tuscan, when a Tuscan version of the French text already existed, reflects the character of a pre-print society in which copyists learnt to make do with and adapt to their own use whatever text they happened to come upon.) Normally written not on expensive parchment but on paper, and without illustrations, they attenuate the chivalric–epic character of the French versions, and seem more popular than the fairly sparse surviving manuscript tradition might suggest.[25] Those that remain to us normally belonged to great patrician families, and are rarely bound together with other works of geography or travel. What was written in them could be remarkably inaccurate (in the preface to a collection of extracts appears the comment: 'Marco Polo is a book that treats of parts of the sea and land . . . the book was made by a gentleman of Venice who went sailing there with his four sons, descendants one after the other, following each the aforesaid book of Marco Polo').[26] One comment we shall see (page 133 below) expressed profound scepticism; it could be that the concluding remarks of two others hint at the same: 'If you want to know yet more, ask someone else, for I, Marco Polo, will seek no more. *Finis*' and 'And if you want to know more, ask someone else for I, Marco, seek no further. *Deo gratias. Amen.*' Otherwise there is nothing to suggest the spirit in which they were received.[27]

It is only when we come to the third major group of 'A'-tradition manuscripts that the form they take would actively contribute to persuading the reader that the material within was authentic. Some time before 1314, his ecclesiastical superiors ordered the Dominican friar, Francesco Pipino of Bologna, to make a Latin translation of the work. It was an appropriate choice since Pipino was a skilled writer, author of a chronicle from the origins of the Franks to the death of the Emperor Henry VII and one who was later to give an account of his own pilgrimage to the Holy Land in 1320.[28] The Dominican Order regarded the Book with immense seriousness, and in his Introduction Pipino directly faced up to the question of its truth:

> But lest the inexperienced Reader should regard as beyond belief the many strange and unheard of things that are related in sundry passages of this Book, let all know Messer Marco Polo, the narrator of these marvels, to be a most respectable, veracious and devout person, of most honourable character, and receiving such good testimony from all his acquaintance, that his many virtues claim entire belief for that which he relates. His Father, Messer Niccolò, a man of the highest respectability, used to relate all these things in the same manner. And his uncle, Messer Maffeo, who is spoken of in the Book, a man of ripe wisdom and piety, in familiar conversation with his Confessor when on his deathbed, maintained unflinchingly that the whole of the contents of this Book were true. Wherefore I have, with a safer conscience, undertaken the labour of this Translation, for the entertainment of my Readers, and to the praise of Our Lord Jesus Christ, the Creator of all things visible and invisible.[29]

The surviving manuscripts are normally on parchment or on fine quality paper. Most are bound up with other works. These are either chronicles – for example, in England, those of Ranulf of Chester or Gerald of Wales – or more generally with other books on the East: with that of Marco Polo's all too brief fellow-traveller, William of Tripoli; with Prince Hetoum; with eastern missionaries such as Odoric of Pordenone. As typical, one can take the two manuscripts of the text in the Hunterian Library of Glasgow University. The first is written on parchment in a fourteenth-century hand, has illuminated initials, and forms part of a quarto volume also containing Odoric of Pordenone. The second, of the fifteenth century, again in quarto, on parchment, with illuminated initials, has been copied by someone who calls himself 'Ricardus plenus amoris fframpton': Richard Full-of-Love-Frampton. It contains, in addition to Marco, an account of the destruction of Troy, the Pseudo-Turpin's *Journey of Charlemagne*, an Odoric, and the *Travels* of Sir John Mandeville. That is to say, other works on the East (including the first war between East and West) for cross-reference and comparison.

We have seen how, in his Preface, Pipino stresses the truth of what is coming. At the same time, he soberly warns his readers that it does not constitute light entertainment. A Dominican friar, he tells us, working at the command of his ecclesiastical superiors, is making this translation in order to stimulate religious zeal and to promote the work of missions:

> And let none deem this task to be vain and unprofitable; for I am of the opinion that the perusal of the Book by the faithful may merit an abounding grace from the Lord; in contemplating the variety, beauty and vastness of God's Creation, as herein displayed in his marvellous works, they may be led to bow in adoring wonder before His Power and Wisdom. Then again in considering the depths of blindness and impurity in which the gentile nations are involved, they may be constrained at once to render thanks to God who had deigned to call his faithful people out of such perilous darkness into his marvellous light, and to pray for the illumination of the hearts of the heathen. Hereby, also, the sloth of undevout Christians may be put to shame, when they see how much more ready the nations of the unbelievers are to worship their idols, than are many of those who have been marked with Christ's token to adore the true God. Moreover, the hearts of some members of the religious orders may be moved to strive for the diffusion of the Christian faith, and by divine aid to carry the name of our Lord Jesus Christ, forgotten among so vast multitudes, to those blinded nations, among whom the harvest is indeed so great, and the labourers so few.[30]

This didactic and religious purpose led Pipino to make many changes in the character of the original work. Rustichello's chivalric rhetoric was eliminated. Gone is the opening address to 'Emperors, Kings, Dukes', etc., and gone, through the very character of the Latin language, the 'What more shall I say?' '*Et que vos en diroie?*' tropes of oral-epic tradition. When, for instance, as we have seen, the three Polos arrive at the court of the Great Khan, Rustichello's original version of the scene (xv) had been modelled on, and frequently used the same words as, his earlier description of the arrival of Tristan at the court of King Arthur.[31] They are greeted in his great palace, surrounded by a very large company of his barons; they kneel and prostrate themselves before him. The Khan bids them rise,[32] greets them with *grant joie et grant feste*, asks many questions on their fortunes. They reply that they have fared well for they have found the Khan safe and well. They then present their credentials from the Pope which please him greatly. In Pipino's version (Pipino I, chapter vii), the great palace, the company of barons, the courtly compliments disappear, and we move rapidly to the handing over of the letters of the Pope whose 'faithful solicitude' the Khan praises. The reduction here of the chivalric element goes together with the immediate focus on the papal letters. So too, as we have seen, the ecclesiastical lessons are reinforced throughout by additions to any dispassionate account of non-Christian religions. These now become 'wretched', 'abominable', 'wicked' or 'insane'.

At the same time, for the straight sequence of chapters found in the original, Pipino substituted a division into three books (the first dealing with West and Central Asia; the second (the only one in fact to carry a title) 'On the Power and Magnificence of Khubilai, Great King of the Tartars'; and the third treating of Japan and the countries bordering the Indian Ocean). These in turn were subdivided into chapters, thus giving it the form of a work to be found upon the desks of scholars. This, taken with the artificiality of his Latin, had the effect of withdrawing Marco from the aura of the world of romance, and of making the material discussed appear much flatter and in a sense more abstract.[33] Here is a work written for learned men and for clerics. As one example, at least, of the context in which it might be found, one can take the inventory of the 234 books in the library of the Franciscans of Gubbio in central Italy, drawn up in 1360. Fifty of the volumes consist of Bibles and biblical commentaries; forty are collections of sermons; twenty deal with law; twenty are works of the early fathers. Apart from Aristotle, there are no classical authors; there are very few contemporary works. Serious religious and ecclesiastical works predominate. Within this library for us today, perhaps Marco Polo's Book, bound up with the travels of Fra Odorico, stands out, but it would not have done so for contemporaries.[34] For them it fitted in easily with the other works beside it.

Though by this time other Latin translations existed,[35] Pipino's was by far the most common. Although it was not the only one which engaged cartographers or serious truth-seekers – the Catalan version, for instance, as we shall see, was drawn upon by the compiler of the *Catalan Atlas* – it was the one most at issue when men seriously discussed the geography of the world, and the gravity with which Marco was presented here must have done much to make his story credible. Some twenty years after Pipino's translation, his fellow Dominican, Jacopo d'Acqui, reveals how strange the Book seemed, how it was sometimes attacked as false, and yet how he holds it to be true:

> This messer Marco was a long time with his father and uncle in Tartary, and he saw there many things and made much wealth, and also learned many things, for he was a man of ability. And so, being in prison in Genoa, he made a book concerning the great wonders of the world, that is to say concerning such of them as he had seen. And what he told in the book was not as much as he had really seen, because of the tongues

of detractors who, being ready to impose their own lies on others, are over hasty to set down as lies what they in their perversity disbelieve, or do not understand. And because there are many great and strange things in that book, which are reckoned past all credence, he was asked by his friends on his deathbed to correct the book by removing everything that went beyond the facts. To which his reply was that he had not told one half of what he had really seen!³⁶

Doubt overcome in the face of what seems incredible, is the reaction too of Antonio Pucci, street singer and poet of the commune of Florence. In his *Libro di varie storie*, written before 1362, Pucci incorporated a great deal from the original Tuscan translation of the Book. He ends by saying that he has decided to leave out many other marvellous things: 'recalling that the supreme poet, Dante, said this [*Inferno*, XVI, 124–6] "Ever to that truth which has the face of a lie, a man as far as he is able, should close his lips, for, though blameless, he will incur shame".'³⁷ Even though it seemed a lie, for Pucci, that is, it was the truth. Not the happiest of endorsements; an easier acceptance of the Book would only come from the testimony of those merchants and missionaries who would follow in Marco's footsteps in the fourteenth century.

Chapter 7

Marco, Merchants and Missionaries

I

'*Q uel ver c'ha faccia di menzogna*' – 'that truth which has the face of a lie', could only find full confirmation in the eighty years which followed Marco Polo's return from the East, a period in which many European merchants and missionaries travelled in Asia.[1] That they should do so was not, it will be seen, in any way the direct result of the publication of Marco's Book. Indeed it could be that the impression it gave of a three to three and a half year journey from Sudak to Beijing would have discouraged travellers. Yet the story has its own intrinsic interest and is also of significance in considering how the geographical importance of the Book was established and confirmed in the later Middle Ages.

Of Latin merchants in Mongol lands our knowledge is limited by their normal obsessive secrecy. Far from putting their *pratiche di mercatura* on public display, even in redacting notarial instruments they often tried to hide their destination under such declarations as that they were going 'over the seas and where God wishes' or 'to various parts of the world'. Consequently we often hear only incidentally and indirectly of merchant activity in the East. (As for instance in the first decades of the fourteenth century a chronicler tells of how a merchant from Cyprus had told the Master of the Temple at Tyre of the country called Hata (Cathay), ruled by the Mongols, 'a large, great and most delightful country' with a city of enormous extent in it called Hansa (Hangzhou?), seat of the Great Khan.[2]) Yet some outlines can be drawn. By the time of the Polos return, Italian merchants were already well established around the Black Sea and in Persia, where the Genoese in particular established excellent relations with the Mongol Ilkhan Arghun.[3] In 1290 as many as 900 of them, it is said, were in his service at Baghdad, building galleys which were to be launched against the Indian-Ocean trade of Egypt under the Mamluk Sultans.[4] In the same period and as a counterpoise, the Venetians were seeking the alliance of the Ilkhans' enemies, the Mamluks and the Kipchak Tartars. These first steps into Asia had been given a new stimulus from 1291, when Acre, the last Christian bastion in the Holy Land, fell to the Mamluks, a disaster which led the Papacy to prohibit all trade with the Muslim powers. At first most Christian merchants interpreted this to mean simply the export of war materials and for a time even their sale came to be permitted in return for payment. (Boniface VIII fixed the terms at a quarter or a fifth of the profit.) Yet this soon was followed by a general embargo; illicit trade grew more dangerous and more expensive, and its value declined; from the early 1320s commerce with Egypt and Syria virtually ceased.[5]

In these circumstances, a strong stimulus was given to the search for new outlets for commerce. One possibility was trade in the West. It was within the context of Muslim advance in the East that the brothers Ugolino and Vadino Vivaldi set out from Genoa in May 1291 with two galleys 'in order to go by the Ocean Sea to the parts of India'. No more was heard of them, and it is not even clear whether they planned to circumnavigate Africa or to cross the Atlantic, but they left behind them a long-lasting memory which may even have influenced the young Columbus.[6] Then again, with the turn of the thirteenth and fourteenth centuries the Genoese and Venetians began to dispatch annual galley convoys to the ports of the English Channel, and navigators began to explore the Azores, Canaries and Atlantic coasts of Africa.[7] Yet the East too still offered great scope for enter-prising investors. From 1295 Persia's Ilkhans were officially Muslims, yet they remained hostile to the Mamluk Sultans. Here was an obvious market to follow up. At Tabriz, Venice came to secure a consulate, and a Domini-can and a Franciscan convent were established in the city. In July 1333, enquiries into heresy by the Dominican Bishop of the town (even *in part-ibus infidelium* the Church could not lay aside its thirst for orthodoxy) revealed that several European merchants – at least five Genoese, two Venetians, and others from Asti, Milan, Pisa and Piacenza – were resident.[8] In the same period the Venetians were prominent at the Ilkhans' new capital of Sultania, and at Ormuz, the island port on the Persian Gulf.

From Persia or from their Black Sea settlements other Italians came to penetrate Central Asia and beyond. Some are even recorded as reaching India by land. In 1338 Giovanni Loredan (who had already, it is known, by that time traded in Cathay) with his brother, Paolo, cousin Andrea and three other Venetian merchants passed from Tana to Astrakhan, south to Urgench, down the Oxus, across the Hindu Kush, to Ghazna and Delhi. Here they presented the Sultan Muhamed ibn-Toghlaq with a clock, a little fountain and other toys for a wealthy man and were rewarded with the huge sum of 200,000 bezants.[9] Others struck out further. As early as 1291 Peter of Lucalongo, 'a faithful Christian and great merchant', perhaps a Venetian or Genoese, is recorded as travelling from Tabriz to India and then

China (crossing on the way the homeward path of the Polos). In 1305 and 1306 a Latin missionary was sending letters to Europe with Venetian merchants who had received the Great Khan's gold tablet, and twenty years later a colony of Genoese and other Italian merchants resided at Zaiton – 'one of the two greatest harbours in the world for commerce' in Marco's Book – on the Formosa Strait.[10]

Records survive up to the 1350s of Venetians who took part in the China trade.[11] But it was the Genoese who were most prominent. The Florentine Francesco di Balduccio Pegolotti's famous 'Advice about the journey to Cathay by the road through Tana, for those going and returning with wares' (see particularly Appendix II), was based on Genoese information from the period 1310–30, and calculates weights according to Genoese measures. And there is a whiff of macho insouciance typical of the Genoese merchant of the day – yet quickly modified – in his account of the itinerary:

> The road from Tana to Cathay is quite safe both by day and by night, according to what the merchants report who have used it – except that if the merchant should die along the road, when going or returning, everything would go to the lord of the country where the merchant dies, and the officers of the lord would take everything – and in like manner if he should die in Cathay [. . .] And there is still another danger; that is, should the lord die and until the new lord who is to rule has been sent for, in that interval sometimes a disorder occurs against the Franks and other foreigners – they call 'Franks' all Christians of countries from the Byzantine Empire westwards – and the road is not safe until the new lord is sent for who is to reign after the one who died.[12]

The truth is that the path was not all that 'safe' and not easy. East of Urgench, through Almalyk, and Zhangye, the way lay along a daunting route of steppes, deserts, high mountains. Still several, clearly, took it. Though they had a certain interest in sugar, ginger and rhubarb, all of which could be bought at very low prices, what the Italians were seeking above all in China was silk, which they would exchange for fine French, German or Italian cloths. How important, and on what scale, was this trade? Some have doubted the existence of any regular intercontinental links and believe that the evidence indicates merely exceptional and intermittent adventures. More plausibly, the trade has been represented in the period 1330–45 as 'a continual and substantial current'. Chinese silk was less esteemed in the West than that of Merv in Turkestan or Talish in Transcaucasia; it formed part, that is, of '*un commerce de masse*', dependent upon quantity rather than quality, and for that very reason must, it is claimed, have been extensive.[13] That view has drawn strength from the discovery at Yangzhou of two Christian tombstones with Gothic lettering, the first for Caterina, daughter of Domenico of the Genoese Ilioni family, dated July 1342, the second for her brother Antonio, dated November 1344. This was the great city which the Book says Marco Polo governed for three years, and where certainly in the 1320s there was a Franciscan convent. Clearly a Genoese merchant colony existed here, one so well established that its members felt secure enough to bring their families with them.[14]

Yet already by the 1340s trade within the Mongol world was becoming more difficult. With Özbeg (1313–41) the Khans of the Golden Horde converted definitively to Islam and thenceforth, however strong the tolerance or pragmatism of Mongol tradition, Christian visitors were likely to find themselves at risk.[15] In 1338, in Central Asia, a pogrom wiped out Christian missionaries and merchants at Almalyk, capital of the Khanate of Chaghadai. Five years later Janibeg, the Kipchak Khan, massacred western merchants on the Black Sea and then besieged Caffa and Tana. That siege was followed by (indeed in the imagination of some western chroniclers of the day it was the direct cause of) the coming of the Black Death, already raging in Asia, to Europe. On the Mediterranean, the Mamluks made further gains. They took Layas, the port of little Armenia, in 1347, and access to Persia became much more arduous. From the 1350s Genoese patricians might go on giving their sons Mongol names ('Tartaro', 'Abaga', 'Casano'),[16] occasional adventurers might be found, like Luchino Tarigo, who took up piracy on the Caspian Sea in 1374,[17] but the great days of Italian trade in Asia were over. During the last quarter of the fourteenth century, this situation was reinforced by the rise of Timur or Tamburlaine, who sacked Sarai and destroyed Tana in 1395. From mid-century, that is, any merchants who could testify to the truth of Marco's Book were very few and far between.

II

In the same period Roman missionaries largely followed in the footsteps of merchants.[18] In Persia their efforts were crowned by the creation of the archbishopric of Sultania (the new capital of the Ilkhans) in 1318. In the Kipchak Khanate there was a Franciscan convent at Sarai well before 1287, and it is possible – though it was to prove a fugitive triumph – that Jerome of Catalonia baptised the Khan Toktai in 1312. Further east bishoprics were established at Matrega (a Black Sea port opposite Soldaia), at Samarkand, Urgench and at Almalyk, where Richard of Burgundy, in another ephemeral success, was to convert the Khan of Chagadhai, before being martyred in 1339. As for China, it was probably Rabban Sauma's mission on behalf of the Ilkhan Arghun and his conversations with Nicholas IV, and stories of the strength of the Nestorian Church there, which first roused papal hopes. In July 1289 Nicholas wrote to Khubilai that he had heard from Arghun, 'who has told us very plainly that your Magnificence has a feeling of great love towards our person and the Roman Church and also towards the nation or people of the Latins'. Warmed by these convictions, he dispatched the Franciscan friar Giovanni da Montecorvino on a mission to China.[19] With the Dominican Niccolò of Pistoia, Montecorvino, who had already spent several years in Persia, left Tabriz in 1291. Hearing of war in Central Asia between Khubilai and Kaidu, they decided to go by sea via India, travelling with the merchant Peter of Lucalongo. In India Niccolò died, but Giovanni, after a stay of some thirteen months, went on to China, arriving at Khanbalikh at the end of 1293, shortly before Khubilai's death. Khubilai's successor, Temur who, despite a strong inclination to Tibetan Buddhism, believed in taking out insurance with whatever religions were going, received him well, and allotted him an annual income, estimated ('according to the calculations of Genoese merchants') in 1326 as the equivalent of 1,200 gold florins.[20]

Almost at once Giovanni quarrelled with his Nestorian fellow Christians in the capital. In that the Roman clergy frequently denied that the Nestorians were Christians this was all too predictable.[21] As a result, he retreated from Khanbalikh to Tenduc, the province ruled, under the suzerainty of the Great Khan, by the Ongut prince, George, supposed descendant of Prester John. George too was a Nestorian but was persuaded to 'convert' to the Latin rite. So, at least, Montecorvino claims (Chinese records declare him to be a convinced Confucian).[22] The truth of this is of little matter since, on George's death in 1298, his people returned to their Nestorian allegiance. Back at Khanbalikh, however, the merchant Lucalongo had flourished, and was to assist the friar by building him a church. Probably, it was he too who put up the money for the purchase of those slaves, forty boys between the ages of seven and eleven, who were to be his earliest converts. They were instructed in Latin and plainchant, and their voices reached, we are told, to the Great Khan in his chamber. Giovanni's ministrations were confined to the Mongol upperclass (he translated the whole of the New Testament and the Psalms into Mongolian), and other Christian groups – Alans of the Greek rite, Armenians and visiting Italians (we have seen Venetian merchants carrying his letters back to Europe). Among these last was a Lombard surgeon who arrived in 1303 and was to disconcert him by broadcasting unfavourable accounts of the work of the Roman Papacy back in Europe.

The indigenous subject people of China Giovanni ignored. Most revealing is a letter of February 1306, where he writes: 'I have had six pictures made of the Old and New Testament for the instruction of the unlearned; and they are written upon in Latin, Tursic [Mongol], and Persian letters so that *all* [*sic*] tongues may read'[23] – a remarkable acknowledgement of the way in which he could be said, like Marco Polo, to have forgotten the native Chinese. Yet among others in China he enjoyed some success. An Armenian merchant built him a church at Zayton and a second at Khanbalikh. He was joined by a German Franciscan in 1306, by which time he claimed to have converted 10,000 souls. In 1307 Pope Clement V appointed him Archbishop of a new archdiocese of Khanbalikh with jurisdiction over the whole of the Mongol Empire. Six Franciscans were ordered to join him as suffragan bishops. Of these one never went, two died in India, but three finally arrived in 1313. Of these two were dead by 1326. As a result of the determination to promulgate a Christianity with rites, exclusively in the Latin language – something which obviously increased the difficulty of ordaining local priests – there was a desperate shortage of missionaries.

This shortage was reinforced by the opening of missionary work in India. Here where 'St Thomas Christians' still existed, Latins had even in the twelfth century occasionally come on pilgrimage to his supposed tomb. In the fourteenth century, interest in the Indian Ocean grew. Between 1312 and 1317, the Dominicans William Adam and Raymond Stephen visited Socotra, an island in the Arabian Sea, still at that time populated by Coptic Christians, preached there for nine months, and from there went on to Ethiopia. Undaunted by their realisation – an insight quite new, revelatory of the new geographical horizons now opening to the West – that 'we who are the true Christians, are not the tenth, no not the twentieth of all men', they both produced their own plans for attacks on Muslim commerce to Egypt. Friar Adam's contribution, with the bloodthirsty title of *De modo Saracenos extirpandi*, suggested a force of forty or fifty vessels, with bases at Ormuz, islands in the Indian Ocean and South Indian ports.[24] Yet it was rather by chance than design that the Roman Church first began to proselytise in India.[25] In 1320, on their way to China, the Dominican Jourdain Cathala or Catalani of Séverac together with four Franciscans and a Genoese merchant stopped at Tana, on the island of Salcette, just north of present-day Bombay. There the Franciscans engaged in disputes with the Muslims, attacked the character of Mohammed and were seized and executed for blasphemy. Jourdain was absent at the time, but the experience, curiously enough, persuaded him to stay on in the subcontinent rather than make his way on to Zaiton. Shortly after, he moved south to Malabar and the Kingdom of Quilon, where, free from Muslim rulers, and with Nestorian Christians dominating the pepper trade, circumstances seemed more auspicious. It was principally to Indian Nestorians, neglected by their mother-Church in Baghdad, that his preaching was addressed. In 1328 he went back to the West, wrote his *Mirabilia* recounting his experiences and recruited more missionaries. Two years later he returned to India, as Bishop of Quilon, setting up a rival field for missionary work to that in China where missionaries were already in short supply. Yet from the end of the 1340s, when anarchy in Persia made access to the Indian Ocean difficult, the enterprise faltered. Giovanni Marignolli, papal envoy to China, visited the church of St George of the Latins of Quilon on his way home in 1346 and had it decorated with pictures. But little is then heard of Latin Christianity in India until the sixteenth century.

Meanwhile, Odoric of Pordenone, another Franciscan, who passed at least three years in China some time between the years 1322 and 1328, recorded the existence of two Franciscan houses in Zaiton, and other convents at Yangzhou (site of the Ilioni family gravestones), and Hangzhou.[26] Yet the mission was isolated and remote. In 1337 the Alans at Khanbalikh, in particular those of the Imperial Guard, felt the need to petition Rome for priests. They found an ally in the Great Khan Toghon Temur who was anxious to establish relations in the West. Accordingly a mission was dispatched to 'the country of the Franks beyond the seven seas where the sun lies down, in order to open the way to frequent passage of ambassadors from us to the Pope and from the Pope to us'. The Great Khan asked too 'that they should bring back from the West horses and other marvels'. With this party there travelled back to the West the Genoese merchant Andrea 'de Nassio'. Pope Benedict XII replied in style, sending as his own ambassadors Giovanni de' Marignolli, a Franciscan who had taught in the University of Bologna, and another Genoese merchant, Andalò da Savignone. They carried rich gifts, jewels, horses and one great horse or warhorse. The embassy, travelling with Andrea 'de Nassio' who returned to report to the Great Khan, sailed from Naples and reached Caffa in March 1339. After a leisurely journey through Central Asia, during which Marignolli rebuilt the Latin church at Almalyk, it reached Khanbalikh in 1342. Here the Great Khan was particularly delighted by the 'heavenly horse'. A dozen court poets, ordered to celebrate its beauty, hailed it as an auspicious omen, signifying that now the most distant regions were showing, by dispatch of tribute, that the Mandate of Heaven extended to the whole world. A painting of it by Chou Long was preserved until the sack of the Summer Palace in 1860.[27]

Marignolli himself stayed for some three or four years in China, returned by sea, and, back in Europe, wrote of the cathedral and other churches of Khanbalikh and the three Franciscan churches in Zaiton.[28] Yet these were years in which the Black Death was raging in Central Asia, and when wars between rival Khans and the emergence of powerful new

Muslim forces were menacing those bishoprics which had been established at Urgench and Almalyk. The routes to China were becoming more difficult, as was shown when Muslims in Central Asia killed the last bishop of Zaiton, Jacopo of Florence, in 1362. In 1370 the arrival of new letters persuaded the Papacy to send Guillaume du Pré as Archbishop of Khanbalikh, together with about twelve Franciscans.[29] If ever they had arrived (or departed) they would have found still more unfavourable conditions. Within the Mongol world the western merchant and missionary had arrived together; now both were in retreat. The Genoese, it is true, continued to trade from Caffa, and Venetians are found at Urgench (1362), Astrakhan (1389), and at Sultania as late as 1399.[30] Yet it is clear that the great days of Asian and in particular Far Eastern commerce had passed. Occasional merchants can be found in China up to 1363; thereafter they disappear. As for the missions, in the second half of the fourteenth century the Mongol dynasties definitively turned to Buddhism or to Islam, and the non-Latin Churches resisted more strongly than ever the call to acknowledge the supremacy of the Roman See.

In so far as China is concerned, the fall of the Yuan dynasty in 1368 and its replacement by the Ming, the replacement, that is, of the foreign Mongol dynasty by supposedly xenophobic native rulers, has frequently been interpreted as one cause for the end of travels to the East. Yet that there was any active hostility from the early Ming to westerners is to be doubted. It is significant that the Chinese *History of the Ming* tells of how, in October 1371, the Emperor Hong-wou gave a merchant of the West, called Nie-koul-louen (Niccolò?), a message for his King (of Naples? of Sicily? the Duke of Milan?), telling him of the accession of the new dynasty. Later, we are told the 'Fou-lin (i.e. the westerners) sent an embassy with tribute in return.[31] Rather than through any hatred of the foreigner on the part of the new rulers of China, it may be supposed that contact was broken off due to the economic difficulties of both Europe and Asia during the second half of the fourteenth century, and because of the political separation of China from the Mongolian steppe-lands through which China was approached. These factors were reinforced for westerners by the expansion of the Ottoman Turks on the Mediterranean, making access to Mesopotamia and the shores of the Black Sea more difficult, and by the rise of the fervent Muslim Timur or Tamerlane in Central Asia. In his *Libellus de notitia orbis* of 1410–14, the Latin Archbishop John III of Sultania gave a depressing report of the situation. Timur has, he reports, destroyed the churches of Georgia, Greater Armenia, Daghestan (on the north-east of the Caspian), Ziquie and the Lower Volga. But there were still Catholics at Baghdad and Kurdistan, and he asserts that he has been in contact with Christians of Cathay whose last archbishop, 'Charles of France', he had known. But the Papacy, he complains, is indifferent to them.[32] Since he was writing at the time of the Great Schism, he might better have written 'the papacies'; for to the three rival Popes, obsessed with their own claims, Asia in these years must have seemed exceptionally remote.

III

If at this juncture one hundred and fifty years of Asian–European connection were being severed, what memory of the contacts remained? In that time there were in the West a fair number of eye-witnesses to the East, even the Far East. There were men like Bargadin of Mayence, known to Philippe of Mézières in Cyprus, who served under the Great Khan for eight years, and who provided enough information on the Mongol world for Mézières to use it in the long drawn-out tedium of his allegorical *Dream of the Old Pilgrim*. (Though with striking inaccuracy – his noble travellers are supposed to visit *in Cathay* 'Sarai, one of the greatest cities of the world'.)[33] Fra Odoric of Pordenone, again, wrote that he had met 'many' in Venice who had seen Quinsai. Merchants and missionaries, speaking to their friends or flocks, could give their own personal testimony to the reality of the essence of Marco Polo's world. Yet such oral witness was by its nature fleeting and temporary. How far did this evidence reach, like Marco Polo's, written form?

In fact a variety of independent accounts were, though without specific reference to his Book, to give testimony to the essential truth of it. First among them was that offered by Prince Hetoum (otherwise Hethum, Hayton, Haytoun), nephew of King Hetoum I of Little Armenia, ruler of those people whom Marco, in an uncharacteristic burst of intolerance, describes as 'wretched cowards, good for nothing but knocking back the booze'.[34] A skilful politician, in 1305 he had, for reasons which have been debated, become a Premonstratensian canon-regular. Two years later, in the convent of the order in Poitiers, he dictated his book in French to Nicolas Falcon. Later, at the request of Clement V, Falcon translated it into Latin; from that Latin text Jean le Long translated it back into French in 1357. It survives in fifteen medieval manuscripts of the original French text and thirty-one manuscripts of the Latin, quite frequently by itself, but often bound up with such works as those of Giovanni di Pian di Carpine, Marco Polo, Jacques de Vitry, John Mandeville and the Alexander stories.[35] Since Little Armenia was a vassal state of the Mongols from the 1240s, Hetoum was in a position to know a great deal about the East. The second part of his work gives a succinct history of the 'Emperors' of the continent since the birth of Christ (Persians, Muslims, Khwarazmins, Mongols). The third speaks specifically of the Mongols from the time of Genghis Khan. The fourth part, added later, consists of yet another of those plans for a crusade which so satisfied the wishful fantasies of the West in this period.

It is the first part – 'The Realms of Asia' – which contains the geographical material. This consists of brief notes on fourteen 'kingdoms'. Of these the first is Cathay, 'the noblest and richest kingdom in the world', bordering on the Ocean Sea with its 'numberless' islands. Its inhabitants 'all have small eyes and little hair in their beards'. In their spiritual beliefs they are simple, but cleverer than all other people in material things; they themselves say that other people see with one eye but they with two. Though not warriors they are skilled in the making of engines of war (mangonels?); they have paper money. Occasionally the second-hand character of this information comes through (Hetoum believes that the Chinese had an alphabet like the Latins); and no knowledge is shown of 'Mangi'. Other chapters mention briefly, and relate to each other across Asia, Telas, land of the Uighurs, home of idolaters who will not kill any living thing; Turkestan, where nomads carry their houses on horseback from place to place; Khwarizm; Comania or Kipchak, extending to the Etyll (the Volga), the greatest river in the world; India, containing Badakhshan with its balas rubies, the tomb of St Thomas, Cambay, the Isle of Ceylon, and more islands in the Ocean Sea. Hetoum continues with Persia – the Oxus (equated with Phison, one of the rivers of Paradise), Bukhara, Samarkand, Isfahan, Nishapur – then Chaldea; Armenia; Media; Mesopotamia; Turkey; and Syria. Here the verbal juxtaposition of one kingdom after another in the text would be a useful aid to a map-maker.

Hetoum's rôle as a monk was ambiguous, for to the end of his life he also played a very active part in politics. After him, considering the extraordinary character of the eastern missions and the interest the orders of friars had in celebrating their own part in them, it is surprising to find – with one major exception which we shall come to in a moment – how few in number, how little diffused, and how cooly received were any reports of them. Such letters as survive, sent home over thousands of miles, bearing moving news for every Christian – by Archbishop Giovanni di Montecorvino, his suffragans Peregrino da Castello[36] and Andrea da Perugia, and then again by Paschal of Vittoria and Fra Menentillo of Spoleto – survive only in one, two or (in one instance) in three copies.[37] Again, the *Book of the Estate of the Great Khan*, written between 1330 and 1334, and dispatched to Pope John XXII by John of Cori, the Dominican Archbishop of Sultania, gave an interesting account of the missionary hopes of the East. (The Great Khan's authority which is absolute, stretches for a journey of six months as the crow flies, and he gives great favours to Christians. In

Cathay there are numerous great cities, as 'Cassay' (Hangzhou) and Khan-balikh where there are three churches. The people are peaceful, wealthy with great abundance of silk, gold and paper money. Archbishop Giovanni Montecorvino is opposed by false, misbelieving Nestorians.) Yet it remains only in one medieval French translation.[38]

Similarly the story of the legate Giovanni Marignolli's journey to and from, and three year stay in, China, appears only in a few brief personal reminiscences inserted, somewhat inappropriately, in his *History of Bohemia*.[39] These are often interesting, if only for the biblical character of his mind ('Phison', one of the four great rivers of Paradise, turns into both the Ganges in India and the Yellow River in China), but they survived in only one complete and one fragmentary manuscript and had no influence on the development of geographical thought. Friar Jourdain Catalani de Séverac's *Mirabilia descripta* was written in 1328 at Avignon, prior to his return to India. It described, often very vividly, 'the many and boundless marvels' of India and the way thither. Yet this too only limped to survival, in one manuscript.[40] Nor do western chronicles carry much on the theme: Johannes Elemosyna (1335/6) and John of Winterthur's Franciscan chronicles say something about the missions but stand virtually alone, and again are each to be read only in one manuscript.[41]

In one case the martyrdom of the four Franciscans at Tana in India was portrayed in art: in the fresco of Ambrogio Lorenzetti (d.1348) in the church of San Francesco at Siena. Then again, one indubitably Mongol face looks out at us from Andrea da Firenze's representation of the *Church Triumphant* (1356) in Santa Maria Novella in Florence (indeed, it has been claimed that the Polos actually appear there beside him – but then whose face has some scholar or other not found in that well-populated fresco?).[42] This does not seem very much and indeed one wonders how far the theme of mission was acceptable to the age. How welcome was the novel perception of William of Adam that 'we who are the true Christians, are not the tenth, no not the twentieth of all men' (shortly to be echoed by Jourdain de Séverac – 'not a twentieth part of people in the world')?[43] Coming at a time when at least tacitly the possibility of converting Muslims had been abandoned, was the whole idea of mission loosing its savour? Recalling, for instance, that Montecorvino was probably the only one of the friars in China to have been capable of preaching in Mongol, was there any covert belief in fourteenth-century Europe (dangerous of course to express openly) that the whole enterprise was futile?

Which leads to the reflection that, however courageous the friars who set out for the East, the martyrdom which some among them received was something which they themselves would have unflinchingly inflicted upon anyone back in Europe who dared to question their own notions.

Throughout Europe it was the friars who acted as Inquisitors into Heretical Depravity. It was they, for example, who on learning that he had expressed doubts on the likelihood of resurrection from death, had dug up and burnt the body of Pietro d'Abano, the learned scholar who had questioned Marco about the inhabitability of the equinoctial regions.[44] In the Italian towns, this was not the least of the many reasons for which, in certain circles, they were intensely disliked. In a story in the *Decameron* (VI,10) Boccaccio shows one Fra Cipolla delivering a sermon on his travels in strange and distant lands (translation of G. H. McWilliam):

> So away I went , and after setting out from Venison, I visited the Greek Calends, then rode at a brisk pace through the Kingdom of Algebra and through Bordello, eventually reaching Bedlam, and not long afterwards, almost dying of thirst, I arrived in Sardintinia. But why bother to mention every single country to which I was directed in my questing spirit? After crossing the Straits of Penury, I found myself passing through Funland and Laughland, both of which countries are thickly populated, besides containing a lot of people. Then I went on to Liarland, where I found a large number of friars belonging to various religious orders including my own, all of whom were forsaking a life of discomfort for the love of God, and paying little heed to the exertions of others so long as they led to their own profit. In all these countries, I coined a great many phrases, which turned out to be the only currency I needed.[45]

And so on – visiting other lands and meeting such interesting characters as 'the Reverend Father Besokindas Tocursemnot', all as evidence for the truth of a bogus relic he is displaying to his congregation. How far, one wonders, were tales of the supposed conversion of tens of thousands in the distant East likely to be received with some quite large measures of scepticism? However, I should remark first that Pastore Stocchi has argued that in this passage Boccaccio, as a good Florentine, is simply displaying a general distaste for travel-narratives which, he holds, were popularly associated with the Book of the Venetian Marco Polo.[46] Second, that many, indeed most learned, literary scholars are keen to emphasise that the essence of the story lies in the triumph of wit and intelligence over gullibility, and that Boccaccio himself cannot justly be seen as anticlerical.

IV

One cannot generalise overmuch from the mentality of the sophisticated. For the account of the in some ways quite unsophisticated friar, the

Franciscan Odorico da Pordenone,[47] did indeed gain a great and deserved popularity. At the command of his provincial minister, it was written down during May 1330 in the convent of Sant'Antonio in Padua, some eight months before his death, and told of the 'many great marvels which I did hear and see when, according to my wish, I crossed the sea and visited the countries of the unbelievers in order to win some harvest of souls'. That first version, dictated to his fellow friar, Guglielmo di Solagna, was followed by a second, some ten years later, reworked in better Latin by Henry of Glatz, who added some reminiscences of other friars. Finally an Italian translation added several touches of fantasy. In its Latin, Italian, French and German versions, it is a work which survives in over a hundred medieval manuscripts.[48]

Born at Villanova near Pordenone in Friuli, after joining his order Odorico had set off from Italy sometime before 1320 in the company of an Irish friar called Brother James. He seems to have stayed some years in the Middle East. In his itinerary he writes of Tabriz and Sultania, of Baghdad and Ormuz. From here he embarked for India, where he tells of the pepper trade of Malabar, of cow worship and suttee, of penitential pilgrimage on the Coromandel Coast, and of the chariot of the Gods under which the believers throw themselves. He visited Tana and, following the rough-hewn conventions of traditional hagiography, gives a long account of the martyrdom of the four Franciscans there. In fact, at this point he managed to secure the bones of the victims and enthusiastically holds forth on their magical properties. They save him from death for instance when 'Saracens' burn down the house in which he was staying. Then, when his ship is becalmed on the passage from India to the East Indies, and the prayers, first of the idolaters and then the Mohammedans fail, a discrete casting of a bone in the waters ensures a fair wind.

He gives accounts of Ceylon, Sumatra and Java, which, for its spices, is 'the second best of all islands that exist', and of Champa on the coast of Annam, with its elephants. Finally he comes to what he calls 'Upper India' or China, to the two house of friars in Zaiton, and the great province of Mangi, with its 'two thousand great cities, cities, I mean of such magnitude that neither Treviso nor Vicenza [two small provincial towns] would be entitled to be numbered among them'. He tells then of visiting Canton (Guangzhou), 'the size of three Venices', Fuzhou and Quinsai, 'this city which is largest in all the world' and which amazes him as much as it did Marco Polo. Then on to Nanjing, Yangzhou, where there was another Franciscan convent, and other towns and cities. Then he comes to Khanbalikh, 'an old city of that famous province of Cathay', where at the centre of the account is the Great Khan's palace and court, his hunting parties, and the splendour of his state. Here, 'where we Brothers Minor have a place appointed in the Khan's court and must always go and give him our bless-ing', Odorico stayed three years. Afterwards he tells of going to Tenduc, and (though this seems improbable) Tibet, 'where dwelleth the Pope of the idolaters'. Finally, in a vivid piece of narrative, he tells of 'a certain valley wherein he saw terrible things', filled with corpses, strange music and heaps of silver which it was fatal to try to remove.

Odorico's work might have been designed as the pendant to Marco Polo's. It is the difference between a travel diary and a geographical textbook. If Marco is noted for abstraction and impersonality and seems deficient in visual perception, Odorico is vivid, gives sudden keen impressions of what he sees: an Islamic wedding feast, the physical appearance of Indians, Suma-trans and of the Chinese ('handsome enough, but colourless, with beards of long, straggling hairs like mousers – cats I mean. And the women are the most beautiful in the world!'). It is wholly characteristic that he should record, as Marco does not, the foot-binding of Chinese ladies. And he himself is continually present in the account. Typical is this passage, where he describes fishing with cormorants in Zhejiang province:

> At the head of the bridge was a hostel in which I was entertained. And mine host, wishing to gratify me, said: 'If thou would like to see good fishing, come with me.' And so he led me on the bridge and I looked and saw in some boats of his that were there certain water-fowl tied upon perches. And these he now tied with a cord round the throat that they might not be able to swallow the fish which they caught. Next he pro-ceeded to put three great baskets into a boat, one at each end and the third in the middle, and then he let the water-fowl loose. Straightway they began to dive into the water, catching great numbers of fish, and even as they caught them putting some of their own accord into the baskets, so that before long all three baskets were full. And mine host then took the cord off their necks and let them dive again to catch fish for their own food. And when they had thus fed they returned to their own perches and were tied up as before. And some of these fish I had for my dinner.[49]

It presents a vignette, never to be found in Marco Polo, of immediacy of experience, a moment of past time caught for ever.

Odorico died in January 1331 and was buried in the Franciscan church of Udine under a tombstone showing a friar with what Colonel Yule has well described as 'a bluff, benevolent, Socratic countenance', grasping a book and preaching to figures kneeling at his feet who represent, it is to be presumed, those whom he has recently converted. Yule has suggested, on the strength of his book, that Odorico's interest or at least participation in missionary work was lukewarm, and even Reichert remarks that he seems to have more interest in the observation of peoples than in conversion.[50] This may be to read too much into his silences. Five months after his death the Patriarch of Aquileia was ordering that accounts of his miracles should be collected.[51] This could simply reflect the financial advantages which might have been perceived in having the relics of a new saint in the diocese. (In the event Odorico was only beatified, and then not until the eighteenth century.) Still, some odour of sanctity must have drifted from him at death for he acquired two fourteenth-century biographies. One was by Johannes von Viktring (d.1345/1347) in his *Liber certarum historiarum.* The second was a *Vita* by an unknown Franciscan, written in 1369, which survives in thirteen manuscripts in which he is claimed (as he himself, in his book, never claims) to have baptised 20,000 heathen.[52]

In the Middle Ages, the manuscript was bound up with a variety of texts: with Marco Polo; with the work of Giovanni di Pian di Carpine, with Holy Land itineraries; with chronicles such as the *Polychronicon* of Ranulph Higden; with the eastern Alexander stories; with academic geography such as the twelfth-century work of Honorius Augustodunensis, or with the tale of *The Three Monks' Journey to Paradise* (in some Italian manuscripts Odorico himself ends his life by making a final journey to Paradise).[53] The connection is with geography, especially missionary geography, and with the East. In these circumstances, however differently Odorico treated his experiences, and however slighter and less comprehensive it was, his book provided a powerful reinforcement to belief in what had been written by Marco Polo.

Yet, quite apart from any merits which it possessed in itself, the importance of Odorico in offering validation of Polo was most markedly increased by the use of his material in another work which came into circulation from about 1366. This was the celebrated *Book of Sir John Mandeville,*[54] in which the author, in the persona of an English knight, purports to tell the story of his travels through the world. In fact no genuine traces of this man have been found and it is clearly a work constructed in its entirety from earlier sources. Among these in particular are Hetoum and Odorico for the Far East, and a pilgrim guide by William of Boldensele for the Holy Land,[55] all as translated into French by one Jean le Long, a Benedictine monk who was from 1365 Abbot of the monastery of Saint Bertin at Saint-Omer. By 1351 this Jean le Long had translated six geographical works from Latin. In addition to the three already mentioned, these were Marco Polo, the Archbishop of Sultania's report between 1330 and 1334, and another narrative of pilgrimage to the Holy Land by the Dominican friar, Ricoldo da Montecroce.[56] In these circumstances and in the absence of any other clear candidate as author, one wonders whether 'Sir John Mandeville' is in fact Jean le Long himself.

Li commence li liures du graunt Taam qui parole de la graunt Ermenie de perste
et decartans et dinde. Et des autres merueille qui y le monde sont.

1. The Polos leave Venice
From *Li Livres du Graunt Caam*, by the artist Johannes, *ca.* 1400. Bodleian Library
Oxford. MS.

2. The TO Map

The first printed map of the world (65 mm. in diameter), from Isidore of Seville's
Etimologiae (Augsburg, 1472), shows the typical form of a TO map. Within the O
of the world, Asia is at the top of the map. The arms of a T are made by the rivers
Don and Nile, and its upright by the Mediterranean which separates Africa from
Europe. Inset are the names of the three sons of Noah whose descendants were
believed to have populated the three continents: Shem, Ham and Japheth. Around
the inner circle of land flows 'the Ocean Sea'. British Library, London.

3. The East *ca.* 1290

A western representation of the East made when the Polos were still in China. At the top is the Last Judgment with the saved on God's right hand. In a roundel below is the Earthly Paradise or Garden of Eden where Adam and Eve eat the Forbidden Fruit, and from where the four great rivers of the world take their origin. Within the O of the world beneath that are a large range of illustrations of the history and myths of the region: 'the Seres who make clothes from silk'; strange creatures like (to the left) the Sciopod who shields himself from the sun with his foot, (below him) the men who feed only on the smell of apples, the Ganges rising in the mountains, and so on. Many of the illustrations refer to Alexander's invasion of India. In the lower half of the illustration, Abraham at Ur in the Chaldees looks out from a castellated window; to his left one sees an enormous tower of Babel, near Babylon. Hereford Cathedral.

4. The Monstrous Races
One of the Blemmyae, a Sciopod, and a 'Wild Man'. These creatures are not in Marco's
Book. But miniaturists commissioned to illustrate it often drew them none the less,
believing that any writing about the East should have such things in it. From the Marco
Polo in *Livre des merveilles*, Bibliothèque Nationale de France, Paris – *ca.* 1400.

5. Difficulties of Illustration

Glancing rapidly over the rubrics, the miniaturist has seen the word 'brothers' (referring to Marco's uncle and father, Niccolò and Maffeo Polo) and has leapt to the conclusion that the Polos were friars. In the same way the words 'gold table' – meaning the small gold tablet which the Great Khan gave as a mark of his protection – has led him to paint a large and splendid gold table. From a Marco Polo manuscript, *ca.* 1400. British Library, London.

6. World Map by Pietro Vesconte

Dating from about 1320, this is one of the first *mappaemundi* in which the techniques of the makers of portolan charts (with a network of loxodromes) were applied to the making of world maps. The East is at the top, Ireland, 'Ybernia', at the bottom. Marco Polo's Book is ignored and there are very few entries on the East. British Library, London.

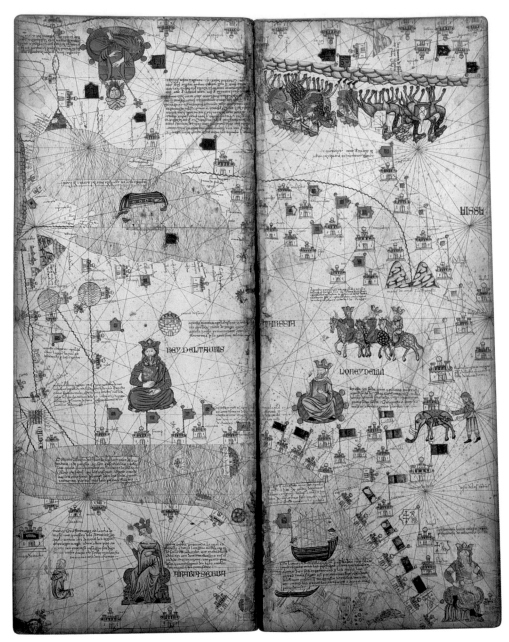

7. *The Catalan Atlas* (The Four Eastern Panels), *ca.* 1380
The Black Sea and western Asia appear in the first panel. In the second, at the top one sees (upside down) a representation of a caravan departing from the Empire of Sareas (i.e. Sarai or the Kipchak Khanate). 'This caravan has left the empire of Sareas to go to Cathay.' In

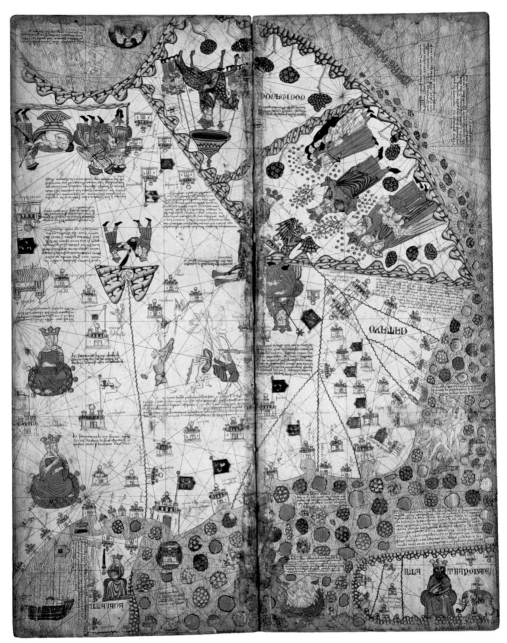

the third panel is the Khan of 'the Empire of Media' (Chaghadai), the ruler of Gog and
Magog (on horseback, top right), Lop, Tenduc, two men hunting for diamonds with eagles
(central) and (bottom) India. For a detail of the fourth panel see illustration 8. Bibliothèque
Nationale, Paris.

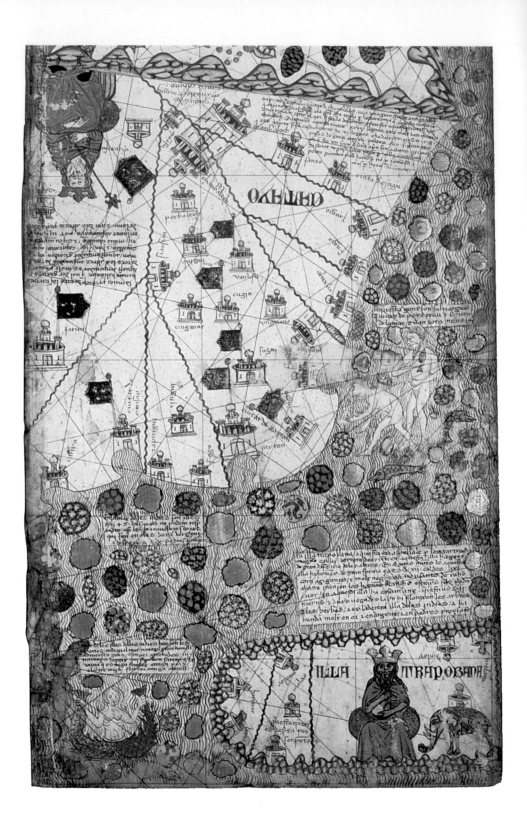

9. Fra Mauro's China, detail

In this map of 1459, from the Biblioteca Nazionale Marciana in Venice, the influence of Marco Polo on his fellow-Venetian cartographer is very apparent. South is at the top of the map, where one sees the Yangtze and its tributaries. The river at the bottom is the Yellow River with a suggestion of its great upper bend. In the centre at the bottom, within 'the noble empire of Cathay', is the city of 'Chanbalec' (Khanbalikh or Beijing). 'Quançu' (Quinsai, or Hangzhou) is placed on the coast with a legend that its circumference is 100 miles and that it has 12,000 bridges. Further south is the 'Regno Magno' (Mangi or the provinces of southern China), which is said to contain 12,000 towns. To the east, at the top, is the Desert of Lop. The illustrations of the towns still give the map a 'medieval' character but offer the impression of a rich and most populous country.

8. *The Catalan Atlas* (South-East Asia)

At the top, almost central, is Khanbalikh (extending for 2 miles), and to its left (upside down) the Great Khan, said to be guarded by 12,000 horsemen. One sees Quinsai, Fugu, Zaiton represented as a great port. In the Sea of Chin are Java and 7,458 islands with the promise of 'gold, silver, spices, precious stones'. 'Trapobana' or Taprabona (often taken in the West to be Ceylon, but here perhaps Java) has an impressive ruler and an Indian elephant, and to the left (not found in Marco's Book), a Siren. Bibliothèque Nationale, Paris.

10. Martin Behaim, Globe
Once again belief in Marco Polo triumphs. Cipangu features prominently in the eastern Atlantic, off the mainland of Mangi, and set amidst Marco's 7,448 islands of the Sea of Chin. Germanisches Nationalmuseum, Nuremberg.

11. Henricus Martellus Germanicus, World Map
At this date the only source for knowledge of Cipangu or Japan in Europe was still Marco Polo. In the British Library *mappamondo* by Martellus of around 1489, Cipangu is not shown. But in this Yale map, said to be executed by him around the same date, it can be seen in the top right-hand corner. In portraying south-west Asia the cartographer has also drawn on Conti. The Beinecke Library, Yale University.

12. The Four Heroes of Geographical Knowledge
In this woodcut of *circa* 1550, Matteo Pagano's world map, based on an earlier planisphere by Giacomo Gastaldi, places within its four corners the figures of Ptolemy, Strabo, Columbus and in the bottom left-hand corner, Marco Polo. This survives in only one copy now in the Map Room of the British Library.

13. (next double spread) Ortelius, Tartary
Since Marco had given only the Mongol or Persian forms of Chinese place names, the first Europeans who arrived by sea on the Chinese coast did not realise that this was the country which he had described. As a result map-makers put a country called Chin or China between 25° and 40° latitude and above that Marco's Mangi and Cathay. So here, in Ortelius' great atlas, the *Theatrum orbis terrarum* of 1587, at 25° there is a port called Chincheo, i.e. Ch'üan-chou (Pinyin Quanzhou), while at 40° another port called Zaiton – which was simply the Mongol name for Ch'üan-chou. Huntington Library, San Marino.

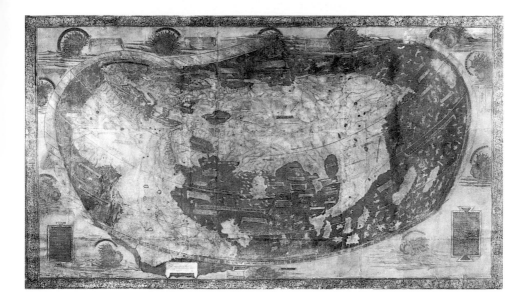

EVROPAE PARS.

SE[...]

Soloski monasterium

Mar Maggiore

Pinego

CONDORA

Colgoyeue

OBDO- RA.

Pechora

Danorum siue Danitarum horda, deiectio siue descensio aut expulsio.

Schiticum prom.

DVCIS MOSCO- VIAE CON- FINII.

Naigatz

Ciremissorum horda

Nephtalitza horda, Nep [...]

Bulgar

Cham Slouoda

Casan

Teron

Kondori

Cingol

Sibir

Crustima

Kytaia lacus.

Viezucano- rum horda.

Turb [...]

Turbonu horda

Bessima

Orlau

Calino

Corolus

Thenishi

Chirai

Chielanorum horda.

Mecrito- rum horda.

ZVIRIA

Hic magnus prouentus culami aromatici.

Abuas medris

CASAN.

Mechet

ASTRACAN

Baschirdorum horda.

BARGV regio palustris

GEOR- GIANI.

Astracan

Sora

Sorana

TARTARIA, Quae Sar- matiam Asiaticam, & vtramque Scythiam veterum comprehendit.

Taugin

Cory

Derbent

Sabran

Cosmay

R. yan

Zibierairorum horda.

TABOR REG:

Girm

Bachu

Mar de Bachu, olim Mare Caspium, et Hyrcanum.

Frutach

TVRCHESTAN Regio vnde essmontani 10. Tribuum soly ante 400. Anos sunt accersiti à Persis contra Ismaelis Mahumedis arma.

Desertum Apastachit.

Tabor seu Tobur, vmbilicarius Tota- rorum regio, vbi libri, olim libro sacro perdidissent, sunt tamen vnus sub uno rege, Qui 1560. in Galliam vnà ad regem Francorum eius nominis primum venit, et postea a Carolo V. Mantue uno sue inside: lituris poenas luit: quia secreto solicitabat Christianos principes ad Iudaismum, de qua re Carolum V. alloquutus erat

Tauris ol. Ecbatana.

TARSE.

CHIORSA- num

Hic Rubini gemme re- periuntur

MAVRENAHER

Lilach

Tanchu

Teras

Sacha

Desertum Caracora- num

Mons Althay, vbi orti Tartari, imperatores sepeliuntur, ab Althay- tone Armeno sub noie Belgi- an describi videntur.

ZAGATAI

Samarchand magni Tamber- quondā sedes.

SIRVISON

Sosech

Satin

Sibuar

TANGVT. asie artē imprimendi ante mille, vt ferunt, annos habuerunt

IESEL. BAS.

SAMARC

Bichend

HAND.

Wazzir

Aesu

CIAR- CIAN.

Catascora

Caracoran

Xanda

Arida

Terment Cheregam.

Arbsiges

Lop.

Caracoran

Cambalu Cataie metropolis, habet 28. mill. in circuitu.

Pons reu [...]

Imaus mons qui ISTIGIAS.

SIM. Etaicam

Desertum Lop.

Chinchi talas

Succuir

His montibus Rhabarbarum prouenit

Cangi

REGNI PERSIAE CONFI- NII.

Georgane Samach

Yelualm Asarest

Chache

SOLITVDINES CASTAE.

Gauta

Sochgi

TENDVCH.

Togara

Talalar nis tan Serme- gan Daran.

TA CALIS TAN.

CAMVL

Sachio

Singui

Camul

Calis

Cuncham

CAINDV.

Casimfu.

Monte Vssonte.

Turfah.

ERGI- gimul.

Sindin fu. Caindu

THEBET

Rosam

MVL.

Lacus Isasius

Caindu

Pharacu

Gin gui.

Sazechian

CARA- ZAN.

Carazan

Caraia

Cacho bach

Baicun [...]

Gin [...]

Continet hęc ta- bula oem Tartariam, cum reliqua Asię Orientalioris ysq, Oce- anū Eoum parte, Magno Chamo obedi- ente: Cuius imperium Obij fl. Kataia la- cu: Volga fl. Mari Caspio, Chesel flu: Vssonte monte, Thebet regione, Ca- romoram fluuio, & Oceano terminatur.

Cum Priuilegio.

PARS

INDIAE

Bror fl. amein.

Sargo

TIPV- RA.

Bonpruo.

MO[...]

Minla lacus.

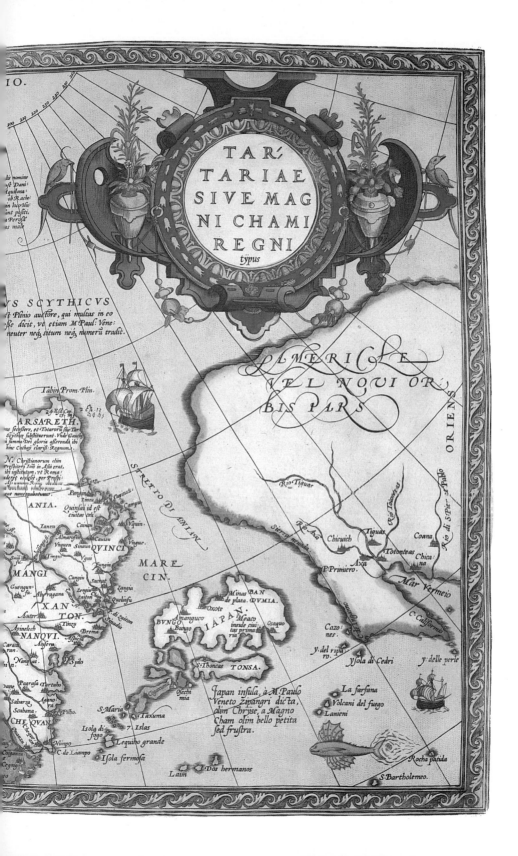

200 210 220 230 240

TAR/
TARIAE
SIVE MAG
NI CHAMI
REGNI
typus

VS SCYTHICVS

st Plinio auctore, qui multas in eo
sse dicit, vt etiam M:Paul: Vene:
neuter neq̃ situm neq̃ numeru tradit.

A MERICLE
VEL NOVI OR
BIS PARS

ORIENS

Tabin Prom: Plin.

24 Est Cap: 2 Pa.17
et 24.45

ARSARETH.
nus secessere, et Totarorū siue Tar
Scythæ substiterunt: Vnde Gaute
à summa Dei gloria asserenda ibi
hinc Cathay clariss: Regnum.

N. Christianorum olim
Presbyteri Iohis in Asia erat,
ibi instituta, vt Roma:
aderat eiusdem, per Presbi:
Asia autem Regis, omnisq̃
Gothium, vmbrarū
que nunc subsidunt

Rio Tiguar

ANIA.
Quinsai id est
ciuitas celi

Pingui   Tinza

Sierra neuada

Chicuich   Tiguas

Coana

Rio de Totontes   Rio di S.Pier Pablo

Totonteas Chica:
na

Pungoi   Cuinci

Almarosu

Camul

Vguin

Sinaus   Vigue.

Vguer
Vgui
Fungin
Sacrat
Langia

Rio Aia   Axa

P.Primiero.

Mar Vermeio

C. Calisornes

C. de Liampo

MANGI

Guengun:
fu

Aberragana
Zenzui   Zaiton

Quelasu

XAN
TON.

Tinzu

Sradia

Brema

Spilo

Spica

QVINCI

MARE
CIN.

Camino

Minas BAN
de plata. DVMIA.

Oxote

BVNGO   Amanguco   Meaco
Bungo   insula cuni
tas prima
ria

Osaguo

IAPAN.

Caza:
nes

y. del ripa
ro.

Ysola di Cedri

y delle perle

S.Thomas   TONSA.

Japan insula, à M. Paulo
Veneto Zipangri dicta,
olim Chryse, a Magno
Cham olim bello petita
sed frustra.

La farsana

Volcani del fuego
Lanieni

NANOVI.

Caracal

Nanguai

Pagrasa   Curtaho

Sabarza
Scabana
Pilbo

S.Maria   Taxuma

Isola di
fogo   7. Islas

Nimpo   Lequiho grande

Isola fermosa

Laim   I. Dos hermanos

Rocha patida

S.Bartholemeo.

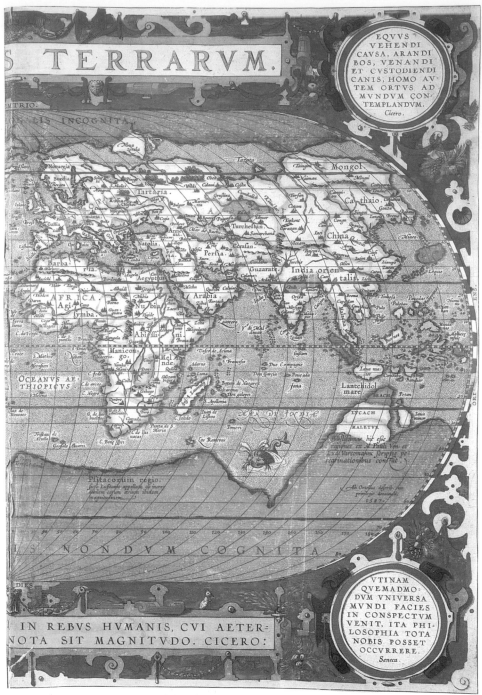

14. Ortelius, Eastern Half of World Map
Ortelius has here taken over Mercator's interpretation of Marco Polo on the kingdoms of Lucach, Boëach and Maletur, which are placed at the peak of a promontory rising from the great *Terra Australis* or *Southern Land Not Yet Discovered* to the south-east of Java. A note under Maletur refers to the travels of Marcus Paulus Venetus and Ludovico Varthema as testimonies to 'the immensely vast regions' found there. Huntington Library, San Marino.

Certainly, recalling that Jean was so fat that he could only walk with difficulty, there is a certain charm in the notion that he might have written himself into the part of a great traveller, that living as he did in a monastery some twenty-five miles from English Calais, Abbot Jean should have fantasised himself into one of those Sir Johns he would often have been seen strutting around in the neighbourhood.

This is guesswork. Yet whoever did in fact write it, the scorn poured out so often upon him as 'an impostor' is wholly out of place. What one has here is a brilliantly constructed work of geography or geographical romance in which an imaginary character leads us with great literary skill on an urbanely written journey through what is conceived as the real world, a marvellous work of *haute vulgarisation* whose readability stands in strong contrast to most of the 'authentic' texts of geography of the day. As a result it achieved immense popularity, surviving in some two hundred and fifty medieval manuscripts (versions in French, Latin, English, Italian and German in the fourteenth century; in Dutch, Gaelic, Danish, Czech and Aragonese in the fifteenth); passing into print between 1478 and 1499 in German, French, Latin, Italian and English; and achieving some eighty editions in eight languages between 1478 and 1592.[57]

Ten of the manuscripts are bound up with Alexander stories, ten with Chaucer's poetry, and ten with Marco Polo. Though Jean le Long had also newly translated Marco Polo from the Latin, the author of *Sir John Mandeville* did not utilise his Book. (Perhaps he felt instinctively that the factual density of the Venetian would destroy his own attempt to create a work of art, as indeed, one might say, it had destroyed the attempt Rustichello had made.) Yet his tale of the East, taken at once to be not simply an educative narrative but an account by a real traveller, added authority to Marco's Book, and until the second half of the sixteenth century was normally accepted as true.[58]

V

Yet before the 1380s one has the impression that the appeal of both Mandeville and Polo too was primarily literary rather than learned. The Florentine chronicler, Giovanni Villani (who had read about Gengis Khan and the Mongols in the chronicle of Hetoum, and who as a merchant may well have had other testimony of Cathay), accepts the reality described in 'the book called Milione which maestro Marco Polo of Venice made which tells much of their power and lordship, since he was for a long time among them'.[59] But no fourteenth-century historian, apart from Pipino, Marco's translator in his own world chronicle, uses his material at any length.[60]

Again, although information about the Mongol world entered the historical sections of the encylopaedias of the later Middle Ages, that which concerned geography was seen there much more rarely. As Reichert has written, 'historical representation' and 'the description of nature' each took their own different ways.[61]

If what Rustichello concocted was a combination of romance and chorography, for his contemporaries the romance dominated. In Fra Filippo di Ferrara's *Liber de introductione loquendi*, a manual of conversation for Dominicans hoping to turn the minds of those with whom they spoke to religion, there are plenty of stories from the Book; and the same anecdotal use of Marco and Odorico is found in a compilation from the Rhineland 'Concerning the Orient', dating from between 1350 and 1361.[62] In its exotic flavour, Marco's Book appealed to that 'medieval orientalism' of which Richard has spoken.[63] It harmonised with, perhaps was the inspiration for, such pageants as that in London in September 1331, when on the eve of a tournament in Cheapside, King Edward III with many knights, 'dressed and masked in the guise of Tartars', rode at vespers, two-by-two through the city, each leading on his right by a silver chain, ladies from among the noblest and fairest of the kingdom, dressed in red tunics and caps of white cameline.[64]

In this the Book blended with, helped to create, the taste of the time and was certainly one of the sources for the eastern elements in the French, Franco-Italian and Italian epics of the later Middle Ages: *Badouin de Sebourc*, the *Entrée d'Espagne* and Andrea da Barberino's *Guerin Meschino*.[65] The vogue was to continue in the Italy of the Renaissance, with Luigi Pulci's *Morgante*, Boiardo's *Orlando innamorato*, and then Ariosto's *Orlando furioso* in which Roland is enamoured of Angelica, beautiful daughter of none other than the King of Cathay. Yet it does not imply, of course, any necessary belief in the truth of the Book. For Jean d'Outremeuse of Liège, in his *Myreur des histoires*, in which the Carolingian hero, Ogier le Danois, conquers Cathay and Mangi, the Book is clearly essentially a romantic source for the invention of yet more romance.[66] Then again, in looking at fourteenth-century eastern exoticism it is difficult to isolate what derives from Marco and what from his successors. When in her *Livre du chemin de large estude*, Christine de Pisan journeys to 'la riche isle de Cathay', she seems to be following Mandeville and Philippe de Mézières rather than Marco,[67] while Chaucer's setting of 'The Squire's Tale' at Sarai is most unlikely to have anything to do with Marco's Book.[68] And at all times what predominated overwhelmingly in this popular vision of 'the East' was the memory of the Mongols. This was not to change until the geographical Renaissance which came to Europe with the development of humanism.

Chapter 8

Marco among the Humanists

I

It was in the years around the turn of the fourteenth and fifteenth centuries that the truth of Marco Polo's Book was most likely to be doubted. As western contacts with the Far East fell away and as those who had visited China died off, there were fewer and fewer in Europe who were able to testify in person to its veracity. It is not then remarkable that precisely in this period we find the only instance from the fourteenth and fifteenth centuries of an explicit declaration of disbelief in it. In the winter of 1392 the Florentine patrician Amelio Bonaguisi was serving as *podestà* in the podestàship ('third-grade') of the village of Cerreto Guidi. In this lonely exile (for the conscientious *podestà* isolated himself from the social life of those subject to his discipline) he spent some of his leisure in writing verse but most of it in copying out a book. In the course of his life, he was to transcribe many works: *A Moral Treatise*, *The Lives and Sentences of the Philosophers*, 'a catalogue of famous cities before and after the Deluge' and an Italian translation of Ovid's *Epistles*.[1] On this occasion he copied the Tuscan version of Marco Polo. And when he had finished it, in language which marvellously echoes the war of fleeting doubts and beliefs in his mind, he explained why:

> to pass the time and to keep melancholy away. Since these seem to me incredible things; and what he says seems to me not so much lies as more than miracles. And yet what he speaks of could be true, but I don't believe it – though in the world one finds very different things from one country to another. But these, it seems to me – though I've enjoyed copying them – are things not to be believed nor to give faith to, so it seems to me.[2]

As an instinctive judgment, given the knowledge available to him, it was not unreasonable. It was not, of course, an informed judgment made by a cosmographer, and it was one which was to receive no explicit (though an occasional inexplicit) echo in the years which followed. Indeed with great justice Folker Reichert has offered a schema in which the Book, seen in the fourteenth century simply as the narration of *mirabilia* and read primarily for literary entertainment, comes, at the turn of the fifteenth century, to be considered as offering genuine geographical knowledge.[3]

Certainly it was some time before cartographers are to be found using it as a source.[4] The first 'transitional' *mappaemundi*, as Woodward has defined them[5] – the first maps, that is, which applied the sophisticated and realistic techniques of the makers of contemporary sea charts or portolan charts to the making of world maps – date from the beginning of the fourteenth century. Yet Marco is ignored in all that have survived. One thinks of the world map of Fra Paolino Minorita which was included in his treatise, the *De mapa mundi* (*ca*.1320). In it Fra Paolino notes some brief details of the East. Of these some seem to derive from a reading of Hetoum: 'Here is the Great Khan', 'Beginning of the kingdom of Cathay'. Others, such as the names Gazaria and Valari are found in Rubruck; and with Rubruck (as against the traditional wisdom of Isidore of Seville) Paolo holds the Caspian to be a closed sea.[6] None the less this is a work which, because it ignores Marco, gives very short measure on most of Asia.

Shortly after Paolino, Pietro Vesconte, a man responsible for many portolan charts, drew a world map (see Illustration 6) to accompany Marin Sanudo's *Liber secretorum fidelium crucis*, one of those many works of the day which offered elaborate plans for a crusade.[7] Vesconte's chart is a slightly improved version of Paolino's, incorporating most of his notes together with some of the remarks from the *De mapa mundi* on the boundaries of Cathay. Otherwise what he has on Asia is sparse and generalised: 'Here are born elephants', etc., while here too are 'The castles of Gog and Magog' which Hetoum mentions but which Marco had explained were really the two quite different peoples, Ung and Mugul. It has been suggested that Vesconte and Sanudo (who in his book mentions Hetoum but not Marco) ignored Marco's Book because their crusade involved the Middle East. Yet in that case why attempt to put in the Far East at all? My own suspicion is that for these men to have attempted to include Marco's material would have represented too complete a break with the accepted idea of what a *mappamundi* was. Then again both Paolino and Vesconte may well have shied away from the immense difficulty of translating the Book into cartographic representation. Though giving frequent indications of bearings and distances, whether in miles or days of travel, it does not of course offer degrees of latitude – something for which in the seventeenth century it would be bizarrely criticised – let alone longitude. It was only, one might say, with the willingness to believe Marco so strongly that one was willing to undertake the whole business of wrestling with all those

'Now let us quit Suju and go on to another which is called Viju, one day's journey distant' – passages that a geographical rather than theological map of the world could be attempted.

Yet it must have been clear, as Marco's Book was followed by those of Odorico and Mandeville, that without an effort to come to terms with the new information no true *mappamundi* was possible. It has been suggested that the first to make the attempt was Angelino Dulcert, map-maker of Majorca. There has survived a map of his from the year 1339, which portrays Europe from the Canaries to the Black Sea. The uneven character of the right-hand margin has suggested to some scholars that the work as we have it is merely a half of what has survived. Since what has survived bears a strong resemblance to the portrayal of Europe in the celebrated *Catalan Atlas*, a work produced some forty years later, and since the *Catalan Atlas* does indeed give a picture of the East which is based on Marco Polo's Book, it has been argued that Dulcert's lost sheets did the same.[8] But a strong objection to the thesis is that the place names of the *Catalan Atlas* seem to be taken from a version of Marco's Book published after 1377, almost forty years, that is, after the Dulcert map. In all it seems rash to speculate on what Dulcert's lost work might have contained. Yet the claims made for it remind us how much our knowledge is circumscribed by the hazards of loss and survival. And how much too, one should add, from arbitrary interference with those documents we still possess. On the last of the eight sheets of the *Medici Atlas*, datable to the third quarter of the fourteenth century, one finds an island marked 'Sipango' and the place name Madagascar, entries which can only be owed to a reading of Marco Polo. Yet closer observation of the style of presentation makes it certain that these are later additions from 'certainly not earlier than the sixteenth century'.[9]

The truth is that the first maps known to us which were strongly influenced by Marco's Book and which still remain to us are those in the *Catalan Atlas* (see Illustrations 7 and 8). This was probably drawn up by the Majorcan Jew Abraham Cresques at some time around 1380.[10] Painted on eight wooden panels, each 69 cm by 39 cm, criss-crossed by the loxodromes of the portolan charts, its eastern material is drawn from both traditional legends and the accounts of travellers. Among these are Odorico; the map, for instance, shows 'Zincolan' (Canton, Guangzhou) and 'Mingio' (Ningbo), of which he but not Marco Polo wrote. But its main source for the East is undoubtedly Marco's Book, perhaps in the version prepared a few years earlier – whether with or without the idea of crusade in mind is not clear – for the Cardinal Juan Fernández de Heredia.[11] Here is found 'the Empire of Sareas' (i.e. of Sarai, the Kipchak Khanate), and a picture of a caravan departing from it ('This caravan has left the empire of Sareas to go to Cathay'). Here are 'the Empire of Media' (the Chaghadai Khanate), Karakorum, and the Great Khan with 12,000 horses. And here are the lands of the Great Khan: 'Chancio' (Zhangye), Khanbalikh (extending for 2 miles), Quinsai, Fugu, Zaiton, Quienfu, Shangdu, in all twenty-nine named Chinese towns. In the Sea of Chin are Java and 7,458 islands (the Rustichello text had 7,448 islands) with the promise of 'gold, silver, spices, precious stones'. Taprabona has an Indian elephant. India, assuming for the first time in maps a peninsula form, has an illustration of suttee. There is much here that is still mythical: Gog and Magog are found enclosed behind a great wall by Alexander, and diamonds are being hunted with eagles, and we seem centuries away from a modern map. Yet here for the first time in the West China assumes on a map a recognisable and, one might say, rational form.[12]

The influence of Marco Polo, working through either the *Catalan Atlas* or some other map dependent upon the Atlas, is shown too, though much more weakly, in *The Book of Knowledge of all Kingdoms and Lordships* which was probably drawn up in the last two decades of the fourteenth century. In this work the author, writing in Spanish, in order to instruct the reader in geographical learning, pretends to be a Franciscan friar who has made a journey through the world. It had, one could say, the same purpose and form as Mandeville's book. Yet it was produced with infinitely less elaboration and art, for it consists of no more than a compilation of names read off the map. None the less we are given here, though in a very confusing manner, the various place names of a journey from Arabia to Java and the Empire of Cathay.[13]

If from the 1380s cartographers began to pay attention to Marco's text, it was some twenty years before literary scholars were to offer it any serious consideration. It was, perhaps surprisingly, with the humanists that the Book of Marco Polo first gained stature. It was with Humanism from the time of Petrarch and Boccaccio – and then more particularly from the time of the growth of Greek learning in the fifteenth century – that the study of geography began to acquire dignity and substance. As far as Marco is concerned, the first indications of this come close to the turn of the fifteenth century with the geographical sections of the *Fons memorabilium universi*, an encyclopaedia in thirty-five books compiled by the schoolmaster–humanist Domenico di Bandino of Arezzo. Bandino describes Marco as the 'the most diligent investigator of eastern shores' and includes very large citations from the Book in his own work. In the biographical section of the *Fons* which details the *viri clari* or 'famous men', Marco is mentioned again, along with other writers on geography such as Pliny, Isidore and Brunetto Latini (while Solinus, Orosius and Albertus Magnus are ignored). He is allotted only three lines, but in them is hailed as the author of the 'delightful book concerning the site, customs and condition of the oriental provinces'. That word 'delightful' (*delectabilem*), it has been suggested, should make us pause, in that the word has a savour of enjoyment remote from works dedicated to serious informative writing (an archetypical academic reaction).[14] Yet of course Rustichello's achievement was indeed to clothe stark facts in a manner 'delightful' for the age.

That said it may be that an important stage in the development of a factual interest in the East is reached with the little work of Bandino's contemporary, the Florentine politician Domenico Silvestri. In his *De insulis et earum proprietatibus*, written around 1400, Silvestri seems to be making serious attempts to discover geographical truth. In discussing the islands of the Indian and China seas he remarks that the Venetian Marco Polo has written that so very many islands existed in India (i.e. the East)[15] that it would be very difficult to speak of them. Could that be true? Silvestri tells us that he is quite prepared to dismiss some assertions about the East. It is his intention to set out only what is testified to by the authority of antiquity (there speaks the humanist), *viva voce* witnesses, or probable conjecture. For instance he refuses to accept Odorico's claim that there are 5,000 islands under the rule of the King of the Tartars. This is one of those statements which he takes to be a lie and which unfortunately weakens the force of the true things Odorico has mentioned. And he would in no way have accepted what Marco Polo had written but for the fact that he has met a Venetian who had been in 'India' and had declared that he himself had seen there many of the things described in his Book. Marco, he remarks again (though here he is guilty of a common misreading[16]), has spoken of dog-headed men. Well, so did Isidore, 'and if we believe him, why not Marco Polo?'[17]

If this does indeed represent a new realism in considering the Book it also implied an urgent need for personal verification of what it said. At the turn of the century this was largely lacking. These were the years when Timur had risen to dominate Central Asia. On behalf of the King of Castille, Ruy González de Clavijo led an embassy to him in 1403 and in his memoirs tells us a little of the lands beyond. At Samarkand he met a merchant who had come in a caravan from Khanbalikh who told him of 'the great wealth and numbers of the people of Cathay' and went on to describe his city as twenty times the size of Tabriz. And on Timur's insistence Ruy's party were given precedence over the emissaries of Cathay. But he is speaking of a world that he clearly thinks of as utterly remote. Again, Johannes Schiltberger, who for many years was Timur's captive, knows China only as a land which Timur had attacked. The narratives of the travels of Bertrand de la Broquière (1432–3) and Pero Tafur (1435–9) display only the most superficial knowledge of the Russian Tartars and neither shows any knowledge of the Far East.[18] In 1410 or 1414 John III,

Archbishop of Sultania in Persia dispatched, at Timur's command, a *Libellus de notitia orbis* to the rulers of Venice, Genoa, Milan, Paris, London and Prague, asking them to ally with his master. But again this pamphlet while displaying a good knowledge of the Middle East is vague and circumstantial on the lands beyond.[19] The embassy of Pietro Rombulo to King George 'of Cathay' (perhaps Tangut?) in 1444–8 was carried out in Ethiopian service and seems to have remained unknown in western Europe.[20] It needed the return to Italy of another Venetian, one Niccolò Conti who had spent some twenty-five years in the East, to give a convincing authentication of Marco Polo and Odorico's accounts.

As a merchant, Conti had travelled in Persia and then passed on by stages via the Red Sea, to India, Malaysia, Sumatra, Java and Vietnam. He had returned via Bengal, Abyssinia and Egypt. In Egypt, in order to save his life and those of his wife and children, he had adopted the Muslim faith. He returned to Italy some time between 1439 and 1442 and went to Pope Eugenius IV then in Florence in order to seek absolution for his apostasy. At the papal court his story was written up by the papal secretary Poggio Bracciolini in a Latin prose narrative which was to have an important influence upon geographical thought on Asia.[21] Conti did not reach China but he told of Chinese merchants of immense wealth and like Marco was deeply impressed by Chinese junks. Again the strangeness of the world described by Conti mirrored and so somehow validated what Marco had spoken of. With this material Poggio incorporated an account of what had been told to him – or rather (there were translation difficulties) what he thought had been told to him – by a representative of the patriarch of a Nestorian Christian kingdom 'from Upper India towards the North, twenty days journey from China'.[22] All this material he included in that humanist classic, the *De varietate fortunae*. Published in 1448 this was a work that appeared in several manuscript versions and was translated, some twenty years later, into Italian. Book IV, containing Conti's story, soon began to circulate separately from the rest of the work and in 1492 this fourth section was edited for print by the Milanese humanist Cristoforo da Bollate under the title *India recognita*.[23]

Conti's account of Asia had its own interest and it was soon remarked that it seemed to offer testimony to the truth of Marco's account. Some time before 1458, a copy of Marco's Book, copied some twenty years before for one of Eugenius IV's bureaucrats, came into the possession of a Venetian patrician. When he had read it he wrote this: 'I, Jacomo Barbarigo, have read this present book of Marco Polo and I have found many things that he says to be true, and this I testify through the revelation of Ser Niccolò Conti, Venetian, who has been a long time in that part of India, and similarly through many Moorish merchants with whom I have spoken.'[24] Similarly the transcriber of a Wolfenbüttel manuscript of the fifteenth century points to Marco's validation from the narratives of Hetoum, Odorico, Mandeville and Conti.[25] The point is made most forcibly in 1502. The Portuguese had already known and used Marco's Book for many years.[26] But it was only then that, together with the fourth book of Poggio's *Historia*, it was translated into their language. In his introduction and dedication to King Manuel the Fortunate, the translator Valentin Fernandes explains that

in the voyage of Niccolò Conti other cities of India are spoken of, besides Calicut and Cochin, which we at the present time have discovered. . . . This work is a witness to the book of Marco Polo who travelled to eastern parts by going from the West to the East in the time of Gregory X. And this Niccolò later, in the time of Eugenius IV, penetrated them by the south and found the same lands described by the said Marco Polo. And this has been the principal cause of my having undertaken the labour of this translation at your command.[27]

II

In the fifteenth century the search for empirical knowledge went hand in hand with an expansion of the number of manuscript texts of the Book and eventually its appearance in print. The Book was first printed in its German version (Nuremberg, 1477, reissued at Augsburg, 1481). This was followed by the Latin translation of Francesco Pipino, the *Liber de consuetudinibus et condicionibus orientalium regionum*, published by Gerard de Leeu at Antwerp between 1485 and 1490, and then by the Venetian dialect text of Venice 1496.[28]

At the same time the century saw a vast expansion in the intellectual horizons of geography.[29] Central to its development was the reception in the West of the leading Greek geographers. Ptolemy's *Geography*, which was first translated into Latin in 1406, gave rise to sophisticated considerations of the size and shape of the known world and of the problem of representing it in the form of a map.[30] Strabo's work, circulating in Italy from 1423, was eventually published in translation in 1469. This offered different interpretations of these problems, together with – and it was this that distinguished it sharply from Ptolemy's survey – an elaborate chorographical study, the sort of material that Ptolemy dismissed as merely 'chit-chat'. These authors introduced fifteenth-century Europe to two different concepts of what for antiquity constituted the true discipline of geography, fruitful subjects for enquiry and debate. That debate, in what was still a manuscript culture where new knowledge passed slowly into general circulation and where old attitudes and beliefs remained strongly entrenched, took some time to develop. This can be seen particularly clearly in the *Ymago Mundi* of the future Cardinal Pierre d'Ailly, completed in August 1410. In its Preface d'Ailly gives the conventional explanation of the learned world of the Middle Ages for a concern with geography: 'It appears that the image of the world or at least the description that one can make of the world in representing it as in a mirror, is not without use for the understanding of Holy Scripture, which frequently mentions the parts, particularly the habitable parts, of the world.'[31] In fact he confines himself to serving up again what had been set down by the standard academic authorities: Pliny, Solinus, Isidore, Sacrobosco, Roger Bacon, Oresme, and makes no effort to reconcile differences between them. Moreover, while writing d'Ailly was happily unaware that a Latin version of Ptolemy's *Geography* was in circulation. Some two years later that embarrassing circumstance was brought to his attention. At which, unabashed, he sat down not to withdraw or re-edit his work but to write two *Compendia* of the *Geography* – 'this great and useful work recently translated from Greek into Latin'[32] – to stand side by side with his unaltered original treatise.

If d'Ailly came across Ptolemy belatedly, he never at any time mentioned Marco Polo. One might be tempted to see in this a silent repudiation. Yet d'Ailly does not consider the work of any traveller: not Rubruck (known to Roger Bacon), not those missionaries to the Mongols found in Vincent de Beauvais' *Encyclopaedia*, nor any writings of the friars who had penetrated Asia in the fourteenth century. As a result his is a work which enjoys all that clarity which comes from being unburdened by too much knowledge and, as such, was to prove a useful textbook for Christopher Columbus. Yet it seems clear from it that at the University of Paris study of cosmography proceeded simply with reference to knowledge acquired in universities and with no glance at what happened outside. Here is a form of scholarship which most humanists were to repudiate, for it was a merit of humanism, one might say, to bring together Ptolemy's learning and Marco's experience. A Munich manuscript of a German translation of Marco Polo, transcribed between 1469 and 1486, goes so far as to end by making Marco recommend Ptolemy for 'further reading'. Here Marco is made to accept the mistaken but common medieval identification of the cosmographer with King Ptolemy Philadelphus II: 'No more will I speak to you of foreign lands. But who wishes to know more will find it in the great scholar and king of Egypt who has not alone written for you of the world but also of the heavens with its stars and the whole firmament. Deo gracias.'[33]

It has often been said that the humanists regarded classical texts with such reverence as to hold them to be above criticism. In so far as geography is concerned that attitude – though we will shortly find one example of it – was rare. During the fifteenth century there was a continuous struggle to distinguish truth and falsehood in the newly discovered texts and to apply what was true to modern needs. In the search to verify or augment the information of the ancients, contemporaries sought out knowledge on distant places both from the classical and the more recent past. This is particularly in evidence at the General Council of the Church which met at Florence between 1439 and 1443. Among the principal aims of the council was the union of the Greek Orthodox Church and other Eastern Christian Churches under the authority of the Roman Pope. At that time, filled with delegates from the whole Christian world, from Constantinople, Russia and many parts of the East, the city must have been almost as crowded, polyglot and overrun by foreigners as it is today. It was at that time that Poggio met his Nestorian Christian 'from "Upper India"'. It was then too that, 'seized with a desire to learn those things which appear to have been unknown to ancient writers, philosophers and even to Ptolemy who was the first to write on this subject', he questioned delegates of the Ethiopian Church about the lands they came from and the source of the Nile.[34]

At the same time we hear of Parentucelli, the future Nicholas V, negotiating with Ethiopian, Armenian and Jacobite Christians through a Venetian interpreter who, we are told, knew a good twenty languages.[35] 'Ethiopian', which is to say 'Coptic', Christians attracted great interest in Florence in these years. Four monks from Egypt and four from a Coptic monastery in Jerusalem were questioned by another papal secretary, Flavio Biondo, who makes a point of telling us about the errors of Ptolemy which they had revealed. Not without the suggestion of a certain pride in his knowingness he warns us that 'Ptolemy was ignorant of many things.'[36] Also found talking to these strangers – and it is here that we come to someone of the greatest importance in considering the influence of Marco Polo – was the Florentine Commune's astrologer, the physician Paolo dal Pozzo Toscanelli. We find him in the cell of Ambrogio Traversari in the monastery of Santa Maria degli Angeli discussing the state of the Coptic Church with an Abyssinian monk, and, again, enquiring of the Cardinal of Kiev about the geography of Russia.[37] We find him, too, with the brilliant Byzantine scholar Gemistus Pletho examining a *Map of the North*, a map of Norway, Iceland and Greenland which Toscanelli had obtained from a Dane, one Clausson Swart, who had visited Florence some years before.[38] Here, fifty-four years before Columbus' First Voyage, these two men are looking at a map on which is marked a part of the New World.

At the Council this same Toscanelli was reunited with a friend from his student days at the University of Padua, Cardinal Nicholas of Cusa. Cusa, remarkable as a theologian and philosopher, was also interested in the principles of cartography. It was he who drew or caused to be drawn one of the first surviving maps of Central Europe and he owned manuscripts of Marco Polo's and of Poggio's account of Niccolò Conti's travels.[39] Later this Cusa was to have in his train a Portuguese cleric called Fernão Martins. And it was in June 1474 to this same Martins, now Canon of Lisbon and adviser to King Afonso V of Portugal, that Toscanelli, at the request of the King, sent a map together with a letter explaining its rationale. Here Toscanelli argues that the shortest way to the Indies lay west across the Atlantic:

> I have spoken with you elsewhere about a shorter way, travelling by sea, to the lands of spices than that which you are taking by Guinea. Your most serene King now requires from me some explanation of this or rather some portrayal which could be taken in and understood by even the moderately learned . . . [Toscanelli therefore sends a map]. . . . It is said that in a most noble port called Zaiton there is such an abundance of navigators with goods that in the whole of the rest of the world there are not so many. It is said that a hundred great ships each year unload pepper there, not to mention other ships bearing other spices. The country is heavily populated, most rich in a multitude of provinces and kingdoms and in cities without number, under a prince who is called the Great Khan, which name in Latin means 'King of Kings', whose palaces and residences are for the most part in the province of Cathay.
>
> His ancestors desired the friendship of Christians, and over two hundred years ago sent ambassadors to the Pope, asking for many men learned in our faith that they might preach; but those sent, hindered on the way, turned back. In the time of Pope Eugenius there came to him an ambassador who told of their great friendship for the Christians, and I had a long talk with him about many things: about the magnitude of the royal buildings, of the great size of the rivers in length and breadth, and the multitude of towns on their banks. . . .
>
> From the city of Lisbon to the west there are [marked on the map] twenty-six spaces, each of which contains two hundred fifty miles, as far as the most noble and very great city of Quinsay. This city is a hundred miles in circumference, and has ten bridges, and its name means City of Heaven, and many wonderful things are told about it, concerning its arts and its revenues. . . . That city lies in the province of Mangi, near the province of Cathay, in which is the royal palace of the king. And from the island of Antillia [an island imagined to exist in the centre of the

Atlantic], known to you, to the very noble island of Cipangu, there are ten spaces. This land is most rich in gold, pearls and precious stones, and the temples and royal palaces are covered with solid gold.[40]

The authenticity of this letter has been doubted. If it was indeed written by Toscanelli it shows that in the Cusa–Martins–Toscanelli circle Marco Polo was taken with immense seriousness. Apart from the visitor to Eugenius IV with whom Toscanelli spoke, and perhaps Niccolò Conti (though Conti never actually visited China), it must be Marco who is the source for the general characterisation of Zaiton (Book II, chapter LXX, of Pipino's Latin version). Either Odorico or Marco (Book II, chapter LXIIII) must be responsible for the supposed 100 miles circumference of Quinsay. All the information on Cipangu must derive from what in Pipino's version is found in Book III, chapter II.[41] Finally, the ambassadors sent to the Pope by the Great Khan to ask for missionaries must be the elder Polos and the missionaries who turned back must be those brief fellow travellers of Marco, the two Dominicans William of Tripoli and Niccolò of Vicenza.

Is the letter genuine? Since the first attack on its authenticity by Henry Vignaud in 1901 two questions have been exhaustively discussed. In the first place, did Toscanelli actually compose the letter and send it, together with a map, to the Portuguese court? Then – a quite separate issue – did Columbus come to hear of the map, enter into correspondence with Toscanelli, and receive a copy of the letter and the map from him?[42] Whatever doubts they may have on a subsequent Toscanelli–Columbus correspondence, the overwhelming majority of scholars accept that the letter to Martins is genuine. A point normally advanced is: What would be the point of forging it? Unfortunately nothing in Columbus scholarship can be resolved so plainly and simply. Cioranescu, for example, has offered a motive together with an explanation of how Columbus came to possess a copy. Following his argument, the letter is the product of Portuguese diplomats, who in the negotiations with Spain on the eve of the Treaty of Tordesillas of June 1494 were seeking to establish a claim to priority over Castille in voyaging in the Atlantic. On his return to Spain in 1496 Columbus was shown the fabrication which he then copied in his papers.[43] More recently, against such scepticism, Parronchi has edited a fifteenth-century Italian treatise on perspective which he holds to be by Toscanelli partly on the grounds of the similarity of tone between the conclusion of that work and the end of the Martins letter.[44] More conclusive for me is the testimony of Fernán Yáñez de Manilla in the *Pleitos* or legal cases of the sixteenth century held to determine the true discoverer of the Indies. Here Fernán recalls how at Palos in 1492, the town boss Martín Yáñez Pinzón recruited the crew for Columbus' ships: 'Friends, come, come with us on this voyage! Here you're creeping about in poverty; come and sail with us! For with God's help we're going to discover a land that they say has houses roofed with gold, and we'll all come back rich and in good fortune.'[45] If, as I believe, Columbus had not read Marco before his First Voyage – it is a question to be considered in the next chapter, those words – 'houses roofed with gold' (inspired, it is to be assumed, by what Columbus himself told Pinzón) – can only come from the Toscanelli letter.

III

Yet though Marco was accepted as an authority in the Toscanelli circle, he did not enjoy a universal confidence among humanists. In 1461 Pope Pius II, the first, perhaps the last, incumbent of the See of Peter, to write of geography while in office, came to pen his *Asia*.[46] Despite its title the work begins by considering the form of the whole earth, setting out, generally without deciding between them, the various opinions of the ancients on such time-honoured questions as the habitability of the equinoctial regions. It goes on to give a description of what Pius calls 'the four parts of the East'. The first of these considers quite briefly India and China, and here we become aware at once of a loud silence on the Polos or anything that might have been learnt from them. This is more significant in that though the work is inspired, above all, by classical authorities – Ptolemy, the newly translated Strabo, Polybius, even Homer – it does, in addition, mention the findings of such medieval authorities as Albertus Magnus. One cannot, that is, simply, explain the omission as springing from any revulsion which so accomplished a humanist might feel on being asked to read Pipino's medieval Latin. Pius' implicit rejection of Polo surely must spring from active scepticism.

Still, Pius himself nurtured at all times and for almost all things a deep-seated tendency towards scepticism. One has only to read in his *Commentarii*, what he has to say about, for instance, the miracles of Joan of Arc (complete with a sneer at the credulity of the French who will believe anything[47]) to gain a sense of those metaphorically raised eyebrows with which he habitually scans life. What he could not do – both since it was written in humanist Latin and then again because it was so much more recent – was ignore Poggio's account of the travels of Niccolò Conti. Yet in Pius' survey the information is held at arm's length and warily surveyed. In the present age Conti has arrived in furthest Asia, 'if those things are true which are said to have been told by him' (a double doubt – not simply whether they are true but whether Conti has actually said them).[48] Yet it is difficult to believe that there is a river longer than the Ganges 'which the Ancients held to exceed all rivers'. Can it be that here there are towns, palaces and temples similar to those of Italy? This is all very different from what the Ancients have said about Scythia. These things are difficult to believe; 'but with the distances involved, they are not easy to disprove'.[49] The point at which the scepticism of Pius takes wing is very obvious: at any attempt to contradict, or add anything to, the wisdom of the Ancients.

IV

Some others are to be found who doubt in a different way. Their views take the form not of openly expressed scepticism but of affirmations of belief which are so tortured as to seem implausible. So, for example, at the end of a series of extracts from the Book in a miscellany of largely pietistic writings from the South German monastery of Tegernsee, the scribe writes this: 'From this history it is seen how wonderful is Almighty God in his works, that seem scarcely credible to men without experience. And yet they much move to belief in the difficult things of the Catholic faith which human reason cannot penetrate. It is finished by me, Brother Osvald Nott, professed monk of Tegernsee.'[50] What Brother Osvald seems to be saying is that by making the effort to believe Marco Polo you will find that your capacity to believe in such difficult doctrines as the Trinity will be strengthened. If so, it is not perhaps the happiest of recommendations. Something of a similar character is found in an elegant fifteenth-century manuscript of the Book probably from Nuremberg. Here the scribe offers this comment:

> Lest the monstrosity of the things and the apparent impossibility of what Marco Polo relates should induce some reserve or make you reluctant to believe what he says, I refer you to the blessed Augustine in his *City of God*, especially in the sixteenth book, but elsewhere; again to Isidore in his *Book of Etymologies*, books XV and XVI; again to the *Concerning the Wonders of the World* of Solinus. . . . In these books you will find many stupendous and scarcely credible things concerning the wonderful variety of creatures and the multiplicity of various forms and human species. But wonderful is God who makes whatever he wishes and whose will is power. It is he who is powerful in all things.[51]

He goes on to cite Pietro d'Abano's accounts of his discussions with Marco. Yet clearly here he is thinking of something else. In Chapter 7 of Book XVI of the *City of God*, St Augustine argues that the monstrous races – the

Cynocephali, Sciopods, and so on – if they exist (for he is agnostic on the subject) – are to be considered as descendants of Adam. These creatures occur again, though without the doubts, in the writings of Isidore of Seville and Solinus. In fact, as has been seen, they feature quite sparingly in Marco Polo. The argument here is, I think, this: that since we have good testimony to the existence of the Cynocephali and so on, we need not disbelieve other, less familiar marvels, such as the Great Khan. It is an interesting testimony to the durability of his influence that St Augustine should be invoked here on the marvellous just as he was two centuries before by Gerald of Wales and Gervase of Tilbury.[52]

To balance such doubts one can point to many others in the second half of the fifteenth century who clearly believed Marco's account. Some offer casual marginal endorsements in the course of writing their own accounts of travel. Anselmo Adorno, merchant of Bruges and Genoa, and coun-sellor to King James III of Scotland, hails him as 'Marco Paulo, excellent and prudent man of most noble soul, to whom among all travellers is owed the highest glory and the crown of triumph'.[53] So too John Capgrave, Prior of King's Lynn, on his return from pilgrimage to Rome around 1450, composed a *Solace of Pilgrimes* in which, so he declares, he wishes to imitate Pythagoras, Plato, St Jerome, John Mandeville and 'also . . . a man of Venys which they called Marcus Paulus; he laboured all the Soldane's lands and descryved on to us the nature of the cuntree, the condiciones of the men and the stately aray of the great Cane household'. At which point a certain modesty intervenes, and Capgrave announces that 'after all these grete cryeris of many wonderful things I wiyl folow with a smal pypyng of such strange sitis as I have seyn'.[54] Fuller and better founded testimonies to belief in the book are not lacking. For instance, the Spaniard Luis de Angulo in his *Book concerning the image or figure of the world*, written in 1456 for *Le bon roi René*, King René I of Anjou, cites extensive passages.[55] Again, in an encyclopaedia, written in the early fifteenth century by the Venetian hydraulic and military engineer Giovanni da Fontana there appears an ample account of 'the Emperor of the Tartars who is called the Great Khan, the splendours of his feasts and the resources of his realms'.[56] Cited very frequently as sources are, Marco, Odorico, Conti and Sir John Mandeville, together with, at one point, 'Costantino of Venice, my faithful friend who wandered for many years through the kingdoms of the Great Khan and told me he had seen many similar things'.[57] In fact, of course, China had ceased to be ruled by the Great Khans from the overthrow of the Mongol dynasty in 1368. Both John III, Archbishop of Sultania, and Jacopo da Sanseverino in his *Libro piccolo di meraviglie* written in the first half of the fifteenth century distinguish the 'Great Khan' and 'the Emperor of China'. Either Constantino believed – as did Poggio, Toscanelli and Columbus – that China was still under Mongol rule, or his interlocutor misunderstood him, or it was perhaps a convention to describe the Emperor as the 'Great Khan'.[58]

V

Most writers of the period considered the Book to be authentic. Yet what did this mean? To what degree did they believe in its authenticity? Do contemporary cartographers throw any light on this? Here too the evidence often appears in no clear-cut form, above all because the different maps they drew up often had different purposes. Even at the beginning of the sixteenth century, the most common *mappaemundi* were the old Macrobian zone-maps and, above all, Isidore of Seville's TO maps, which reached the status of print as early as 1478. Here were traditional representations with which the common reader felt comfortable, and which printers clearly felt most appropriate for the texts of hallowed antiquity which they normally accompanied. Then again, turning to the humanism of the *avant garde*, the first world maps of the Ptolemaic atlases, because they were seeking, above all, a correspondence with Ptolemy's text, simply reproduced the world maps found in Byzantine manuscripts of the work, which – it is a long controversy – may or may not go back to classical times but certainly displayed no interest in modern information on Asia.

In fact, of the 330 *mappaemundi* which have survived from between 1400 and 1492, almost all were either of Macrobian or Isidorean design or formed part of the new Ptolemaic atlases.[59] Apart from these, there were only twelve principal cartographers and one globe maker who sought to portray the whole of the world between 1400 and 1492 and whose work has, if only in part, survived. Appendix III lists the fifteen maps and one globe from their hands which remain. Of the first nine of these, three of their cartographers ignore Marco's Book: Andreas Walsperger, his anonymous follower, and the designer of the so-called 'Genoese' World Map (who does however incorporate material from Niccolò Conti). The other six include information from the Book, though of a very limited and superficial kind, suggesting sometimes, as with the Borgia planisphere, an attempt to produce not a work of science but simply a pleasant decorative representation, sometimes simply haste in attempts to resumé very difficult material. However, in none of these first nine maps – even those of Walsperger and his follower – does it seem to me that the treatment of Marco's material necessarily represents disbelief. There were great difficulties in any attempt to give appropriate weight to his story amid the others – those of Ptolemy and of the ecclesiastical tradition – which were also in existence. It was easy for a writer to dash off a few lines on the theme 'excellent and most prudent observer'. But a cartographer was continually faced with the problem of making active choices. If Quinsai exists, where is it to be placed? And in what relation to Cipangu – if it exists? What shape is Cipangu to be given? Who are we to trust in locating Prester John? And so on. Fifteenth-century map-makers (apart from those pioneers directly concerned with Ptolemy) have very often been branded for conservatism.[60] Perhaps this has been exaggerated. But where it is true, its cause must surely lie in the temptation, faced with the difficulties of choice, simply to copy what was most accessible and uncontentious of what had gone before.

An obvious example is our tenth world map of the period, the anonymous Catalan *Mappamundi* (*ca.*1450–60), which is almost wholly based on the *Catalan Atlas* produced some seventy to eighty years before,[61] and which as a result is very strongly under Marco Polo's influence. It was only in rare moments that a cartographer would come, with great patience and a strong passion for truth, to re-examine the Book in a determined effort to incorporate all that could be understood of it into existing knowledge. Such a man, one who should be hailed as a great hero of the Italian Renaissance, was the Venetian Camaldolese monk, Fra Mauro, '*cosmographus incomparabilis*', in his *Mappamundi* of 1457–9.[62] This most brilliant authority, seeking to reconcile Ptolemy, traditional knowledge and experience, consulted among many other witnesses Muslim seamen, and from them learnt enough to deny Ptolemy's beliefs both in the uninhabitability of the equatorial zone and the landlocked character of the Indian Ocean. Could it have been their testimony which allowed him to place such trust in Marco's work? In China (see Illustration 9), where one sees clearly the two principal rivers, the Yangtze and the Huang He, he has taken almost all the names of the towns from Marco. They appear with elegant Gothic representations in red, blue and green, and with annotations largely drawn from Marco's text. All the north-east is called 'Chataio' (Cathay) and shows 'Canbalech'. Chausay (Quinsai) is placed on the coast with a legend that its circumference is 100 miles and that it has 12,000 bridges. Lower down is the 'Regno Magno' (i.e. Mangi), which is said to contain 12,000 towns. To the east, there emerges a large peninsula called the 'Regno de Zaiton', with a 'magnifico porto de Zaiton'.

Opposite that port the 'ixola de Zimpagu' (Cipangu)' is portrayed – perhaps the first representation, however fanciful and inaccurate, of Japan in European cartography – as lying just north of 'Java major'.[63] Against Marco's text, Prester John has been sent to Abyssinia. In the eastern seas, Fra Mauro, who derives the names of his islands largely from Conti, follows Marco in writing that lack of space has forced him to omit many islands. Although the map still has a 'medieval' character, with occasional references to historical events and to myths, none the less, like Marco, Mauro rejects Gog and Magog in favour of the tribes 'Hung e Mongul', and like him too, though more specifically, rejects the customary monstrous races ('*quasi incredibili*').

Overall the map represents a triumph for the persuasiveness of Marco's Book, and was perhaps influential in moving the two other important map-makers of the age to endorse the Book. Of these the first is the enigmatic Henricus Martellus Germanicus, of whom we know very little, but that he worked in Florence in the map-making workshop of Francesco Rosselli. In his *Mappamundi* in the British Library, which has been dated as of 1489 or 1490, one finds Ciamba (Champa), and some slight but clear detail on China: Mangi and 'Quinsey'. 'Cataio' here appears not as a province but a city, though otherwise what is shown of south-west Asia seems to derive from Marco and Conti. Cipangu is not shown.[64] But in his Yale map, dated to around 1489, executed according to the Second Projection of Ptolemy, Cipangu appears 90° west of the Canary Islands (see Illustration 11). In conformity with Toscanelli's theory, Lisbon is 105° from Cipangu and 135° from Quinsai.[65] If that date is correct, Martellus had an explicit belief in the existence of Japan – and hence in the truth of Marco Polo – before Columbus' First Voyage.[66]

As remarkable as this work in its way is the Terrestrial Globe whose mapping is the work of Martin Behaim (Nuremberg, 1492) (see Illustration 10). This is the first representation to mention Marco: 'The whole world according to the length and breadth with the art of geometry, namely the one part as described by Ptolemy in his book called "Cosmographia Ptolemaei" and the remainder from what the knight Marco Polo of Venice caused to be written down in 1250 [*sic*]'. It shows Conchim (Anan), 'Thebet', the Kingdoms of Cathay and Mangi, Quinsai and Zaiton, Tartaria, together with Cipangu at 25° east of China ('The most noble and richest island of the East . . . [here] are found gold and shrubs yielding spices'); and the imaginary island of Antillia of which Toscanelli had written. From Europe to Asia Behaim marks an oceanic space of 130°. Both Quinsai (of which Marco Polo makes so much) and the great port of Zaiton are absent. On Prester John, Behaim hedges his bets by placing him both in India and Africa. Ravenstein's study of the map concluded from many examples where the same place name is positioned in widely different regions (as for instance 'Bangala' which appears in the centre of Cathay and then a second time to the east of the Indus) that the globe was con-structed from two maps based on different translations of Marco's Book. In the place names in fact one can see the influence of both Pipino's Latin and an Italian text.[67]

This evidence shows that there was no uniform response to Marco Polo among cartographers. Clearly, even those who willed his truth were likely to seize upon different aspects of the Book. There is, for example, a great contrast in their approach to the East between those two eminent cartographers, Fra Mauro with all his decoration and detail, and Henricus Martellus who cultivates a Ptolemaic austerity and concentrates on essentials. Yet both, like Behaim, finally accept Japan's existence. That they should have done so is remarkable. Most of what Marco writes about it is extravagant nonsense, and no other traveller had ever spoken of it. In accepting its existence the cartographers, like the theoretician, Toscanelli, were making powerful leaps of faith in the honesty of Marco Polo. How far, one must now ask, was Columbus himself, on his four voyages, similarly dependent on an act of faith in the Venetian?

Chapter 9

Columbus and After

I

Here is a Book which revealed something of new lands, their names, something of their riches, and which spoke in particular of the realm of the Great Khan, its government, wealth and splendour. Could such material, combined with the learning of humanism, have influenced Portuguese attempts to reach Asia, Columbus' 'Enterprise of the Indies' and the other European ventures in the age of exploration?

On this subject large claims have been made. Certainly, the Portuguese knew of Marco from at least the early years of the fifteenth century. One story has it that his Book was presented by the Venetian Senate to Prince Pedro, brother of that Prince Henry who is sometimes known as 'Henry the Navigator'. So at least Valentin Fernandes asserted in the dedication to King Manuel the Fortunate in his Portuguese translation of 1502:

> Concerning this matter I heard in this city of yours [Lisbon], most prudent King, that the Venetians had hidden the present book for many years in their treasure-house. And at the time that the Infante Dom Pedro of glorious memory, your uncle, arrived in Venice, and after the great feasts and honours which were tendered him because of the privileges which they enjoy in your realms, as well as the fact that he merited it, they offered him a worthy gift, the said book about Marco Polo, that he might be guided by it, since he was desirous of seeing and travelling throughout the world. It is said that this book is in the Torre de Tumbo [the royal archive]. If that is so who should know better than Your Royal Highness?[1]

Pedro visited Venice in April 1428. But the tale of the Book being 'hidden' and then drawn from the Venetians' 'treasure-house', whatever that might be, has a mythic ring, the testimony is of late date and the final question suggests doubts about the matter in the translator's own mind. It could well be no more than an attempt to engage the King's interest by associating the work with his relative.

However it is true that a Latin version appears in the library catalogue of King Duarte (1433–8), while in his *Cronica do descobrimiento e conquista da Guiné* of 1453 Gomes Eannes da Zurara shows that his is familiar with it.[2] And Jafuda Cresques, son of the man who produced the *Catalan Atlas* which draws so heavily upon the Book, is said to have been summoned – though here again the evidence is late – from Majorca to Portugal by Prince Henry.[3] Yet the Book can have had little relevance to the early stages of Portuguese exploration which were concerned not at all with Asia but with Atlantic islands and the African coastline.[4] Reference to 'the Indies' only comes with papal bulls to the Portuguese royal house as late as the 1450s (and may even then be referring to Abyssinia). From that decade one can trace at least the indirect influence of the Book. Clearly this is present, as we have seen, in the map drawn up by Fra Mauro for King Afonso V and the letter of advice (in the event not followed) which Paolo dal Pozzo Toscanelli dispatched to the Portuguese court in June 1474.

One reference has been taken as suggesting that thereafter Marco's Book was not well regarded by the Portuguese. In the first *Decade* of his *Asia*, Joam de Barros wrote that when Columbus came to court to offer his project to John II (which most take to be in 1484) he had 'read a good deal of Marco Polo who spoke somewhat of oriental regions, of the kingdom of Cathay, and of the mighty Isle of Cipango', and that the King had rejected him because, among other things, sceptical about one whose ideas were 'founded on imagination and ideas about the Isle of Cipango'.[5] But Barros, writing in the 1540s (possibly even the early 1550s), is a late source. It could be that he felt patriotically bound by then to excuse the King's rejection of what had turned out to be a splendid offer. The story that at this point Columbus was drawing upon Marco Polo's description of Japan and the Far East served this purpose quite well in two respects. In the first place it was coming to be appreciated in the 1540s that Japan was not at all likely to be reached by sailing directly across the Atlantic. In the second the Portuguese were encountering difficulties in attempting to match up the China they had discovered with the Mangi and Cathay of the Great Khan. But that the Portuguese were sceptical in the fifteenth century (or indeed that the Book had been read by Columbus back in the 1480s) is unlikely. Certainly it is true that their scepticism or perhaps indifference was to grow. In 1502 Valentin Fernandes presented his Portuguese translation of Marco and Conti as throwing light on those islands 'which we at the present time have discovered', yet that confident pronouncement excited little interest in the years that followed.

Turning to Columbus and his 'Enterprise of the Indies', the view of him as directly indebted to Marco Polo has until very recently won almost unanimous support and Columbus' most distinguished biographers – Ballesteros, Morison, Fernández-Armesto – assume that reading Marco Polo played an important part in the formulation of his plans before 1492.[6] The claim was first put forward in the life of the Admiral ascribed to his son Fernando. This presents a picture of a learned, university-trained sage who plans his expedition only after having studied deeply a wide variety of geographical sources. Fernando mentions Aristotle, Strabo, Solinus, Mandeville, Julius Capitolinus and others, together of course, with Marco Polo.[7] Whether the biography was actually written by Fernando is much in question these days,[8] and, quite apart from that, several things in it are demonstrably false. Yet this has not weakened the claims of those who see an intimate Polo–Columbus connection. After all there is the testimony of Barros' *Asia* (though, as we have seen, it is rather late), and above all there is Columbus' library. The Biblioteca Colombina of Seville still preserves several printed books which Columbus owned and in which his signature appears. Among them the most important are Ptolemy's *Cosmography*; Pliny's *Natural History*; the *Ymago Mundi* with other texts of Pierre d'Ailly, the *Asia* of Pius II, and the Book of Marco Polo.

Several of these are annotated with postils or marginal comments; in all there are over 2,000 of them. On some occasions they simply repeat a word in the text but on others the comment is extensive. Their standard of Latin is extremely poor; the handwriting generally excellent, of considerable beauty, without emendation, almost as if copied from drafts. Some palaeographers, following their arcane calling, have detected four hands here; some three; some two; some again, one hand alone. (One scholar has asserted that Columbus marked his own contributions with a cross, presumably for the purpose of allowing scholars in future ages to make the identification.[9]) I would think myself that the question of how many people were writing the postils, and which of them represent Columbus' own contribution, has not all that much importance in that they were unlikely to have been set down in the course of solitary and private reading. What may be imagined is a group – Columbus, his brother Bartolomeo, a friendly priest perhaps, anyone who can be found who has some claim to know Latin – gathering round, laboriously to decipher and comment on the texts. What has more importance is when they were written. The normal assumption, of course, is that the majority of them were made before 1492, that they are the tell-tale spoor of Columbus' studies in preparation for his great enterprise. If so, it would follow that by examining them one can discover how Columbus' mind was working before he set out on his First Voyage, what his plan was, what he was looking for.

The version of Marco Polo which survives in the Biblioteca Colombina is the Latin translation of Francesco Pipino, the *Liber de consuetudinibus et condicionibus orientalium regionum*, published between 1485 and 1490, by, it is thought, Gerard de Leeu at Antwerp. This bears 366 postils: far fewer than those to Pierre d'Ailly (898 postils) or Pius II (853). Most readers, consulting either the original or the excellent facsimile edited by Juan Gil, will agree with him in seeing three different hands.[10] Of these Gil identifies the first as 'the Anonymous Amanuensis', perhaps Gaspar de Gorricio, a monk of the Carthusian monastery of Seville, who was born in northern Italy.[11] The second he calls 'the Curious Reader', whom he thinks is probably Columbus' son, Don Fernando, writing considerably later. The third is the Admiral himself. The 'Curious Reader' is assumed to be the author of all those annotations which refer to astrologers (*iudicium astrolgiae*), magicians (*incantatores*), wonders (the 'Paradise' of the Old Man of the Mountain) and interesting sexual or domestic practices (for example, husbands' loan of wives to guests in Camul – '*ospitandi peregrinos modus mirabilis*', as the glossator puts it). Columbus himself is assumed to be the writer of notes on gold, jewels, spices, St Thomas's Tomb in India and falcons.[12] As I have suggested, it may be doubted whether individual hands have much importance here. My guess is that those by the side of Christian miracles ('*Nota, magnum miraculum*' etc.) came directly from the interest of Columbus. But most of the postils are simple notations of place names and products. There are many mundane entries such as 'rice, palm wine' or on the mineral oil of Armenia, but many others seem like some miser's bright recollections of an Aladdin's cave, speaking of precious metals and the products of the spice trade: 'great treasures', 'pepper, cinnamon, nuts', 'much incense', 'mines of silver', 'here are found rubies, topazes, sapphires, pearls in great abundance, silver'. Against tales of the Great Khan's wealth: 'gold, silver, precious stones'; against Cipangu are the postils: 'gold in the greatest abundance', 'red pearls', and, by the story of the jewel inserted in warriors' flesh to give invulnerability, 'stone of wondrous virtue'; in the islands 'infinite spices, whitest pepper', 'pepper, nutmegs, cloves and other spices in abundance', 'perfumes in abundance'. Mentions of ships too are regularly marked – 'ships of India', ' ships in the greatest abundance', 'many ships', 'ships in the very greatest multitude', and – a linking of interests – at the account of Aden, 'naves multas cum aromatibus'.

But quite naturally – since this sort of thing is absent from Marco's Book – there is little note taken of theoretical geography. There are a few passages referring to the equator. At 'Samara' (Sumatra), to the text (Pipino, III, xvi), 'in this kingdom the arctic pole is not seen', appears the gloss 'ultra equinocialem'; and again at Comarin (Pipino, III, xxxii) 'ultra equinocialem', then 30 miles north, 'sub equinociale'. But there are no notes of distances between towns or between provinces, and there is no evidence for any attempt from the descriptions of the three Polo's journeys, to trace the landward extent of Asia (which descriptions, as we have seen, would have been in fact deeply misleading). The Book's main value to Columbus, that is, would have lain in its description of eastern riches, all those things capable of persuading a patron that a westward journey could be profitable. Yet of course tales of Asian riches whether ultimately deriving from Marco and other writings or from knowledge of the wealth derived from the spice trade were commonplace in the fifteenth century and direct knowledge of Marco was not at all necessary for this. Certainly, if we accept the authenticity of the Toscanelli letter, and are prepared to agree that Columbus had seen and copied it during his residence in Lisbon, then it could be said that Columbus had a grasp, at least at second hand, of almost everything that was relevant for his purposes in Polo's Book. From the letter he would have learnt of the Great Khan, his request, two hundred years before, for Christian missionaries, of the port of Zaiton notable for its trade in pepper, of the towns along the Yangtze, of Quinsai, of the City of Heaven. He would also have known the tale that in 'the most noble island of Japan' the roofs were tiled with gold.

There is in fact very good evidence that Columbus' first direct knowledge of the Book came well after his First Voyage. This appears in a letter sent between December 1497 and early spring 1498 by the Bristol merchant John Day to the Almirante Mayor (certainly none other than Columbus). With some other English merchants, Day was established in Sanlúcar de Barrameda at the mouth of the Guadalquivir, where his main business was selling cloth to Genoese traders. With this dispatch he tells Columbus of the recent voyage of John Cabot from Bristol and says that (as I read it) at Columbus' request, he is sending him a copy of Marco Polo's Book.[13] Faced with this letter, those who believe that Columbus and his friends annotated the Latin Marco Polo now in the Biblioteca Colombina before 1492 have to argue that what Day sent to Columbus was a different, perhaps better, version. Yet, confining ourselves to printed texts, by 1498 there were only two other possible choices: the German translation of 1477 and the Venetian of 1496/7. Professor Quinn, a very distinguished authority, has argued for the Venetian. Yet this does not, like the Latin text, appear in any inventory of the Colombina, while it seems unlikely that the Venetian text would have been marketed in England (or anywhere else outside Venice and the Veneto). And my own suspicion is that, poor as Columbus' Latin was, he would have found it rather easier to read the Latin than the Venetian version.[14] Again, it is improbable that this would have been seen as more satisfactory than the 'short' version of Pepino – not really shorter on anything likely to have interested Columbus – in that peculiar climate where any work in Latin was likely to be taken as more authoritative than one in Venetian.

Then again, two of what seem to be Columbus' postils (both, as it happens, marked with a cross) date from after the Second Voyage. The first is to Book III, chapter 8, which identifies the port of Zaiton with Cape Alpha et Omega (Alfaeto), that is to say the easterly tip of Cuba (today's Punta de Maisi). This can only have been written after Columbus had dis-covered the promontory and declared it to be the end of the East and the beginning of the West as he did on that voyage.[15] Then again chapter 31 of Book III, 'The Kingdom of Coilum' (i.e. Quilon, on the Malabar Coast), opens with the sentence: 'Proceeding on the plain from the kingdom of Moabar [Maabar on the Coromandel Coast] towards the south-west for around 500 miles one finds Coilum, where dwell many Christians and Jews and idolaters.' Against the chapter heading and this sentence there appears the cross and the words 'vide Colocut'. Calicut, whose Zamorin or Sea-Rajah exercised government over Quilon at the end of the fifteenth century, does not appear in Marco's Book. However, it was referred to in Poggio's account of the travels of Conti. Yet, as chance has it, in the first, rather rare, publication of this work in 1492, the name is omitted. Accordingly the balance of probabilities is that this postil must be owed to information brought back by Vasco da Gama from the Malabar Coast towards the end of 1499.[16]

These two passages cannot by themselves of course prove that the bulk of the postils were not written before the First Voyage. Then again, though Columbus may not have received this particular copy of the Book in the Colombina before 1498, it could be argued that he may have read another copy or some other version of Marco before 1492. Since Queen Isabella possessed a manuscript of the Aragonese version,[17] it would be reasonable to think that he might well have consulted this in the four months between the Capitulations of Santa Fe (when the Crown accepted his project) and his departure from Palos. Accordingly we must now turn to the principal source for the First Voyage to find out whether any direct knowledge of Marco's Book is to be found there. This is the *Diario*, a paraphrase of Columbus' journal of the time made by the evangelical historian Las Casas.[18] This is not entirely satisfactory as an authority, being simply a summary by someone who had his own axes to grind, yet that said it must be confessed that it reveals no decisive evidence that Columbus read Marco Polo and some suggestion that he did not. (Indeed it offers very little evidence for any reading at all; the only work actually cited, and then very vaguely, is Pliny in the entry for 12 November.[19]) In the prologue which Las Casas says he gives in full, Columbus declares how he had given the monarchs a report (here and throughout I cite the translation of O. Dunn and J. E. Kelley): 'about the lands of India and about a prince who is called "Grand Khan" which in our Spanish language means "King of Kings"; how many times he and his predecessors had sent to Rome to ask for men learned in our Holy Faith in order that they might instruct him in it and how the Holy Father had never provided them. . . .'[20] This passage could be seen as an exaggerated elaboration of the Book's description of how Khubilai had sent the Polos to the Papacy to ask for 'men learned in the liberal arts'. But it might as easily be taken as an extended commentary on what appears in the Toscanelli letter.

The Great Khan has a prominent place in the *Diario*, and at the time of Columbus' departure was clearly in the front of everyone's minds. Before he embarked Ferdinand and Isabella gave Columbus three letters of credence, opening with the words, 'To the most serene . . .', with a space for the name to be inserted. Las Casas says these were 'royal letters of recommendation for the Great Khan and for all the kings and lords of India of any other region he might find in the lands which he might discover'. (For a moment one could believe that these letters, dated from Granada 17 April 1492, are drawing upon the same vein of rhetoric found at the opening of Rustichello's version of Marco: 'To kings and the first of their blood and friends [they begin] and to the illustrious and notable nobles and magnificent men, to the dukes, marquesses, counts, viscounts, barons, lords and ladies of the land, to communities and singular persons. . . .'[21]) Certainly, again, throughout the *Diario* Columbus is deeply engaged with thoughts of Cipangu and Cathay. As early as 6 October, four weeks out of sight of land Columbus decides that he has sailed past Cipangu and that it will be better to go on to 'the mainland', i.e. Cathay. On 13 October – the day after striking land at San Salvador – he is planning to go 'southwest to seek gold and precious stones . . . I want to go to see if I can find the island of Cipangu.' On 21 October, at Isabella, the natives point to an island which they call 'Colba' which 'I believe must be Cipangu . . . I have already decided to go to the mainland and to the city of Quinsay and to give your Highnesses' letters to the Great Khan and to ask for, and to come with, a reply.' Two days later he is planning to depart for the isle of Cuba 'which I believe must be Cipangu'. Off the coast of Cuba at the beginning of November 1492 indeed he sends off his ambassador Rodrigo de Xerez, with his interpreter Luis de Torres and two Indians, in order to meet the Great Khan. Off they go up the Cacoyuguin valley to present his sovereigns' letters to that great potentate.[22]

Yet there are many indications that these notions do not spring from a reading of Marco Polo. On the 24th Columbus sets sail for Cuba which I heard from these people was very large and of great commerce and that there were there gold and spices and great ships and merchants. I believe it is so according to signs that all the Indians of these islands and those I have with me make (because I do not understand them through speech) and that this is the island of Cipangu of which marvellous things are told. And in the spheres that I saw and in world maps it is in this region.

There is no reference here to Marco Polo, only to 'spheres' and 'world maps'. When Cuba is reached Columbus decides instead that it forms part of the Chinese mainland. Here he learns of a river beyond Cabo de Palmas:

The Admiral decided to go as far as that river and send a gift to the king of that land and send him the Monarch's letter. In the Admiral's opinion he was 42 degrees N of the equinoctial line, if the text from which I have transcribed this is not corrupt,[23] and he says he will endeavour to go to the Great Khan who he thought was in that region or to the city of Cathay which is in the Great Khan's possession, which he says is very large *according to what he was told* before he left (author's italics).

Gil points out that had Columbus read Polo he could not have thought of Cathay as a city.[24] For Columbus' annotations on the Colombina text make quite clear that it was no such thing.[25] (He also points out that one of Columbus' captains, Vincente Yáñez Pinzón, was still thinking of it as a city as late as 1499.) Then again how significant is the passage I have italicised? Does this suggest a knowledge of the East based at that time upon discussion rather than reading?

On 1 November Columbus sends an Indian ashore to assure the natives that his men mean no harm and are not subjects of the Great Khan, with whom at this stage he believed they were at war. The *Diario* continues: 'It is certain, says the Admiral, that this is the mainland and that I am, he says, before Zaitun and Quinsai, more or less a hundred leagues distant from one or the other. . . .' No reader of the Book could have believed that the Cuban coastline bore any resemblance to the world of great cities between these two centres, and the Book itself gives no basis for the calculation of distance. Columbus has arrived at his 'hundred leagues' simply by marking off a position with dividers on a map. This will be one of 'the maps of the world' showing the 'innumerable' islands in the East, of which the *Diario* entry for 14 November makes mention, with perhaps also (as in Fra Mauro's map) some graphic representation of the Great Khan upon it. All the evidence, that is to say, seems to suggest that Columbus' vision derives from maps rather than any reading of Marco Polo. This, of course, must be some map which, like the Borgia planisphere or the Martellus *mappa-mundi* of 1488–90, does indeed show Cathay as a city.[26] (The cartographical error is owed, I would guess, to an overhasty reading of some texts of Sir John Mandeville, which describe the province of Cathay, then switch suddenly to its old (unnamed) and new, named, principal cities. Here the reader could find it easy to presume that the old city was also called Cathay.)[27]

The truth is that though, of course, the indirect, long-term influence of Marco Polo is ever-present, it is impossible to point to any evidence of Columbus' personal direct reading of Marco's Book in the *Diario*.[28] Immensely convincing is Gil's argument that Columbus in 1492 was a man who truly and without false modesty was indeed as he was to describe himself, '*non doto en letra . . . lego marinero*', a simple, unlearned sailor, one who first turns to books not in order to find materials to persuade a patron to back his enterprise, but rather – some five years after returning from his First Voyage – in order to discover what it is that he has discovered. The 'bookish' Columbus is also absent from the reports of the Second Voyage. Andrés Bernáldez, parish priest of Los Palacios, with whom Columbus lodged on his return, held him to have been seeking 'the province and city [again] of Catayo which is under the dominion of the Great Khan'. For Bernáldez the sole source referred to is not Polo but *The Book of Sir John Mandeville*, where 'anyone who wishes to know the truth of this . . . will see that the city of Catayo is very rich and that its district has the name of the city'.[29]

One should add that the reports of the Third and Fourth Voyages, undertaken when Columbus had actually read the Book which John Day had sent him, seem in a curious way to reflect less of its influence than did the first two when its influence came to him only indirectly. Remarkably little is to be found in them. On 16 August 1498, having just set sail from Paria and the pearl fisheries of Margarita, Columbus wrote of having seen 'very fine pears and bright red pearls which Marco Polo says are worth more than the white'.[30] (The Latin version, though not Rustichello's, does indeed say this in discussing Cipangu [III, II,] at which point, in Columbus' copy, appears the marginal annotation 'Margarite rubee'). This is the only surviving passage in any of his works in which Columbus actually mentions Marco Polo by name. On the Fourth Voyage, Columbus' delusions, born of remote Marco Polo influence a long time before, were as strong as ever. 'On 13 May, I reached the province of Mago, which marches with that of Cathay . . .' (in fact the southern coast of Cuba).[31] On the island a crossbowman hit an animal that 'seemed to be a *gato paulo*, except that it was much larger and had the face of a man'. Columbus had read of the Gatpauls (perhaps some form of boar) in his Latin Marco, and had marked them 'Gatti pauli'.[32] Earlier, on the Mosquito Coast, off Panama, he was preparing to set off in search of 'the mines of gold of the province of Ciamba'. This again is perhaps the result of the reading of Marco Polo, who spells out the products of Ciamba (Champa, an Indo-Chinese kingdom of south and central Vietnam), or rather – since no version of the Book tells of gold as being among them – a confused recollection of reading it.[33] These few remarks comprise the sum total of his references to the text of the Book.

II

None the less, partly as a result of the discoveries of Columbus and of those who followed, partly through the spread of printing, the Book began to gain much greater popularity than previously. Some twenty-four editions were published during the sixteenth century. The Portuguese translation of 1502 was followed the next year by a Castillian version from the hand of Rodrigo Fernández de Santaella, Archdeacon of Seville and confessor of Ferdinand and Isabella.[34] If the principal aim of these was to offer knowledge to the two countries most closely involved in exploration, others were issued to satisfy a more disinterested curiosity. Among them was a work first published at Basel in 1532, the *Novus orbis regionum ac insularum veteribus incognitarum* ('The New World of regions and islands unknown to the ancients'), a collection of travel narratives which included the voyages of Cadamosto, Columbus, Vespucci and Hetoum. Compiled by Johann Huttich, it was introduced by Simon Grynaeus, a humanist well known in his day and professor of Greek at Heidelberg, and published simultaneously at Basel and Paris. Marco appears here in a Latin text taken not directly from Pipino but from a translation made specially for the occasion from the Portuguese version of 1502. Despite this disadvantage, the *Novus orbis* – no doubt because couched in the language of learning as written by a humanist – was taken by many as the standard compilation of voyages in the period and was reprinted in 1537, 1555 and 1585, with subsequent translations from it into German and French. (The original French or Franco-Italian had been translated into Italian; from that tongue Pepino had rendered it into Latin, from which it passed into Portuguese and then with Huttich into Latin again. This Latin version was then retranslated into French – a curious *ronde*.) Grynaeus praises Marco as one of the few medieval authors of value to the geographer and appended to his work a map by Sebastian Münster which showed Mexico (Temistitan), then, a short distance to the west, 'Zipangu', then, further west, an 'Archipelago of 7,448 islands', and finally a mainland with Cathay, Quinsay and Tangut.[35]

The tradition of the *Novus orbis* was continued by Raynerius Reineck who in 1585 published his *Historia orientalis* in two volumes, a collection of chronicles, including Marco's and Hetoum's, together with (this was just fourteen years after the Christian victory over the Turks at Lepanto) miscellaneous crusading material. But it was the Venetians who were principally responsible for keeping Marco's fame alive. There were six republications of the Venetian-language text of 1496 up to 1597 and as many as nine more up to 1672. Yet the unfamiliarity of the Venetian language denied that version any general European audience. This was very clearly understood by Giambattista Ramusio (1485–1557), the most distinguished among the men of his century who publicised the extent and significance of the discoveries in Asia and the Americas, and the man who first presented Marco as a Venetian hero.[36] Not a patrician but a member of the citizen class, Ramusio followed a career in the Venetian administrative service. He accompanied embassies to Paris and elsewhere in Europe and in Venice was employed as Secretary to the Senate and then to the Council of the Ten. He had all the energetic effectiveness to be expected of one who occupied those posts and all the scholarly instincts of one who was at the same time curator of the Marciana Library. His interests included Greek literature, Latin inscriptions and medicine; and 'speaking French as though born in Paris' he had translated Villehardouin's *Chronicle of the Conquest of Constantinople* into Italian. Among his friends were Girolamo Fracastoro (distinguished medical scientist, inventor of the word *syphilis*), the *cosmografo* of the Venetian Republic Jacopo Gastaldi, the printers Aldo Manuzio and the Giunti, the humanist diplomat Andrea Navagero, and the Venetian poet who wrote in Tuscan and in the purest classical Latin, Pietro Bembo.

It may be that Ramusio's early travels with ambassadors first excited his interest in geography. Certainly the Venetian diplomatic service was a principal means through which Ramusio began to build up his collection of source materials towards the understanding of those changes which had so recently and rapidly come to Europe's knowledge of the world. As early as 1520 we find a friend writing to him from Buda with information obtained from a German cosmologist about Muscovy and the Tartars. When four years later Andrea Navagero was appointed as ambassador of the Serenissima to Charles V in Spain, Ramusio seized the opportunity to enlist his services in acquiring knowledge of Spanish explorations. In this Navagero was eminently successful. He made the acquaintance of Peter Martyr, Italian chronicler of the Spanish discoveries, and sent Ramusio an Italian version of Martyr's account of their exploits, together with information which he himself had gleaned about Columbus. More than this, he acquired a copy of *The Natural History of the Indies*, written by a Spanish colonist, former resident in Italy and Italophile, Gonzalo Fernández de Oviedo y Valdés. As a result, in 1534 Ramusio published a composite volume in Italian translation, containing these works together with a narrative of the recent conquest of Peru. But still before that, charmed with Oviedo's work, Ramusio, Bembo and Fracastoro opened a transcontinental correspondence with its author, now returned to the distant Indies, which was to continue for many years.

It was almost two decades later that Ramusio started to publish the three volumes of the *Navigazioni e viaggi*, his compilation of travel narratives in their (not Venetian but) Tuscan translation. These were planned according to a coherent scheme designed to produce a 'reform' (a word much in the air at the time) of geography and cartography. It was not until 1559, which is to say two years after his death, that the second volume (the last of the three to be published) emerged from the press. It was this volume, reprinted in 1574, 1583 and 1606, which contained his edition of Marco's Book. In it he drew together Pipino's Latin version with a manuscript now lost containing what is often much fuller material from a tradition which had hitherto been submerged but which is unquestionably authentic (found in what is referred to as the Z text). To this he added a preface in which, drawing upon Venetian legend or gossip, he provided an account of the Polos. It is he who tells the famous story of the three men returning in Mongol dress, having almost forgotten their Venetian tongue, whose relatives cannot recognise them until they reveal the jewels they carry with them. Little of this can be relied upon and some of it (as for instance the remark that Marco's collaborator was a Genoese writing in Latin) is all too patently false. Yet what Ramusio succeeds in doing – clearly thinking of the fame of the *Genoese* Columbus (whom none the less he greatly admired) – is to put forward the claims of Marco as a man of greatness as an explorer.

There is a very real sense in which Ramusio changed the subject of Marco's Book, which became now not Asia but, as his title states, 'The Voyages (*Viaggi*) of Marco Polo'. How marvellous, he broods, the extent of those journeys through regions which the ancients wrote of as *terra incognita*! And if the things told here seem fables, you will find extraordinary things too in Strabo, Pliny and Herodotus. If you are amazed at the riches of Quinsai, think of Hernan Cortés on Temistitan (i.e. Tenochtitlán–Mexico of the Aztecs). Surely, he suggests, the Polos were greater than Columbus?

Many times I have considered within myself the question as to which was the most marvellous voyage, that made by land by these our Venetian gentlemen or that made by sea by the aforesaid Lord Don

Cristoforo and if I am not deceived by affection for my country it seems likely to me that that by land should be placed in front of that by sea, it being necessary to take note of the enormous greatness of soul with which so difficult an enterprise was carried out and brought to a conclusion along such extraordinary length and harshness of the route and the lack of food not for days but months. . . .[37]

By comparison, he remarks (here, unfortunately, falling into bathos), Columbus, after all, had been merely blown by the wind. And no European had dared to follow in the footsteps of Marco Polo whereas 'The year following the discovery of these Eastern [i.e. West] Indies there immediately returned many ships, and every day to the present time infinite numbers go there as a matter of course and these parts are so known and have so much commerce that it is greater now than between Italy, Spain and England.' It is curious that Ramusio was unaware of the fourteenth-century merchant and missionary involvement in the East. And it is curious too that in this instance a man whose vision included Europe and the whole world, one who was certainly no petty nationalist, should indeed have failed to realise that whatever the merits of Marco Polo it was precisely the fact that men of the sixteenth century were following Columbus which made him the more significant figure.

Yet a similar 'affection for my country' had already persuaded one Englishman to agree with him:

I know that Marco Polo the Venetian, Ludovico Varthema, Christopher Columbus, Amerigo Vespucci, Pinzón, Alvise Cadamosto, Alfonso di Negro and Ferdinand Cortés and many others whom I omit were great travellers through the earth. . . . Yet of all those I have mentioned, one alone, Polo the Venetian, who had been a little before him, and our Mandeville, is more illustrious and more worthy of praise, for having opened the world to the following generations.[38]

Since the English writer had gone, or was supposed to have gone, by land, then sure enough land-travel must attract the greater honour and glory. Certainly the country which had accepted John Cabot's interpretation of Marco's Book stood by it confidently. In his *Brief Summe of Geographie*, written in 1540–1, Roger Barlow portrayed the East according to Marco.[39] John Frampton who translated it from the Spanish version of Santaella some forty years later tells us that he embarked upon it, 'perswading that it might give greater lighte to our seamen if ever this nation chaunced to find a passage out of the frozen Zone to the South Seas'.[40] And it was an Englishman who first started off all that 'fame by accretion' which was to be Marco's (that he had brought back tagliatelle, printing, gunpowder and the like to Europe). Dr William Gilbert (of whom it was to be written – by none less than Dryden – 'Gilbert shall live till loadstones cease to draw' – on balance a false prophecy) asserted in his *De magnete* (London 1600),[41] that it was Marco from his stay in China who had introduced Europe to knowledge of the compass: 'the Venetian Paolo learnt of the compass around 1260 and brought it to Europe' – an example of the magnetism of a *name* for attracting all that could be associated with it.

Venice of course remained the particular centre for his glorification. Already in 1553 the Council of the Ten had specified that Giacomo Gastaldi should base his wall-maps of Asia for the Doge's Palace on the Book. Not that they needed to insist; in his planisphere, produced three years before, Gastaldi had filled the four corners of his map with four heroes of geographical knowledge, the ancients Ptolemy and Strabo, the moderns Columbus and Marco Polo. His three large maps of Asia produced in 1561 include all the names mentioned in Ramusio's edition of Marco Polo.[42] And Italians in general seem to have gone along with the Venetian position. In 1563 Ignazio Danti, the celebrated cartographer who was to design the maps in the map galleries of the Vatican, decorated part of the Palazzo Vecchio in Florence with a series of maps. Two of these, 'Giapan overo Cipangu isola' and 'The ultimate parts known of the Western Indies' (*sic*), draw heavily upon Marco even though more accurate material was available at the time.[43]

III

Ramusio's argument for believing in the substance of Marco's Book (if you doubt Quinsai, think of Mexico) though not particularly logical must have had strong force in the mid-sixteenth and even seventeenth centuries when so many marvellous new things were being revealed. Yet the Book could still be treated with a certain scepticism by non-geographers. In the Fifth Book of *Pantagruel*, chapter 31 treats of *How in the land of Satin we saw Hearsay, who kept a school of vouching*. Here one finds 'a diminutive, monstrous, mis-shapen old fellow called Hearsay', surrounded by innumerable men and women who 'could most fluently talk with you of prodigious things' – as for instance the Pyramids of Egypt, the Troglodytes, the Blemmyae, the Hyperborei, and so on, 'every individual word of it by Hearsay'. Among Hearsay's most devoted followers are in particular writers on geography such as Herodotus, Pliny, Solinus, Pomponius Mela, Strabo, Pope Pius II, Jacques Cartier, Hetoum the Armenian, Ludovico Varthema and, of course, Marco Polo the Venetian.[44]

So too Sir Robert Burton in the *The Anatomy of Melancholy* (1621) writes of the spirits of the Desert of Lop and the straight streets of Cambalu, but then in whimsical mood plans an imagined journey by air where he will discover

> whether *Marcus Polus* the *Venetians* narration be true or false, of that great City of *Quinsay* and *Cambalu*, whether there be any such places, or that as *Matth Riccius* the Jesuite hath written *China* and *Cataia* be all one, the great *Cham* of *Tartary* and King of *China* bee the same; *Xuntaine* and *Quinsay* and the citty of *Cambalu* bee that new Pacquin,or such a wall 400 leagues long to part *China* from *Tartary*; whether *Presbyter John* be in *Asia* or *Africke*, *M. Polus Venetian* puts him in *Asia*, the most received opinioun is, that he is Emperour of the Abisinnes, which of old was *Aethiopia*, now *Nubia* under the *Aequator* in *Africke*.[45]

In this flying machine, he tells us, 'I would censure all *Plinies, Solinus, Strabos, S John Mandevills, Olaus Magnus, Marcus Polus* lies . . .'

Again the non-geographer could simply ignore him. In his *De la vicissitude ou variété des choses en l'universe* (Paris, 1577),[46] Louis Le Roy, speaks of 'the Great Cham' of Cathay and the magnificence of his domain. He gives from Hetoum an account of the early history of the dynasty and reports, again from Hetoum, that striking remark that the Cathayans believe that only they see with two eyes. From some contemporary authority Le Roy writes of the esteem in which letters are held among them and how public offices go not to birth or riches but only to learning, wisdom and virtue.

Geographers had to take the Book more seriously. One of the first questions which Columbus' discovery posed was: 'Is this "New World" which he has discovered, as he believes, the Asia of Marco Polo?'[47] – a question which took in a second enquiry: 'How far can one trust what one reads in Marco Polo?' In so far as Spanish opinion is concerned it is clear that few agreed with the Admiral's claim that he had come upon the lands of the Great Khan.[48] The map of 1500 from the hand of Juan de la Cosa who was Columbus' pilot includes no names from Polo; nor indeed, though they attempt to unite the new knowledge with the ideas of Ptolemy, do the three sketch-maps of Alessandro Zorzi which are supposed to illustrate the views of Columbus' own brother Bartolomeo in 1503.[49] In his introduction to Pomponius Mela's *De situ orbis* published at Salamanca in 1498, Francisco Nuñez de la Yerva declares roundly that Columbus has not found India (i.e. Asia).[50] When five years later Santaella translated Marco into Castillian it is not impossible that his principal purpose was to publicise the view that Asia was one thing, the new discoveries another. In his preface Santaella asserts this to the reader in a remarkably confident way. Nor, he adds with some asperity – challenging another notion dear to Columbus – are the new islands of the Antilles and Hispaniola at all the same as the biblical Tarsis and Orphir.[51] After which one is neither surprised at the silence about Marco's Book in Vespucci's letters nor at the resounding attack upon it in Martín Fernández de Enciso's *Suma de Geographía* of 1519. Enciso uses Pliny, Strabo, Ptolemy, but (reflecting on the chapters on Tangut in Marco Polo's Book, though without mentioning him by name) remarks:

> From the Ganges to that part of the East that is furthest India called Cathay where were the lands of Prester John and of Gog and Magog, there is no authentic writing . . . because though some merchants have passed there, they have seen little and what they have written of it is doubtful and in little order, and so in all of little faith.

At the same time – and it is an interesting example of how selective our scepticism is always likely to be – while rejecting the bulk of the Book he gives the fullest and most respectful credence to Marco's tale (XIII) of a mountain moving in response to the prayers of a Christian holy man.[52] Marco still continued to be read by some in Spain. When in the Pacific during the Magellan/El Cano circumnavigation an inventory was taken of the goods of the dead *contador* Iñigo Ortiz de Perea sure enough there is found among them 'un libro de Marco Pablo' – valued at $1\frac{1}{2}$ ducats (a sailor might earn 3 ducats a month).[53] Yet this is not typical. It is clear that the great Las Casas, missionary cleric and historian of the discovery of the New World, who seems to know everything about the explorers of his own day, knew nothing of Marco Polo whom he mistook for Paolo dal Pozzo Toscanelli.[54]

Much the same picture emerges among the Portuguese. There are early signs of belief that Columbus had reached the Asia of Marco Polo. On his first return from India in 1499, Vasco da Gama passed 'eleven thousand islands . . . and those should be the ones that have been discovered [by Columbus] for the King of Castile'.[55] In the dedication of the 1502 translation into Portuguese Valentin Fernandez observes that India has been discovered by Vasco da Gama, while 'the much honoured Hidalgo Gaspar Cortereal in his navigations to the north has reached the lordship of the Great Khan [in fact Newfoundland]'. But these endorsements soon evaporate, and with them disappears any interest in Marco Polo. (The Portuguese translation of 1502 survives today in only five copies, which suggests a small print run and demand.) As we shall see, the Portuguese were for a time prepared to trust the Book on the ports of Cathay. Antonio Galvano in his (to use the title of Richard Hakluyt's translation)

Discoveries of the World from their first original unto the year of our Lord 1555 praised him for discovery of the land route to the East in what might be thought of as over-enthuasiastic terms:

> And although at the first his booke was taken for a fabulous thing, yet now there is better credit given unto it; for that by the late experiences of the trauailers and merchants of these daies unto those parts, the names of the countreys, cities, and townes, anchorages, with their situations, latitudes [these are not, of course, found in the Book], and commodities are now found true, as he and other historiographers of that time have reported.[56]

But Professor Cortesão's claim that in Portugal, from the *Mappamundo* of Cantino (1502) to the *Atlas* of Homem-Reineless (1519) one can find the influence of Ptolemy but not of Marco, is broadly true. In general caution prevailed. Diego Homem for instance does not recognise the existence of Japan in his maps of 1558, 1561 and 1568 (though the 1568 map does accept towns called Quinsai, Cambaluc, Tangut and Cataio).[57]

By contrast the geographers of Italy and northern Europe gave greater credence to the Book. Here Englishmen and Italians came together. In 1497 John Cabot returned from his expedition on behalf of Henry VII. In August of that year the Venetian merchant Lorenzo Pasqualigo wrote to his family in Venice: 'That Venetian of ours who went with a small ship from Bristol to find new islands has come back and says he has discovered mainland 700 leagues away which is the country of the Grand Khan.' Four months later the Duke of Milan's ambassador was writing of how King Henry 'has gained part of Asia without a stroke of the sword'. 'Zoane' Cabot has found fish, brazil-wood and silk there, and further south, 'he proposed to keep along the coast from the place at which he touched, more and more towards the coast, until he reaches an island which he calls Cipango, situated in the equinoctial region where he believes that all the spices of the world have their origin, as well as the jewels'.[58] Marco is not actually mentioned here, but he does not need to be. He is part of the climate.

Eventually – though perhaps more slowly than is generally recognised – the conviction that the New World was an outcrop of Asia died away. But Italian interest in Marco's Book survived. Among Italian cartographers, Giovanni Matteo Contarini (1506) shows Cuba, to the west of it 'Zipangu', and then a mainland with both a province and city of Cathay, Quinsai, Tangut and Ciamba. In his *Mappamundo* (Rome, 1507 or 1508) Johannes Ruysch closely follows Marco, accepting Marco's Java minor, Java maior, Canpicio, the Desert of Lop, Cathaya (as a city), Cianfu, Quinsai,

Tibet, Tangut, Mangi, Ciandu, Zaito, Ciamba and Loac. And he follows Columbus' final conclusions in identifying 'Cipangu': 'Marco Polo says there is a very large island called Sipango. . . . There is great abundance of gold and all kinds of gems. But as the islands discovered by the Spaniards occupy this spot, we do not locate this in India here, being of the opinion that what the Spaniards call Spagnola [Hispaniola] is really Sipango.'[59]

A daring break with this tradition came with the map of 1507 by Martin Waldseemüller of Strassburg, which shows first a new continent, America, then to the west Sipangu, and then finally the mainland of Asia.[60] Yet Waldseemüller himself soon came to have cold feet about this formula, and very great confusion surrounded the identity of the New World for a long time yet. In his *Opusculum geographicum* of 1533 Johannes Schöner writes, 'Behind the Sinae and the Seres . . . many countries were discovered by one Marco Polo a Venetian and others, and the sea coasts of these countries have now recently again been explored by Columbus and Vespucci in navigating the Indian Ocean.'[61] In particular the riches of Tenochtitlán–Mexico looted by Cortés caused many in the 1520s and 1530s (indeed in one case as late as the 1590s) to think that this city with its bridges and canals, its mass of people and the splendour of its wealth, must have been Marco's Quinsai; while others fastened on place name similarities, holding that 'Messigo' must be Mansi; Tamago, Tibet and so on.[62]

IV

It should be added that the attempts of cartographers to interpret Marco's Book led to frequent error. Since Marco had given only the Mongol or Persian forms of Chinese place names, the first Europeans who arrived by sea on the Chinese coast did not realise at all that this was the country which he had described. Hence both Portuguese and French portolan charts of the 1540s put a country called Cin or China between 25° and 40° of latitude, and above that Marco's Cataio and Mangi. Here one sees at 25° a port called Chincheo, i.e. Ch'üan-chou (Pinyin Quanzhou), while at 40° one sees a port called Zaiton – which was the Mongol name for Ch'üan-chou.[63] This misapprehension passed swiftly to the cartographers of northern Europe (see Illustration 13). And to literature too. In Book XI (ll.385–91) of *Paradise Lost* (first published in 1667), Milton has Adam ascend the loftiest hill of Paradise in order to look upon the sites of future kingdoms:

> His Eye might there command wherever stood
> City of old or modern Fame, the Seat
> Of mightiest Empire, from the destin'd Walls

Of Cambalu, seat of Cathaian Khan,
And Samarkand by Oxus, Temir's Throne,
To Paquin of Sinaean Kings, and thence
To Agra and Lahor of Great Mogul

Remembering perhaps a world map of Ortelius, the poet like the cartographer has not realised that Cathayan Cambalu and Peking are one and the same place.

The Book gave rise to a second profound misunderstanding (see Illustration 14).[64] In chapters CLXIV–CLXV Marco declares that leaving the island of Java and sailing 700 miles south-south-west, one arrived at the two islands called Sandur and Condur. Going from these for 500 miles one came to the province of Locac. In the Ramusio version this Locac is said to be a mainland. It is a good country, rich, and with its own king; the people are idolaters with their own language. They grow brazil-wood; gold is found there 'in incredible quantity' as also elephants and porcelain shells used in currency. The King does not encourage visits of strangers who might get to know of its treasures and resources. Then leaving Locac and going south for another 500 miles one comes to an island called Pentain, 'a very savage place'. A further 60 miles on and then 30 miles south-east one comes to the island kingdom of Malaiur where 'they have great merchandise of all things, with spices, for these they have in great abundance'.

As they stand it is difficult today to make anything of these chapters. Quite plausibly – in that chapter CLXIII immediately before deals with Champa – Colonel Yule suggested that when Marco wrote of leaving the island of Java this was a lapse of the pen for 'when leaving Champa' (i.e. today's South and Central Vietnam). In this way he was able to identify 'Locac' with its idolaters, gold, unwelcoming king and so on, as Siam. This being so, 'Pentain' would be an island at the end of the Malacca Straits and – acknowledging 'a good deal of confusion' – the supposed island kingdom of Malaiur would be the Malay peninsula. Not having Yule's knowledge of Asia, early modern cartographers simply accepted what they read, that this was a description of what lay in the 1,790 miles below – not Champa – but Java. The first to do this was Gerard Mercator in his globe of 1541 (which has seventy-three place names from the Book).[65] To complicate matters Mercator consulted two versions of Marco's work. In the first he read the name Lucach (*sic*). In the second, which he found in the Grynaeus–Huttich *New World* collection, that name had been corrupted to Boëach.[66] As a result he portrayed a huge promontory rising up towards Java from the Terra Australis, the great southern landmass. At its tip is 'Beach' (a further corruption) with the legend 'Goldbearing province which few from other regions visit on account of the incivility of the people'. To its south-west appears what we know to be Beach's other form, the kingdom of Lucach. Below it is Maletur (Marco's Malaiur) with the inscription 'Kingdom in which is a mighty store of spices'. Opposite Maletur is the island of 'Petan' and to the west of Petan the island of Java Minor (i.e. Sumatra). In the long inscription on the promontory Mercator writes that Book III of Marcus Paulus Venetus, collated with Book VI of Ludovico Varthema, are the testimonies to 'the immensely vast regions' which exist here. (Varthema was a Bolognese merchant whose account of eastern travel written in 1510 does indeed tell of a voyage to Java, though in no way justifying Mercator's assumptions.)

This scheme was followed in Mercator's extremely influential World Map of 1569, and from there passed to most cartographers of northern Europe. It is found in the world maps of – to cite only a few – Ortelius (1564, 1571 and 1587), of Cornelius Wytfliet (1605) and of Hondius (1630). It was only in the second half of the seventeenth century that the Kingdom of Beach starts to disappear from the atlases. As late as 1664 Thévenot, the French publicist who in his *Relation de divers voyages curieux* was belatedly seeking to do for France what Hakluyt and Purchas had done for England, was arguing for the existence of this great southern world to the south-east of Java on the grounds that Marco Polo had learnt of it from the Chinese.[67]

All this adds up to a very considerable distortion. Could it have been a fruitful distortion? In July 1619 Commander Frederick de Houtman bound for Batavia with two ships 'suddenly came upon the southland of Beach in 32°20″' – that is to say just south of today's Perth in Western Australia, an area which a Dutch map of twenty years later identifies with 'Beach Provincia aurifera'.[68] This prompts the thought that the maps of Mercator and those following in his tradition could have led Dutch seamen, never averse to the sight of 'a gold-bearing province', to keep a weather eye out for it. It is a long way, of course, from conceding this possibility to going along with that colossal snob and fervent Venetian patriot by adoption, Vitale Terrarossa, who in the 1680s was to argue that it was Marco 'a Venetian patrician' who had discovered Australia – just as, he says, 'the Venetian patricians', the Zeni brothers had discovered America in the fourteenth century and had by their writings inspired Columbus to get there. One stresses the 'patrician' aspect here in conformity with the fervour of Terrarossa's own sentiments.[69] Patriotism by itself can persuade us of a great deal; when combined with class prejudice it can convince us of almost anything.

Chapter 10

Jesuits, Imperialists and a Conclusion

I

From the seventeenth century the Book lost much of its influence as a work of geography and often came to be read as a curiosity, for entertainment or other reasons. (In Florence, for instance, many, inspired by Lionardo Salviati's vision of an ideal Italian language, to be created from selected writings from the fourteenth century – *il buon secolo della lingua* – drew upon what Salviati described as the *Ottimo* or 'best' Tuscan translation (TA).[1] Yet despite this distinction, this version did not actually reach print until 1827.) In a way any discussion of the Book in this later period is likely to be patchy and unsystematic, in that its presence in the consciousness of the reading public was intermittent and haphazard. Yet there is a fascination in seeing the *fortuna* of the work playing itself out to the Victorians and beyond.

Certainly new editions testified to the Book's continuing popularity in the seventeenth century. It was reissued twice in Latin, on eight occasions in the Venetian-language text of 1496, and once in German, Dutch, Spanish and English. The Latin edition published at Berlin in 1671 by the orientalist Andreas Müller of Greiffenhagen has a certain interest as representing a first example of the Polo–scholarship industry. Müller collated two texts (that of the *Novus orbis* and a manuscript of Pipino's Latin translation – in fact a pointless exercise since the first ultimately derived from the second), provided an elaborate index, and accompanied this with a *Disquisitio geographica et historica de Chataja*, discussing such topics as whether Cathay was the same as China.[2] Müller ignored, or was not aware of, Ramusio's Italian version with which a comparison would have been much more appropriate. In fact, some fifty years earlier Samuel Purchas in his celebrated *Hakluytus Posthumus or Purchas his Pilgrimes*[3] had given a free translation in summary of Ramusio's Italian translation together with a strong defence of this as the best text of the Book. He says that he possessed a translation into English made by Hakluyt from the Latin. (This seems to have disappeared; presumably it was taken from the *Novus orbis*.) But

The Latine is Latten, compared to Ramusio's Gold. And hee which hath the Latine hath but Marco Polos Carkasse, or not so much, but a few bones, yea sometimes stones rather than bones; things diverse, averse, adverse, perverted in manner, disjoynted in manner, beyond beliefe. I have seen some Authors maymed but never any so mangled and so mingled, so present and so absent, as this vulgar Latine of Marco Polo. . . . many which have read M. Paulus never saw M. Polo nor know the worth of the worthiest Voyage, that perhaps any one man hath ever written.[4]

With Georg Horn, in his *De originibus Americanis libri quattuor*, published at The Hague in 1652, doubts about the Latin text were accompanied by regrets at 'the interpolation' (though is this merely a euphemism?) of falsehood in all the available versions:

It is to be regretted that some impostor has interpolated so many falsehoods into Marco Polo's *Voyages*. For who believes what he writes about Quinsai, that there are 12,000 stone bridges there, constructed with arches so high that ships with upright masts can sail under them? And how many errors have entered the catalogue of the Emperors of Tartary? For if we except Genghis, Möngke and Khubilai, the others are very corrupt. . . . Purchas realised the defect, writing 'I have seen many corrupt authors, but none more so than the Latin edition of Polo the Venetian.'[5]

Horn too draws attention to a striking omission in the Book: 'That the [Great] Wall is more recent than 1200 is shown by the fact that Polo the Venetian never refers to it, though he would not have passed it over if it were already there.' Scepticism about the truth of the Book might perhaps at this point have triumphed but for the fact that in the writings of the Catholic missionaries in China of the sixteenth and seventeenth centuries – writings which obviously superseded his authority – Marco was still treated with great respect. In his *Relation of the Things of China* written in 1575–6 the Augustinian friar Martín de Rada was the first to realise (in opposition to the Jesuits at the court of Akbar) that 'the country which we commonly call China was called by Marco Polo the Venetian the kingdom of Cathay, perhaps because it was then so called; for when he came there which was about the year 1312, it was ruled by the Tartars'.[6] This recognition allowed Marco the praise of another Augustinian friar, Juan Gonzalez de Mendoza in his *Historia de las cosas mas notables del gran Reyno de la China* (Rome, 1585, translated into English, 1589). The brilliant Jesuit missionary Matteo Ricci came independently to the same conclusion. In 1605 Ricci heard of men in the province of Shaanxi who were descendants of Christians (to which Marco had referred) and knew something, though very little, of the Christian faith. 'From this we understand that there is absolutely no doubt that China is Marco Polo the Venetian's Cathay and that what he says is quite true, that there are Christians in Cathay for in his days they would have been many.'[7]

Most influential of the Jesuit authors was Martino Martini in his *Novus atlas Sinensis* published at Amsterdam in 1655, a work which provided many valuable maps and remarkably comprehensive geographical information from Chinese sources. For all his knowledge of these Martini also read Odorico and Hetoum, and consistently and frequently speaks highly of Marco, identifying the names he gave to localities and justifying his descriptions. 'I hold it a duty', he writes, 'to free that most noble patrician from the accusation of mendacity and from the other calumnies to which he has been subject; the more so because his accusers who have so lightly condemned in him things they cannot understand are far worthier of reproof.' Martini's work became immediately the leading authority. It was reprinted in French in Volume XI of *L'Asie* of Johan Blaeu's *Le grand atlas ou cosmographie Blaviane* (Amsterdam, 1663). Finally it served as the basis for the lavishly illustrated popularising work of another Jesuit, Athanasius Kircher's *China Illustrata* (Amsterdam, 1667; and in translation *La Chine*, Amsterdam, 1670). Kircher himself refers quite frequently to that *oculatus inspector Paulus Marcus Venetus*: 'There is none among all ancient authors who have spoken of the kingdoms of the East who have treated so fully of these matters nor who have given so perfect a description as he'. Kircher's praise was adulterated – he complained, anachronistically enough, that Marco ignored latitude and longitude, and he set off a long-enduring wild goose chase in being the first to attempt to trace his route to and from China.[8] Another member of the order, the Portuguese Gabriel de Magalhães, whose writings on China eventually reached print in 1688, criticised (in fact inaccurately) Polo for claiming that paper money existed in China under the Mongols, but was the first to identify the 'Pulisanghinz' bridge of which he wrote in chapter CV.[9] Sixty years later another learned Jesuit publicist, J. B. du Halde, though virtually ignoring his Book as a source, would also affirm Marco's credibility.[10]

Yet whatever elders among the orders might pronounce in public, junior members might well privately reject. Domingo Navarrete who was in China between 1658 and 1670 tells of hearing two Jesuits in Canton arguing whether Marco's book or Martini's was the more fantastic in its claims.[11] With the eighteenth century, when colonial rivalry between France, Spain and Britain and the ever-growing importance of world trade prompted many collected editions of travels – collections in which Marco's work still featured prominently[12] – there came the first published denunciation of it. This was attached to the text in the fourth volume of *The New Col-*

lection of Voyages and Travels, commonly known, from the name of its publisher Thomas Astley, as *Astley's Voyages*.[13] The anonymous editor here lays out various criticisms of the Book at some length: Chinese cities are given their Mongol names; no latitudes are given for places; distances and bearings are unreliable, so that it is difficult to order localities on a map. Much of it, he asserts, is superficial; there was, for example, hardly any account of the Mongol capital of Karakorum. The historical content is 'full of Errors and Fables' – as that Tartar magicians could raise storms and deflect them from the Khan's palace. And (this written in London two years after the Catholic Prince Charles had almost been carried to the throne by an insurgence of terrifying highlanders) it reeked of papistry. Considering the story of the holy man who moved a mountain, the writer remarks that like the friars Marco 'made no Scruple any more than they, to tell a Lie to serve his Religion'.

Moreover Marco has mistaken the succession of the Khans. All this raised grave doubts:

> Is it possible that our *Venetian* could have given no better Account of Things, if he understood the Languages and was in such Favour at Court as he pretends? Hence there is Room to suspect that he never was either in *Tartary* or *Katay*. For why might he not have penned all he hath written of those countries from the Reports of others, as well as most of what he relates of other Countries and Islands, which makes the greater Part of his Work, and are, for the general, more exactly described? His Account of the several Parts of *India* and Coasts of *Africa*, seems to be taken from the Books or Mouthe of the Mohammedans; most of the Names being such as are given them by the *Arabian* and *Persian* Authors.
>
> Had our *Venetian* been really on the Spot, with those Advantages he had of informing himself, how is it possible he could have made not the least Mention of the Great Wall: the most remarkable Thing in all *China* or perhaps in the whole World? It is in vain to say with *Martini*, that he entered China by the Southern Provinces. After all, supposing he had not seen this Wonder of China, he could not possibly but have heard of it. In short the most we can do in favour of Polo is to suppose that in Case he was in the Countries, which he describes as an Eye-Witness, he never kept a regular journal of his Travels, as he pretends, but when he returned to *Venice*, drew up his Relation on the Strength of his Memory, which in many Things deceived him; and inserted as his own Remarks, the idle reports of others, which he had taken for granted, without further Enquiry. It would be no difficult Matter for a Person, who had conversed much with Travellers into those Parts of the World, to sit

down and write a much better Relation than Polo has done: notwith-
standing, it must be confessed, that he is the Father of modern
Discoveries, and he led the Way to all the rest.

Astley's *New Collection* had a considerable international success. It was
translated (together with its prefaces) into French as *L'Histoire générale des
voyages* (Paris, 1746–70) under the editorship of none other than the Abbé
Prévost, author of *Manon Lescaut*; and into German (*Allgemeine Historie der
Reisen*, Leipzig, 1750). Its views on Marco, complete with anti-Catholic
comments were taken up in a general work on medieval history published
in 1829 by K. D. Hüllmann. Hüllmann believed that Marco's work was 'an
ecclesiastical fiction, devised as a book of travels', written 'to kindle enthusiasm for the conversion of the Mongols, and so to facilitate commerce
through their domains'; that what Marco wrote were 'recollections of the
bazaar and travel books of traders from those countries'.[14] Yet otherwise
the eighteenth-century no-nonsense, Grub-Street comments of the editor
of *Astley's Voyages* seem to have had little resonance. The attitude of the
Enlightenment was summed up by one of its most eminent historians,
William Robertson in his *An Historical Disquisition concerning the Knowledge which the Ancients had of India* (London, 1791). Robertson considered
the Book 'the most complete survey hitherto made of the East, and the
most complete description of it ever given by any European', and met
the various objections which had been made against it. Marco could
not (thinking perhaps less of the criticisms of Astley than of Athanasius
Kircher) as a merchant be expected to know latitude and longitude, and it
was quite natural that he should use Mongol names for Chinese places.
Moreover: 'Columbus, as well as the men of science with whom he corre-
sponded, placed such confidence in the veracity of his relations, that upon
them the speculations and theories, which led to the discovery of the
New World, were in great measure founded. Life of Columbus by his
Son, c.7 and 8.'[15]

Robertson's remarks were published in the year before the celebrated
embassy of Lord Macartney to Peking in which the British government
attempted to secure an exchange of ambassadors and entry into commercial relations with China. Macartney took with him his life-long friend and
fellow Anglo-Irishman, George Staunton. Staunton's son, George Thomas
Staunton, then aged twelve and (as a result of a crash-course with a missionary order in Italy) the only member of the delegation to speak any
Chinese, accompanied them as a page. In 1797 the elder George Staunton
published *An Authentic Account of an Embassy from the King of Great Britain
to the Emperor of China* wherein, in addition to relating the events of the
embassy, he took time off to identify Marco's Quinsai and to explain why

the Venetian had made no mention of the Great Wall (like Martini he decided he had arrived through the Tibetan mountains).

The Macartney mission, combined with an ever-increasing involvement in the East, was responsible for a new interest in Marco Polo's Book in Britain. It was another Anglo–Irishman, William Marsden, one whose mind had been deeply formed by experience of the Empire, who brought about the first scholarly edition of the text. Marsden had served for eight years in the office of Writer for the East India Company at Sumatra. On his return he was employed as Second Secretary, and then between 1804 and 1807 – that momentous period of British naval history – as First Secretary of the Admiralty. By instinct a scholar, he took part in the 'philosophical breakfasts' of Sir Joseph Banks, wrote a *History of Sumatra* (1783), a *Dictionary and Grammar of the Malayan Language* (1812) and a *Numismata orientalia illustrata* (1823–5). His *The Travels of Marco Polo* (London, 1818) consisted of an English translation of Ramusio's text, together with an eighty-page introduction. Marsden followed Ramusio's editorial remarks too readily and he gave new life to Kircher's misleading interpretation of the work as an itinerary. Yet he approached the Book with a passionate determination to illustrate its truth and elucidate its difficulties. He examined the different manuscript traditions and, in notes at the end of each chapter, gave interesting illustrations of the text, derived often from his network of contacts in the East. So for instance after the section in which Marco speaks of 'the pears of enormous size' to be found in Quinsai, he remarks: 'Mr Henry Browne, who for many years filled the situation of Chief of the Company's Factory at Canton, assures me that he has seen pears, supposed to have been produced in the province of Fo-kien, the bulk of which equalled that of a moderate sized wine decanter.'

His profound sympathy for the Book was quickened by Macartney's embassy and British dreams of entering China. Commenting on Niccolò Polo's introduction of Marco to the Great Khan, he remarks: 'It is impossible for those who have read the account of Lord Macartney's Embassy not to be struck with the resemblance between this scene and that which passed at Johol in 1793 when Sir George Staunton presented his son, the present Sir George Thomas Staunton, to the venerable Kien Long.'[16]

The Book, he thought, suffered from 'a deficiency of skill in literary composition on the part of the author'. Yet its merit lay in its essential truth:

> Of those who in the present day declare their want of faith, and make the character of Marco Polo the subject of pleasantry, it is probable that the greater proportion have but superficially read his work; and there is reason to believe that the number of these, who, having deliberately perused it, continue to think the narrative fictitious, is very inconsiderable.[17]

II

From Marsden's time it is probable that the Book has never been out of print. From that time too it has been the constant subject of learned enquiry.[18] In 1865 the distinguished sinologist, M. G. Pauthier, edited *Le Livre de Marco Polo citoyen de Venise, conseiller privé et commissaire impérial de Khoubilai-Khaân*, a work whose title, emphasising Marco's supposed status as an imperial official, sets the scene for the mass of valuable citations from Chinese official sources. This vision of Marco as the high official of a foreign imperialist dynasty was followed by the very similar interpretation of Henry Yule (London, 1871; second edition, 1875; third edition, posthumous, 1903). Colonel Yule came from one of those many Victorian Scottish families whose very considerable abilities and self-confidence were dedicated to the service of the British Empire. His father was an officer of the Bengal Army, served as Assistant to the Resident in Lucknow and Oudh, and collected (and studied) a large library of Arabic and Persian manuscripts. His uncle, a colonel with the East India Company, served as Resident of Java when under British occupation. One of his cousins became a general in the Royal Engineers; his first wife's father was a general in the Bengal Army, his second wife was the daughter of a member of the Bengal civil service. One of his brothers died at the head of the Ninth Lancers during the Mutiny; another was a distinguished 'civilian' (i.e. civil officer) in the Bengal Service who, on shooting his four-hundredth tiger, decided to stop recording the numbers of those others he would slaughter. Yule himself, brought up to the classics at the Edinburgh High School, went on to become an officer in the Bengal Engineers, served in the Sikh wars, the Mutiny, and went as secretary of a mission to the King of Burma. With restless energy, he translated Schiller into English verse, lectured on fortification, reported on the frontier passes between Aracan and Burma and organised the defences of Singapore.

As a result of his friendship with the Governor-General Lord Dalhousie, a fellow Scot, Yule was appointed Under-Secretary, then Secretary, to the Government of Public Works, which was concerned with irrigation and railways. Yule also became an intimate of Dalhousie's successor Lord Canning. When Canning retired in 1862, Yule, now forty-two and weary of India, overhastily resigned his commission and elected to go too, believing that through him he would secure 'congenial employment' back in Britain. But his friend's untimely death a few months later shattered his hopes. It was in these circumstances that he found alternative occupation in scholarship, notably with his editions for the Hakluyt Society: the *Travels of Friar Jordanus*; the *Cathay and the Way Thither*; then the Marco Polo; and such other works as an *Essay on the Geography of the Oxus Region* (1872), which was promptly circulated by the Russian government among its officers in Central Asia. Later he became a member of the India Council, of the Army Sanitary Committee (where he negotiated with Florence Nightingale – 'She immediately finds out all I don't know'), a firm supporter of Lord Salisbury, and one calling, amidst the strident voices of many others, for revenge for the death of General Gordon.[19]

An arch-representative of the age of imperialism then, very appropriate for the editor of a book by the servant of an earlier imperialism. Certainly Yule's edition bears constant testimony to information drawn from a vast network of servants of the later Empire: 'very extensive private correspondence to nearly all parts of Europe and many centres in Asia'. There abound such comments as (discussing Marco on Hormuz): 'An application to Colonel Pelly, the very able British Resident at Bushire, brought me from his own personal knowledge the information that I sought, and the following particulars are compiled from the letters with which he has favoured me'. For the determination of (as he believed) Marco's route in Persia, Yule draws on 'the journey taken by Major R. M. Smith R. E. in 1866' (that 'R. E.' being the mark of Yule's loyalty to his corps; and for the Royal Engineers of course geography was a particular concern). To learn about Kishm, 'application was made through Colonel Maclagan to Pandit Manphul C.S.I., a very intelligent Hindu gentleman, who resided for some time in Badakshan as agent of the Panjab Government'. There they all are, those loyal servants of the Queen, Major P. Moleswoth Sykes, Colonel Goldsmid, Lieutenant Kempthorne, 'my brother officer, Major T. G. Montgomerie R. E.' (model for Colonel Creighton in Kipling's *Kim*, inventor – though this Yule does not tell us – of the 'moonchees'-system, by which native Indians were sent in disguise to make secret maps of Central Asia[20]), Mr E. Stack of the Indian Civil Service, General Cunningham, and famous names in the 'Great Game' like Younghusband and Bell (who was, though Yule of course again says nothing of this, Director of Military Intelligence of the Indian Army), 'Mr William Johnson of the Indian Service' (the first European to reach the Taklamakan from India) and many more. And with them are those loyal servants of the Czar, playing on the other side, Colonel Nikolai Prejevalsky, and all the Lieutenants Roborovsky and K. P. Koslovs and Generals Pievtsov.[21] And then too the missionaries, those colonialists of the soul: the Right Reverend G. E. Moule (who was Anglican bishop of Marco's Quinsai), the Rev. Mr Jaeschke, writing from Tibet, 'the Rev. D. D. Green an American missionary at Ning po'. The testimony of these men stands alongside Arrian's account of Alexander's expedition, the writings of Idrisi, Odorico, Ibn Battuta and the *Yuan shih*.

In their travels through Asia these men always seem to have had Marco Polo with them, either in their hand or their head. They too were exploring an unknown world. These were the days when Baron Ferdinand von

Richthofen had just invented the phrase (not, as most today believe, of immemorial antiquity) 'The Silk Road' and when Sven Hedin and Aurel Stein were mounting their first expeditions. In the introduction to the second edition of his Marco Polo, Yule reflected on the growth in knowledge of Asia which had occurred in the four years since the publication of the first:

> Karakorum, for a brief space the seat of the widest empire the world has known, has been visited; the ruins of SHANG-TU, the 'Xanadu of Cublay Khan', have been explored; PAMIR and TANGUT have been penetrated from side to side; the famous mountain road of SHEN-SI has been traversed and described; the mysterious CAINDU has been unveiled; the publication of my lamented friend Lieutenant Garnier's great work on the French Exploration of Indo-China has provided a mass of illustration of that YUN-NAN for which but the other day Marco Polo was well-nigh the most recent authority. Nay, the last two years have thrown a promise of light even on what seemed the wildest of Marco's stories, and the bones of a veritable RUC from New Zealand lie on the table of Professor Owen's Cabinet.

In his introduction to the third edition Henri Cordier wrote in the same vein: 'Since the last edition was published more than twenty-five years ago, Persia has been more thoroughly studied; new routes have been explored in Central Asia, Karakorum has been finally described, and Western and South-Western China have been opened up to our knowledge in many directions.' It was all still going on. 'As this sheet goes finally to press we hear of the exploration of Pamir by officers of Mr Forsyth's Mission', remarks Yule on one passage in that same edition. To which Henri Cordier, in the third, adds the comment, 'I have made use of the information collected by them'. The Book could still reveal errors in the cartography of the nineteenth century. It spoke for instance of the cold felt on descending the mountains of Kerman. At which Yule mentions a communication he has received from Major Oliver St John who had surveyed a section of them in 1872: 'Yet practically this chain is ignored in all our maps!'

In his edition of the Book Yule freely acknowledged his own limited mastery of Asian languages – 'a fair familiarity with Hindustani for many years and some reminiscences of elementary Persian'. Yet his Edinburgh education had given him a good knowledge of the classics and a powerful curiosity had caused him to acquire a reasonable acquaintance with medieval western vernacular literature. More than that he possessed in abundance what his editor called that 'earnest wish to be exact' which is the characteristic of the true scholar; his professional skills were drawn into play with the many maps he drew; and, to a very remarkable extent, he seems to be interested in everything he finds in the Book. Time and time again his notes expand to full essays: 3,000 words on the Dong or Wild Yak (with information from three British and one Russian officer who have shot one); 7,000 words on Prester John, 1,000 words identifying Marco's 'Bargelac' as the species of sand-grouse '*Syrrhaptes Pallasii*'; 5,000 words on the Sensin (complete with engraving of a Tibetan Bacsi); 7,000 words on the astrologers of Khanbalikh; 2,000 on what exactly Polo meant by 'buckram', and other extensive exposition. Most of all he had a passionate sympathy with the subject. In many ways Yule's edition is the most satisfactory to read today because it gives the impression – reinforced by the reproduction of about one hundred and seventy woodcuts of Asia taken from Victorian contemporaries – that everything in the Book is still alive and in some way contemporary.

III

Throughout its history the power of the Book has obviously never derived, as have other works of great influence, from brilliant intellectual or imaginative ability. It came rather from a careful, common-sense and well-organised transmission of what in its heyday was hitherto unknown information. This material, originating from diligent accumulation of records and notes, is set down in a spirit which seeks to omit all that is not true. Often irrespective of their merits, the fortune of books such as this depends above all and in a stronger way than others whose text is less passive, upon the intellectual and social milieux in which they are read. At its inception and in its early years, Marco Polo's Book enjoyed an extensive readership. Yet though in the course of the fourteenth century its truth could be verified by many merchants and missionaries who travelled east, and was confirmed by some who wrote accounts of what they had seen there, it still had a primarily literary function; it was basically treated, like many other geographical works of the time, as a book of wonders. And this despite Marco's rejection of false wonders in favour of truth. Again, although its Latin version was designed to reach a learned audience, it was not until 1380 that we find a cartographer who draws upon it. Meanwhile even as a collection of geographical wonders its fame was challenged from the 1360s by the appearance of the much more brilliantly presented work attributed to Sir John Mandeville.

It was the coming of Humanism, with all of Humanism's fascination with geography and the ancient geographers, which powerfully enhanced its vitality. It was in the fifteenth century that the Book entered its prime, when it was passionately studied by scholars like Toscanelli and humanist map-makers like Fra Mauro and Henricus Martellus. It was in this era that the name of Marco Polo came to be associated with those of Strabo and

Ptolemy from classical antiquity, the time when Martin Behaim announced that his globe showed: 'the whole world . . . namely the one part as described by Ptolemy . . . and the remainder from what the knight Marco Polo of Venice caused to be written down'. It is that combination, one might almost say, which, in so far as the science of geography is concerned, accounts for the discovery of America. This was the supreme moment of the Book. Though Columbus had not read it before his First Voyage, there was a real sense in which he did not need to; by then its contents were part of the mental climate; for Europe the Great Khan still lived and reigned, a hundred and thirty years after his expulsion from China. In the sixteenth century printing widened its readership, and, as the example of Mercator's great southern continent bending northwards to the East Indies shows, it could still exercise great influence for the diffusion, when misunderstood, of falsehood as well as truth. In the seventeenth century, greater European knowledge of Asia, and particularly the writings of the Jesuit fathers in China, inevitably reduced its impact; eighteenth-century Augustan ratio-nalism could look upon it at times uneasily; yet with the nineteenth, amidst the consolidation of European empires in the East, it was to attain cult status as a work of scholarly and romantic interest.

Habent sua fata libelli; books, books too, have their destiny. As to whether today that of Marco Polo lives on, different readers in my experience give different answers. For those who have no taste for a chivalric-epic prose style it has no literary merits. (Even for those who do, those merits, it must be confessed, are few.) And that the barrier of its impersonality limits general interest is well demonstrated by the difficulties met with by those who have tried to transmute it into any other art. The reserve of the author, his refusal to cast his life and work as an adventure, has left meagre oppor-tunities for adaptation. This has been well demonstrated in a painful film (with Gary Cooper) and more recently a television series in many episodes (featuring an international cast including John Gielguid as a Doge of Venice and Burt Lancaster as Pope Gregory X). Coleridge's 'Kubla Khan' (1816), born of a reading of Purchas' summary of Ramusio under the influence of opium, has a minimal relation to the text. And Italo Calvino's *Invisible Cities*, where Marco tells tales of real and unreal cities to the Great Khan, serves only as a playful commentary upon language, narration, the relation of author to reader, of the geographer's words to the thing actually described, and the contrast between what the historian tells us and that reality of which he seeks to tell.

Is the Book now to be seen as little more than 'the tedious enumeration of Chinese cities or the stories we have all heard before'?[22] Has it become simply a happy hunting ground for scholars, a source for such towering but somehow unvital erudition as is displayed by Paul Pelliot in the three (posthumously published) volumes of his *Notes on Marco Polo* (1959–63)?

The life-span of Pelliot, that most learned pupil of the *École Française d'Extrême Orient*, who began his career as a youthful linguistic genius, swashbuckling through Asia in Gallic style,[23] and ended as a man either reviled as a colonialist manuscript-thief or mocked as one whose knowledge of life was confined to 'a book-lined study', marks off the changes which have come to Asian–European relations in the twentieth century, and the difference between his generation and Yule's. Certainly Marco's work can never be as powerful as when it was first written. For us, as Foscolo Benedetto has remarked, information on the Mongols brings neither terror nor hope. For Venetians of the thirteenth century the name Batu recalled those days when the fires of the Tartar camps could be seen from the campanile of San Marco; that of Arghun spoke of hopes that by the evangelisation of the Ilkhans the whole world might become Christian.[24] Many of Marco's *merveilles* are no longer marvellous – coal, oil, the magnet, sago, paper money – while others seem merely ridiculous. Very few among us have any interest in the commerce of thirteenth-century Asia. Nor is it now a revelation to learn that a rich urban civilisation existed at that time on the other side of the world.

All true. Yet the Book, though in some ways a sport, is still a landmark in the history of geography and as such an enlargement of the human spirit, a *merveille*. And with all its clumsiness it still gives out for those with a Gothic taste its own curious poetry, and the flavour of the author's own enigmatic personality. It is instructive to attempt to compare Marco with another great traveller of the next generation, namely Abu 'Abdullah ibn Battuta, whose *A Gift to the Observers concerning the Curiosities of the Cities and Marvels encountered in Travels* was written in cooperation with his own Rustichello, one Ibn Juzayy. Ibn Battuta left Morocco in 1325 and passed the next twenty-nine years in voyaging. After going on the Haj through the Mamluk kingdom of Egypt to Arabia and Mecca, he journeyed on to Dehli, Ceylon, Bengal and China.[25] And when he returned to his native Ceuta in 1349, there were still other travels ahead for him, to the Nasrid Kingdom of Granada in Spain, and then to the Kingdom of Mali. In everything he does a seemingly unquenchable energy breaks through: 'I have indeed – praise be to God – attained my desire in this world, which was to tread through the earth, and I have attained in this respect what no other person has attained to my knowledge'. There is an echo here of Pietro d'Abano's praise of Marco. And in some ways one can see similarities. In Ibn Battuta's tale, too, one suspects, there is, as in Rustichello's version of Marco, exaggeration of the rôle he is playing at the courts of the rulers at which he stays, most notably of all when, at the court of the Sultan Muhammad Tughluq (a sort of Muslim mad-King Ludwig of Bavaria), he is made *qadi* of Delhi (almost as impressive in its way as Marco's supposed governorship of Yangzhou) and is then appointed as his ambassador to China (in the same way that Marco is said to have been sent to India on behalf of the Great Khan).

Yet there are more, and more important, ways in which the two men differ. Ibn Battuta's tale, planned in the tradition of the *rihla*, or Arab travel-narrative, is not a geography like Marco's work, but essentially an autobiography, replete with adventures – muggings, shipwrecks, attacks and capture by pirates, robberies by warrior bands, changes in status from great wealth to great poverty and back again. It reads like a picaresque novel. The author tells us all about his plans to take over the Maldive Islands from their ruler, and refers in passing to his many marriages to, and divorces from, a lengthy sequence of wives. Through all of which he exudes an enormous self-satisfaction. Always one up, even when he is temporarily vanquished we know that our hero with one bound will throw off his coils and triumph again. This is miles from the impersonality, the supreme reticence, of Marco. Yet there is a deeper difference between the two books which could be in part the explanation of that dissimilarity. It is that in many ways Ibn Battuta is always at home. Either being, or posing as, a specialist in Islamic law, he lodges everywhere with scholars and sufis; wherever he goes he is in the House of Islam, with those fellow Muslims who have spread throughout the whole of the East. At Alexandria in Egypt a holy man prophesies to him that he will visit three sufis known to him, two in India, one in China – which indeed he does. And then in Granada he finds sufis from Samarkand. In one way his work can be looked on as an epic tribute to Muslim solidarity and charity towards their co-religionists from foreign lands.

This is very different from the Polos who do not seem to have found any similar prop in the 'heretic' Nestorian Church. In China Marco is always an alien. And perhaps too in Venice when he returns. And in the manner of aliens he does not willingly choose to communicate anything of his own personality to us. That impersonality which limits access, at the same time speaks of his mind. There is something touching in all that stoic silence about his own adventures, sufferings, joys. What stands in its place is clear, serious, normally (when his admiration for the Great Khan does not stand in his way) dispassionate, objective. One is tempted to say 'scientific'. Yet there was something not wholly inappropriate in Rustichello's portrayal of Marco as a knight errant engaged on a *queste*. With no academic training such as that enjoyed by the friars Rubruck and Giovanni di Pian di Carpine, without their motive for composition, and with no easily identifiable self-interest at stake, he opened vast horizons for the West, and gave to Europe a work which was to be a powerful element in its discovery of the world in the centuries which followed.

Appendix I

A Note on Manuscripts of the Book

The autograph of the Book begun by Marco and Rustichello in prison in Genoa does not survive, and the texts of some hundred and fifty medieval and Renaissance manuscripts which do survive often differ sharply from each other. In order to guide the reader through the various families of manuscripts to which it is therefore sometimes necessary to allude, I give here a simplified and summary account of the conclusions upon them, as expounded in great detail by L. Foscolo Benedetto, and Moule-Pelliot (for whose editions see above pp. 5–7).

Manuscripts of the Book fall into two general categories, denoted respectively A and B:

1. In **category A,** the manuscript which most scholars, and which this present work, take to be the earliest and closest to the original is 'F', the early fourteenth-century version written in Franco-Italian (Bibliothèque Nationale, ms. fr. 1116) called sometimes 'the Geographic Text'. (For Dr Wehr's, as it seems to me mistaken, arguments against this view, see above pp. 53–56.)

From not this text but from others in Franco-Italian very close to it were taken: first, a translation into northern French (FG) from which derive the three manuscripts, B3, B4 and B5 (see above pp. 6, 55). Allied to this group are some ten other extant manuscripts in French. From other Franco-Italian texts in this category derive translations into Tuscan (TB, found in five surviving manuscripts) and into Venetian (VA, six extant manuscripts).

From this Venetian translation, VA, was made the Latin translation (P) by Fra Francesco Pipino, executed between 1310 and 1317, another translation into Tuscan (TB, six manuscripts), and a German translation.

From Pipino's Latin version (P), which survives in about seventy manuscripts, were translated the Czech and Irish Gaelic versions, and a Venetian translation (back, that is, into the language from which Pipino had taken it).

2. **Category B** is represented in very few manuscripts, but is of great importance, containing much material which is not to be found in the A texts, with several passages which, as I argue on p. 58 above, it might well have been dangerous to broadcast too generally at the time. Its most important manuscript representative is a Latin version copied in the 1470s, now in Toledo (the Z text). It is also clear that the Italian version published in 1559 by Giambattista Ramusio derives from a Latin manuscript or manuscripts from this family.

As I have explained (above, p. 58) Foscolo Benedetto and Moule-Pelliot assumed that both the A and B traditions derive directly from a lost copy of one original autograph, and that an approximation to one original text can be obtained by putting together material from both families. On the other hand it could be that Marco made more than one version of his Book. The first (A) would be that begun in prison with Rustichello, and designed for general consumption. The second (B), could represent a more personal authorial statement, which for that very reason enjoyed a much more limited circulation.

SIMPLIFIED STEMMA

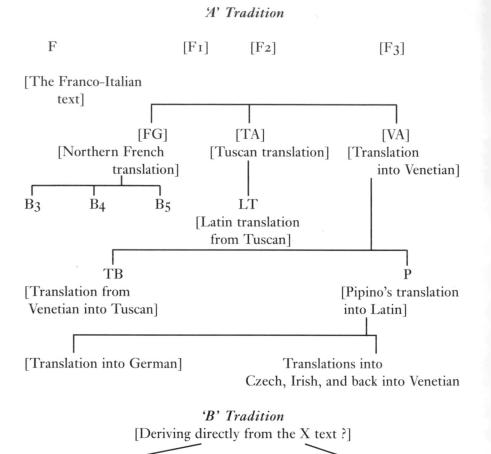

X
Lost work written in prison in Genoa

'A' Tradition

F   [F1]   [F2]   [F3]

[The Franco–Italian
text]

[FG]   [TA]   [VA]
[Northern French   [Tuscan translation] [Translation
translation]   into Venetian]

B3   B4   B5   LT
[Latin translation
from Tuscan]

TB   P
[Translation from   [Pipino's translation
Venetian into Tuscan]   into Latin]

[Translation into German]   Translations into
Czech, Irish, and back into Venetian

'B' Tradition
[Deriving directly from the X text ?]

Z   Ramusio's Italian text
[The Latin Toledo manuscript]

Appendix II

Times of Travel to China by Land

All the periods of time given in the text for the land journeys of the Polos to and from China present problems, especially if, as seems probable, they were able to use the *yam* or Mongol postal system. In chapter v, Niccolò and Maffeo, in company with the embassy of the Ilkhan of Persia, take a 'whole year' to travel from Bukhara to Northern China. Their journey from the Great Khan's court to Layas (IX) takes them three years: 'And this because they could not always ride, because of the bad weather, and the snow and the swollen rivers'. The return to China (XIV) takes three and a half years, 'and this was for the snow and the rain and the great floods, and because they were not able to ride in winter as in summer'. The explanations for these very long time spans seem weak, and no stronger seem the explanations for them bravely tendered by modern readers. It has been suggested that part of the delay in the Polos' return to China might be because Gregory X had ordered them to call on the Ilkhans on the way, in order to negotiate a joint enterprise against the Mamluks. But there is no evidence at all for this speculation, and it seems improbable that they would be singled out for this mission when it would delay still further the papal reply to the Great Khan's message. A. J. Charignon suggested that the 'three and a half years' is intended to describe the length of time that the elder Polos were absent from Khubilai's court, which would be 1268–72.[1] But this is quite at variance with what is said in the Book.

My own guess would be that Rustichello is exaggerating the length of time in order to give his readers the impression of great distances. In his merchant handbook, *La pratica di mercatura*, Francesco Pegolotti, drawing principally upon Genoese material from between 1310 and 1330, assumes that the normal time of travel for merchants (who would not, of course, be using the *yam*) along 'the road from Tana to Cathay' would be around nine months. This text survives in only one, fifteenth-century manuscript, but Bautier has discovered a *pratica della mercatura* from around 1315 which draws on the same sources as Pegolotti for a description of the journey to Cathay.[2] These offer the following itinerary:

Tana to Astrakhan *(10–12 by horse-wagon)*	25 days by ox-wagon
Astrakhan to Sarai (on the Lower Volga)	1 by water
Sarai to Saracanco (i.e. Saraichik, near Guryev on the R. Ural)	8 by water
	[Alternatively . . . *Astrakhan to Saracanco* (directly) *8 days by water or road]*
Saracanco to Utrar (Utrar, on the Syr-Daria, north-west of Tashkent)	50 days in camel wagon
	[Alternatively – Sarai to *Utrar, via Urgench (Organdi,* *the old capital of Khwarezm,* *southeast of Aral Lake)* *55–60 days in camel wagon]*
Utrar to Almalyk ('Amalecco', the Chaghadai capital, standing to the north-west of today's Ining, at the meeting of routes between southern Russia and India)	45 days by pack-ass
Almalyk to 'Camesu' Yule, [*Cathay*, 148 n. 2] identifies this as Kan-chau (*Pinyin*, Zhangye in Gansu), Marco's 'Canpiciou', 'the capital and place of government of the whole province of Tangut', to the west of the Yellow River)	70 days by pack-ass
'Camesu' to 'the River' (For 'the River' Yule [*Cathay*, 148 n.3] suggests the Grand Canal. Lopez and	

Raymond [p. 356 n.51]
say the Yangtze,
which seems too far south)   45 days by horse

'River' to Quinsai
(= Hangzhou)   [no figure]

Quinsai to Khanbalikh   30 days

Total 274 days plus time from Grand Canal to Quinsai

There are several indications that Pegolotti is in no way abbreviating the times involved.

1. It can be seen, for instance, that he calculates seventy days for the distance between Almalyk and Zhangye. Here Yule remarks that the author of the *Masálak-al-Absár* (apparently written between 1371 and 1374) allowed only forty days between them, 'showing that the time named by Pegolotti is most ample allowance. The same author allows forty days from Kamchui [today Zhangye] to Khanbalikh.'[3]

2. Again, in his letter to the Pope from Khanbalikh, 8 January 1305, Giovanni di Montecorvino gives a more optimistic account of the time-scale for the land voyage:

> With regard to the way I make known that through the land of Toctai [the Kipchak Khan], Emperor of the northern Tartars, is the shorter way and safer, so that they will be able to come with the envoys [from Tana?] within five or six months. But the other road (by sea) is very long and dangerous, with two voyages of which the first is like the distance between Acre and the province of Provence, but the other is like the distance between Acre and England, and it might happen that they would scarcely accomplish that route in two years.[4]

3. There are some other measures of comparison for journeys through the Central Asian part of the itinerary. The Taoist sage Ch'ang Chun, aged seventy-two, went from the Chinese border (leaving March 1221) to Perwali in Kashmir (arrived May 1222), via the northern edge of the Gobi Desert, Urumchi, Tashkent, Samarkand, in fourteen months.[5] Giovanni di Pian di Carpine took a little over six months and three weeks from Kiev to the Great Khan's camp near Karakorum (riding with the *yam* from the Volga) and six months to return in 1246–7.[6] In 1253 William of Rubruck took seven months and a week to go from Soldaia to the camp of Möngke near Karakorum (7 May to 27 December). He left Karakorum in the second half

of July 1254, arrived at Gorighos in Little Armenia on 17 May 1255 and landed in Cyprus 16 June (say roughly eleven months from Karakorum to Cyprus).[7] In 1254 King Hetoum I of Little Armenia took eight months from Karakorum to Sis in Little Armenia.[8]

On occasions, delays were obviously possible. So, for instance, Venetian merchants bound for India in 1338, were blocked by ice for fifty days at Astrakhan.[9] But Rustichello's figures still seem very grossly exaggerated.

Appendix III

Marco Polo and World Maps of the Fifteenth Century

Excluded here (see illustrations) are Macrobian zone and TO maps, together with traditional world maps from Ptolemaic atlases. Also ignored are the Laon Globe (which is lost), and 'the Vinland Map', now generally acknowledged to be a forgery.[1] There remain:

1. Albertin de Virga's *World Map* (present location unknown, *ca.*1411–15). This shows Cathay (Catajo), Zaiton etc., materials which certainly derive, at least in part, from a reading of Marco. Yet the confusion in the naming of an island: 'Caparu [i.e. for Cipangu or Japan] sive Java Magna' reveals a hasty and careless attempt to digest the Book.[2]

2. Andrea Bianco's *World Map* (1436), a circular *mappamundi* forms part of an atlas produced by Bianco which is now in the Biblioteca Marciana in Venice. It shows 'the Empire of Cathay' and a representation of the Great Khan, together with an Indian Ocean with its many islands as revealed in Marco's Book. Marco's Prester John is here banished to Africa. (News, however distorted, of the Christian Negus of Abyssinia was spreading in the fifteenth century.) But Gog and Magog, rejected by Polo, are here reaffirmed, and the Terrestrial Paradise is sited above Cathay. Bianco, Master (*ammiraglio*) and *uomo di consiglio* of the Venetian galleys in the eastern trade, was obviously a serious enquirer, and he is said to have helped later in the production of the great world map of Fra Mauro (on which see below, 11). The atlas also contains a Ptolemaic world map. R. A. Skelton has speculated that Bianco is deliberately putting side by side the two different world pictures. Overall one has the sense of the difficulty in his mind of reconciling the different traditions, and of placing Marco within them.[3]

3–5. Giovanni Leardo produced three world maps: one now at Verona (1442) which is very summary; one at Vicenza (1448); one at New York (1452 or 1453). As with Bianco there is some slight Polo influence in all three, but with their representations of the Terrestrial Paradise in the East, these works follow basically the ecclesiastical tradition.[4]

6. Andreas Walsperger (1448). In the cosmographical table, now in the Vatican Library, transcribed between 1447 and 1455 by the monk Friedrich Ammann in the Benedictine monastery of St Emmeram in Bavaria, the sources given include Ptolemy, Honorius of Augustodunensis, 'Marcum den Venediger', and Pomponius Mela. (Mandeville and Lucidarius are specifically excluded as unreliable.)[5] On the other hand, Walsperger, a Benedictine who apparently had links with St Emmeram and who executed this work at Constance in 1448 is, with the author of its copy (7 below), the only major cartographer to ignore Marco almost completely in this period. Claiming to be constructed 'from the cosmography of Ptolemy', it records Quinsai, but is otherwise a mixture of different traditions, showing the Earthly Paradise, Monstrous Races around the Antarctic ('anthropophagi who eat the flesh of men'), a Prester John in India, and an 'Empire of Cathay' with a capital called 'Waldach' to the north of the Caspian.[6]

7. Anon. *ca.*1470, the Zeitz map (Bell collection, Minneapolis). This map derives in its entirety from Walsperger; 'Waldach' appears again as the capital of Cathay, etc.[7]

8. Circular 'Borgia' planisphere (first half of fifteenth century, now in the Vatican Library). Engraved on bronze, this is a work which I would think to have been drawn up simply for decorative purposes. There is a measure of knowledge of the East, some of which could derive from a vague knowledge of Marco or other writers ('From Organti to Cathay camels go in four months'; 'Lower India or Serica' where is 'the city [*sic*]' of Cathay 'in which the Emperor Great Khan has his seat'; 'Cambalec'; Upper India 'where is the body of the blessed Thomas'), and so on. But together with these things, the Caspian is shown as a branch of the ocean rather than an inland sea which no serious enquirer can have believed after the thirteenth century.[8]

9. The (so-called) 'Anonymous Genoese' Elliptical World Map (1457, in the Biblioteca Nazionale, Florence). 'This is the true description of cosmographers . . . in which frivolous stories are rejected'. Since it shows Venice as the most important town in Italy, the traditional title of this map can be discounted. Ptolemy is used for southern Asia. The influence of Conti is clear – with Java Maior (Borneo); Java Minor (Java); Sanday and Bandan, Ceylon and the Ganges Delta. But China is quite empty, and

there is no Japan. Accordingly it would seem that Marco's information has either not been considered or has been thought of as too difficult to deal with.[9]

10. The anonymous Catalan *Mappamundi* (*ca.*1450–60 Biblioteca Estense, Modena). This work, whose legends are often in Catalan, derives from the *Catalan Atlas*, of which it is a less elaborate version. Accordingly, sure enough, Marco is a major source; though in line with common fifteenth-century belief Prester John is now found in Africa.[10]

11. Fra Mauro, *Mappamundi* (1457–9) (see Illustration 9, and cf. above p. 148]. It was executed for King Afonso V of Portugal, and survives in a copy of around 1459 in the Biblioteca Marciana in Venice.

12. Fragment, Venetian style (*ca.*1460), in the Topkapi Sarai. This has legends borrowed from Marco Polo, and is possibly by Fra Mauro.[11]

13–14. Henricus Martellus Germanicus. In Yale University Library (see above Illustration 11). To which should be added that if in the British Library *Mappamundi* of Martellus (which is dated 1489 or 1490), 'Cataio' appears not as a province but a city, it may be questioned whether at that time Martellus had any direct knowledge of Maro Polo. Vietor dates the Yale map 'around 1489'. But could the presence of Japan in the map in fact mean that between the drawing of the British Library map and the Yale map, Martellus has heard of Columbus' claim to have come across Cipangu? Should, that is, the date be post 1492?

That question could be more satisfactorily answered if the three manuscripts of his *Insularium illustratum* (at Florence, Leiden and London) could be accurately dated. In these Martellus gives a detailed map of 'Cinpangu Insula', showing rivers, mountains and several cities.[12] A legend, deriving immediately from Marco, says that ships go there from the province of Quinsai in winter and return home in summer. On the east coast are represented a forest of nutmeg trees and a legend echoes Marco in saying that 'the island' is 150,000 paces from Mangi and is very large.

15. Paris Map (*ca.*1490, Bibliothèque Nationale). Charles de la Roncière argued that this work was presented to the Spanish monarchs by Columbus in 1491, a claim which has excited much controversy.[13] For what purpose Columbus should have presented Ferdinand and Isabella with a large chart of Europe and Africa together with, inset to the left of it, a comparatively diminutive *Mappamondo*, I have nowhere seen explained. However that may be, it may be conceded that this is a work of a type which Columbus might well have seen. It contains legends from

Pierre d'Ailly's *Imago Mundi*, a representation of the Earthly Paradise in the vicinity of Japan, and no elements derived from Marco Polo.

16. Martin Behaim, Terrestrial Globe (Nuremberg, 1492). See above p. 149, and Illustration 10. The globe (which has been much restored), 20 inches in diameter, was painted and inscribed by Glockenthon and Gegenhart on the basis of a chart by Behaim, citizen of Nuremberg and for many years a merchant and adventurer in Portugal.

Notes

Introduction

1 L. Olschki, *Marco Polo's Precursors* (Baltimore, 1943), 14 n. 27; S. E. Morison, *The Great Explorers: the European Discovery of America* (New York, 1978), 370; M. Collis, *Marco Polo* (London, 1959), 59; G. Caraci, 'Viaggi fra Venezia ed il Levante fino al XIV secolo e relativa produzione cartografica' in *Venezia e il Levante fino al secolo XV*, ed., A. Pertusi (Florence, 1973), 156–7; A. Margarido, 'La vision de l'autre (Africain et Indien d'Amèrique) dans la Renaissance portugaise' in *L'Humanisme portugais de l'Europe* (Paris, 1984), 512–13; M. de Gandillac, 'Sur quelques voyages utopiques' in *Voyager à la Renaissance* (Paris, 1987), 548; E. Vicentini, 'Il Milione di Marco Polo come portolano', *Italica*, 71 (1994), 145; A. E. Nordenskiöld, *Periplus* (Stockholm, 1897), 140.

2 See below pp. 109, 111–14.

Chapter 1   *Images of Asia and the Coming of the Mongols*

1 L. Réau, *Iconographie de l'Art chrétien* (Paris, 1955–9), vol. 2, 236–55; U. Monneret de Villard, *Le leggende orientali sui Magi Evangelici* (Vatican, 1952); B. Hamilton, 'Prester John and the Three Kings of Cologne', *Studies in Medieval History Presented to R. H. C. Davis*, ed. H. Mayr-Hartung and R. I. Moore (London, 1985) and now in *Prester John, the Mongols and the Ten Lost Tribes*, ed. C. F. Beckingham and B. Hamilton (Aldershot, 1996); J. B. Friedman, *The Monstrous Races in Medieval Art and Thought* (London, 1951), 172–4.

2 Yule-Cordier [above p. 6, *Note on citation of texts*], vol. 2, 425–6, 431–2; J. K. Wright, *The Geographical Lore of the Time of the Crusader* (New York, 1925; reprinted London, 1965), 272.

3 So Jacopo da Voragine in the *Legenda Aurea*, ed. T. Graesse (Osnabrück, 1969), 540–8; cf. Réau, *Iconographie*, vol. 2, 427; vol. 3, pt 1, 111, 180.

4 B. A. Lees, *Alfred the Great* (London, 1919), 190–3.

5 *Die ältesten lateinischen Thomasakten*, ed. K. Zelzer (Berlin, 1977); Voragine, *Legenda Aurea* ch. 5; F. Spadafora in *Biblioteca Sanctorum* (Rome, 1969), vol. 12, 535–9.

6 G. Cary, *The Medieval Alexander*, ed. D. J. A. Ross (Cambridge, 1967); D. J. A. Ross, *Alexander historiatus: A Guide to Medieval Illustrated Alexander Literature* (London, 1963); P. Meyer, *Alexandre le Grand dans la littérature française du Moyen Age* (Geneva, 1970); W. J. Aerts *et al.*, (eds.) *Alexander the Great in the Middle Ages* (Nijmegen, 1978).

7 A. R. Anderson, *Alexander's Gate, Gog and Magog and the Inclosed Nations* (Cambridge, Mass., 1932).

8 In translation, with kindred texts in *Le meraviglie dell'India*, ed. G. Tardiola (Rome, 1991), 63–91.

9 R. Wittkower, 'Marvels of the East: A Study in the History of Monsters', *Journal of the Warburg and Courtauld Institutes*, 5 (1942), 159–97; J. B. Friedman, *The Monstrous Races* (London, 1951); J. Le Goff, 'L'Occident médiévale et l'océan Indien: un horizon onirique' in his *Pour un autre Moyen Age* (Paris, 1977), 280–93.

10 'De adventu patriachae Indorum ad urbem sub Callisto papa II' in F. Zarncke, 'Der Priester Johannes' in *Abhandlungen der philologisch-historischen Classe der Königlich sächsischen Gesellschaft der Wissenschaften*, 7 (1879); on this theme *Prester John, the Mongols and the Ten Lost Tribes*, cited above, note 1.

11 Otto of Freising, *Chronicon*, ed. A. Hofmeister (*S.R.G. in u. sch.*, Hanover and Leipzig, 1912), vol. 7, 33; in English translation by C. C. Mierow, *The Two Cities* (New York, 1966), 443–4; C. F.

Beckingham, 'The achievements of Prester John', *Between Islam and Christendom* (London, 1983) article I.

12 *La lettera del Prete Gianni*, ed. G. Zaganelli (Parma, 1990); C. E. Nowell, 'The historical Prester John', *Speculum*, 28 (1953), 435–45; J. Richard, 'L' extrême-orient légendaire au Moyen Age: Roi David et Prêtre Jean', *Annales d'Ethiopie*, vol. 2 (1957), 225–42 and in his *Orient et Occident au Moyen Age: contacts et relations (XIIᵉ–XVᵉ siècles)* (London, 1976), article XXV; V. Slessarev, *Prester John, the Letter and the Legend* (Minneapolis, 1959); Beckingham 'Achievements of Prester John'.

13 L. Olschki, *Storia letteraria delle scoperte* (Florence, 1937), 283–4.

14 *Prester John, the Mongols and the Ten Lost Tribes* (see note 1), 184–7.

15 G. F. Hourani, *Arab Seafaring in the Indian Ocean in Ancient and Early Medieval Times* (Princeton, 1951), 66–79.

16 G. T. H. Kimble, *Geography in the Middle Ages* (London, 1938), ch. 3.

17 D. Abulafia, 'Asia, Africa and the Trade of Medieval Europe', *The Cambridge Economic History*, vol. 2, 2nd edn by M. M. Postan and E. Miller (Cambridge, 1987), 437–45.

18 H. Yule, *Cathay and the Way Thither*, 2nd edn revised by H. Cordier (London, Hakluyt, 1915; photo-reproduction, New York, 1967), 255.

19 S. Maqbul Ahmad, 'Cartography of al-Sharif al-Idrisi' in *Cartography in the Traditional Islamic and South Asian Societies (The History of Cartography*, vol. 2, pt 1, ed. J. B. Harley and D. Woodward, London, 1992), 156.

20 S. D. Goitein, 'From the Mediterranean to India', *Speculum*, 29 (1954), 181–97; *idem*, 'Letters and documents on the India Trade in medieval times', *Islamic Culture*, 37 (1963), 188–205.

21 *The Itinerary of Benjamin of Tudela*, ed. M. N. Adler (London, 1907), 62–3. This work has been in part incorporated in a recent reprint of *Jewish Travellers in the Middle Ages*, ed. E. N. Adler (New York, 1987). *The City of Light*, translated and edited by David Selbourne (London, 1997), an account of a supposed visit to China in the 1270s by one Jacob, Jew of Ancona, is a fake (for an amusing discussion, see the review by Bernard Wasserstein and David Wasserstein, 'Jacopo Spurioso', *Times Literary Supplement*, no 4937, 14 November 1997, 15–16).

22 Helpful accounts in D. Attwater, *The Christian Churches of the East* (Milwaukee, 1948).

23 J. Dauvillier, 'Les provinces chaldéennes "de l'extérieur" au Moyen Age', *Mélanges F. Cavallera* (Toulouse, 1948), 261–316, and in his *Histoire des institutions des églises orientales au Moyen Age* (London, 1983), article I.

24 J. Richard, *La Papauté et les missions d'Orient au Moyen Age (XIIIᵉ–XVᵉ siècles)* (Rome, 1977), 19–20.

25 D. Sinor, 'Un voyageur du treizième siècle: le Dominicain Julien de Hongrie', *Bulletin of the School of Oriental and African Studies*, 14 (1952), 589–602; and in his *Inner Asia and its Contacts with Medieval Europe* (London, 1977).

26 A.-D. von den Brincken, 'Le Nestorianisme vu par l'Occident' in *1274: Année Charnière: Mutations et Continuités* (Paris, 1977), 73–84, here p. 76.

27 J. J. Saunders, *The History of the Mongol Conquests* (London, 1971); D. Morgan, *The Mongols* (Oxford, 1986); M. Weiers, *Die Mongolen* (Darmstadt, 1986).

28 On Mongol-West relations H. Franke, 'Sino-Western contacts under the Mongol empire', *Journal of the Hong Kong Branch of the Royal Asiatic Society*, 6 (1966), 49–72; J. Richard, 'The Mongols and the Franks', *Journal of Asian History*, 3 (1969), 45–57, and in his *Orient et Occident*, article XXVII; G. A. Bezzola, *Die Mongolen in abendländischer Sicht 1220–1270* (Bern and Munich, 1974); D. Sinor, 'The Mongols and Western Europe' in *A History of the Crusades*, ed. K. M. Setton, vol. 3: *The Fourteenth and Fifteenth Centuries*, ed. H. W. Hazard (London, 1975), 513–44.

29 R. Southern, *Western Views of Islam in the Middle Ages* (Cambridge, Mass., 1962), 45–7; Bezzola, *Die Mongolen*, 14–28.

30 Sinor, 'Un voyageur du treizième siècle'.

31 Matthew Paris, *English History*, trans. J. A. Giles (London, 1852), vol. 1, 131–2.

32 On this Bezzola, *Die Mongolen*, 34–6, and Monneret de Villard, *Le Leggende orientali*, 182–236.

33 Matthew Paris, *English History*, vol. 1, 312, 356, 467; vol. 2, 131; vol. 3, 353, 453. See J. J. Saunders, 'Matthew Paris and the Mongols', *Essays in Medieval History presented to Bertie Wilkinson*, ed. T. A. Sandquist and M. R. Powicke (Toronto, 1969), 116–32; S. Menache, 'Tartars, Jews, Saracens and the Jewish-Mongol "Plot" of 1241', *History*, 263 (1996), 319–42; C. Burnett and P. Gautier Dalché, 'Attitudes towards the Mongols in Medieval Literature: the xxii Kings of Gog and Magog from the court of Frederick II to Jean de Mandeville', *Viator*, 22 (1991), 153–67.

34 F. Babinger, 'Maestro Ruggiero delle Puglie: relatore pre-poliano sui Tartari' in *Nel VII centenario della nascita di Marco Polo*, ed. R. Almagià (Venice, 1955), 53–61.

35 P. Jackson, 'The Crusade against the Mongols', *Journal of Ecclesiastical History*, vol. 42 (1991), 1–18.

36 For what follows, I. de Rachelwiltz, *Papal Envoys to the Great Khan* (London, 1971); Richard, *La papauté*, 63–98.

37 See Simon de Saint Quentin, *Histoire des Tartares*, ed. J. Richard (Paris, 1965); and the articles by G. G. Guzman, 'Simon of Saint-Quentin and the Dominican Mission to the Mongol Baiju: a reappraisal', *Speculum*, 46 (1971), 232–49; *idem*, 'Simon of Saint-Quentin as historian of the Mongols and Seljuk Turks', *Medievalia et Humanistica*, 49, n.s. 3 (1972), 155–78; G. G. Guzman, 'The Encyclopedist Vincent of Beauvais and his Mongol extracts from John of Plano Carpini and Simon of Saint-Quentin', *Speculum*, 49 (1974), 287–307.

38 See below, notes 39 and 40.

39 Benedict's shorter version, which survives in two manuscripts, is in *Sinica Franciscana*, ed. A. van den Wyngaert (Quaracchi, 1929), vol. 1, 135–41; translated into English by 'a Nun of Stanbrook Abbey' in *The Mongol Mission*, ed. C. Dawson (London, 1955; reprinted as *Mission to Asia*, New York, 1987), 79–84. The longer version, existing in only one manuscript, has been edited by A. Önnerors, *Hystoria Tartarorum C. de Bridia monachi* (Berlin, 1967), and with translation and commentary by G. D. Painter in *The Vinland Map and the Tartar Relation*, ed. R. A. Skelton, T. E. Marston and G. D. Painter (London, 1965), 21–106. F. R. Maddison's doubts on its authenticity (in his, 'A sceptical view of the Tartar Relation', pp. 187–91 in ed. H. G. Wallis (ed.), 'The strange case of the Vinland Map; A Symposium', *Geographical Journal*, cxl, [1974] 183–211) seem to have found no followers.

40 The shorter, in eight chapters, survives in twelve manuscripts and a later abridgement. The second version which has a ninth chapter describing the itinerary exists in three manuscripts. Edited in *Sinica Franciscana*, vol. 1, 3–134, it too is translated in *The Mongol Mission*, 3–76 (see n. 39 above). More recently it has been re-edited, together with an Italian translation, as *Storia dei Mongoli*, ed. E. Menestò, with contributions by P. Daffinà, C. Leonardi, M. C. Lungarotti and L. Petech (Spoleto, 1989). For another manuscript to those detailed in Menestò, see F. E. Reichert, *Begegnungen mit China: Die Entdeckung Ostasiens im Mittelalter* (Sigmaringen, 1992), 152.

41 J. Fried, 'Auf der Suche nach der Wirklichkeit. Die Mongolen und die europäische Erfahrungswissenschaft im 13. Jahrhundert', *Historische Zeitschrift*, 243 (1986), 287–332, here 304–5, 315–16; for an enthusiastic assessment, J. K. Hyde, 'Ethnographers in search of an audience' in his *Literacy and its Uses: Studies on late medieval Italy*, ed. D. Waley (Manchester, 1993), 162–216, here 173–83.

42 *Storia dei Mongoli*, ed. Menestò, 229, translated in *The Mongol Mission*, 4.

43 Rachelwiltz, *Papal Envoys*, 106–7; F. W. Cleaves, 'An early Mongol version of the Alexander Romance', *Harvard Journal of Asiatic Studies*, 22 (1959), 1–99.

44 *Storia dei Mongoli*, ed. Menestò, 229–30, and Daffinà's notes, 407–9.

45 *Ibid.*, 257–8.

46 *Ibid.*, 289–90; Painter in *The Vinland Map*, 104–6, sought to make sense of these names; but compare Daffinà's notes to Menestò, 467–71.

47 Salimbene de Adam, *Cronica*, ed. G. Scalia (Bari, 1966), 197–8. The famous Franciscan preacher, Berthold of Regensburg, would introduce the Mongols in his sermons, drawing on Giovanni di Pian di Carpine and other sources, but with no geographical references, and merely to hold up Mongol vices as a mirror to the sinfulness of Christians: J. Hanske and A. Kuotsala, 'Berthold von Regensburg, O. F. M. and the Mongol-Medieval Sermon as a historical source', *Archivium Franciscanum Historicum*, 89 (1996), 425–45.

48 Translated from the Persian by A. J. Boyle in Rachelwiltz, *Papal Envoys*, 213–14.

49 This was later included in the *Speculum Historiale* of Vincent de Beauvais. H. Yule, *Cathay*, vol. 1, 262–3 (where the old French translation from Guillaume de Nangis' *Vie de Saint Louis* is printed); vol. 4, 266; F. E. Reichert, *Begegnungen mit China* (Sigmaringen, 1992), 72; on the growing influence of Christianity at Möngke's court, B. Spuler, 'Le Christianisme chez les Mongols aux XIIIᵉ et XIVᵉ siècles' in *1274: Année charnière*, 45–54.

50 Something on this in Joinville's life of the King, writing in his mid-eighties of events some fifty years before, in *Memoirs of the Crusades by Villehardouin and de Joinville*, trans. F. Marzialis (London, 1908), 168–9, 253–9.

51 For this mission Guillaume de Rubruck, *Itinerarium* in *Sinica Franciscana*, vol. 1, 147–332. English translations in *Mongol Mission*, 89–220; and with commentary, *The Mission of Friar William of Rubruck: His Journey to the Court of the Great Khan Möngke, 1253–1255*, ed. P. Jackson and D. O. Morgan (London, Hakluyt, 1990); French version and commentary, Rubruck, *Voyage dans l'Empire Mongol 1253–1255*, ed. C. Kappler and R. Kappler (Paris, 1985).

52 See L. Olschki, *Guillaume Boucher, A French Artist at the Court of the Khans* (Baltimore, 1946).

53 Reichert, *Begegnungen*, 112.

54 *Ibid.*, 88–111.

55 R. Vaughan, *Chronicles of Matthew Paris* (Cambridge, 1958), 153–4.

56 See above notes 40 and 41. One of the few chroniclers to use Giovanni is the Dominican, Francesco Pipino (the translator of Marco Polo into Latin) in his *Chronicon* (Foscolo Benedetto cxxxvii–cxxxviii).

57 See Guzman's articles cited in note 38 above.

58 Reichert, *Begegnungen*, 218–19, cites Martin of Troppau (d.1278), Ranulf Higden (d.1364), Henry of Hereford (d.1370), Paulinus Minorita (d.1344), Giovanni Colonna, Guillaume de Nangis, the anonymous author of the *Flores temporum* (1290–4), and Saint Antoninus of Florence (d.1459) in his *Chronicorum opus*.

59 *The Opus Majus of Roger Bacon*, ed. J. H. Bridges (Oxford, 1897), vol. 1, 303, 305, 323, 400; vol. 2, 368, 383, 387–8. See A.-D. von den Brincken, 'Le Nestorianisme vu par l'Occident' in *1274: Année charnière*, 78; Reichert, *Begegnungen*, 230–1. On the manuscripts of the *Opus Majus*, see *Roger Bacon: Essays*, ed. A. G. Little (Oxford, 1914), 379.

60 The fullest list for Rubruck is still in *The Texts and Versions of John de Plano Carpini and William de Rubruquis*, ed. C. R. Beazley (London, 1903), xvii–xix, which refers to five (and a possible, lost sixth) medieval manuscripts, of which four are from England.

61 J. Heers, *Marco Polo* (Paris, 1983), 125–8; M. Chahin, *The Kingdom of Armenia* (London, 1987), ch. 25. King Hetoum I (1226–1270) visited the Mongol court in 1254: J. A. Boyle 'The journey of Het 'um I, King of Little Armenia, to the Court of the Great Khan Möngke', *Central Asiatic Journal*, 9 (1964), 175–81, and in his *The Mongol World Empire 1206–1370* (London, 1977). G. G. Guzman, in his 'European clerical envoys to the Mongols. Reports of western merchants in Eastern Europe and Central Asia 1231–1255', *Journal of Modern History*, vol. 22 (1996), 53–67, observes, however, that merchants in this period appear to have provided Europe with little information on the Mongols.

62 B. Cecchetti, 'Testamento di Pietro Vioni veneziano fatto in Tauris [Persia] MCCLXIV [*sic*] X decembre', *Archivio Veneto*, 26 (1883), 161–5; for the date A.

Stussi, 'Un testamento volgare scritto in Persia nel 1263', *L'Italia dialettale*, n. s. 11 (1962), 24; E. Ashtor, *Levant Trade in the Later Middle Ages* (Princeton, 1984), 58. This Pietro's father, Vitale, owned a palace in S. Giovanni Grisostomo in Venice which may well be the same 'Milione' bought by the Polo family, Heers, *Marco Polo*, 41.

63 J. Richard, 'Les Mongols et l'Occident: deux siècles de contacts' in *1274, Anné charnière*, 91 (and in his *Croisés, missionnaires et voyageurs*, London, 1983, article XIV).

64 For what follows see J. A. Boyle, 'The Il-Khans of Persia and the Christian West', *History Today*, and in his *The Mongol World Empire*, vol. 13; J. Richard, 'Le début des relations entre la papauté et les Mongols de Perse', *Journal Asiatique*, 237 (1949), 291–7, and in his *Les Relations entre l'Orient et l'Occident du Moyen Age* (London, 1977). For background D. Morgan, *Medieval Persia 1040–1797* (London, 1988), chs 7 and 8.

65 See C. Brunel, 'David Ashby, auteur méconnu des "Faites des Tartares"', *Romania*, 79 (1958), 39–46. Ashby's treatise, surviving in only one manuscript, was destroyed in 1904.

66 See W. Budge, *The Monks of Kûblâ Khân* (London, 1929); A. C. Moule, *Christians in China before the year 1550* (London, 1930), ch. 4; J. Richard, 'La mission en Europe de Rabban Çauma et l'union des églises', in his *Orient et Occident au Moyen Age: contacts et relations (XIIe–XIVe s.)* (London, 1976); M. Rossabi, *Voyager from Xanadu: Rabban Sauma and the first Journey from China to the West* (London, 1992).

67 See below p. 120. It is probably no coincidence that it was in 1288 that the Catalan missionary enthusiast, Ramon Llull wrote his account of a mystical conversion of a Mongol, the *Liber Tartari et Christiani*, on which E. Allison Peers, *Ramon Llull: a Biography* (London, 1929), 197–200.

68 Heers, *Marco Polo*, 99; L. F. Salzmann, *Medieval Byways* (London, 1913), 45–50.

69 S. Schein, 'Gesta Dei per Mongolos 1300: the Genesis of a non-event', *English Historical Review*, 94 (1979), 805–19.

Chapter 2   *The Polos*

1 Pauthier's identification (ix, 361) of Marco with a Po-loh who was a commissioner of the Great Khan's Privy Council has been shown to be mistaken: Li Tse-fen, 'Reality and myth in the Milione of Marco Polo' (in Chinese) *The Eastern Miscellany*, October/November 1977, translated by I. N. Molinari, 'Un articolo d'autore cinese su Marco Polo e la Cina', Supplement no. 30, *Istituto Orientale di Napoli: Annali*, 42 (1982), fasc. 1, 9–17. 54–60.

2 For analogous biographical sources with a similar 'unmodern' sense of literary sincerity, J. Larner, 'Traditions of literary biography in Boccaccio's Life of Dante', *Towns and Townspeople in Medieval and Renaissance Europe: Essays in Memory of J. K. Hyde*, ed., B. Pullan and S. Reynolds, *Bulletin of the John Rylands University Library of Manchester*, 72, (1990), 107–17; P. Rubin, 'What men saw: Vasari's Life of Leonardo da Vinci and the Image of the Renaissance Artist', *Art History*, 13 (1990), 34–46.

3 V. Bertolucci Pizzorusso, 'Enunciazione e produzione del testo nel *Milione*', *Studi mediolatini e volgari*, 25 (1977), 5–43, here 21–2.

4 G. Orlandini, 'Marco Polo e la sua famiglia', *Archivio Veneto Tridentino*, 9 (1926), 68. See too R. Gallo, 'Marco Polo: la sua famiglia e il suo libro' in *Nel VII centenario della nascita di Marco Polo*, ed. R. Almagià (Venice, 1955), 65–193.

5 Heers, *Marco Polo*, 124–5.

6 Ibid., 60, 118–24; F. Thiriet, *La Roumanie vénetienne au Moyen Age* (Paris, 1959), 37, 46, 91, 341.

7 See G. I. Bratianu, *Recherches sur le commerce génois dans la Mer Noire au XIIIe siècle* (Paris, 1924), and Heers, *Marco Polo*, passim.

8 Yule-Cordier, vol. 1, 3.

9 Compare L. Olschki, *Marco Polo's Precursors* (Baltimore, 1943), 73–4, with the account of the 1338 expedition in R. S. Lopez, 'L'extrême frontière de l'Europe médiévale', *Le Moyen Age* (1963), 488.

10 As suggested by F. C. Lane, *Venice: A Maritime Republic* (Baltimore, 1973), 80.

[11] Not 'in 1262': P. Jackson, 'The dissolution of the Mongol empire', *Central Asiatic Journal*, 22 (1978), 233–4.

[12] Yule-Cordier, vol. 1, 9 n. 5. At this point Birac is said to be 'king' of Bukhara. Yet he ruled 1266–70; Moule-Pelliot, vol. 1, 22–3.

[13] H. Franke, 'Sino-Western contacts', in his *China Under Western Rule* (Aldershot, 1994), 54–5.

[14] Pipino, I, ii, ed. Prásek, 8.

[15] M. Bihl (with transcripts of letters by A. C. Moule) 'De duabus epistolis fratrum minorum tartariae aquilonis an. 1323', *Archivium Franciscanum historicum*, 16 (1923), 89–112, here 109.

[16] Olschki, *Marco Polo's Precursors*, 86.

[17] See Appendix II.

[18] M. H. Laurent, 'Grégoire X et Marco Polo (1266–71)', *Mèlanges d'archéologie et d'histoire*, 58 (1941–6), 132–44; Moule-Pelliot, vol. 1, 23–5.

[19] Boncompagno da Signa in his *De malo senectutis*, in P. Molmenti, *Venice*, trans. H. F. Brown, (London, 1906), 45.

[20] Martin da Canal, *Les Estoires de Venise*, ed. A. Limentani (Florence, 1972), 128–30; 246–62; 288–300; 328–32; E. Muir's *Civic Ritual in Renaissance Venice* (Princeton, 1981) has much interesting discussion of pre-Renaissance ceremonies.

[21] Molmenti, *Venice*, 115, from Martin da Canal.

[22] *Merchant Culture in Fourteenth Century Venice: the Zibaldone da Canal*, translated and introduced J. E. Dotson (Binghamton, 1994), 10; original text, A. Stussi, *Zibaldone manoscritto mercantile del sec. XIV* (Venice, 1967).

[23] *Merchant Culture*, 50–1.

[24] See the articles of G. Arnaldi, 'Scuole nella Marca Trevigiana e a Venezia nel secolo XIII'; L. Renzi, 'Il francese come lingua letteraria e il franco-lombardo'; G. Folena, 'Tradizione e cultura trobadorica nelle corti e nelle città venete'; M. Cortelazzo, 'La cultura mecantile e marinaresca'; and A. Limentani, 'Martin da Canal e "Les Estoires de Venise"' in *Storia della cultura veneta*, ed. G. Arnaldi (Vicenza, 1976) vol. 1; F. Brugnoli, 'I toscani nel Veneto e le cerchie toscaneggianti' in *ibid.*, vol. 2; A. Monteverdi, 'Lingua e letteratura a Venezia nel secolo di Marco Polo' in *Storia della civiltà veneziana*, ed. V. Branca, F. Braudel, A. Tenenti (Florence, 1979) vol. 1 – where for Venetian *volgare* see particularly 360–1.

[25] Moule-Pelliot's suggestion (vol. 1, 25–6 n. 2) that Marco might have met Rustichello, his future collaborator, at this time rests on, first, a belief in the truth of Rustichello's claim that he drew the material for his *Méliadus* from a work owned by Edward I, and, second, on the speculation that Rustichello might have met Edward in the Holy Land rather than in Italy before or after that time.

[26] Visconti learnt of his election 23 October 1271; on the 11th or 18th of November he sailed for Brindisi; Laurent, 'Gregoire X et Marco Polo', 137.

[27] Fra William is presumably the author of the *De statu Saracenorum et Mahomete pseudopropheta eorum et eorum lege et fide*, redacted in 1273, published by H. Prutz, *Kulturgeschichte der Kreuzzüge* (Berlin, 1883), 572–98. On this work see U. Monneret de Villard, *Lo studio dell'Islam in Europa nel XII e XIII secolo* (Vatican, 1944), 70; P. A. Throop, *Criticism of the Crusade* (Amsterdam, 1940), ch. 5, refers to four manuscripts, three in Latin, one in French. This William of Tripoli, who was a Dominican, cannot be, as has been suggested, the Franciscan, Guillaume Champenois mentioned in the *Geste des Chiprois* under the year 1239 (see Throop, *Criticism*, 118 n. 19).

[28] R. Amitai-Preiss, *Mongols and Mamlukes: The Mamluk-Ilkhanid War 1260–1281* (Cambridge, 1995), 125–7; P. Thorau, *The Lion of Egypt: Sultan Baybars I and the Near East in the Thirteenth Century*, trans. P. M. Holt (London, 1992), 204–10.

[29] Bertolucci Pizzorusso, 'Enunciazione . . . Milione', *Studimediolatinc e volgari*, 25 (1977), 20–1.

[30] D. Morgan, *The Mongols* (Oxford, 1986), 110–11; M. Rossabi, 'The Muslims in the Early Yüan Dynasty' in *China under Mongol Rule*, ed. J. D. Langlois (Princeton, 1981), 257–95. See, too, M. Rossabi's *Khubilai Khan: His Life and Times* (London, 1988), 178–84; F. E. Reichert, *Begegnungen mit China* (Sigmaringen, 1992), 115, n. 315.

31 Yule-Cordier, vol. 1, 27 n. 1; vol. 3, 74.
32 Chapter XVI; on Khubilai's missions, W. W. Rockhill, 'Notes on the relations and trade of China with the Eastern Archipelago and the Coast of the Indian Ocean during the Fourteenth Century. Pt. i', *T'oung Pao*, 15 (1914), 430–43.
33 M. Rossabi, 'The reign of Khubilai Khan' in *The Cambridge History of China*, vol. 6: *Alien Regimes and Border States 907–1368*, ed. H. Franke and D. Twitchett (Cambridge, 1994), 416–18; J. W. Haeger, 'Marco Polo in China? Problems with internal evidence', *Bulletin of Sung and Yuan Studies*, 14 (1978), 27.
34 F. W. Cleaves, 'A Chinese source bearing on Marco Polo's departure and a Persian source on his arrival in Persia', *Harvard Journal of Asiatic Studies*, 15 (1952), 419–506. Rashid al-Din mentions only Khwaja (whom Polo calls Coja) in the embassy; J. A. Boyle, 'Marco Polo and his Description of the World', *History Today* (1971), 765 (and in his *The Mongol World Empire 1266–1370*, London, 1977, article XV). Boyle thinks that he ignores the Polos because they were not official emissaries; D. Morgan, *The Mongols*, (Oxford, 1986), 193, because mere Franks were unworthy of his pen.
35 As appears from Maffeo's will of 6 February 1310 at which time only 1,000 *hyperpyra* had been recovered, Orlandini, 'Marco Polo', 14. Maffeo's will also refers to the 'three gold tablets which were of the *magni chani* of the Tartars', ibid., 27, and, later, mentions the *fraterna compagnia*.
36 Moule-Pelliot, vol. 1, 34–5.
37 Yule-Cordier, vol. 1, 52–3.
38 See above p. 28.
39 R. Gallo, 'Nuovi documenti riguardanti Marco Polo e la sua famiglia', *Atti dell' Istituto Veneto di Scienze, lettere ed arti: Classe di scienze morali e lettere*, 116 (1958), 313–15.
40 Foscolo Benedetto, cxciv.
41 *Ibid.*, ccxii–ccxiv; Yule-Cordier, vol. 1, 120.
42 See below, page 55.
43 Orlandini, 'Marco Polo', 58–62; Moule-Pelliot, vol. 1, 554ff.
44 Moule-Pelliot, vol. 1, 30.
45 Foscolo Benedetto, cxciv; translated Yule-Cordier, vol. 1, 54.

Chapter 3 *Marco Polo and Rustichello*

1 C. Segre, 'Marco Polo, Filologia e industria culturale' in C. Segre, G. Ronchi, M. Milanesi, *Avventure del "Milione"* (Parma, 1983), 10–14.
2 V. Bertolucci Pizzorusso, 'Lingue e stili nel "Milione"', in *L'epopea delle scoperte*, ed. R. Zorzi (Venice, 1994), 63.
3 *Milione. Le Divisament dou monde*, ed. G. Ronchi (Milan, 1982), 1, line 7.
4 J. Heers, *Marco Polo* (Paris, 1983), 277.
5 G. Bertoni in a review (characterised by a singular meanness of spirit) of Foscolo Benedetto in *Giornale storico della letteratura italiana*, 92 (1928), argued, 286–7 for 'Rusticiano'. But see L. Foscolo Benedetto, 'Non Rusticiano ma Rustichello', in his *Uomini e Tempi: Pagine varie di critica e storia* (Milan, 1953), 63–70.
6 Heers, *Marco Polo*, 283–4, citing E. Cristiani, *Nobilità e Popolo nel comune de Pisa* (Naples, 1962), 470; G. della Guerra, *Rustichello da Pisa* (Pisa, 1955); A. Joris, 'Autour du Divisament du Monde. Rusticien de Pise et l'empereur Henri VII de Luxembourg (1310–1313)', *Le Moyen Age* (1994), 353–68; R. Morozzo della Rocca, 'Sulle orme di Polo', *L'Italia che scrive*, 37, 11.10 (Oct. 1954), 120.
7 Foscolo Benedetto, xiv–xviii; Bertolucci Pizzorusso, 'Lingue e stili', 65–6; cf. E. Löseth, *Le Roman en prose de Tristan, le roman de Palamedes et la compilation de Rusticien de Pise* (Paris, 1891, *Bibliothèque de l'École des Hautes Études*, 82 1890 [sic], reprinted New York, 1970), 423–74.
8 See E. G. Gardner, *The Arthurian Legend in Italian Literature* (London, 1938); A. Viscardi, 'Arthurian influences in Italian Literature 1200–1500' in *Arthurian Literature in the Middle Ages*, ed. R. S. Loomis (Oxford, 1959), ch. 32; D. Branca, *I romanzi italiani di Tristano e la 'Tavola ritonda'* (Florence, 1968); A. Viscardi, *Letteratura Franco-Italiana* (Modena, 1941); S. Roncaglia, 'La Letteratura franco-veneta' in *Storia di letteratura italiana*, ed. E. Cecchi and N. Sapegno, *Il Trecento* (Milan, 1965), vol. 2, 727–59; L. Renzi, 'Il francese come lingua letteraria e il franco-lombardo' in *Storia della cultura*

veneta, ed. G. Arnaldi (Vicenza, 1976), vol. 1, 563–89; and J. Critchley, *Marco Polo's Book* (Aldershot, 1992), 19–22.

9 Compare R. S. Loomis, 'Edward I, Arthurian Enthusiast', *Speculum*, 28 (1953), 114–27; with M. Prestwich, *Edward I* (London, 1988), 117–20 (who, however, believes the Rustichello story). Against loan or gift of the book, Critchley, *Marco Polo's Book*, 4–8.

10 On chivalric-epic prose style see J. Frappier, *Étude sur "La mort le roi Artu"* (Geneva, 1968), ch. 7; Limentani in Martin da Canal, *Les Estoires de Venise* (Florence, 1972), ccxliii–ccliii; cccii–ccciii.

11 Foscolo-Benedetto, xix–xxvi.

12 V. Bertolucci Pizzorusso, 'Enunciazione e produzione', *Studi mediolatini e volgari* 25 (1977), 8.

13 Ramusio, 233; Moule-Pelliot, vol. 1, 73.

14 B. Wehr, 'A propos de la genèse du "Devisement dou Monde" de Marco Polo', *Le passage à l'écrit des langues romanes*, ed. M. Selig, B. Frank, J. Hartmann (Tübingen, 1993, *Scripta Oralia*, 46), 299–326.

15 G. P. Cuttino, *English Diplomatic Administration 1259–1339* (2nd edn, Oxford, 1971), 175–6.

16 Moule-Pelliot, vol. 2, CXXVIII–CXXIX; F. E. Reichert, *Begegnungen mit China* (Sigmaringen, 1992), 147, 157.

17 Foscolo Benedetto, xxxix, LVI–LVIII; J. Petit, 'Un capitaine du règne de Philippe le Bel: Thibault de Chepoy', *Le Moyen Age*, 10 (1897), 224–39, here 232–4.

18 *Milione. Le Divisament*, chs 223–8, Reichert, *Begegnungen*, 147.

19 See E. Vinaver, *The Rise of Romance* (Oxford, 1971), ch. v.

20 Marco Polo, *Milione*, ed. V. Bertolucci Pizzorusso (Milan, 1975), 468–9. This edition is essential for consideration of the early Tuscan texts.

21 C. E. Pickford, 'Miscellaneous French Prose Romances' in *Arthurian Literature in the Middle Ages*, ed. R. S. Loomis (Oxford, 1959), 352.

22 Yule-Cordier, vol. 2, 456, 462.

23 *Ibid.*, vol. 1, Yule's introduction, lxxxiii.

24 Heers, *Marco Polo*, 315.

25 Moule-Pelliot, vol. 1, 40–1.

26 See below, page 127.

27 So Reichert, *Begegnungen*, 157. Critchley, *Marco Polo's Book*, 173–7.

28 P. Demiéville, 'La situation religeuse en Chine au temps de Marco Polo', in *Oriente Poliano: studi e conferenze . . . in occasione del VII Centenario della nascita di Marco Polo* (Rome, 1957), 193–236, here, 223–4.

29 See A. N. Waldron, 'The problem of the Great Wall', *Harvard Journal of Asiatic Studies*, 42 (1983), 643–63.

30 Heers, *Marco Polo*, 174.

31 P. Pelliot, *Notes on Marco Polo*, ed. L. Hambis (Paris, 1959–73), vol. 1, 366, 603–6, 803, 813, 842.

32 *Ibid.*, vol. 1, 652–61.

33 Yule-Cordier, vol. 1,448 n.1; vol. 2, 74; P. Pelliot, 'Kao-Tch'ang, Qoco, Houo-Tcheou et Qara-Khodja', *Journal Asiatique*, s.10, 19 (1912), 592.

34 H. Franke, 'Sino-Western contacts under the Mongol Empire', 53–4, in his *China under Mongol Rule* (Aldershot, 1994), article VII; R. Trauzettel, 'Die Yüan-Dynastie' in *Die Mongolen*, ed. M. Weiers (Darmstadt, 1986), 233 suspects that Marco had been no further than Karakorum and had gained most of his knowledge from merchants who had been there. F. Wood, *Did Marco Polo go to China?* (London, 1995), denies that the Polos got any further than Bukhara, thus reviving the thesis of *Astley's Voyages* (London, 1747), see below pp. 174–5.

35 Yule-Cordier, vol. 1, 380.

36 L. Olschki, *L'Asia di Marco Polo: introduzione alla lettura a allo studio del Milione* (Venice, 1957), 193 n. 47; for the Persian cosmographer who presented a terrestrial globe to Khubilai in 1267, R. J. Smith, *Chinese Maps* (Hong Kong, 1996), 45–6; Yule-Cordier, vol. 1, 455–6. This is not, of course, to say that the Chinese did not produce their own maps.

37 Wood, *Did Marco Polo go to China?*, 130, 146, 148. See the will in G. Orlandini, 'Marco Polo e la su famiglia?', *Archivio Veneto Tridentino*, vol. 9 (1926), 25–31.

38 See below pp.111–13.

39 See H. Franke, 'Some sinological remarks on Rashid al-Din's history of China' in his *China under Mongol Rule* (Aldershot, 1994), vol. 3; J. A. G. Boyle, 'Rashid al-

Din: the first world historian', in his *The Mongol World Empire 1206–1370* (London, 1977), article XXIX.

40 Li Tse-fen, 'Reality and myth in the Milione of Marco Polo' (in Chinese) *The Eastern Miscellany*, October/November 1977, translated by I. N. Molinari, 'Un articolo d'autore cinese su Marco Polo e la Cina', Supplement no. 30, *Istituto Orientale di Napoli: Annali*, 42 (1982), fasc. ii, 17. A. C. Moule, *Christians in China before the year 1500* (London, 1930), 139 n. 19. On the other hand Peng Hai, 'When was Marco Polo in Yangzhou?' (in Chinese), *Lishi Yanjiu* (1980), accepts his governorship and dates it to 1282–5. In the case of Yangzhou, Wood, *Did Marco Polo go to China?*, 132–3, reports a Chinese scholar's suggestion that what Rustichello originally wrote was that Marco 'sejourna' or stayed there for three years, and that this was incorrectly copied as 'governa'. But the phrase the F text uses is '*seigneurie ceste cité*' which seems much less capable of being misread in this way.

41 Li Tse-fen, 'Reality and myth', 29–32, 65ff. A. C. Moule, *Quinsai with other notes on Marco Polo* (Cambridge, 1957), 70–8. And before these, Yule, vol. 2, 128–31.

42 Critchley, *Marco Polo's Book*, 38–42.

43 *Ibid.*, xii xiii.

44 Li Tse-fen, 'Reality and myth', *passim*.

45 H. Franke, 'Could the Mongol emperors read and write Chinese?', *Asia Minor* (1953), 29–30 (and in his *China under Mongol Rule*, article V).

46 Rossabi, 'The Muslims' in *China under Mongol Rule*, ed. J. D. Langlois (Princeton, 1981), 257–95. See, too, M. Rossabi, *Khubilai Khan* (London, 1988), 178–84. For a bibliography, Reichert, *Begegnungen*, 115 n. 315.

47 Ramusio, 166–69 on whom Moule, *Quinsai*, 79–88.

48 Critchley, *Marco Polo's Book*, 78–9, citing P. H-c. Ch'en, *Chinese Legal Tradition under the Mongols* (Princeton, 1979), 134–5; Olschki, *L'Asia*, 172–6.

49 C. Bauer, 'Venezianische Salzhandelspolitik bis zum Ende des 14. Jahrhunderts', *Vierteljahrschrift für Wirtschaftsgeschichte*, 22 (1930), 273–323, and now, above all, J. C. Hocquet, *Le sel et la fortune de Venise* (Lille, 1978–9).

50 J. W. Haeger, 'Marco Polo in China? Problems with internal evidence', *Bulletin of Sung and Yuan Studies*, 14 (1978), 22–30.

51 *Ibid.*, 25.

52 On Marco's Peking, Wood, *Did Marco Polo go to China?*, 82–8.

53 Haeger, 'Marco Polo in China?', 28.

Chapter 4   *The Making of the Book*

1 Chapter CLX, 19. Good on this, D. Rieger, 'Marco Polo und Rustichello da Pisa. Der Reisende und sein Erzähler', *Reise und Reiseliteratur in der Frühen Neuzeit*, ed. X. von Ertzdorff and D. Neukirch (Amsterdam, 1992), 289–312.

2 For other doubts: W. Lentz, 'War Marco Polo auf dem Pamir?', *Zeitung der Deutschen Morgenländischen Gesellschaft*, 86 (1933), 1–32.

3 U. Tucci, 'I primi viaggiatori e l'opera di Marco Polo' in *Storia della cultural veneta*, ed. G. Folena, vol. 1 (Vicenza, 1976), 650. Tucci's comments on the absence of any references in the work to 'i valori artistici' (649) should be seen in relation to the fact that such values were not found in western literature of the thirteenth century, and only very occasionally in that of the fourteenth.

4 F. Borlandi, 'Alle origini del libro di Marco Polo' in *Studi in onore de A. Fanfani*, vol. 1 (Milan, 1962), 105–47. Similar in A. Carile, 'Territorio e ambiente nel 'Divisament dou Monde', *Studi veneziani*, 1 (1977), 13 36 and E. Vicentini, 'Il Milione di Marco Polo come portolano', *Italica*, 71:2 (1994), 145–52.

5 Foscolo Benedetto, ccx–ccxi.

6 See, below, pp. 118, 187–9.

7 R. S. Lopez, 'Nouveaux documents sur les marchands italiens en Chine à l'époque mongole', *Académie des Inscriptions et Belles Lettres: Comptes Rendus* (1977), 452; L. Petech, (Les marchands italiens dans l'empire mongole), *Revue Asiatique*, 1977, 250; 1962, 552), claims that there is less on commerce in Polo's Book than that of the friar Odorico, an overstatement. Against his own thesis Carile (note 4, above) very fairly cites two

passages: 'hi vienent maintes nes con maintes mercandies . . . draps d'ore et de soie . . . et de maintes autres couses que nos ne vos conteron eci' (CXCII) and 'il hi a encore maintes autres mercandies de quelz ne firai memoire nostre livre parce que trop seroit longaine matiere a mentovoir' (CLXXXVII). In fact these are taken from the northern-French translation and do not occur in the F version, but stress the vagueness often found in Marco's accounts of trade, which at this point the translator by these remarks feels himself compelled to underline.

8 J. Heers, *Marco Polo* (Paris, 1983), 258–9.

9 P. Pelliot, *Notes on Marco Polo*, ed. L. Hambis (Paris, 1959–73), vol. 2, 872–4.

10 T. Allsen, 'Mongolian princes and their merchant partners', *Asia Major*, 3rd. series, vol. 2, pt 2 (1989), 82–126.

11 Heers, *Marco Polo*, 168–70, who, however, detects in Marco a mercantile mentality, 172–4. Lopez, 'Nouveaux documents', 452, remarks on the absence of notices on organisations of voyages, volume of business, conditions and problems of markets, concluding that Marco is 'souvent trop anxieux de se montrer gentilhomme pour se pencher sur les menus détails du commerce'. On merchant secrecy, Heers, *Marco Polo* 168, and F. E. Reichert, *Begegnungen mit China* (Singmaringen, 1992), 79–80.

12 L. Olschki, *L'Asia di Marco Polo* (Venice, 1957, [and in English translation, Berkeley and Los Angeles, 1960]), 109–18, 178. Compare p. 112: 'i tre Veneziani si sentirano sempre come apostoli laici della fede' with p. 119 'Perciò Marco Polo non fu né mercante né missionario . . .'

13 See below, p. 113.

14 On whom Yule-Cordier, vol. 1, 348.

15 Yule-Cordier, vol. 2, 323–8.

16 Ramusio, 193; Moule-Pelliot, vol. 1, 254–5.

17 Above, p. 24.

18 Only in Ramusio, II, 156–7.

19 Moule-Pelliot, vol. 1, 96; vol. 2, 21; it appears too in the summary of the Book by Jacopo d'Acqui (Foscolo Benedetto, cxcii–cxcviiii).

20 C. Segre, 'Marco Polo' in C. Segre, G. Ronchi, M. Milanesi, *Avventure del 'Milione'* (Parma, 1983), 15.

21 J. Heers, 'De Marco Polo', 135; and *idem*, *Marco Polo*, 317, 322–30.

22 Brunetto Latini, *Li Livres dou Tresor*, ed. F. J. Carmody (Berkeley, 1948), 109–21; Ristoro d'Arezzo, *La composizione del Mondo colle sue cascioni*, ed. A. Morino (Florence, 1976), 134–7 for the geography.

23 Foscolo Benedetto, xxxvi [A2]; xxxviii [B1].

24 U. Monneret de Villard, *Le Leggende orientali* (Vatican, 1952), 182–236.

25 F. M. Rogers, *The Travels of the Infante Dom Pedro of Portugal* (Cambridge, Mass., 1961), ch. 6.

26 Gerald of Wales, *The History and Topography of Ireland*, trans. J. J. O'Meara (Harmondsworth, 1982), 57.

27 *Ibid.*, 57–8.

28 Gervais de Tilbury, *Le Livre des Merveilles*, trans. A. Duchesne (Paris, 1992), 20–2.

29 P.-Y. Badel, 'Lire la merveille selon Marco Polo', *Revue des Sciences humaines*, 183 (1981), 7–16, here 11–12.

30 On the concept, J. Le Goff, 'The Marvellous in the Medieval West' in his *The Medieval Imagination*, trans. A. Goldhammer (Chicago, 1988), 27–44.

31 Yule-Cordier, vol. 2, 194.

32 Olschki, *L'Asia*, 385–91.

33 H. Yule, *Cathay and the Way Thither*, rev. H. Cordier (London, 1915; New York, 1967), vol. 2, 239.

34 Though, as Olschki points out, *L'Asia*, 342, Chau Ju-Kua knew there was not much gold in Japan.

35 Pelliot, *Notes*, vol. 2, 671–725 (isle of women); Yule-Cordier, vol. 3, 109–10 (dog-headed barbarians); 120–1 (two islands, male and female); 120 (the Rukh) are all found in Chau Ju-Kua's *Description of Barbarous Peoples*. For the Rukh in Arab folk-lore, R. Irwin, *The Arabian Nights: A Companion* (Harmondsworth, 1995), 207.

36 J. Needham, with Wang Ling, *Science and Civilisation in China*, vol. 3, (Mathematics and the Sciences of the Heavens and the Earth), (Cambridge, 1959), 503ff; R. J. Smith, *Chinese Maps* (Hong Kong, 1996), 16–19.

37 'tuit les homes de ceste ysle ont chief come chien et dens et iaux come chiens; car je voç

di qu'il sunt tuit senblable a chief de grant chienz mastin'; cf. Yule-Cordier, vol. 2, 311.

38 R. Wittkower, 'Marco Polo and the pictorial tradition of the marvels of the East', *Oriente Poliano*, 156.

39 C. W. Bynum, 'Wonder', *American Historical Review*, 10, 2 (1997), 20. I find remarkable the assertion of M. B. Campbell, *The Witness and the Other World: Exotic European Travel Writing, 400–1600* (Ithaca, 1985), 88, that Marco's description of the East – drawing at this point specifically on his description of the rhinoceros – is 'not exactly a corrective' to the *mirabilia* tradition of earlier centuries.

40 See J. Richard, *Les récits des voyages et des pèlerinages* (Brepols, 1981).

41 J. K. Hyde, 'Medieval Descriptions of Cities', *Bulletin of the John Rylands Library*, 48 (1986), 308–41.

42 *Gesta Hammaburgensis Ecclesiae Pontificium*, ed. B. Schmeidler (Scriptores r. Germ. in u. schol., Hanover, 1917); in English translation by F. J. Tschau (New York, 1959). R. Bartlett, *Gerald of Wales 1146–1233* (Oxford, 1982), 174 n. 72, points out that Adam of Bremen had access to a text which incorporated some sections (4, 9–11) of Tacitus' *Germania*, and so to some, however slight, knowledge of classical chorography. King Alfred of England's frequently cited description of northern waters, inserted in his description of Orosius (surviving in only one manuscript) consists merely of 2½ pages by Ohthere and 2 pages by Wulfstan. See R. Pauli's version of Orosius in his *Life of Alfred the Great*, trans. B. Thorpe (London, 1853), 249–57.

43 'aliis alienam nationibus et valde diversam'. I cite the translation of M. Richter, in his *Geraldus Cambrensis: The Growth of the Welsh Nation* (Aberystwyth, 1976), 64.

44 Bartlett, *Gerald of Wales*, 213–17.

45 See above, pp. 26–7.

46 Needham, *Science and Civilisation in China*, vol. 3, ch. 22; Smith, *Chinese Maps*, chs 1 and 2.

47 Chau Ju-Kua, *On the Chinese and Arab Trade*, ed. and trans. F. Hirth and W. W. Rockhill (St Petersburg, 1911), 153.

48 Needham, *Science and Civilisation in China*, vol. 3, 519.

49 'The Wonder of the Capital' translated by A. C. Moule, *New China Review* (1921), 12–17.

50 E. Balazs, 'Marco Polo and the Capital of China' in his *Chinese Civilisation and Bureaucracy* (New Haven, 1964) (in Italian in *Oriente Poliano*), 79–100.

51 Needham, *Science and Civilisation in China*, vol. 3, 254; H. Franke, 'The exploration of the Yellow River sources under emperor Qubilai in 1281' in his *China under Mongol Rule*, article IX.

52 As, from the first half of the century, the description by the Sinicised Kitan minister Yeh-lü Ch'u-ts'ai, of the itinerary of the army of Genghis Khan to Persia in 1219–24 (English translation from a fragmentary version in E. Bretschneider, *Medieval Researches from Eastern Asiatic Sources*, London, 1888, vol. 1, 9–24); the full text has now been discovered, I. de Rachelwiltz, 'Yeh-lü Ch'u-ts'ai (1189–1243). 'Buddhist idealist and Confucian Statesmen' in *Confucian Personalities*, ed. A. F. Wright and D. Twitchett (Stanford, 1962) 360 n. 4. Also the accounts of the anonymous envoy of the Kin Emperor to Persia and the Hindu Kush in 1220 (translated in Bretschneider, *Medieval Researches*, vol. 1, 25–34), and of the Taoist monk, Chhiu Chhang-Chhun's visit to Genghis Khan in Afghanistan (*ibid.*, vol. 1, 35–108, and by Arthur Waley, *The Travels of an Alchemist. The Journey of the Taoist Ch'ang-ch'un* (London, 1931). Closer to our period, there are descriptions of Ch'ang Te's embassy of 1259 on behalf of the Great Khan Möngke to his brother, Hülegü in Persia (later written up by Liu Yu and presented to Khubilai (Bretschneider, *Medieval Researches*, vol. 1, 109–15)), and of the peregrinations of Yeh-lü Hi-liang in Central Asia between 1260 and 1262 (*ibid.*, 109–15.6). We have, too, an account of Cambodia by Chou Ta-Kuan, written while acting as a counsellor of an embassy sent there in 1297 (translated by Pelliot in *Bulletin de l'École Française d'Extrême Orient*, 1902, and from there into English in J. Mirsky (ed.) *The Great Chinese Travellers*, London,

1965, 203–33). On Khubilai's missions, Rockhill, 'Notes on the relations and trade', 430–43.

53 Smith, *Chinese Maps*, 15–16.

54 Needham, *Science and Civilisation in China*, vol. 3, 533ff; Bretschneider, *Medieval Researches* vol. 2, 3–136. For a map of China excluding the countries of the barbarians, drawn up between 1311 and 1320, *The 'Mongol Atlas' of China by Chu Ssu-Pen and the Kuang-yu-t'u*, ed. W. Fuchs (Beijing, 1946). C. D. K. Yee's 'Cartography in China' in *The History of Cartography*, vol. 2, pt 2, *Cartography in the Traditional East and Southeast Asian Societies*, ed. J. B. Harley and D. Woodward (London, 1994), 34–202, 228–31, warns against simply looking for the ideals and mathematical traditions of western cartography in examining Chinese geographical traditions. In the same work, G. H. Herb, 'Mongolian Cartography' (682–5) notes that no Mongolian maps survive from before the eighteenth century.

55 Guillaume de Rubruck, *Itinerarium* in *Sinica Franciscana*, vol. 1, 171.

56 Friar Jordanus, *The Wonders of the East*, ed. H. Yule (London, Hakluyt, 1863), 55.

57 Not too much significance should be attached to this word. Cf. J. Needham, *The Grand Titration: Science and Society in East and West* (London, 1969), 117: 'The standard of life was often higher in China; it is well known that Marco Polo thought Hangchow a paradise' and p. 171: 'In Marco Polo's time Hangchow was like a paradise compared to Venice or other dirty towns of Europe'. But the use of the word among Italians to describe a (western) city was not uncommon at that time and would come quite naturally to Rustichello. See e.g., Bonvesin della Riva, *De magnalibus Mediolani*, ed. M. Corti (Milan, 1974), 46: 'Who shall attentively and diligently observe all that is here, though he tour the whole world, will never find a similar paradise of delights' and *Statuti di Brescia dell'anno MCC-CXIII* (xvi), 1606: 'since it is said that cities are made in similitude of Paradise', provisions are made for the adornment of the city. On the cleanliness of European cities in the period see the (perhaps optimistic) study of L. Thorndike, 'Sanitation, baths, and street-cleaning in the Renaissance', *Speculum*, 3 (1928), 192–203.

58 Ramusio, 29.

59 Francesco Balducci Pegolotti, 'Avisamento del viaggio del Gattaio', *La Practica della Mercatura*, ed. A. Evans (Cambridge, 1936), 22, in R. Lopez and W. W. *Medieval Trade* (New York, 1955), Raymond, 537: 'there is still another danger, that is, that should the lord die [and] until the new lord who is to rule has been sent for, in that interval sometimes a disorder occurs against the Franks and other foreigners – they call "Franks" all Christians of countries from the Byzantine Empire westwards – and the road (from Tana to Cathay] is not safe until the new lord is sent for who is to reign after the one who died'.

60 See R. Starn, *Contrary Commonwealth: The Theme of Exile in Medieval and Renaissance Italy* (London, 1982).

61 Moule-Pelliot, vol. 1, 28, 523.

Chapter 5   *The Description of the World*

1 Ramusio, 68, omitting the Queen's letter to Bayan.

2 For this convention, Bertolucci Pizzorusso, 'Enunciazione . . . *Milione*', *Studi mediolatini e volgari*, 25 (1977)', 35–7.

3 C. Deluz, 'Villes et organisation de l'espace: La Chine de Marco Polo' in *Villes, bonnes villes, cités et capitales. Études d'historie urbaine (XII*e*–XVIII*e *siècle) offertes à Bernard Chevalier* (Caen, 1993), 161–8.

4 Ramusio, 249.

5 See above p. 82.

6 E.g. ch. LXVII, 1; (War of Prester John and Genghis Khan). On this as a formula, E. Baumgartner 'Les techniques narratives dans le roman en prose' in *The Legacy of Chrétien de Troyes*, ed. N. J. Lacy, D. Kelly and K. Busby vol. 1 (Amsterdam, 1987).

7 L. Olschki, *L'Asia di Marco Polo* (Venice, 1957; English trans. Bereley and Los Angeles, 1960), 299–301.

8 L. Olschki, 'I palazzi del Gran Cane e la

reggia di Bisanzo', in his *Storia letteraria delle scoperte geografiche: Studi e ricerche* (Florence, 1937), 73–104.

9 See below Appendix I.

10 F. E. Reichert, *Begegnungen mit China* (Sigmaringen, 1992), 91–6, 114–20, for a discussion of Marco's portrayal of China.

11 See, for instance, P. Olbricht, *Das Post-wesen in China unter der Mongolen-herrschaft im 13. und 14. Jahrhundert* (Wiesbaden, 1954); H. Franke, *Geld und Wirtschaft in China unter der Mongolen-Herrschaft* (Leipzig, 1949), 13, 44–5.

12 See H. R. Clark, *Community, Trade, and Networks: Southern Fujian Province from the Third to the Thirteenth Century* (Cambridge, 1991), ch. 7.

13 A. C. Moule, *Quinsay* (Cambridge, 1957), 42.

14 Reichert, *Begegnungen*, 156, points to other Chinese matters in Z but not F: pepper consumption in Quinsai; manners of maidens in Cathay; speech and writing in Mangi; Manichean beliefs in southeastern China.

15 Olschki, *L'Asia*, 391–408.

16 *The Cambridge History of China*, vol. 6: *Alien Regimes and Border States 907–1368*, ed. H. Franke and D. Twitchett (Cambridge, 1994), vol. 6 704.

17 Olschki, *L'Asia*, 160–1; Kawwazoc Shoji, 'Japan and East Asia' in *The Cambridge History of Japan, Medieval Japan*, ed. Kozo Yamamura (Cambridge, 1990), vol. 3, 411.

18 Yule-Cordier, vol. 2, 413–14.

19 In general J. Critchley, *Marco Polo's Book* (Aldershot, 1992), 68–76.

20 M. T. Hodgen, *Early Anthropology in the Sixteenth and Seventeenth Centuries* (Philadelphia, 1971), 94–103.

21 S. M. Islam, *The Ethics of Travel from Marco Polo to Kafka* (Manchester, 1996), 165–7. As an afterthought the thesis is modified on page 207: 'Marco Polo's world is not yet quite Eurocentric'. Dr Islam normally uses the English translation of the Book by R. Latham in the Penguin Classics (Harmondsworth, 1958), without distinguishing (as it does) the various texts of the work that are drawn upon.

22 *The Travels of Ibn Battuta A.D. 1325–1354*, trans. H. A. R. Gibb and C. F.

Beckingham (London, Hakluyt, 1994), vol. 4, 911–12; and see Benjamin of Tudela, *The Itinerary* ed. N. M. Adler (London, 1907), 66.

23 Above, pp. 79.

24 Yule-Cordier, vol. 2, 288.

25 Ramusio, 235.

26 Yule-Cordier, vol. 2, 76.

27 Ramusio, 242.

28 *Milione. Le Divisament* ch. lxxxii, 7–10; Ramusio, 159–60.

29 Ramusio, 249.

30 *Ibid.*, 168.

31 *Ibid.*, 193–4. Ramusio actually heads this chapter 'Della religione de' *Tartari* e usanze loro', but it is clearly the Cathayans of whom Marco is treating.

32 *Ibid.*, 235–7. Further discussion of Marco's portrayal of the Chinese in Critchley, *Marco Polo's Book*, 125–9.

33 E.g. below p. 124.

34 Islam, *The Ethics of Travel*, 155.

35 Olschki, *L'Asia*, 230–49.

36 At this point the Chepoy text adds those remarks on Mohammed's supposed commands to work evil against Christians which in the F text, chapter xxx and in Ramusio, 100, are applied (see below) to the Muslims of Tabriz.

37 See N. Daniel, *Islam and the West: The Making of an Image* (Edinburgh, 1960); R. W. Southern, *Western Views of Islam in the Middle Ages* (Cambridge, 1982); J. Tolan, 'Anti-hagiography: Embrico of Mainz's *Vita Mahumeti*', *Journal of Medieval History*, xxii (1996), 25–41.

38 Yule-Cordier, vol. 1, 216.

39 Pipino (citing here book and chapter numbers) III, 14; and cf. e.g., 12, 26, 41, 45, 60, and so on; with Critchley, *Marco Polo's Book*, 144–5. In a similar way the Ramusio text, 191, remarks that, before the preaching of the priests of the idolaters the Mongols had not practised charity, holding that the poor were cursed of God.

Chapter 6   *Varieties of the Book*

1 See above, p. 1–2.

2 L. Olschki, 'Marco Polo, Dante Alighieri e la cosmografia medievale', *Oriente Poliano: Studi e conferenze tenute . . . in*

occasione del VII Centenario della nascita di Marco Polo (Rome, 1957), 45–65, here pp. 57, 70; G. Bertolucci, 'Polo, Marco', *Enciclopedia Dantesca* (Rome, 1973), vol. 4, 589.

3 The count depends on whether one accepts fragments and abbreviations. Segre in *Milione. Le Divisament* xv, writes of 130. To Moule-Pelliot's 120 must be added the further 20 or so Latin translations identified by Wehr (p. 320) from Kristeller's *Iter Italicum*.

4 J. W. Bennett, *The Rediscovery of Sir John Mandeville* (New York, 1954), 263–334. Compare the more than 600 manuscripts of Dante's *Divine Comedy* (G. Folena, 'La tradizione delle opere di Dante Alighieri' in *Atti del Congresso Internazionale di Studi Danteschi*, Florence, 1965), vol. 1, 46. Or again (though similarly, a very different genre) Jacopo da Voragine's *Legend of the Saints* (*Legenda Aurea*) written in the 1260s, has left 800 manuscripts of its Latin text (plus translations into French, Spanish, Italian, Provençal, English, Dutch, High and Low German and Bohemian), and, at least, 156 printed editions between 1470–1500; S. L. Reames, *The Legenda Aurea: A Reexamination of its Paradoxical History* (London, 1985).

For historical texts, see B. Guenée, *Histoire et culture historique dans l'Occident médiéval* (Paris, 1980), 250–2, from which I take the following examples: John of Salisbury, *Historia Pontificalis* – 1; *Histoire de Guillaume le Maréchal* – 1; Saxo Gramaticus – 3; Froissart, *Chronicles* – 49; Einhard – 80; *Grandes Chroniques de France* – 106; Ranulph Higden, *Polychronicon* – 118; Bede, *Historia Ecclesiastica* – 164; Turpin, *Historia Karoli Magni* – 170; Justin, *Epitome* – 207; Orosius – 245; Valerius Maximus – 419. See too J. Crick, *His-toria Regum Britanniae of Geoffrey of Monmouth III. A summary catalogue of the manuscripts* (Woodbridge, 1990), reveals 215 manuscripts.

5 Foscolo Benedetto, ccxiv.

6 As is, three years later, her servant, Thierry d'Hirec, Bishop of Arras. Foscolo Benedetto, xlv.

7 For contemporary views on the truthfulness of stories in the prose epic style see in general note 23 below.

8 Foscolo Benedetto, xxxiv.

9 *Ibid.*, xxxvi [A2]; xxxviii [B1].

10 See S. Reynolds, 'Social mentalities and the case of medieval scepticism', *Transactions of the Royal Historical Society*, 6th ser., 1 (1991), 21–41.

11 Foscolo Benedetto, cxv.

12 'Tertia die invenimus Tartaros inter quos cum intravi visum fuit mihi quod ingrederer quoddam alium seculum', *Sinica Franciscana*, 1, 93. Cf. Peregrino di Castello who describes himself as 'episcopus in mundo alio constitutus': F. E. Reichert, *Begegnungen mit China* (Singmaringen, 1992), 134.

13 Foscolo Benedetto, cxxi.

14 For a recent study of this phenomenon, I. M. Higgins, *Writing East: the 'Travels' of Sir John Mandeville* (Philadelphia, 1997).

15 W. Stokes, 'The Gaelic abridgement of the Book of Marco Polo' in *Zeitschrift für celtische Philologie*, 1 (1897), 246–7, 365 (texts, 245–73; 362–438). For the manuscript, *The Book of Mac Carthaigh Riabhach Otherwise the Book of Lismore* (facsimiles in collotype of Irish Manuscripts, vol. 5 Dublin, 1950).

16 Foscolo Benedetto, xxxiv–xxxv.

17 *Ibid.*, xxxv–xxxvi. See H. O[mant], *Livres des Merveilles: Reproduction des 265 miniatures du manuscript français 2810 de la Bibliothèque Nationale* (Paris, 1907); J. Porcher, *French Miniatures from Illuminated Manuscripts* (London, 1960), 69 and plate 65; M. Meiss, *French Painting in the Time of Jean de Berry: The Late Fourteenth Century and the Patronage of the Duke* (London, 1967), 314 (ascribed to Boucicaut Master and collaborator), 403 n. 12; *idem*, *French Painting in the Time of Jean de Berry: The Boucicaut Master* (London, 1968), 80, 85–98. This volume included all the texts translated into French by Jean le Long (see below p. 130), together with Mandeville.

18 Foscolo Benedetto, xxxvii–xxxviii.

19 *Ibid.*, xxviii–xxix. O. Pächt and J. J G. Alexander, *Illuminated Manuscripts in the Bodleian Library Oxford* (Oxford, 1973), vol. 3, 792 and 793. P. Ménard, 'L'illustration du "Devisement du Monde" de Marco Polo', *Bulletin de la Société Nationale des Antiquaires de France*

(1985), 85–9, remarks that there are in fact only four surviving manuscripts with more than a few illustrations: London, British Museum, Ms. Royal 19 D.1, mid-fourteenth century, with 19 miniatures; Oxford, The Bodleian Library 264, *ca.* 1400, with 38 miniatures; Bibliothèque Nationale de France fr. 2810 executed *ca.* 1410 for John the Fearless, Duke of Burgundy, with 84 miniatures; and Bibliothèque L'Arsenal, Paris 5219 of the sixteenth century with 197 miniatures.

[20] Reichert, *Begegnungen*, 252.

[21] See D. J. A. Ross, 'Methods of Book Production in a XIVth Century French Miscellany, London B. M. Ms. Royal 19 D.1', *Scriptorium*, 6 (1952), 63–75. In his *L'Asia de Marco Polo*, 115 and fig. 3, Olschki was mistaken in seeing the appearance of the Polos in friars' habit in this manuscript as significant. In the next miniature they appear in secular costume.

[22] See R. Wittkower, 'Marco Polo and the pictorial tradition of the marvels of the East', in *Oriente Poliano*, 155–72.

[23] C. Segre, 'Marco Polo', 18. Yet was Arthurian literature seen as fiction? As early as 1190 William of Newburgh had criticised tales about him as made up either from 'an inordinate love of lying, or for the sake of pleasing the Britons', and another Englishman, Ranulph of Higden, in the early part of the four-teenth century, has been hostile. However, around 1314, Francesco da Barberino (*I documenti d'amore*, ed. F. Egidi [Rome, 1905], vol. 1, 101) had advised his readers to read Tristan but to ignore accounts of the paladins on the grounds of their untruthfulness. (So, too, in thir-teenth-century France, Alberic des Trois Fontaines was persuaded that poems about the paladins were composed of 'fables . . . in great part most false'; J. Crosland, *The Old French Epic*, Oxford, 1951, p. 100.) Those narrating tales about Charlemagne and the paladins were likely to jump the other way. In the Franco-Italian verse epic, the *Entrée d'Espagne* (ed. A. Thomas, Paris, 1913, vol. 1, 2), written around 1320, the anonymous Paduan poet prefaces the work with an assurance that here the reader will find not 'fables of Arthur' but the truth. This,

despite the fact that among the sources for the *Entrée*, feature, not only Carolin-gian romances, and, it has been sug-gested, Marco Polo, but also the very 'fables of Arthur' of which the author complains. Again, in his wholly imagi-nary epic, *La Guerra d'Attila* (ed. G. Stenardo, Modena, 1941, vol. 1, 3–4) Niccolò da Casola assures us that we will find not fables of Tristan and Yseult, of Geneviève and Arthur, but *une ystoire verables*. In Italy, one would think, Arthurian stories were, at least, highly suspect, as Boccaccio (*Il comento alla Divina Comedia e gli altri scritti intorno a Dante*, ed. D. Guerri, Bari, 1918, vol. 2, 144) puts it, 'per qual ch'io creda più composte a beneplacito che seconda la verità'. Yet, when in the Renaissance, an Italian went to England and carefully demolished the time-hallowed myths about him, he was bitterly attacked by English patriots who stubbornly rejected his findings (E. K. Chambers, *Arthur of Britain*, London, 1927, ch. 4).

[24] Foscolo Benedetto, cv–cviii.

[25] It appears, together with school-books, Boccaccio's *Filostrato*, *leggendari*, and *cantari*, in the inventory of an early fifteenth-century Florentine bookseller: A. De La Mare, 'The Shop of a Floren-tine "Cartolaio" in 1426' in *Studi offerti a Roberto Ridolfi*, ed. B. Maracchi Biagia-relli and D. E. Rhodes (Florence, 1973), 237–48.

[26] Foscolo Benedetto, cxi. See too 'This book is called the navigation of Messer Marco Polo – and it belongs to me Piero del Ricio and my brother, 1458' (Bertolucci Piz-zorusso, 328), or 'at Venice on the Rialto it is placed in chains that all may read it' (Foscolo Benedetto, ccx–ccxi). It is fair to add, however, that J. Heers ('Le projet de Chrisophe Columb' in *Colombeis*, Genoa, 1986, vol. 1, 24), has seen great signifi-cance in the form of the first, and F. Bor-landi ('Alle origini del libro' (Milan, 1962), 105–47) in that of the latter.

[27] Foscolo Benedetto, cvi–cvii.

[28] L. Manzoni, 'Fra Francesco Pipino', *Atti e memorie della R. Deputazione di storia patria per la Romagna*, ser, 3, vol. 13 (1895), 257–334; G. Zaccagnini, 'Francesco Pipino, traduttore del

"Milione", cronista e viaggiatore in Oriente nel secolo XIV', *Atti e memorie della R. Deputazione di storia patria per l'Emilia e la Romagna*, vol. 1 (1935–6), 61–95. From Pipino's version, which survives in about seventy manuscripts (B. Wehr, 'A propos de la gènese . . .', *Le passage à l'ecrit des langues romanes*, ed. M. Selig *et al.* (Tübingen, 1993), 320), were translated, before the invention of printing, the Czech, the Irish and a Venetian translation (back, that is, into the language from which Pipino had taken it). After the coming of printing it was the source of a Portuguese translation (and from this a Latin version, by Grynaeus (*Novus Orbis*, Basle, 1552); an unpublished German version; two French translations, of which one achieved print.

29 Pipino, 1–2; translated Yule, vol. 2, 448.

30 *Ibid.*

31 Foscolo Benedetto, xx–xxi.

32 Contrary to Dr Wehr's views on the priority of Pipino's text over Rustichello's, it is surely significant that this moment, which has already been mirrored in the *Méliadus*: 'M. Tristan s'enienoille a ses pies, mais li roi ne le souffre pas, ainz le drece heramant . . .' (Foscolo Benedetto, xxi), is retained in Pipino's Latin (I, 7, ed. Prásek, 130): 'ingressi ad Regem procierunt cum reverencia maxima coram eo., qui alacriter eos suscipiens iussit, ut surgerent . . .'.

33 Bertolucci Pizzorusso, 335–7, suggests that the Bibliothèque Nationale ms. lat. 3195, which consists of a fusion of Pipino with a Latin translation of the Tuscan translation, was made by someone who disliked the generic and abstract character of Pipino's work.

34 K. W. Humphreys, *The Book Provisions of Medieval Friars* (Amsterdam, 1964), 105–6. For Fra Odorico rather than Odericus Vitalis here, see Critchley, *Marco Polo's Book*, 156.

35 See Foscolo Benedetto, cv; cxix; and in general his ch. vi.

36 Foscolo Benedetto, cxciv; translated Yule-Cordier, vol. 1, 54.

37 Antonio Pucci, *Libro di varie storie*, ed. A. Varvaro (Palermo, 1957), 35. The work survives in the author's autograph revision and in five manuscript copies.

Chapter 7   *Marco, Merchants and Missionaries*

1 F. E. Reichert, *Begegnungen mit China* (Singmaringen, 1992), 75–86.

2 *Les Gestes de Chiprois: Recueil de chroniques françoises écrites en Orient aux XIIIᵉ et XIVᵉ siècles*, ed. G. Reynaud (Geneva, 1887), 294.

3 J. Heers, *Marco Polo* (Paris, 1983), 97–100.

4 J. H. Richard, 'Les navigations des occidentaux sur l'Océan Indien et la Mer caspienne (XIIᵉ–XIVᵉ siècles), in *Orient et Occident au Moyen Age: contacts et relations (XIIᵉ–XVᵉ s.)* (London, 1976), article XXXI, 359–60; see too *idem*, 'Isol le Pisan: Un aventurier franc gouverneur d'une province mongole?', in *ibid.*, article XXX.

5 A. Ashtor, *Levant Trade in the Later Middle Ages* (Princeton, 1983), ch. 1; L. Petech, 'Les marchands italiens dans l'empire mongol', *Revue Asiatique*, 250 (1962), 549–74; F. Surdich, 'Gli esploratori genovesi del period medievale', *Studi di storia delle esplorazioni*, vol. 1 (1978), 11–117.

6 A. Magnaghi, *Precursori di Colombo? Il tentativo di viaggio transoceanico dei Genovesi fratelli Vivaldi nel 1291* (Memorie della R. Società Geografica Italiana, 13, Rome, 1935); G. Moore, 'La spedizione dei fratelli Vivaldi e nuovi documenti d'archivio', *Atti della Società Ligure di Storia Patria*, n.s. 12 (1972), 387–410.

7 See F. Fernández-Armesto, *Before Columbus: Exploration and Colonisation from the Mediterranean to the Atlantic 1229–1492* (London, 1987), *passim*.

8 Petech, 'Les marchands italiens', 569.

9 R. S. Lopez, 'Venezia e le grandi linee dell'espansione commerciale nel secolo XIII' in *La civiltà veneziana del secolo di Marco Polo* (Venice, 1955), 39–82 (this provides a corrected version of an important document first printed in *idem*, 'Nuove luci sugli italiani in Estremo Oriente prima di Colombo', *Studi Colombiani*, vol. 3, Genoa, 1951, 337–98); *idem*, 'L'extrême frontière du commerce de l'Europe médièvale', *Le Moyen Age* (1963), 479–90. I am uncertain of the extent of trade with India; *multi merca-*

tores latini are said to have witnessed the execution of four Franciscan friars at Tana in 1321 (see below p. 121), though the apologist is here perhaps simply claiming necessary witnesses to a martyrdom.

10 *Sinica Franciscana*, I, 342–3, 375–6; Petech, 'Les marchands italiens', 555–6.

11 R. Morozzo della Rocca, 'Catay' in *Miscellenea in onore di R. Cessi*, vol. I (Rome, 1958), 299–303.

12 R. S. Lopez and W. W. Raymond, *Medieval Trade in the Mediterranean World* (New York, 1955), 357.

13 R. H. Bautier, 'Les relations', in *Sociétés et compagnies de commerce . . .*, ed. M. Mollat (Paris, 1970), 308–9 for merely intermittent trade. But see R. Lopez, 'European merchants in the medieval Indies', *Journal of Economic History*, vol. 3 (1942), 164–84; *idem*, 'China silk in Europe in the Yüan period', *Journal of the American Oriental Society*, 72 (1952), 72–76; *idem*, 'Nouveaux documents sur les marchands italiens en Cine à l'époque mongole', *Comptes rendus de l'Académie des Inscriptions et Belles-Lettres* (1977), 445–58; M. Balard, 'Precursori di Cristoforo Colombo: i Genovesi in Estremo Orient nel XIV secolo', *Studi Colombiani*, vol. 3; *idem*, *La Mer Noire et la Romanie génoise XIIIe–XVe siècles* (London, 1989), article XIV; *idem*, 'Les Gênois en Asie centrale et en Extrême Orient au XIVe siècle: un cas exceptionnel?' in *Economies et sociétés au Moyen Age: Mélanges offerts à Edouard Perroy* (Paris, 1973), 68, 1–89, for arguments that the numbers of merchants going to India and China were 'not small'.

14 Not of the Viglioni family (of Venice), as was once believed; see Lopez, 'Nouveaux documents', 456–7. The tombstone of Caterina shows a Virgin and Child at the top, with, below, a representation of the martyrdom of St Catherine of Alexandria. F. A. Rouleau, 'The Yangchow Latin tombstone as a Landmark of Medieval Christianity', *Harvard Journal of Asiatic Studies*, 17 (1954), 346–65; Reichert, *Begegnungen*, 80 n. 90.

15 J. Richard, 'La conversion de Berke et les débuts de l'Islamisation de la Horde d'Or', *Revue des études islamiques* (1967), 173–84, and in his *Orient et Occident*, article XXIX.

16 Lopez, 'L'extrême', 482.

17 Balard, *La Roumanie*, 858–62.

18 On the missions, A. C. Moule, *Christians in China* (London, 1930); J. Richard, *La papauté et les missions d'Orient* (Rome, 1997); *idem*, *Orient et Occident*; R. E. Loenertz, *La société des Frères Pérégrinants: Etude sur l'Orient Dominicain*, vol. I (Rome, 1937).

19 J. Richard, 'Essor et déclin de l'Eglise catholique de Chine au XIVe siècle' in his *Orient et Occident*, XXIII. The letters from China of Giovanni da Monte Corvino, Peregrino da Castello and Andrea da Perugia, are edited in *Sinica Franciscana*, I, 340–77; in translation in *Mission to Asia*, 224–37; and in translation with commentary, H. Yule, *Cathay*, vol. 3 (rev. H. Cordier, London 1915; New York, 1967), 1–75 and Moule, *Christians*, ch. 7.

20 *Sinica Franiscana*, vol. I, 375.

21 See the comment of the Dominican Archbishop of Sultania in 1328: 'Of these Nestorians there are more than thirty thousand living in the said empire of Cathay and they are very rich people but greatly dread and fear *Christians*', Moule, *Christians*, 250.

22 L. Carrington Goodrich, 'Westerners and Central Asians in Yuan China', in *Oriente Poliano*, 7–8.

23 Moule, *Christians*, 178.

24 Richard, *La Papauté*, 170; *idem*, 'Les premiers missionaires latins en Ethiopie (XIIe–XIVe siècles)' in his *Orient et Occident*, article XXIV; *idem*, 'Les navigations', *ibid.*, 360–1.

25 J. Richard, 'Les missionaires latins dans l' Inde au XIVe siècle', *Studi Veneziani*, vol. 12 (1970), 231–42, and in his *Orient et Occident*, article XXV; J. D. Ryan, 'European travelers before Columbus: The fourteenth-century's discovery of India', *Catholic Historical Review*, 79 (1993), 648–70. On Friar Jordanus, *The Wonders of the East*, trans. H. Yule (London, Hakluyt, 1863); Jourdain Catalani de Séverac, *Mirabilia descripta; Les Merveilles de l'Asie*, ed. H. Cordier (Paris, 1925; Latin text and French translation); Yule, *Cathay*, vol. 3, 75–80; Moule, *Christians*, 210–13.

26 *Sinica Franciscana*, vol. I, 413–95; translation in Yule, *Cathay*, vol. 2.

27 B. Z. Kedar, 'Chi era Andrea Franco?', *Atti della Società Ligure di Storia Patria*, n.s. 17 (1977), 369–77, shows that the merchant in Toghan Temur's embassy was not Andalò da Savignano but 'Andrea de Nassio'. See too Petech, 'Les marchands italiens', 554–5; H. Franke, 'Some western contacts under the Mongol Empire', *Journal of the Hong Kong Branch of the Royal Asiatic Society*, 6 (1966), 58; *idem*, 'Das "himmlische Pferd" des Johann von Marignola', *Archiv für Kulturgeschichte*, 50 (1968), 33–40; Reichert, *Begegnungen*, 84 n. 117.

28 *Sinica Franciscana*, vol. 1, 524–60; translation Yule, *Cathay*, vol. 3, 177–269.

29 Richard, *La Papauté*, 154 n. 133; J. I. Catto, 'Guillaume du Pré and the Tartars', *Archivium Franciscanum Historicum*, 60 (1967), 210–13.

30 R. Morozzo della Rocca, 'Sulle orme di Polo', *L'Italia che scrive* (October 1954), 121.

31 Petech, 'Les marchands italiens', 557–8; On the Ming attitude to foreigners, J. D. Langlois (ed.) *China under Mongol Rule* (Princeton, 1981), 9, 19.

32 'Der "Libellus de notitia orbis" Johannes III (de Galonifontibus?) O.P., Erzbischofs von Sultanyeh', ed. A. Kern, *Archivium fratrum praedicatorum*, 8 (1938), 82–123; Richard, *La Papauté*, 256–7.

33 Phillipe de Mézières, *Le songe du vieil pélerin*, ed. G. W. Coopland (Cambridge, 1969), 222–9.

34 Chapter XX, 6, 'cheitif et vilç et ne ont nulle bonté for qu'il sunt buen beveor'.

35 Hayton, *La Fleur des histories de la terre d'Orient*, ed. C. Kohler (*Recueil des Historiens des Croisades, Histoires Arménien*, vol. 2), introduction xxii–cxlii; French text, 113–253; Latin text, 255–363. Jean le Long's version of 1351 appears in five manuscripts. There are two other versions of the French text. For Juan Fernández de Heredia, grand-master of the Order of St John of Jerusalem (1377–96) it was translated into Aragonese. It was printed in French on four occasions, in Latin on six (1529, 1532 with Simon Grynaeus, *Novus Orbis*, 1563). There were English translations by Richard Pynson (1520–30), and by Purchas; and translations into German,

Dutch and Italian (Ramusio, 1559). Hetoum, *A Lytell Chronycle*, ed. G. Burger (London, 1988), reprints Pynson's version with valuable comment.

36 Moule, *Christians*, 210 n. 68 upholds the authenticity of Peregrino's letter.

37 *Sinica Franciscana*, vol. 1, 340–77, 501–6; English translations, Yule, *Cathay*, vol. 3, 45–75, 81–8; Moule, *Christians*, ch. VII.

38 'Le Livre du Grant Caan', ed. M. Jacquet, *Journal Asiatique*, 6 (1830), 57–72; L. de Backer, *L'Extrême Orient au Moyen Age* (Paris, 1877), 335–46; English translations, Yule, *Cathay*, vol. 3, 89–103; Moule, *Christians*, 249–51.

39 *Sinica Franciscana*, vol. 1, 524–650; English translation, Yule, *Cathay*, vol. 3, 209–69.

40 See above, note 25.

41 Moule, *Christians*, 209 n. 67; Reichert, *Begegnungen*, 217.

42 M. G. Chiappori, 'I tre Polo nella "Ecclesia militans" de Andrea Bonaiuti in S. Maria Novella a Firenze', *Quaderni Medievali*, 15 (1983), 27–51.

43 Cited in Richard, *La Papauté*, 170, 292.

44 A. Murray, 'The Epicureans', in *Intellectuals and Writers in Fourteenth-Century Europe*, ed. P. Boitani and A. Torti (Cambridge, 1986), 161–2.

45 Boccaccio, *The Decameron*, translated G. H. McWilliam (Harmondsworth, 1972), 511.

46 M. Pastore Stocchi, 'Dioneo e l'orazione di frate Cipolla', *Studi sul Boccaccio*, 10 (1977–8), 201–15. In the *Decameron*, one story (X, 3) is set in China but there seems to be no influence from the Book. Boccaccio's treatise, *De montibus, silvis, fontibus, lacibus, fluminibus, stagnis seu paludibus et de nominibus maris*, ignores the Polos because it is a classical reference book concerned not with geography as such as with the identification of classical toponyms; see again M. Pastore Stocchi, *Tradizione medievale e gusto umanistico nel 'De montibus' del Boccaccio* (Padua, 1962), 42 n. 12.

47 *Sinica Franciscana*, vol. 1, 381–495; *Les voyages en Asie du bienheureux frère Odoric de Pordenone*, ed. H. Cordier (*Recueil de voyages et documents*, vol. 10, Paris, 1891); in English translation, Yule, *Cathay*, vol. 2; Odorico da Pordenone, *Relazione del*

Viaggio in Oriente e in Cina (1314?–1330), ed. Camera di Commercio, Industria, Artigianato e Agricoltura di Pordenone (Pordenone, 1982) – with texts taken from T. Domenichelli, *Sopra la vita e i viaggi del beato Odorico da Pordenone dell'ordine de' Minori* (Prato, 1881). See too Reichert, *Begegnungen*, 148–51.

48 On the manuscripts, the conclusions of G. C. Testa, 'Bozza per un censimento dei manoscritti odoricioni' in *Odorico da Pordenone e la Cina; atti del convegno storico internazionale. Pordenone 28–9 maggio 1982*, ed. G. Melis (Pordenone, 1983), 117–50, are modified by Reichert, *Begegnungen*, 172–5. And see L. Monaco, 'I volgarizzamenti italiani della relazione di Odorico da Pordenone', *Studi mediolatini e volgari*, 26 (1978–9), 179–220; F. Romana Camaroto, 'Odorico da Pordenone', *La Rassegna della letteratura italiana*, (1991).

49 Translated Yule, *Cathay*, vol. 2, 190.

50 Reichert, *Begegnungen*, 120.

51 Yule, *Cathay*, 2, 212–13.

52 *Ibid.*, 214–15. These are translated into English with comment by A. C. Moule, 'A life of Odoric of Pordenone', *T'oung Pao*, 20 (1921), 275–90.

53 Yule, *Cathay*, 2, 173–6, 181–2. On the three monks, H. R. Patch, *The Other World* (Cambridge, Mass., 1950), ch. 5 'Journeys to Paradise'.

54 Excellent modern version, *The Travels of Sir John Mandeville*, translated C. W. R. D. Moseley (Harmondsworth, 1983). On whom, M. Letts, *Sir John Mandeville: the Man and His Book* (London, 1949); J. W. Bennett, *The Rediscovery of Sir John Mandeville* (Oxford, 1954); C. Deluz, *Le livre de Jean de Mandeville: une 'Géographie' au XIVe siècle* (Louvain-la-Neuve, 1988); M. C. Seymour, *Sir John Mandeville* (Aldershot, 1993), and see too Higgins (above p. 208, n. 14).

55 See 'Itinerarius Guilielmi de Boldensele', ed. C. L. Grotefend, *Zeitschrift des Historischen Vereins für Niedersachsen* (1852; reprinted Hanover, 1855), 236–86. On him, A. S. Atiya, *The Crusade in the Later Middle Ages* (London, 1938), 160–1.

56 The translations were printed at Paris in 1529 under the title, *Lhystoire merveilleuse plaisante et recreative du grand empereur de tartarie seigneur des tartares*, nommé le Grand Can. From the manuscript all, apart from Marco Polo, are edited in L. de Backer, *L'Extrême Orient au Moyen Age* (Paris, 1877). For Jean le Long, *ibid.*, 7–14, and O. Holder-Egger in *Chronica monasterii Sancti Bertini auctore Iohanne Longo*, *MGH.SS.* 25, 736–47.

57 Deluz, *Le livre de Jean de Mandeville*, 271–2, 309. See too Jacopo da Sanseverino, *Libro piccolo di meraviglie*, ed. M. Guglielminetti (Milan, 1985), for another journey, inspired by Mandeville, which survives in two manuscripts.

58 The only medieval cosmographer known to me who casts doubt on Mandeville is the monk Friedrich Ammann who, in his cosmographical table transcribed between 1447 and 1455, gives his sources as Ptolemy, Honorius of Augustodunensis, 'Marcum den Venediger', and Pomponius Mela, but specifically excludes Mandeville and Lucidarius; D. B. Durand, *The Vienna-Klosterneuburg Map Corpus of the Fifteenth Century: A Study in the Transition from Medieval to Modern Science* (Leiden, 1952), 176, 371–2.

59 Giovanni Villani, *Cronica*, ed. F. Gherardi Dragomanni (Florence, 1844), vol. 1, 209–11 (Bk 5, ch. 29).

60 Reichert, *Begegnungen*, 220–2.

61 *Ibid.*, 229; Reichert points out that Vincent of Beauvais discusses the Tartars in the *Speculum Historiale* but ignores them in the *Speculum naturale*.

62 Reichert, *Begegnungen*, 197–9, citing R. Creytens, 'Le manuel de conversation de Philippe de Ferrare O. P. (d.1350?)', *Archivium Fratrum Praedicatorum*, 15 (1945), 107–35. Philippe's treatise has not been published. For the German material, Reichert, *Begegnungen*, 232.

63 J. Richard, 'La vogue de l'Orient dans la littérature occidentale du Moyen Age', in his *Les relations entre l'Orient et l'Occident au Moyen Age* (London, 1977), 506.

64 *Annales Paulini* in *Chronicles of the Reigns of Edward I and Edward II*, ed. W. Stubbs (Rolls Series vol. 76, 1882), vol. 1, 354–5.

65 Reichert, *Begegnungen*, 208–12.

66 *Ibid.*, 222–4; Bennett, *Sir John*, 91–4, 97–110; see Richard, 'La vogue', 558, for lost verse tale of Ogier in China.

67 Reichert, *Begegnungen*, 207.

68 Yule-Cordier, vol. 1, 128–9.

Chapter 8   *Marco among the Humanists*

1   G. Mazzatinti, *Firenze: Biblioteca Nazionale Centrale (Inventari dei manoscritti delle biblioteche d'Italia)*, 8 (Forlì, 1896), 172–3.
2   Marco Polo, *Milione. Versione toscana del Trecento*, 333.
3   F. E. Reichert, *Begegnungen mit China* (Sigmaringen, 1992), 276, 232–3.
4   The map in the Doges's Palace in the fourteenth century which, it is said, derived from Marco's Book, was destroyed by fire in 1483, and it is impossible to have any confirmation that this was so: R. Gallo, 'Le mappe geografiche del Palazzo Ducale di Venezia', *Archivio Veneto* (1943), 47–89.
5   Harley and Woodward, *Cartography* 295–8.
6   R. Almagià, *Planisferi carte nautiche, e affini dal secolo XIV al XVII esistenti nella Biblioteca Apostolica Vaticana* (*Monumenta Cartographica Vaticana*, vol. 1, Vatican, 1944), plate 1, 3–6; B. Degenhart and A. Schnitt, 'M. Sanudo und Paolino veneto', *Römische Jahrbuch für Kunstgeschichte*, 14 (1973), 1–137.
7   Almagià, *Planisferi*, 15–17, 20–3; M. Destombes, *Mappemondes AD 1200–1500* (Amsterdam, 1964), 246; O. and M. Dilke, 'Mapping a crusade – propaganda and war in 14th century Palestine', *History Today*, 39 (August 1989), 31–5. Vesconte's map survives in six copies with loxodromes, one without; Paolino's two surviving copies have none, Degenhart and Schnitt, 'M. Sanudo', 105.
8   A. Cortesão, *History of Portuguese Cartography* (Coimbra, 1969), vol. 2, 39–48; M. de la Roncière and M. Mollat du Jourdin, *Les Portulans Cartes marines du XIIIᵉ au XVIIᵉ siècle* (Fribourg, 1984), 7.
9   Cortesão, *History of Portuguese Cartography*, vol. 2, 290–1; G. T. H. Kimble, 'The Laurentian World Map with special reference to its portrayal of Africa', *Imago Mundi*, 1 (1935), 29–33; L. Bagrow, *History of Cartography*, revised and enlarged by R. A. Skelton (London, 1964), plate 36.
10   *Mapamundi: the Catalan Atlas of the Year 1375*, ed. C. Grosjean (Zurich,

1978); *El atlas catalán de Cresques Abraham* (Barcelona, 1977); P. Yoeli, 'Abraham and Yehuda Cresques and the Catalan Atlas', *Cartographic Journal*, 7 (1970), 17–27; H. Cordier, 'L'Extrême Orient dans l'atlas catalan de Charles V', *Bulletin de geographie historique et descriptive* (1895), 19–63. In identifying Cresques' toponyms I have found particularly useful the first chapter of C. A. Semans, 'Mapping the Unknown: Jesuit Cartography in China 1583–1773' (Ph.D. Diss., University of California Berkeley, 1987), a work more comprehensive than its title suggests. Fernández-Armesto (*Before Columbus*, London, 1987, 159) argues for 'ca.1380'.
11   Compare J. J. Nitti, in the preface to his edition of *Juan Fernández de Heredia's Aragonese Version of the 'Libro de Marco Polo'* (Madison, 1980) and A. Luttrell, 'Greek histories translated and compiled for Juan Fernández de Heredia, Master of Rhodes, 1377–1396' in his *The Hospitallers in Cyprus, Rhodes, Greece, and the West 1291–1440* (London, 1978), article XX, 407.
12   Others in this style, M. Destombes, 'Fragments of two medieval maps at the Topkapu Saray Library' *Imago Mundi* (1955), vol. 12, 150–2: probably by the same author. The surviving fragments show some of Asia, with names of Central Asia from Marco Polo in Catalan. China is missing.
13   *Libro del conosçimiento de todos los reynos e señoríos*, ed. M. Jimenez de la Espada (Madrid, 1877); and in *Sinica Franciscana*, 1, 566–75; in translation, *Book of the Knowledge of all the Kingdoms, Lands, and Lordships that are in the World*, ed. C. Markham (London, 1912). It survives in four manuscripts; Markham dated the earliest to 1350–60, which is too early, see Fernández-Armesto, *Before Columbus*, 259 n. 4.
14   Foscolo Benedetto, ccxvi–ccxvii; A. T. Hankey, 'Bandini, Domenico' in *Dizionario Biografico Italiano*, v (1903); idem, 'The successive revisions and surviving codices of the Fons memorabilium universi of Domenco di Bandino', *Rinascimento* (1960), vol. 2, 3–49; idem, 'The library of Domenico di Bandino',

Rinascimento, vol. 8 (1957), 177–207; Reichert, *Begegnungen*, 258–9.

15 China was often seen as part of India. The *Book of Knowledge* thinks of it as *India la alta*; Franciscans generally speak of it as *India magna*; Marignolli as *India maxima* – Reichert, *Begegnungen*, 222–7; and see above chapter 1, note 3.

16 See above p. 82.

17 C. Percoraro, 'Domenico Silvestri, "De insulis et earum proprietatibus"', *Atti della Accademia di Scienze, lettere e Arti di Palermo*, 14 (1953–4), 30–1, 38; Reichert, *Begegnungen*, 233–4.

18 See *The Bondage and Travels of Johann Schiltberger (1396–1427)*, ed. J. Buchan Telfer (London, 1879); Ruy Gonzáles de Clavijo, *Embajada a Tamorlan*, ed. F. Lopez Estrada (Madrid, 1943), in English translation as *Embassy to Tamerlane*, ed. G. Le Strange (London, 1925); Bertrandon de la Broquière, *Le Voyage d'Outremer*, ed. C. Schefer (Paris, 1892); Pero Tafur, *Andanças e viajes de Pero Tafur por diversas partes del Mundo avidos (1435–39)*, ed. Jimenez de la Espada (*Colecciòn de libros españoles raros e curiosos*, vol. 8, Madrid, 1874); in English, *Travels and Adventures 1435–39*, translated M. Letts (London, 1926). Reichert, *Begegnungen*, 254–6, 43.

19 'Der "Libellus de notitia orbis"', ed. Kern.

20 Reichert, *Begegnungen*, 257 n. 17, citing C. Traselli, 'Un italiano in Etiopa nel XV secolo: Pietro Rombulo da Messina', *Rassegna di Studi Etiopici*, 1 (1941), 173–202.

21 Poggio Bracciolini, *Historie de varietate fortunae libri quattuor* (Lutetiae Parisiorum, 1723), reprinted *Opera Omnia*, (Turin, 1968), vol. 2, 126–52. There is a new edition edited by O. Merisalo, published by the *Annales Academiae Scientiarum Fennicae* (Helsinki, 1993); English translations: 'The travels of Nicolò Conti in the East' in *India in the Fifteenth Century*, ed. R. H. Major (London, Hakluyt, 1857) and *Narratives of Eastern Travel by Poggio Bracciolini and Ludovico de Varthema*, translation by J. Winter Jones, revised L. D. Hammond (Cambridge, Mass., 1963); and an Italian version in *Viaggi in Persia, India e Giava*.

di Niccolò Conti, Girolamo Adorno, e Girolamo da Santo Stefano, ed. M. Longhena (Milan, 1929). For discussion, F. Surdich, 'Conti, Niccolò de', *Dizionario Biografico Italiano*, vol. 25 (1983); and T. C. Schmidt, 'Die Entdeckung des Ostens und der Humanismus: Niccolò de' Conti und Poggio Bracciolinis "Historia de Varietate Fortunae"', *Mitteilungen des Instituts für Österreichische Geschichtsforschung*, 103 (1995), 392–418. The story that Conti dictated his account as 'penance' for his apostacy derives from a late tradition, 'Discorso sopra il viaggio de Niccolò de Conti veneziano'; in G. B. Ramusio, *Navigazioni e viaggi*, ed. M. Milanesi (Turin, 1978–85), vol. 2, 785–6.

22 Poggio Bracciolini, *Historia*, 148–9. This could well be the same man who, in the time of Eugenius IV, spoke to Toscanelli about the realm of the Great Khan: 'for a long time, on many things, on the greatness of the royal buildings . . . the multitude of cities, on one river . . . two hundred cities, and marble bridges . . .'. These subjects are not discussed by Conti.

23 See M. Longhena, 'I manoscritti del quarto libro del De Varietate Fortunae di Poggio Bracciolini', *Bollettino della Società Geografica Italiana*, series 7, vol. 2 (1925), 191–215 and Schmidt, 'Die Entdeckung des Ostens', 409–12, with summary of Merisalo's findings.

24 Foscolo Benedetto, cxl. The German cleric in Rome who copied this manuscript in April 1458 carefully transcribed Barbarigo's comment as well (*ibid.*, cxli). This was then bound up with such other works relating to the East as a *Book of Mahommed*, and the *Letter of Prester John*.

25 Reichert, *Begegnungen*, 268.

26 See below p. 152.

27 Edited in F. M. Esteves Pereira, *Marco Polo* (Lisbon, 1922), 78 verso.

28 See Shinobu Iwamura, *Manuscripts and Printed Editions of Marco Polo's Travels* (Tokyo, 1949); C. Sanz, *El Libro de Marco Polo: Notas historicas y biblograficas*, (Madrid, 1959).

29 M. Milanese, 'La rinascita della geografia dell' Europa (1350–1480)' in *Atti del convegno 'Europa e Mediterraneo tra Medio*

Evo e prima Età moderna. L'osservatore italiano', ed. G. Gensini (Centro de Studi sulla Civiltà del Tardo Medioevo, San Miniato, Collana Studi e Ricerche, 4, 1992), 35–59; G. Uzielli, *Paolo dal Pozzo Toscanelli: Iniziatore della scoperta d'America* (Florence, 1892); *Raccolta*, vol. 5, pt.1; D. B. Quinn, 'The Italian Renaissance and Columbus', *Renaissance Studies*, 6 (September/December 1992); 352–9; S. Gentile, *Firenze e la scoperta dell'America. Umanesimo e geografia nel 400 fiorentino. Catalogo dell'esposizione, Biblioteca Medicea Laurenziana 992–3* (Florence, 1992); J. Larner, 'The Church and the Quattrocento Renaissance in Geography', *Renaissance Studies* (1998), 26–39.

30 O. A. W. Dilke, 'The culmination of Greek cartography in Ptolemy' in *The History of Cartography*, vol. 1 (London, 1987), ed. J. B. Harley and D. Woodward.

31 Pierre d'Ailly, *Ymago Mundi*, ed. E. Buron, vol. 1 (Paris, 1930), 152. The first edition appeared in a varied collection of treatises (including d'Ailly's own and those of his pupil, Jean Gerson), published in a volume without title, colophon, date, pagination or indication of printer. It came from the press of John of Westphalia, printer of Louvain, between 1480 and 1483. Buron's work reprints, with French translation, the *Ymago Mundi*, the *Compendium Cosmographiae Ptolemaei*, the *Compendium Cosmographiae Ptolomaei*, *Tractatus Secundus*, and an *Epilogus mappae mundi*.

32 *Ymago Mundi*, ed. Buron, vol. 3, 620 (*Compendium Cosmographiae*, chap. 12).

33 *Der mitteldeutsche Marco Polo*, ed. H. von Tscharner (*Deutsche Texte des Mittelalters*, vol. 40, Berlin, 1935), xiv.

34 Poggio Bracciolini, *Historia*, 149–52.

35 C. Vasoli, 'Profilo di un papa umanista: Tommaso Parentucelli', in his *Studi sulla cultura del Rinascimento* (Manduria, 1968), 89–90; J. Gill, *The Council of Florence* (Cambridge, 1959), 321–7, for negotiations with Copts.

36 *Scritti inediti e rari di Biondo Flavio*, ed., B. Nogara (Rome, 1927), 22–4.

37 On his life and works: G. Uzielli, *Paolo dal Pozzo Toscanelli: Iniziatore della scoperta d'America* (Florence, 1892); *idem, La*

vita e i tempi di Paolo dal Pozzo Toscanelli (*Raccolta di Documenti e Studi pubblicati dalla R. Commissione Colombiniana*, vol. 5, pt 1, Rome, 1894); and E. Garin, 'Ritratto di Paolo dal Pozzo Toscanelli' in his *La cultura filosofica del Rinascimento italiano: Ricerche e documenti* (2nd edn, Florence, 1979), 313–34. On the meetings with the Abyssinian, C. L. Stinger, *Humanism and the Church Fathers: Ambrogio Traversari (1386–1439) and Christian Antiquity in the Italian Renaissance* (Albany, 1977), 46; with the cardinal, M. V. Anastos, 'Pletho, Strabo and Columbus', reprinted from *Mélanges Henri Grégoire*, vol. 4 (Brussels, 1953), in his *Studies in Byzantine Intellectual History* (Variorum, London, 1979), 5.

38 A. Diller, 'A Geographical Treatise by George Gemistos Pletho', *Isis*, 27 (1937), 447–8; C. M. Woodhouse, *George Gemistos Plethon: The Last of the Hellenes*, (Oxford, 1986), 183; A. Diller, 'The autographs of George Gemistus Plethon', *Scriptorium*, 10 (1956), 32–3.

39 P. M. Watts, *Nicholas Cusanus: A Fifteenth-Century Vision of Man* (Leiden, 1982), 212; D. B. Durand, *The Vienna-Klosterneuburg Map Corpus . . .* (Leiden, 1952), 525–6; T. Campbell, *Earliest Printed Maps 1472–1500* (London, 1987), 35–55. For Cusanus' manuscript of Marco Polo (now British Library, Addit. 19952) see Foscolo Benedetto, cxxxvii.

40 For a convenient text and translation of the Latin letter H. Vignaud, *Toscanelli and Columbus* (London, 1902, an amplification of the French edition, Paris, 1901); though for these sections (from pp. 294–5, 298–300, 302) I have given my own translation. For Martins as a signatory to Cusa's will (1464), and as an interlocutor in his dialogue *De non aliud*, E. Vansteenberghe, *Le cardinal Nicholas de Cues 1401–1464* (Paris 1920; reprinted Frankfurt am Main, 1965), 252, n. 1.

41 Ed. Prásek, *Manka Pavlova 2 Benátek* (Prague, 1902), 141 (Quinsay), 153 (Cipangu), 150 (Zaiton).

42 For introductions to the 'bibliografia sterminata', I. Luzzana Caraci, *Colombo vero e falso: La costruzione delle Historie fernandine* (Genoa, 1989), 153–71, and, with an edition of the texts, *Colección Docu-*

mental del Descubrimiento (1470–1506), ed. J. Pérez de Tudela, C. Secco Serrano, R. Ezquerra Abalia, E. López Oto (Bilbao, 1994), vol. 1, 13–30.

[43] A. Cioranescu, 'Portugal y las cartas de Toscanelli', *Estudios Americanos*, 14 (1957), 1–17.

[44] A. Parronchi, *Studi su la 'dolce' prospectiva* (Milan, 1964), 593, which prints the *Della prospettiva*, 599–641.

[45] M. Manzano and A. M. Manzano, *Los Pinzones y el Descubrimiento de América* (Madrid, 1988), vol. 1, 40.

[46] This was first printed as *Historia Rerum Ubique Gestarum cum locorum descriptione non finita. Asia Minor incipit* (Venice, John of Cologne, 1477). I cite from the edition of Pius's work published under the (similarly misleading) title *Asiae Europaeque elegantis descriptio* at Cologne in 1531. For a consideration of the work see N. Casella, 'Pio II tra geografia e storia: la "Cosmographia"', *Archivio della Società Romana di Storia Patria*, series 3, vol. 26 (1974), 35–112. As Reichert, *Begegnungen*, 261, observes, those scholars who have seen the influence of either Marco or Odorico in this work are in error.

[47] E. S. Piccolomini: Papa Pio II, *I Commentarii*, ed. L. Totaro (Milan, 1984), i, 1110.

[48] *Asiae*, 18.

[49] *Ibid.*, 19, 27–8.

[50] Foscolo Benedetto, cxxxviii.

[51] *Ibid.*, cxxxviii–cxxxix.

[52] Later a copy of this same manuscript came into the hands of the Nuremberg humanist, Hartman Schedel, who was to give the work a ringing *Commendatio*, Foscolo Benedetto, cxxxix; Reichert, *Begegnungen*, 187.

[53] *Itinéraire d'Anselme Adorno en Terre Sainte (1470 1471)*, ed. J. Heers and G. de Groer (Paris, 1978), 28.

[54] John Capgrave, *Ye Solace of Pilgrimes*, ed. C. A. Mills (Oxford, 1911), 1.

[55] Reichert, *Begegnungen*, 261. See R. Fernández Pousa, 'Un "Imago Mundi" español: Ludovicus de Angulo: De imagine seu figura mundi, Lion, 1456', *Revista de Indias*, 2 (1941), 39–65. The work survives in only one manuscript. In Antoine de la Sale's *La Salade*

(*Oeuvres Complètes*, vol. 1), ed. F. Desonay (Liège, 1935), written some time before 1449 for King René's son, whose tutor Antoine was, the description of Asia (pp. 131–63) follows Hetoum rather than Marco.

[56] Fontana's work was published under the pseudonym 'Pompilius Azalus of Piacenza', as *De omnibus rebus naturalibus quae continentur in mundo* (Venice, 1544). For the eastern passages, Book 5, chapters 12–36. On this work, L. Thorndike, *A History of Magic and Experimental Science* (New York, 1923–41), vol. 4, 150–63.

[57] P. Azalus (= G. da Fontana), *De omnibus rebus*, 119.

[58] Reichert, *Begegnungen*, 255 n. 6.

[59] Harley and Woodward, *Cartography*, 365–7, for a list of later medieval *mappaemundi* to 1469; Destombes, *Mappemondes*, for 1200–1500. For some general reflections (Comune de Venezia: VII Centenario della Nascita de Marco Polo), *Mostra 'L'Asia' nella Cartografia degli Occidentali*, ed. T. Gasparrini Leporace (Venice, 1954) and G. Caraci, 'Viaggi fra Venezia ed il Levante fino al XIV secolo e relativa produzione cartografica', in *Venezia e il Levante fino al secolo XV*, ed. A. Pertusi, (Florence, 1973), vol. 1, 147–84; R. A. Skelton, *Explorers' Maps; Chapters in the Cartographic Record of Geographical Discovery* (London, 1970), ch. 1; P. Whitfield, *New Found Lands: Maps in the History of Exploration* (London, 1998), ch. 2.

[60] Bagrow, *History*, 69–73, 91; W. I. J. Flint, *The Imaginative Landscape of Christopher Columbus* (Princeton, 1992), 38.

[61] Although in her edition of the Catalan fourteenth-century text, *Viatges de Marco Polo* (Barcelona, 1958, p. 18), Annamaria Gallina asserts (rather than demonstrates, and without reference to the fourteenth-century *Catalan Atlas*) that a manuscript from the family of this text lies behind the Modena Catalan map.

[62] See Appendix III.

[63] G. Kish, 'Two Fifteenth-Century Maps of "Zipangu": Notes on the early cartography of Japan', *Yale University Library Gazette*, 40 (1966), 206–14; W. F.

Washburn, 'Japan on early European maps', *Pacific Historical Review*, 21 (1952), 222–3.

[64] R. Almagià, 'I mappamondi di Enrico Martelli e alcuni concetti geografici di Cristoforo Colombo', *La Bibliofilia*, 42 (1940), 288–311.

[65] Destombes, *Mappemondes*, 229–34; A. O. Vietor, 'A pre-Columbian map of the world, circa 1489', *Yale University Library Gazette*, 37 (1963), 8–12 (reprinted in *Imago Mundi*, xvii [1963], 95–6).

[66] But see Appendix II.

[67] E. G. Ravenstein, *Martin Behaim: His Life and Globe* (London, 1908); Destombes, *Mappemondes*, 234–5; H. Vignaud, *Toscanelli and Columbus* (London, 1902) 180–2 and n. 172.

Chapter 9   *Columbus and After*

[1] *Marco Polo*, ed. F. M. Esteves Pereira (Lisbon, 1922), 78. I cite the translation of F. M. Rogers, *The Travels of the Infante Dom Pedro of Portugal* (Cambridge, Mass., 1961), 47.

[2] Eannes da Zurara, *Cronica*, ed. J. de Braganca (Opporto, 1937), vol. 1, 267; vol. 2, 189; Esteves Pereira, *Marco Paulo*, xix, xxx–xxxiii.

[3] B. W. Diffie and G. D. Winius, *Foundations of the Portuguese Empire (1415–1580)* (Minneapolis, 1970), 116–17.

[4] F. Fernández Armesto, *Before Columbus* (London, 1987), 175–85.

[5] Joam de Barros, *Asia: dos feitos que os Portugueses fizeram no descobrimiento e conquista dos mares e terras do oriente. Da primeira decada*, ed. A. Baiao (Coimbra, 1932), Book III, ch. 11, 112–13, which passage Bartolomé de Las Casas translated in his *Historia de las Indias* (Mexico and Buenos Aires, 1965) vol. 1, 149–50; C. E. Nowell, 'The Toscanelli letter and Columbus', *Hispanic American Historical Review*, 17 (1937), 346–8.

[6] For a recent review of the evidence, published perhaps before the discussions of Juan Gil (see note 10 below) were available, F. E. Reichert, 'Columbus und Marco Polo – Asien in America. Zur Literaturgeschichte der Entdeckungen',

Zeitschrift für Historische Forschung, 15 (1988), Heft 1, 1–63.

[7] F. Colombo, *Historie della vita e dei fatti dell'Ammiraglio Cristoforo Colombo* (Venice, 1571), chs 6 and 7. There is an edition by R. Caddeo (Milan, 1930), and an English translation by Benjamin Keen, *The Life of Admiral Christopher Columbus by his son Ferdinand* (New Brunswick, 1959).

[8] I. Luzzana Caraci, *Colmbo vero e falso: La costruzione delle Historie fernandine* (Genoa, 1989); E. V. L. Prati, 'Nuove ricerche su Cristoforo Colombo nella Venezia del tardo Cinquecento: Le historie di Don Fernando', in *L'epopea delle scoperte*, ed. R. Zorzi (Florence, 1994), 135–61.

[9] The fullest study of the handwriting is F. Streicher, 'Die Kolumbus-Originale. Eine paläographische Studie', *Gesammelte Aufsätze zur Kulturgeschichte Spaniens: Spanische Forschungen der Görresgesellschaft*, 1 (1928), 196–250; though its conclusions have found very little support, see, e.g., S. E. Morison, *Christopher Columbus Admiral of the Ocean Sea*, 1 (Boston, 1942), 127–8. For a succinct discussion by Juan Gil, *Cristóbal Colón, Textos y documentos completos*, ed. C. Varela (Madrid, 1984), lvi–lxii.

[10] The facsimile version has been edited by Juan Gil, *El Libro de Marco Polo: Ejemplar anotado por Cristóbal Colón y que se conserva en la Biblioteca Capitular y Colombina de Sevilla* (*Tabula Americae*, vol. 5, Madrid, Testimonio Compañia Ed., 1986), which I refer to as Gil, *El Libro*. This volume is to be distinguished from *El libro de Marco Polo anotado por Cristóbal Colón: El libro de Marco Polo, version de Rodrigo de Santaella*, ed. J. Gil (Madrid, Alianza, 1987), in which Gil prints a translation not of the first printed Latin version but of a version which he has 'corrected', together with what he believes to be the different postils (marked off by different typography) of Columbus, Fernando Colón and Gaspar de Gorricio. This is preceded by Gil's essay 'Libros, descubridores y sabios en la Sevilla del quinientos'. I refer to the whole work as Gil, 'Libros'. The postils

(together with a brief extract of the text to which they referred) were first published as 'Scritti di Cristoforo Colombo' and 'Autografi di Cristoforo Colombo con prefazione e trascrizione diplomatica', ed. C. de Lollis, in vol. 1, pt 2, 2 and vol. 3 respectively of the *Raccolta di documenti e studi pubblicati dalla R. Commissione Colombiana del quarto centenario della scoperta dell'America* (Rome, 1892–4). As both the facsimile of 1986 (colossally expensive) and the de Lollis editions are difficult to get hold of, a useful work is Maro Polo, *Il Milione con le postille di Cristoforo Colombo*, ed. L. Giovannini (Rome, 1985), which translates the (uncorrected) Colombina printed text into Italian, and gives, with some corrections of de Lollis' edition from the original volume, the Latin of Columbus' annotations.

11 On whom, P. Gribaudi, 'Il P. Gaspar Gorrizio de Novara', *Bollettino storico bibliografico subalpino*, 40 (1938), 1–87; and M. Serrano y Sanz, 'El Archivo Colombino de la Cartuja de las Cuevas', *Bóletin de la R. Academia de la Historia*, 96 (1930), 157–70.

12 Gil, *El Libro*, 116–18.

13 L.-A. Vigneras, 'New Light on the 1497 Cabot Voyage to America', *Hispanic American Historical Review*, 36 (1956), 503–9; D. B. Quinn, 'John Day and Columbus', *Geographical Journal*, 133 (1967), 205–9; idem, *England and the Discovery of America, 1481–1620* (London, 1973), 103–11.

14 *Biblioteca Colombina, Catálogo de sus libros impresos*, ed. S. Arbolí y Faraudo, with notes by S. de la Rosa y López (Seville, 1888–1948); A. M. Huntington, *Catalogue of the Library of Ferdinand Columbus* (New York, 1905; reprinted, 1967) – a facsimile of F. Cólon's unfinished mss. catalogue of 4,231 books.

15 'Portus Zaizen id est caput de alpha & omega'; cf. Las Casas, *Historia*, (Bk I, ch. 50) 1, 250–1; *The Four Voyages of Columbus*, ed. C. Jane (London, Hakluyt, 1930–33), vol. 1, 115 and n.6; Reichert, 'Columbus', 31.

16 Reichert, 'Columbus', 31–2.

17 *Juan Fernández de Heredia's Aragonese Version*, xxvi; Gil, 'Libros', vi.

18 *Diario of Christopher Columbus' First Voyage to America 1492–1493*, ed. O. Dunn and J. E. Kelley Jr. (Norman, 1989); D. Henige, *In Search of Columbus: The Sources for the First Voyage* (Tucson, 1991).

19 Gil, 'Libros', vii, remarks that it is so exceptional that it was perhaps added later.

20 *Diario*, ed. Dunn and Kelley, 17.

21 *Colección documental del Descubrimiento* vol. 1, 71. But for similar formulas, J. Critchley, *Marco Polo's Book*, (Aldershot, 1992), 2–4.

22 *Diario*, ed. Dunn and Kelley, 2 November 1492. They returned on the evening of 5 November.

23 He was in fact 21 degrees north; Las Casa repeats this observation in his *Historia*, 1, 44.

24 Gil, 'Libros', viii; idem, *El Libro*, 16–17.

25 Pipinio, II, x – 'Cambalu civitas Cathay provintia'; ibid., xvi – Cathay provincia.

26 Both in the *Carta de Colón* of 1493 (in *The Four Voyages of Columbus*, ed. Jane) and in the version of that letter in the *Libro Copiador de Cristóbal Colón*, ed. A. Rumeu de Armas (Madrid, 1989), vol. 2, 435, Columbus refers to his belief that La Juana (i.e. Cuba) was the mainland 'provincia del Catayo'. Presumably he has seen one of those maps, such as that of G. M. Contarini (see below p. 167) which show Catayo both as a city and a province.

27 See, for instance, John Mandeville, *The Travels*, trans. C. W. R. D. Mosley (Harmondsworth, 1983), 141.

28 Gil, *El Libro*, 166. On the 6, 13, 15, 16 January 1493 the *Diario* records Columbus as hearing of 'an island where there were women only'. Has he come to believe this through a memory of 'islands of men and women' in Marco's Book? The postil to the Colombina Pipino (III, xxxII) reads 'duas insulas masculina feminina'. Yet the whole legend is very old, goes back to, or is kin to, that of the Amazons, and (found for instance in Chinese tradition) was extensively diffused quite independently of the Book. See Yule-Cordier, vol. 2, 405–6; it is mentioned too by Jordanus and Conti.

29 *The Four Voyages*, ed. Jane, vol. 1, 116.

30 Las Casas, *Historia*, vol. 2 (67), Bk I, ch. 148, citing the Admiral's own words.

31 *The Four Voyages*, ed. Jane, 94–5.

32 *Ibid.*, 100–1 and n. 3; cf. Pipino, III, XXXII – 'Ibi [in Comari, i.e. around Cape Comorin in India] sunt cati qui dicuntur pauli, valde diversi ab aliis'.

33 *The Four Voyages*, ed. Jane, 80–1; Pepino, III, IX X; Yule, vol. 2, 266–8.

34 Reprinted as *Libro de Las Cosas Maravillosas de Marco Polo*, introduction by R. Benítiz Claros (Madrid, 1947).

35 K. Nebenzahl, *Maps from the Age of Discovery* (London, 1990), 98–9.

36 For what follows, A. Gerbi, *Nature in the New World: From Christopher Columbus to Gonzalo Fernández de Oviedo*, translated J. Moyle (Pittsburgh, 1985), 165–73; S. Grande, 'Le relazioni geografiche fra P. Bembo, G. Fracastoro, G. B. Ramusio, G. Gastaldi', *Memorie della Società Geografica*, 12 (1905), 93–197; A. di Piero, 'Della vita e degli studi di G. B. Ramusio', *Archivio Veneto*, new series 4 (1902), 5–112; G. Lucchetta, 'Viaggiatori e racconti di viaggi nel Cinquecento' in *Storia della cultura veneta*, ed. G. Arnoldi and M. P. Stocchi (Vicenza, 1980), 482–9. And see Marica Milanesi's introduction to volume 1 of her edition of Ramusio's *Navigazioni e viaggi* (Turin, 1978–85), and her *Tolomeo sostituito: Studi di storia delle conoscenze geografiche nel XVI secolo* (Milan, 1984), chapter 1. See above, chapter 8, note 21.

37 Ramusio, *Navigazioni e viaggi*, ed. Milanesi, vol. 3, 23–4.

38 John Leland, *Commentarii de scriptoribus Britannicis* (Oxford, 1549), vol. 2, 367.

39 Roger Barlow, *Brief Summe of Geographie*, ed. E. G. R. Taylor (London, 1932), 135ff.

40 John Frampton, *The Most Noble and Famous Travels of Marcus Paulus* (London, 1579), cited in Skelton, *Explorers* 14.

41 William Gilbert, *De magnete* (London, 1600), 4.

42 This was executed in 1553; 'rinfrescata' in 1761 by Francesco Griselini. R. Gallo, 'La mappa dell'Asia della Sala dello Scudo nel Palazzo Ducale e il Milione di Marco Polo' in *Nel VII Centenario*,

195–232. A. E. Nordenskiöld, 'The influence of the "Travels of Marco Polo" on Jacopo Gastaldi's Maps of Asia', *Geographical Journal* (April 1899), 396–406 (Italian version, 'Intorno alla influenza dei "Viaggi di Marco Polo"', *Revista Geografica Italiana*, 8, 1901, 496–511). The maps are illustrated in Nordenskiöld's *Periplus*, plates 54–5.

43 G. Kish, 'The Japan of the "Mural Atlas" of the Palazzo Vecchio, Florence', *Imago Mundi*, 8 (1951), 52–4. Cf. A. Kammerer, *La découverte de la Chine par les Portugais au XVIᵉ siècle et la cartographie des portulans* avec des notes de toponymie chinoise par P. Pelliot (Leiden, *T'oung Pao*, supplément au Teme. 39, 1944), 45–6. The portolan of Lopo Homem of 1554 first displays the word 'Japan', though Gastaldi may have got there first with 'Giapam' in '1550'.

44 *The Complete Works of Doctor Francis Rabelais*, translated by Sir Thomas Urquhart, vol. 2 (London, 1927), 634–7; *Oeuvres Complètes*, ed. G. Demerson (Paris, 1973), 876 (where ch. 30). If actually written, as most believe, by François Rabelais then to be dated to around 1551–2.

45 *The Anatomy of Melancholy*, ed. T. Faulkner *et al.* (Oxford, 1989–90), vol. 2, 34, 38.

46 Louis Le Roy, *De la vicissitude . . .* (Paris, 1577), Bk 9, 91–3.

47 In general on this Reichert, 'Columbus', 46–53.

48 Gil, 'Libros', xxix–xxxi.

49 *Ibid.*; Nebenzahl, *Maps from the Age of Discovery*, 31–2, 38–9.

50 W. G. L. Randles, *De la terre plate au globe terrestre* (Paris, 1980), 370.

51 *Libro de Las Cosas Maravillosas*, 12, 15.

52 Gil, 'Libros', xlvi, xlix.

53 Gil, *El Libro*, 107–8; Gil, 'Libros', L.

54 Las Casas, *Historia*, vol. 1, 62, 251 'Marco Paulo, físico florentin'.

55 Reichert, 'Columbus', 49.

56 *Discoveries of the World . . .* (London, 1862), (Hakluyt's translation of 1601 from the Portuguese of Galvano's work published in 1563), 48–9.

57 *Portugaliae Monumenta Cartographica*, ed. A. Cortesão and A. Teixeira da Mota (Lisbon, 1960), vol. 1, 294–5 and *passim*.

58 J. A. Williamson, *The Cabot Voyages and Bristol Discovery under Henry VII* (Cambridge, 1962), 207–10.

59 Nebenzahl, *Maps from the Age of Discovery*, 45–51.

60 *Ibid.*, 52–5.

61 Cited in Skelton, *Explorers*, 16–17; for other cartographers with Polo influence: Pietro Apiano (1520), Oronce Fine (1531), Giulio de Musis (1554), see Almagià, 'Marco'. But many other examples could be adduced.

62 Reichert, 'Columbus', 53–5.

63 Kammerer, *La découverte de la Chine, Explorers*, 103–4.

64 Yule-Cordier, vol. 2, 277–80; Skelton, *La découverte de la Chine, Explorers*, 13.

65 R. W. Shirley, *The Mapping of the World: Early Printed World Maps 1472–1700* (London, 1984), 88–9, plate 68; the great promontory of Beach has not yet appeared in Mercator's double cordiform world map of 1538.

66 M. Pauli Veneti, *De regionibus orientalibus libri iii*, in *Novus orbis regionum ac insularum veteribus incognitarum* (Basel,1532), Bk 3, ch. 11 – De provincia Boëach.

67 *Early Voyages to Terra Australis now called Australia*, ed. R. H. Major (London, 1859), xiv–xviii.

68 J. C. Beaglehole, *The Exploration of the Pacific*, 2nd edn (London, 1947), 138–9.

69 Vitale Terrarossa, *Riflessioni geografiche circa le terre incognite distese in ossequio perpetuo della nobiltà veneziana . . . nella quali . . . si pruova che i Patrizi di Venezia prima d'ogni altro hanno all' Italia & all'Europa, discoperte tutte le terre anticamente incognite, anco l'America e la Terra Australis . . .* (Padua, 1686). It was republished the following year, F. Ambrosini, *Paesi e mari ignoti: America e colonialismo europeo nella cultura veneziana (secoli XVI–XVII)* (Venice, 1982), 178–9.

Chapter 10   *Jesuits, Imperialists and a Conclusion*

1 I must thank Professor J. R. Woodhouse for raising this with me. On the edition of the Ottimo text by Baldelli Boni in 1827, see Bertolucci Pizzorusso' Enunciazione', 340.

2 The supplementary material was apparently republished later as *De Sinarum Magnaeque Tartariae rebus commentatio alphabetica, ex auctoris commentariis super M. Poli* (n.d., n.p. but probably Berlin, 1675).

3 Samuel Purchas, *Hakluytus Posthumus . . .* , vol. 11 (London, 1906; original London, 1625), 188–308.

4 *Ibid.*, 187, 306.

5 Georg Horn, *De originibus Americanis libri quattuor* (The Hague, 1652), 23.

6 *South China in the Sixteenth Century*, ed. C. R. Boxer (London, 1953), 260; D. F. Lach, *Asia in the Making of Europe* (1965–1993), vol. 3, pt 4 1575–78.

7 A. C. Moule, *Christians in China* (London, 1930), 9–10; Matteo Ricci and Nicolas Trigault, *Histoire de l'expédition chrétienne au royaume del la Chine 1582–1610*, ed. J. Shis, G. Bessiere, J. Dehergne (n.p., 1978), 71 (Bk 1 ch. 2); 181 (Bk 4 ch. 3). So too, Diego de Pantoja in the Jesuit letterbook from Peking of 1602, Lach, *Asia in the Making of Europe*, vol. 3, pt 1, 319–20.

8 Pars secunda, ch. 6, 87–90.

9 Lach, *Asia in the Making of Europe*, vol. 3, 424; vol. 4, 1693, 1729, citing his *Nouvelle Relation de la Chine* (Paris, 1688, 1689), translated by John Ogilby as *A New History of China* (London, 1688).

10 *Description géographique de la Chine*, 4 vols (Paris, 1735), vol. 1, 435, 437–8; vol. 4, 581–2. It was translated shortly after into English by the Irishman Green and the Scotsman Guthrie; 'Green said of Guthrie that he knew no English, and Guthrie of Green that he knew no French' – *Boswell's Life of Johnson*, ed. G. B. Hill and L. F. Powell (Oxford, 1934), vol. 4, 30.

11 J. S. Cummins, *A Question of Rites. Friar Domingo Navarrete and the Jesuits in China* (Aldershot, 1993), 211.

12 E.g. J. Harris, *Navigantium atque Itinerantium Bibliotheca or Collections of Voyages and Travels* (2nd edn of 1715 and 3rd of 1744), said to be from Ramusio, in fact from the summary of Purchas; Pierre Bergeron, *Recueil de divers voyages curieux faits en Tartarie, en Perse et ailleurs*, 2 vols, (Leiden, 1729) and *Voyages faits principalement en Asie*, vol. 2 (La Haye, 1735), based on Müller.

[13] Published in London in 1747, 582–3.

[14] K. D. Hüllmann's *Städtewesen des Mittelalters* (Bonn, 1829), is noted in Yule-Cordier, vol. 1, 115–16.

[15] W. Robertson, *An Historical Disquisition* (London, 1791) 122, 237.

[16] *The Travels of Marco Polo*, ed. W. Marsden (London, 1818), ix.

[17] *Ibid.*, xxv.

[18] Of particular note before Pauthier, Placido Zurla's *Di Marco Polo e degli altri viaggiatori veneziani più illustri* (Venice, 1818–19); the publication by M. Roux under the auspices of the Société de Géographie de Paris of the Rustichello version of the text (the so-called *Geographic Edition*) in 1824; the 'Crusca' edition of an Italian version *Il Milione di Marco Polo* with a very influential commentary by G. Baldelli Boni (Florence, 1827).

[19] The life by his daughter prefaced to the third edition of Yule-Cordier has considerable period interest. See too Coutts-Trotter in the *Dictionary of National Biography*, and R. J. Bingle, 'Henry Yule, India and Cathay' in *Compassing the Vast Globe of the Earth*, ed. R. C. Bridges and P. E. Hair (London, 1996), 143–63.

[20] See P. Hopkirk, *Trespassers on the Roof of the World* (London, 1982), chs 2 and 3.

[21] For the background P. Hopkirk, *Foreign Devils on the Silk Road* (Newton Abbot, 1981); and *idem*, *The Great Game* (London, 1990).

[22] J. Critchley, *Marco Polo's Book* (Aldershot, 1992), 179.

[23] See Hopkirk, *Foreign Devils*, ch. 13.

[24] Foscolo Benedetto, 'Grandezza di Marco Polo', in his *Uomini e Tempi*, 73.

[25] *The Travels of Ibn Battuta A. D. 1325–1354*, translated by H. A. R. Gibb, 3 vols (London, 1938–71), and C. F. Beckinglam (1994); and Ross E. Dunn *The Adventures of Ibn Battuta: A Muslim Traveler of the 14th Century* (London, 1986).

Appendix II   *Times of Travel to China by Land*

[1] J. Critchley, *Marco Polo's Book* (Aldershot, 1992), 67, refers to the letter (to A. C. Moule) written by A. J. Charignon. Although the Book says (chapter lxii) that the Polos spent three years in 'Canpiciou', it does not specify when, and it is improbable that it would be while on an embassy from the West to the Great Khan.

[2] Francesco Balducci Pegolotti, 'Avisamento del viaggio del Gattaio', *La pratica della mercatura*, ed. A. Evans (Cambridge, 1936), 21–3 (in translation, R. S. Lopez and W. W. Raymond, *Medieval Trade in the Mediterranean World*, New York, 1955, 355–8 and H. Yule, *Cathay* rev. H. Cordier (London 1915; New York, 1967), vol. 3, 137–73); R. H. Bautier, 'Les relations économiques des Occident avec les pays d'Orient au Moyen Age. Points de vue et documents' in *Sociétés et compagnies de commerce en Orient et dans l'Ocean Indien*, ed. M. Mollat (Paris, 1970), 311–16 (and in Bautier's *Commerce méditeranéen et banquiers italiens au Moyen Age*, London, 1992, IV).

[3] H. Yule, *Cathay*, vol. 3, 148 n.2; E. Thomas, *Chronicles of the Pathán Kings of Delhi* (London, 1871), 203–4, n.1.

[4] In translation by A. C. Moule, *Christians in China* (London, 1930), 195.

[5] *The Times Atlas of World Exploration*, ed. F. Fernández-Armesto (London, 1991), 19.

[6] *Storia dei Mongoli*, ed. E. Menestò, chap. 9.

[7] *The Mission of Friar William of Rubruck*, ed. Jackson and Morgan, xi–xv.

[8] J. A. Boyle, 'The Journey of Het 'um I', *Central Asiatic Journal*, 9 (1964), 175–89

[9] R. S. Lopez, 'Nuove luci' *Studi Colombiani*, vol. 3 (Genoa, 1951), 395.

Appendix III   *Marco Polo and World Maps of the Fifteenth Century*

[1] M. Monmonnier, 'The Vinland Map, Columbus, and Italian-American Pride', in his *Drawing the Line: Tales of Maps and Cartocontroversy* (New York, 1995), ch. 3.

[2] M. Destombes, *Mappemondes* (Amsterdam, 1964), 205–7; F. V. Wieser, *Die Weltkarte des Albertin de Virga* (Innsbruck, 1912).

[3] Destombes, *Mappemondes*, 246–7, R. A. Skelton, T. E. Marston, G. D. Painter,

The Vinland Map and the Tartar Relation (London, 1965), 124–7; A. E. Nordenskiöld, *Periplus: An Essay on the Early History of Charts and Sailing Directions* (Stockholm, 1897), 19; V. I. J. Flint, *The Imaginative Landscape of Christopher Columbus* (Princeton, 1992), 20–1, 163–4.

4 Destombes, *Mappemondes*, 208–11; J. K. Wright, *Leardo Map of the World* (New York, 1928); P. Durazzo, *Il planisfero di Giovanni Leardo* (Mantua, 1885); Nordenskiöld, *Periplus*, 61. Gasparrini Leporace in *Mostra L'Asia*, 19 thinks Leardo used the Book for the 1453 map but not those of 1442 or 1448.

5 D. B. Durand, *The Vienna-Klosterneuburg Map Corpus . . .* (Leiden, 1952), 176, 371–2.

6 Destombes, *Mappemondes*, 211–14; Durand, *Map Corpus*, 209–13; J. B. Friedman, *The Monstrous Races . . .* (London, 1951), 56–8; Almagià, *Planisferi*, 30–31, plate 12.

7 Destombes, *Mappemondes*, 214–17; H. Winter, 'A circular map in a Ptolemaic MS', *Imago Mundi*, 10 (1953), 15–22.

8 Destombes, *Mappemondes*, 239–41; Almagià, *Planisferi*, 27–9, plate 11.

9 Destombes, *Mappemondes*, 222–3; E. L. Stevenson, *Genoese World Map 1457. Facsimile and Critical Text* (New York, 1912). Appendix II of Merisalo's edition of Bracciolini, *De varietate fortunae*, reproduces the verbal citations of Conti on the map.

10 Destombes, *Mappemondes*, 217–21; G. T. H. Kimble, *Catalan World Map of Modena* (facsimile), (London, 1934).

11 Destombes, *Mappemondes*, 228–9; *idem*, 'Fragments', 151–2.

12 R. Almagià, 'I mappamondi'; G. Kish, 'Two fifteenth-century maps of "Zipangu" . . .' *Yale University Library Gazette*, 40 (1996), 224.

13 Destombes, *Mappemondes*, 185; De la Roncière and Mollat du Jourdin, 21; Flint, 164–8; D. B. Quinn, 'Columbus and the North: England, Iceland, and Ireland', *William and Mary Quarterly* (1992), 289–91.

Works Cited

Versions of the Text

The Book of Ser Marco Polo the Venetian, ed. H. Yule, 3rd edn, revised by H. Cordier (London, 1903); reprinted 2 vols (New York, 1993)

The Description of the World, ed. A. C. Moule and P. Pelliot (London, 1938)

'The Gaelic abridgement of the Book of Marco Polo', trans. W. Stokes, *Zeitschrift für celtische Philologie*, 1 (1897)

Juan Fernández de Heredia's Aragonese Version of the 'Libro de Marco Polo', ed. J. J. Nitti (Madison, 1980)

Libro de Las Cosas Maravillosas de Marco Polo, introduction by R. Benítiz Claros (Madrid, 1947)

El libro de Marco Polo anotado por Cristóbal Colón: El libro de Marco Polo, version de Rodrigo de Santaella, ed. J. Gil (Madrid, 1987)

El Libro de Marco Polo: Ejemplar anotado por Cristóbal Colón y que se conserva en la Biblioteca Capitular y Colombina de Sevilla, ed. J. Gil, (*Tabula Americae*, vol. 5, Madrid, Testimento Compañía Editiones, 1986)

Le Livre de Marco Polo citoyen de Venise, conseiller privé et commissaire impérial de Khoubilai-Khaân, ed. M. G. Pauthier (Paris, 1865)

Marco Polo, ed. F. M. Esteves Pereira (Lisbon, 1922)

M. Pauli Veneti De regionibus Orientalibus libri iii, in S. Grynaeus, *Novus orbis regionum ac insularum veteribus incognitarum* (Basel, 1532)

Marka Pavlova z Benátek, Milion, ed. J. V. Prásek (Prague, 1902)

Il Milione, ed. L. Foscolo Benedetto (Florence, 1928)

Il Milione di Marco Polo, ed. G. Baldclli Boni (Florence, 1827)

Milione. Le Divisament dou monde, ed. G. Ronchi (Milan, 1982)

Milione. Versione toscana del Trecento, ed. V. Bertolucci Pizzorusso (Milan, 1975)

Il Milione con le postille di Cristoforo Colombo, ed. L. Giovannini (Rome, 1985)

Der mitteldeutsche Marco Polo, ed. H. von Tscharner (*Deutsche Texte des Mittelalters*, 40, Berlin, 1935)

The most noble and famous travels of Marcus Paulus, trans. John Frampton, (London, 1579)

Ramusio, G. B., *Navigazioni e viaggi*, ed. M. Milanesi, vol. 3 (Turin, 1980)

———. *Navigazioni e viaggi*. (Venice, 1559; facsimile, Amsterdam, 1968)

The Travels of Marco Polo, ed. William Marsden (London, 1818)

Viatges de Marco Polo: Verió catalana del segle XIV, ed. A. Gallina (Barcelona, 1958)

Other Works

Authors born before 1500 are listed under their first names Further, those few works and compilations, particularly in Italian, referred to mainly by title in the text are thus listed below.

Abulafia, D., 'Asia, Africa and the Trade of Medieval Europe', *The Cambridge Economic History*, vol. 2, 2nd edn by M. M. Postan and E. Miller (Cambridge, 1987)

Adam of Bremen, *Gesta Hammaburgensis Ecclesiae Pontificium*, ed. B. Schmeidler (Scriptores r. Germ. in u. schol., Hanover, 1917)

———. *History of the Archbishops of Hamburg-Bremen*, English translation by F. J. Tschau (New York, 1959)

Aerts, W. J. *et al.* (eds) *Alexander the Great in the Middle Ages* (Nijmegen, 1978)

Allsen, T., 'Mongolian princes and their merchant partners', *Asia Major*, 3rd, series vol. 2, pt 2 (1989)

Almagià, R., 'I mappamondi di Enrico Martelli e alcuni concetti geografici di Cristoforo Colombo', *La Bibliofilia*, 42 (1940)

———. *Planisferi carte nautiche, e affini dal secolo XIV al XVII esistenti nella Biblioteca Apostolica Vaticana* (*Monumenta Cartographica Vaticana*, 1, Vatican, 1944)

Ambrosini, F., *Paesi e mari ignoti: America e colonialismo europeo nella cultura veneziana (secoli XVI-XVII)*, (Venice 1982)

Amitai-Preiss, R., *Mongols and Mamlukes: The Mamluk-Ilkhanid War 1260–1281* (Cambridge, 1995)

Anastos, M. V., 'Pletho, Strabo and Columbus', reprinted from *Mélanges Henri Grégoire*, vol. 4 (Brussels, 1953), in his *Studies in Byzantine Intellectual History* (London, 1979)

Anderson, A. R., *Alexander's Gate, Gog and Magog and the Inclosed Nations* (Cambridge, Mass., 1932)

Antoine de la Sale's *La Salade* (*Oeuvres Complètes*, vol. 1), ed. F. Desonay (Liège, 1935)

Antonio Pucci, *Libro di varie storie*, ed. A. Varvaro (Palermo, 1957)

Arnaldi, G., 'Scuole nella Marca Trevigiana e a Venezia nel secolo XIII', in *Storia della cultura veneta*, vol. 1

Ashtor, A., *Levant Trade in the Later Middle Ages* (Princeton, 1983)

Astley's Voyages [i.e. *The New Collection of Voyages and Travels*] (London, Thomas Astley, 1747)

Atiya, A. S., *The Crusade in the Later Middle Ages* (London, 1938)

Attwater, D., *The Christian Churches of the East* (Milwaukee, 1948)

Azalus, Pompilius, *De omnibus rebus naturalibus quae continentur in mundo* (Venice, 1544)

Babinger, F., 'Maestro Ruggiero delle Puglie: relatore pre-poliano sui Tartari' in *Nel VII centenario*

Backer, L. de, *L'Extrême Orient au Moyen Age* (Paris, 1877)

Badel, P.-Y., 'Lire la merveille selon Marco Polo', *Revue des Sciences humaines*, 183 (1981)

Bagrow, L., *History of Cartography*, revised and enlarged by R. A. Skelton (London, 1964)

Balard, M., 'Les Gênois en Asie centrale et en Extrême-Orient au XIVᵉ siècle: un cas exceptionnel?' in *Economies et sociétés au Moyen Age: Mélanges offerts à Edouard Perroy* (Paris, 1973)

———. *La Mer Noire et la Romanie génoise aux XIIIᵉ–XVᵉ siècles* (London, 1989)

———. 'Precursori di Cristoforo Colombo: i Genovesi in Estremo Orient nel XIV secolo', *Studi Colombiani*, vol. 3

Balazs, E., 'Marco Polo and the Capital of China' in his *Chinese Civilisation and Bureaucracy* (New Haven, 1964) (in Italian in *Oriente Poliano*)

Barros, J. de, *Asia: dos feitos que os Portugueses fizeram no descobrimiento e conquista dos mares e terras do oriente. Da primeira decada*, ed. A. Baiao (Coimbra, 1932)

Bartlett, R., *Gerald of Wales 1146–1233* (Oxford, 1982)

Bauer, C., 'Venezianische Salzhandelspolitik bis zum Ende des 14. Jahrhunderts', *Vierteljahresschrift für Wirtschaftsgeschichte*, 22 (1930)

Baumgartner, E., 'Les techniques narratives dans le roman en prose' in *The Legacy of Chrétien de Troyes*, ed. N. J. Lacy, D. Kelly and K. Busby, vol. 1 (Amsterdam, 1987)

Bautier, R. H., 'Les relations économiques des Occident avec les pays d' Orient au Moyen Age. Points de vue et documents.' in *Sociétés et compagnies de commerce en Orient et dans l'Ocean Indien*, ed. M. Mollat (Paris, 1970)

———. *Commerce méditerranéen et banquiers italiens au Moyen Age* (London, 1992)

Beaglehole, J. C., *The Exploration of the Pacific*, 2nd edn (London, 1947)

Beckingham, C. F., 'The achievements of Prester John', *Between Islam and Christendom* (London, 1983), article I

Benjamin of Tudela, *The Itinerary*, ed. M. N. Adler (London, 1907)

Bennett, J. W., *The Rediscovery of Sir John Mandeville* (New York, 1954)

Bergeron, P., *Recueil de divers voyages curieux faits en Tartarie, en Perse et ailleurs*, 2 vols (Leiden, 1729)

———. *Voyages faits principalement en Asie*, 2 vols (La Haye, 1735)

Bertolucci, G., 'Polo, Marco', *Enciclopedia Dantesca*, vol. 4 (Rome, 1973)

Bertolucci Pizzorusso, V., 'Enunciazione e produzione del testo nel *Milione*', *Studi mediolatini e volgari*, 25 (1977)

———. 'Lingue e stili nel "Milione"', in *L'epopea delle scoperte*, ed. R. Zorzi (Venice, 1994)

Bertrandon de la Broquière, *Le Voyage d'Outremer*, ed. C. Schefer (Paris, 1892)

Bezzola, G. A., *Die Mongolen in abendländischer Sicht 1220–1270* (Bern and Munich, 1974)

Biblioteca Colombina, Catálogo de sus libros impresos, ed. S. Arbolí y Faraudo, with notes by S. de la Rosa y López (Seville, 1888–1948)

Bihl, M. (with transcripts of letters by A. C. Moule), 'De duabus epistolis Fratrum Minorum Tartariae Aquilonis an. 1323', *Archivium Franciscanum Historicum*, 16 (1923)

Bingle, R. J., 'Henry Yule, India and Cathay' in *Compassing the Vast Globe of the Earth*, ed. R. C. Bridges and P. E. Hair (Hakluyt, London, 1996)

Biondo Flavio, *Scritti inediti e rari*, ed. B. Nogara (Rome, 1927)

Blaeu, J., *Le Grand Atlas ou Cosmographie Blaviane* (Amsterdam, 1663)

Bonvesin della Riva, *De magnalibus Mediolani*, ed. M. Corti (Milan, 1974)

Book of Mac Carthaigh Riabhach Otherwise the Book of Lismore (facsimiles in collotype of Irish manuscripts, vol. 5 [Dublin, 1950])

Book of the Knowledge of all the Kingdoms, Lands, and Lordships that are in the World, ed. C. Markham (London, 1912)

Borlandi, F., 'Alle origini del libro di Marco Polo' in *Studi in onore de A. Fanfani*, vol. 1 (Milan, 1962)

Boxer, C. R. (ed.) *South China in the Sixteenth Century* (London, 1953)

Boyle, J. A., 'The journey of Het 'um I, King of Little Armenia, to the Court of the Great Khan Möngke', *Central Asiatic Journal*, 9 (1964)

————. 'Marco Polo and his Description of the World', *History Today* (1971)

————. *The Mongol World Empire 1206–1370* (London, 1977)

————. 'Rashid al-Din: the first world historian', in *The Mongol World Empire*, article XXIX

Branca, D., *I romanzi italiani di Tristano e la 'Tavola ritonda'* (Florence, 1968)

Bratianu, G. I., *Recherches sur le commerce génois dans la Mer Noire au XIIIe siècle* (Paris, 1924)

Bretschneider, E., *Medieval Researches from Eastern Asiatic Sources*, 2 vols (London, 1888)

Brincken, A.-D. von, 'Le Nestorianisme vu par l'Occident' in *1274: Année Charnière: Mutations et Continuités* (Paris, 1977)

Brugnoli, F., 'I toscani nel Veneto e le cerchie toscaneggianti' in *Storia della cultura veneta*, vol. 2

Brunel, C., 'David Ashby, auteur méconnu des "Faites des Tartares"', *Romania*, vol. 79 (1958)

Brunetto Latini, *Li Livres dou Tresor*, ed. F. J. Carmody (Berkeley, 1948)

Budge, W., *The Monks of Kûblâ Khân* (London, 1929)

Burnett, C. and Gautier Dalché, P., 'Attitudes towards the Mongols in Medieval Literature: the xxii Kings of Gog and Magog from the court of Frederick II to Jean de Mandeville', *Viator*, 22 (1991)

Burton, R., *The Anatomy of Melancholy*, ed. T. Faulkner *et al.* (Oxford, 1989–90)

Bynum, C. W., 'Wonder', *American Historical Review* (1997)

C. de Bridia, *Hystoria Tartarorum*, ed. A. Önnerors (Berlin, 1967)

————. *Hystoria Tartarorum* with translation and commentary by G. D. Painter in *The Vinland Map and the Tartar Relation*

Cambridge History of China, vol. 6: *Alien Regimes and Border States 907–1368*, ed. H. Franke and D. Twitchett (Cambridge, 1994)

Campbell, M. B., *The Witness and the Other World: Exotic European Travel Writing, 400–1600* (Ithaca, 1985)

Campbell, T., *The Earliest Printed Maps 1472–1500* (London, 1987)

Caraci, G., 'Viaggi fra Venezia ed il Levante fino al XIV secolo e relativa produzione cartografica', in *Venezia e il Levante fino al secolo XV*, ed. A. Pertusi, vol. 1 (Florence, 1973)

Carile, A., 'Territorio e ambiente nel 'Divisament dou Monde', *Studi veneziani*, vol. 1 (1977)

Carrington Goodrich, L., 'Westerners and Central Asians in Yuan China', in *Oriente Poliano*

Cary, G., *The Medieval Alexander*, ed. D. J. A. Ross (Cambridge, 1967)

Casella, N., 'Pio II tra geografia e storia: la "Cosmographia"', *Archivio della Società Romana di Storia Patria*, series 3, vol. 26 (1974)

Catto, J. I., 'Guillaume du Pré and the Tartars', *Archivium Franciscanum Historicum*, 60 (1967)

Cecchetti, B., 'Testamento di Pietro Vioni veneziano fatto in Tauris [Persia] MCCLXIV [*sic*] X decembre', *Archivio Veneto*, 26 (1883)

Chahin, M., *The Kingdom of Armenia* (London, 1987)

Chambers, E. K., *Arthur of Britain* (London, 1927)

Chao, 'The Wonder of the Capital' trans. A. C. Moule, *New China Review* (1921)

Chau Ju-Kua, *On the Chinese and Arab Trade*, ed. and trans. F. Hirth and W. W. Rockhill (St Petersburg, 1911)

Chiappori, M. G., 'I tre Polo nella "Ecclesia militans" de Andrea Bonaiuti in S. Maria Novella a Firenze', *Quaderni Medievali*, 15 (1983)

Chronica monasterii Sancti Bertini auctore Iohanne Longo, *MGH.SS*, vol. 25, ed. O. Holder-Egger

Chronicles of the Reigns of Edward I and Edward II, ed. W. Stubbs, vol. 76 (Rolls Series, 1882)

Cioranescu, A., 'Portugal y las cartas de Toscanelli', *Estudios Americanos*, 14 (1957)

Cleaves, F. W., 'A Chinese source bearing on Marco Polo's departure and a Persian source on his arrival in Persia', *Harvard Journal of Asiatic Studies*, vol. 15 (1952)

————. 'An early Mongol version of the Alexander Romance', *Harvard Journal of Asiatic Studies*, 22 (1959), 1–99

Colección Documental del Descubrimiento (1470–1506), ed. J. Pérez de Tudela, C. Secco Serrano, R. Ezquerra Abalia, E. López Oto (Bilbao, 1994)

Collis, M., *Marco Polo* (London, 1959)

Colombo, F., *Historie della vita e dei fatti dell'Ammiraglio Cristoforo Colombo* (Venice, 1571)

————. *Historie*, ed. R. Caddeo (Milan, 1930)

————. *The Life of Admiral Christopher Colombus by his son Ferdinand*, trans. B. Keen (New Brunswick, 1959)

[Columbus] *Libro Copiador de Cristóbal Colón*, ed. A. Rumeu de Armas (Madrid, 1989)

Cordier, H., 'L'Extrême Orient dans l'atlas catalan de Charles V', *Bulletin de geographie historique et descriptive* (1895)

Cortelazzo, M., 'La cultura mercantile e marinaresca', in *Storia della cultura veneta*

Cortesão, A., *History of Portuguese Cartography* (Coimbra, 1969)

Creytens, R., 'Le manuel de conversation de Philippe de Ferrare O.P. (†1350?)', *Archivum Fratrum Praedicatorum*, vol. 15 (1945)

Crick, J., *Historia Regum Britanniae of Geoffrey of Monmouth. A summary catalogue of the manuscripts* (Woodbridge, 1990)

Cristiani, E., *Nobilità e Popolo nel comune de Pisa* (Naples, 1962)

Critchley, J., *Marco Polo's Book* (Aldershot, 1992)

Crone, G. R., 'Fra Mauro's Representation of the Indian Ocean and the Eastern Islands' in *Studi Colombiniani*, vol. 3

Crosland, J., *The Old French Epic* (Oxford, 1951)

Cummins, J. S., *A Question of Rites. Friar Domingo Navarrete and the Jesuits in China* (Aldershot, 1993)

Cuttino, G. P., *English Diplomatic Administration 1259–1339* (2nd edn, Oxford, 1971)

Daniel, N., *Islam and the West: The Making of an Image* (Edinburgh, 1960)

Dauvillier, J., *Histoire des institutions des églises orientales au Moyen Age* (London, 1983)

————. 'Les provinces chaldéennes "de l'extérieur" au Moyen Age', *Mélanges F. Cavallera* (Toulouse, 1948)

Dawson, C. (ed.) *The Mongol Mission* (London, 1955; reprinted as *Mission to Asia*, New York, 1987)

Degenhart, B. and Schnitt, A., 'M. Sanudo und Paolino veneto', *Römische Jahrbuch für Kunstgeschichte*, 14 (1973)

De La Mare, A., 'The Shop of a Florentine "Cartolaio" in 1426' in *Studi offerti a Roberto Ridolfi*, ed. B. Maracchi Biagiarelli and D. E. Rhodes (Florence, 1973)

Deluz, C., *Le livre de Jean de Mandeville: une 'Géographie' au XIVe siècle* (Louvain-la-Neuve, 1988)

Deluz, C., 'Villes et organisation de l'espace: La Chine de Marco Polo' in *Villes, bonnes villes, cités et capitales. Études d'historie urbaine (XIIe–XVIIIe siècle) offertes à Bernard Chevalier* (Caen, 1993)

Demiéville, P., 'La situation religeuse en Chine au temps de Marco Polo', in *Oriente Poliano*

Destombes, M., 'Fragments of two medieval maps at the Topkapu Saray Library' *Imago Mundi*, vol. 12 (1955)

———. *Mappemondes AD 1200–1500* (Amsterdam, 1964)

Diario of Christopher Columbus' First Voyage to America 1492–1493, ed. O. Dunn and J. E. Kelley Jr (Norman, 1989)

Diffie, B. W. and Winius, G. D., *Foundations of the Portuguese Empire (1415–1580)* (Minneapolis, 1970)

Dilke, O. A. W., 'The culmination of Greek cartography in Ptolemy' in *The History of Cartography*, ed. J. B. Harley and D. Woodward vol. 1 (London, 1987)

Dilke, O. and Dilke, M., 'Mapping a crusade – propaganda and war in 14th century Palestine', *History Today*, no. 39 (August 1989)

Diller, A., 'A Geographical Treatise by George Gemistos Pletho', *Isis*, vol. 27 (1937)

———. 'The autographs of George Gemistus Plethon', *Scriptorium*, vol. 10 (1956)

Domenichelli, T., *Sopra la vita e i viaggi del beato Odorico da Pordenone dell'ordine de' Minori* (Prato, 1881)

Dunn, R. E., *The Adventures of Ibn Battuta: A Muslim Traveller of the Fourteenth Century* (London, 1986)

Durand, D. B., *The Vienna-Klosterneuburg Map Corpus of the Fifteenth Century: a Study in the Transition from Medieval to Modern Science* (Leiden, 1952)

Durazzo, P., *Il planisfero di Giovanni Leardo* (Mantua, 1885)

El atlas catalán de Cresques Abraham (Barcelona, 1977)

Fernández-Armesto, F., *Before Columbus: Exploration and Colonisation from the Mediterranean to the Atlantic 1229–1492* (London, 1987)

Fernández Pousa, F., 'Un "Imago Mundi" español: Ludovicus de Angulo: De imagine seu figura mundi, Lion, 1456', *Revista de Indias*, vol. 2 (1941)

Folena, G., 'La tradizione delle opere di Dante Alighieri' in *Atti del Congresso Internazionale di Studi Danteschi*, vol. 1 (Florence, 1965)

———. 'Tradizione e cultura trobadorica nelle corti e nelle città venete', in *Storia della cultura veneta*

Foscolo Benedetto, L., 'Non Rusticiano ma Rustichello', in his *Uomini e Tempi: Pagine varie di critica e storia* (Milan, 1953)

———. 'Grandezza di Marco Polo', in *Uomini e Tempi*

Flint, V. I. J., *The Imaginative Landscape of Christopher Columbus* (Princeton, 1992)

Francesco Balducci Pegolotti, 'Avisamento del viaggio del Gattaio', *La Pratica della Mercatura*, ed. A. Evans (Cambridge, 1936)

Francesco da Barberino, *I documenti d'amore*, ed. F. Egidi (Rome, 1905)

Franke, H., *China under Mongol Rule* (Aldershot, 1994)

———. 'Could the Mongol emperors read and write Chinese?', *Asia Minor* (1953)

Franke, H. 'The exploration of the Yellow River sources under Emperor Qubilai in 1281' in his *China under Mongol Rule*, section 9

———. *Geld und Wirtschaft in China unter der Mongolen-Herrschaft* (Leipzig, 1949)

———. 'Das "himmlische Pferd" des Johann von Marignola', *Archiv für Kulturgeschichte*, 50 (1968)

———. 'Sino-Western contacts under the Mongol Empire', sections 53–4, in his *China under Mongol Rule*

———. 'Some sinological remarks on Rashid al-Din's history of China' in *China under Mongol Rule*, section 3, (Aldershot, 1994)

———. 'Some Western contacts under the Mongol Empire', *Journal of the Hong Kong Branch of the Royal Asiatic Society*, series 6, vol. 58 (1966)

Frappier, J., *Étude sur 'La mort le roi Artu'* (Geneva, 1968)

Fried, J., 'Auf der Suche nach der Wirklichkeit. Die Mongolen und die europäische Erfahrungswissenschaft im 13. Jahrhundert', *Historische Zeitschrift*, 243 (1986)

Friedman, J. B., *The Monstrous Races in Medieval Art and Thought* (London, 1951)

Gallo, R., 'Marco Polo: la sua famiglia e il suo libro' in *Nel VII centenario*

———. 'La mappa dell'Asia della Sala dello Scudo nel Palazzo Ducale e il Milione di Marco Polo' in *Nel VII centenario*

———. 'Le mappe geografiche del Palazzo Ducale di Venezia', *Archivio Veneto* (1943)

———. 'Nuovi documenti riguardanti Marco Polo e la sua famiglia', *Atti dell' Istituto Veneto di Scienze, lettere ed arti: Classe di scienze morali e lettere*, vol. 116 (1958)

Gandillac, M. de, 'Sur quelques voyages utopiques' in his *Voyager à la Renaissance* (Paris, 1987)

Gardner, E. G., *The Arthurian Legend in Italian Literature* (London, 1938)

Garin, E., 'Ritratto di Paolo dal Pozzo Toscanelli' in his *La cultura filosofica del Rinascimento italiano: Ricerche e documenti*, 2nd edn (Florence, 1979)

Gentile, S., *Firenze e la scoperta dell'America. Umanesimo e geografia nel 400 fiorentino. Catalogo dell'esposizione, Biblioteca Medicea Laurenziana* (Florence, 1992)

Gerald of Wales, *The History and Topography of Ireland*, trans. J. J. O'Meara (Harmondsworth, 1982)

Gervais de Tilbury, *Le Livre des Merveilles*, trans. A. Duchesne (Paris, 1992)

Gestes de Chiprois: Recueil de chroniques françoises écrites en Orient aux XIIIᵉ et XIVᵉ siècles, Les, ed. G. Reynaud (Geneva, 1887)

Gil, J., *Cristóbal Colón, Textos y documentos completos*, ed. C. Varela (Madrid, 1984)

Gill, J., *The Council of Florence* (Cambridge, 1959)

Giovanni Boccaccio, *Il comento alla Divina Comedia e gli altri scritti intorno a Dante*, ed. D. Guerri (Bari, 1918)

———. *The Decameron*, trans. G. H. McWilliam (Harmondsworth, 1972)

Giovanni di Pian di Carpine, *Storia dei Mongoli*, ed. E. Menestò, with contributions by P. Daffinà, C. Leonardi, M. C. Lungarotti and L. Petech (Spoleto, 1989)

Giovanni Villani, *Cronica*, ed. F. Gherardi Dragomanni (Florence, 1844)

Goitein, S. D., 'From the Mediterranean to India', *Speculum*, 29 (1954)

———.'Letters and documents on the India Trade in medieval times', *Islamic Culture*, 37 (1963)

Gomes Eannes da Zurara, *Cronica do Descobrimiento e Conquista da Guiné*, ed., J. de Bragança (Opporto, 1937),

Gribaudi, P., 'Il P. Gaspar Gorrizio de Novara', *Bollettino storico bibliografico subalpino*, 40 (1938)

Guenée, B., *Histoire et culture historique dans l'Occident médiéval* (Paris, 1980)

Guerra, G. della, *Rustichello da Pisa* (Pisa, 1955)

Guilielmus de Boldensele, 'Itinerarius', ed. C. L. Grotefend, *Zeitschrift des Historischen Vereins für Niedersachsen* (1852, reprinted Hanover, 1855)

Guillaume de Rubruck, *Itinerarium* in *Sinica Franciscana*, vol. 1

————. *The Mission of Friar William of Rubruck: His Journey to the Court of the Great Khan Möngke, 1253–1255*, ed. P. Jackson and D. O. Morgan (London, 1990)

————. *Voyage dans l'Empire Mongol 1253–1255*, ed. C. Kappler and R. Kappler (Paris, 1985)

————. *The Texts and Versions of John de Plano Carpini and William de Rubruquis*, ed. C. R. Beazley (London, 1903)

Guzman, G. G., 'The Encyclopedist Vincent of Beauvais and his Mongol extracts from John of Plano Carpini and Simon of Saint-Quentin', *Speculum*, 49 (1974)

————. 'European clerical envoys to the Mongols. Reports of western merchants in Eastern Europe and Central Asia 1231–1255', *Journal of Modern History*, vol. 22 (1996)

————.'Simon of Saint-Quentin and the Dominican Mission to the Mongol Baiju: a reappraisal', *Speculum*, 46 (1971)

————. 'Simon of Saint-Quentin as historian of the Mongols and Seljuk Turks', *Medievalia et Humanistica* (1972)

Haeger, J. W., 'Marco Polo in China? Problems with internal evidence', *Bulletin of Sung and Yuan Studies*, 14 (1978)

Halde, J. B. du, *Description géographique de la Chine* (Paris, 1735)

Hamann, G., 'Fra Mauro und die italienische Kartographie seiner Zeit als Quellen zur frühen Entdeckungsgeschichte', *Mitteilungen des Instituts für Österreichische Geschichtsforschung*, 78 (1970)

Hamilton, B., 'Prester John and the Three Kings of Cologne', *Studies in Medieval History Presented to R. H. C. Davis*, ed. H. Mayr-Harting and R. I. Moore (London, 1985)

Hankey, A. T., 'Bandini, Domenico ' in *Dizionario Biografico Italiano*, vol. 5 (1903)

————. 'The successive revisions and surviving codices of the Fons memorabilium of Domenico di Bandino', *Rinascimento*, vol. 2 (1960)

Hanske, J. and Kuotsala, A., 'Berthold von Regensburg, O. F. M. and the Mongol-Medieval Sermon as a historical source', *Archivium Franciscanum Historicum*, 89 (1996)

Harley, J. B. and Woodward, D. (eds) *Cartography in the Traditional Islamic and South Asian Societies* (*The History of Cartography*, vol. 2, pt 1; London, 1992)

Harris, J., *Navigantium atque Itinerantium Bibliotheca or Collections of Voyages and Travels* (London, 1715)

Heers, J., 'Le projet de Chrisophe Columb' in *Colombeis*, vol. 1 (Genoa, 1986)

————. *Marco Polo* (Paris, 1983)

Heers, J. and Groer, de G. (eds) *Itinéraire en Terre Sainte (1970–1971)*, (Paris, 1978)

Henige, D., *In Search of Columbus: The Sources for the First Voyage* (Tucson, 1991)

[Hetoum/Haytoun/Hayton], *La Fleur des histoires de la terre d'Orient*, ed. C. Kohler (*Recueil de Historiens des Croisades, Histoires Arméniens*, vol. 2)

Hetoum, *A Lytell Chronycle*, ed. G. Burger (London, 1988)

Higgins, I. M., *Writing East: the Travels of Sir John Mandeville* (Philadelphia, 1997)

Hocquet, J. C., *Le sel et la fortune de Venise* (Lille, 1978–9)

Hodgen, M. T., *Early Anthropology in the Sixteenth and Seventeenth Centuries* (Philadelphia, 1971)

Hopkirk, P., *Foreign Devils on the Silk Road* (Newton Abbot, 1981)

———. *Trespassers on the Roof of the World* (London, 1982)

———. *The Great Game* (London, 1990)

Horn, G., *De originibus Americanis Libri quattuor* (The Hague, 1652)

Hourani, G. F., *Arab Seafaring in the Indian Ocean in Ancient and Early Medieval Times* (Princeton, 1951)

Humphreys, K. W., *The Book Provisions of Medieval Friars* (Amsterdam, 1964)

Huntington, A. M., *Catalogue of the Library of Ferdinand Columbus* (New York, 1905; reprinted 1967)

Hyde, J. K., 'Ethnographers in search of an audience' in his *Literacy and its Uses: Studies on Late Medieval Italy*, ed. D. Waley (Manchester, 1993)

———. 'Medieval Descriptions of Cities', *Bulletin of the John Rylands Library*, 48 (1986)

Lhystoire merveilleuse plaisante et recreative du grand empereur de tartarie seigneur des tartares, nommé le Grand Can (Paris, 1529)

Ibn Battuta, *The Travels A.D. 1325–1354*, vols 1–3, trans. H. A. R. Gibb (London, 1958–71) vol. 4 trans. C. F. Beckingham (London, 1994)

Irwin, R., *The Arabian Nights: A Companion* (Harmondsworth, 1995)

Islam, S. M., *The Ethics of Travel from Marco Polo to Kafka* (Manchester, 1996)

Iwanczak, W., 'Entre l'espace ptolémaïque et l'empirie: les cartes de fra Mauro', *Médiévales: Langue, Textes, Histoire*, vol. 18 (1990)

Jackson, P., 'The Crusade against the Mongols', *Journal of Ecclesiastical History*, 42 (1991)

———. 'The dissolution of the Mongol empire', *Central Asiatic Journal*, 22 (1978)

Jacopo da Sanseverino, *Libro piccolo di meraviglie*, ed. M. Guglielminetti (Milan, 1985)

Jacopo da Voragine, *Legenda Aurea*, ed. T. Graesse (Osnabrück, 1969)

Johann Schiltberger, *The Bondage and Travels of Johann Schiltberger (1396–1427)*, ed. J. Buchan Telfer (London, 1879)

John Capgrave, *Ye Solace of Pilgrimes*, ed. C. A. Mills (Oxford, 1911)

John Mandeville, *The Travels*, trans. C. W. R. D. Moseley (Harmondsworth, 1983)

Jordanus, *The Wonders of the East*, ed. H. Yule (London, 1863)

Jourdain Catalani de Séverac, *Mirabilia Descripta; Les Merveilles de l'Asie*, ed. H. Cordier (Paris, 1925)

Joris, S., 'Autour du Divisament du Monde. Rusticien de Pise et l'empereur Henri VII de Luxembourg (1310–1313)', *Le Moyen Age* (1994)

Juan González de Mendoza, *Historia de las cosas mas notables del gran Reyna de la China* (Rome, 1985)

Kammerer, A., *La découverte de la Chine par les Portugais au XVIe siècle et la cartographie des portulans avec des notes de toponymie chinoise par P. Pelliot* (Leiden, *T'oung Pao*, supplément au Tome 39, 1944)

Kawwazoe Shoji, 'Japan and East Asia' in *The Cambridge History of Japan*, vol. 3 *Medieval Japan*, ed. Kozo Yamamura (Cambridge, 1990)

Kedar, B. Z., 'Chi era Andrea Franco?', *Atti della Società Ligure di Storia Patria*, n.s., vol. 17 (1977)

Kimble, G. T. H., *Catalan World Map of Modena (facsimile)*, (London, 1934)

———. *Geography in the Middle Ages* (London, 1938)

———. 'The Laurentian World Map with special reference to its portrayal of Africa', *Imago Mundi*, vol. 1 (1935)

Kircher, A., *China Illustrata* (Amsterdam, 1667)

Kish, G., 'Two fifteenth-century maps of "Zipangu": Notes on the early cartography of Japan', *Yale University Library Gazette*, 40 (1966)

———. 'The Japan of the "Mural Atlas of the Palazzo Vecchio, Florence"', *Imago Mundi*, vol. 8 (1951)

Lach, D. F., *Asia in the Making of Europe* (Chicago, 1965–93)

Lane, F. C., *Venice: A Maritime Republic* (Baltimore, 1973)

Langlois, J. D. (ed.) *China under Mongol Rule* (Princeton, 1981)

Larner, J., 'The Church and the Quattrocento Renaissance in Geography', *Renaissance Studies* (1998)

———. 'Traditions of literary biography in Boccaccio's Life of Dante', in *Towns and Townspeople in Medieval and Renaissance Europe: Essays in Memory of J. K. Hyde*, ed. B. Pullan and S. Reynolds, *Bulletin of the John Rylands University Library of Manchester*, 72, (1990)

La lettera del Prete Gianni, ed. G. Zaganelli (Parma, 1990)

Las Casas, Bartolomé de, *Historia delos Indias* (Mexico and Buenos Aires, 1965)

Laurent, M. H., 'Grégoire X et Marco Polo (1266–71)', *Mèlanges d'archéologie et d'histoire*, 38 (1941–6)

Lees, B. A., *Alfred the Great* (London, 1919)

Le Goff, J., 'The Marvellous in the Medieval West' in his *The Medieval Imagination* trans. Arthur Goldhammer (London, 1988)

———. 'L'Occident médiévale et l'océan Indien: un horizon onirique' in his *Pour un autre Moyen Age* (Paris, 1977)

Leland, J., *Commentarii de scriptoribus Britannicis* (Oxford, 1549)

'Le Livre du Grant Caan', ed. M. Jacquet, *Journal Asiatique*, 6 (1830)

Lentz, W., 'War Marco Polo auf dem Pamir?', *Zeitung der Deutschen Morgenländischen Gesellschaft*, 86 (1933)

Letts, M., *Sir John Mandeville: the Man and His Book* (London, 1949)

'Der "Libellus de notitia orbis" Johannes III (de Galonifontibus?) O. P., Erzbischofs von Sultanyeh', ed. A. Kern, *Archivium Fratrum Praedicatorum*, vol. 8 (1938)

Libro del cononsçimiento de todos los reynos e señoríos, ed. M. Jimenez de la Espada (Madrid, 1877)

Limentani, A., 'Martin da Canal e "Les Estoires de Venise"'; in *Storia della cultura veneta*, vol. 1

Li Tse-fen, 'Reality and myth in the Milione of Marco Polo' (in Chinese) *The Eastern Miscellany*, October/November 1977, trans. I. N. Molinari, 'Un articolo d'autore cinese su Marco Polo e la Cina', Supplement no. 30, *Istituto Orientale di Napoli: Annali*, vol. 42 (1982), fasc. 1

Lo Jung-Pang, 'Chinese shipping and East-West trade from the Tenth to the Forteenth Century' in *Sociétés*, ed. Mollat

Loenertz, R. E., *La société des Frères Pérégrinants: Etude sur l'Orient Dominicain*, vol. 1 (Rome, 1937)

Longhena, M., 'I manoscritti del quarto libro del De Varietate Fortunae di Poggio Bracciolini', *Bollettino della Società Geografica Italiana*, series 7, vol. 2 (1925)

Loomis, R. S., 'Edward I, Arthurian Enthusiast', *Speculum*, 28 (1953)

Lopez, R., 'China silk in Europe in the Yüan period', *Journal of the American Oriental Society*, 72 (1952)

———. 'European merchants in the medieval Indies', *Journal of Economic History*, vol. 3 (1942)

———. 'L'extrême frontière de l'Europe médiévale', *Le Moyen Age* (1963)

———. 'Nouveaux documents sur les marchands italiens en Chine à l'époque mongole', *Académie des Inscriptions et Belles Lettres: Comptes Rendus* (1977)

———. 'Nuove luci sugli italiani in Estremo Oriente prima di Colombo', *Studi Colombiani*, vol. 3 (Genoa, 1951)

———. 'Venezia e le grandi linee dell'espansione commerciale nel secolo XIII' in *La civiltà veneziana del secolo di Marco Polo* (Venice, 1955)

Lopez, R. S., and Raymond, W. W., *Medieval Trade in the Mediterranean World* (New York, 1955)

Löseth, E., *Le Roman en prose de Tristan, le roman de Palamedes et la compilation de Rusticien de Pise* (Paris, 1891, *Bibliothèque de l'École des Hautes Études*, vol. 82 1890 [*sic*], reprinted New York, 1970)

Luttrell, A., 'Greek histories translated and compiled for Juan Fernández de Heredia, Master of Rhodes, 1377–1396' in his *The Hospitallers in Cyprus, Rhodes, Greece, and the West 1291–1440*, vol. 20 (London, 1978)

Luzzana Caraci, I., *Colombo vero e falso: La costruzione delle Historie fernandine* (Genoa, 1989)

Maqbul Ahmad, S., 'Cartography of al-Sharif al-Idrisi' in *Cartography in the Traditional Islamic and South Asian Societies*, ed J. B. Harley and D. Woodward

Magnaghi, A., *Precursori di Colombo? Il tentativo di viaggio transoceanico dei Genovesi fratelli Vivaldi nel 1291* (Memorie della R. Società Geografica Italiana, vol. 18, Rome, 1935)

Major, R. H. (ed.) *Early Voyages to Terra Australis now called Australia* (London, 1859)

Manzano, M., and Manzano, A. M., *Los Pinzones y el Descubrimiento de América* (Madrid, 1988)

Manzoni, L., 'Fra Francesco Pipino', *Atti e memorie della R. Deputazione di storia patria per la Romagna*, series 3, vol. 13 (1895)

Mapamundi: the Catalan Atlas of the Year 1375, ed. C. Grosjean (Zurich, 1978)

Margarido, A., 'La vision de l'autre (Africain et Indien d'Amèrique) dans la Renaissance portugaise' in *L'Humanisme portugais de l'Europe* (Paris, 1984)

Martin da Canal, *Les Estoires de Venise*, ed. A. Limentani (Florence, 1972)

Martini, M., *Novus Atlas Sinensis* (Amsterdam, 1655)

Matthew Paris, *English History (1253–1273)*, trans. J. A. Giles (London, 1852)

Mauro, Fra, *IL Mappamondo di Fra Mauro*, ed. T. Gasparrini Leporace (Rome, 1956)

Mazzatinti, G., *Firenze: Biblioteca Nazionale Centrale (Inventari dei manoscritti delle biblioteche d'Italia*, vol. 8 (Forlì, 1896)

Meiss, M., *French Painting in the Time of Jean de Berry: The Boucicaut Master* (London, 1968)

———. *French Painting in the time of Jean de Berry: The Late Fourteenth Century and the Patronage of the Duke* (London, 1967)

Menache, S., 'Tartars, Jews, Saracens and the Jewish-Mongol "Plot" of 1241', *History*, 263 (1996), 319–42

Ménard, P., 'L'illustration du "Devisement du Monde" de Marco Polo', *Bulletin de la Société Nationale des Antiquaires de France* (1985)

Merchant Culture in Fourteenth Century Venice: The Zibaldone da Canal, trans. and intro. J. E. Dotson (Binghamton, 1994)

Le meraviglie dell'India, ed. G. Tardiola (Rome, 1991)

Meyer, P., *Alexandre le Grand dans la littérature française du Moyen Age* (Geneva, 1970)

Milanese, M., 'La rinascita della geografia dell' Europa (1350–1480)' in *Atti del convegno 'Europa e Mediterraneo tra Medio Evo e prima Età moderna. L'osservatore italiano'*, ed. G. Gensini (Centro de Studi sulla Civiltà del Tardo Medioevo, San Miniato, Collana Studi e Ricerche, vol. 4, 1992)

1274: Année Charnière: Mutations et Continuités (Paris, 1977)

Mirsky, J. (ed.) *The Great Chinese Travellers* (London, 1965)

Molmenti, P., *Venice*, trans. H. F. Brown (London, 1906)

Monaco, L., 'I volgarizzamenti italiani della relazione di Odorico da Pordenone', *Studi mediolatini e volgari*, 26 (1978–9)

'Mongol Atlas' of China by Chu Ssu-Pen and the Kuang-yu-t'u, The, ed. W. Fuchs (Beijing, 1946)

Monmonnier, M., *Drawing the Line: Tales of Maps and Cartocontroversy* (New York, 1995)

Monneret de Villard, U., *Le leggende orientali sui Magi Evangelici* (Vatican, 1952)

———. *Lo studio dell'Islam in Europa nel XII e XIII secolo* (Vatican, 1944)

Monteverdi, A., 'Lingua e letteratura a Venezia nel secolo di Marco Polo' in *Storia della civiltà veneziana*, ed. V. Branca, F. Braudel, vol. 1 (Florence, 1979)

Moore, G., 'La spedizione dei fratelli Vivaldi e nuovi documenti d'archivio', *Atti della Società Ligure di Storia Patria*, n.s., vol. 12 (1972)

Morgan, D., *The Mongols* (Oxford, 1986)

———. *Medieval Persia 1040–1797* (London, 1988)

Morison, S. E., *Columbus Admiral of the Ocean Sea* (Boston, 1942)

———. *The Great Explorers: the European Discovery of America* (New York, 1978)

Morozzo della Rocca, R., 'Catay' in *Miscellenea in onore di R. Cessi*, vol. 1 (Rome, 1958)

———. 'Sulle orme di Polo', *L'Italia che scrive* (October 1954)

Mostra 'L'Asia' nella Cartografia degli Occidentali, ed. T. Gasparrini Leporace (Venice, 1954)

Moule, A. C., *Christians in China before the year 1550* (London, 1930)

———. 'A life of Odoric of Pordenone', *T'oung Pao*, 20 (1921)

———. *Quinsay* (Cambridge, 1957)

Muir, E., *Civic Ritual in Renaissance Venice* (Princeton, 1981)

Müller, A., *De Sinarum Magnaeque Tartariae rebus commentatio alphabetica, et commentariis super M Poli* (Berlin?, 1675?)

Murray, A., 'The Epicureans', in *Intellectuals and Writers in Fourteenth-Century Europe*, ed. P. Boitani and A. Torti (Cambridge, 1986)

Nebenzahl, K., *Maps from the Age of Discovery* (London, 1990)

Needham, J., *The Grand Titration: Science and Society in East and West* (London, 1969)

Needham, J., with Wang Ling, *Science and Civilisation in China*, vol. 3, (Mathematics and the Sciences of the Heavens and the Earth), (Cambridge, 1959)

Nel VII centenario della nascita di Marco Polo, ed. R. Almagià (Venice, 1955)

Niccolò da Casola, *La Guerra d'Attila*, ed. G. Stenardo (Modena, 1941)

Nordenskiöld, A. E., 'The influence of the "Travels of Marco Polo" on Jacopo Gastaldi's Maps of Asia', *Geographical Journal* (April 1899). (Italian version, 'Intorno alla influenza dei "Viaggi di Marco Polo" ', *Rivista Geografica Italiana*, 8, 1901)

———. *Periplus: An Essay on the Early History of Charts and Sailing Directions* (Stockholm, 1897)

Nowell, C. E. 'The historical Prester John', *Speculum*, 28 (1953)

———. 'The Toscanelli letter and Columbus', *Hispanic American Historical Review*, 17 (1937)

Odorico da Pordenone, *Les voyages en Asie du bienheureux frère* ed. H. Cordier (*Recueil de voyages et documents*, vol. 10, Paris, 1891)

———. *Relazione del Viaggio in Oriente e in Cina (1314?–1330)*, ed. Camera di Commercio, Industria, Artigianato e Agricoltura di Pordenone (Pordenone, 1982)

Olbricht, P., *Das Postwesen in China unter der Mongolenherrschaft im 13. und 14. Jahrhundert* (Wiesbaden, 1954)

Olschki, L., *L'Asia di Marco Polo: introduzione alla lettura a allo studio del Milione* (Venice, 1957) (English trans., Berkeley and Los Angeles, 1960)

———. *Guillaume Boucher, A French Artist at the Court of the Khans* (Baltimore, 1946)

———. 'Marco Polo, Dante Alighieri e la cosmografia medievale', in *Oriente Poliano*

———. *Marco Polo's Precursors* (Baltimore, 1943)

———. *Storia letteraria delle scoperte* (Florence, 1937)

O[mant], H., *Livres des Merveilles: Reproduction des 265 miniatures du manuscript français 2810 de la Bibliothèque Nationale* (Paris, 1907)

Oriente Poliano: Studi e conferenze tenute . . . in occasione del VII Centenario della nascita di Marco Polo (Rome, 1957)

Orlandini, G., 'Marco Polo e la sua famiglia', *Archivio Veneto Tridentino*, vol. 9 (1926)

Otto of Freising, *Chronicon*, ed. A. Hofmeister (*S.R.G. in u. sch.*, Hanover and Leipzig, 1912) trans. C. C. Mierow, *The Two Cities* (New York, 1966)

Pächt, P., and Alexander, J. G., *Illuminated Manuscripts in the Bodleian Library Oxford*, vol. 3 (Oxford, 1973)

Parronchi, A., *Studi su la 'dolce' prospectiva* (Milan, 1964)

Pastore Stocchi, P., 'Dioneo e l'orazione di frate Cipolla', *Studi sul Boccaccio*, 10 (1977–8)

———. *Tradizione medievale e gusto umanistico nel 'De montibus' del Boccaccio* (Padua, 1962)

Patch, H. R., *The Other World* (Cambridge, Mass., 1950)

Pauli, P., *Life of Alfred the Great*, trans. B. Thorpe (London, 1853)

Peers, E. Allison, *Ramon Llull: a Biography* (London, 1929)

Pelliot, P., 'Kao-Tch'ang, Qoco, Houo-Tcheou et Qara-Khodja', *Journal Asiatique*, series 10, vol. 19 (1912)

———. *Notes on Marco Polo*, ed. L. Hambis (Paris, 1959–73)

Peng Hai, 'When was Marco Polo in Yangzhou?' (in Chinese), *Lishi Yanjiu* (1980)

Percoraro, C., 'Domenico Silvestri, "De insulis et earum proprietatibus"', *Atti della Accademia di Scienze, lettere e arti di Palermo*, vol. 14 (1953–4)

Pero Tafur, *Andanças e viajes de Pero Tafur por diversas partes del Mundo avidos (1435–39)*, ed. Jimenez de la Espada (*Collecciòn de libros españoles raros e curiosos*, vol. 8, Madrid, 1874)

———. *Travels and Adventures 1435–39*, trans. M. Letts (London, 1926)

Petech, L., 'Les marchands italiens dans l'empire mongol', *Revue Asiatique*, 250 (1962)

Petit, J., 'Un capitaine du règne de Philippe le Bel: Thibault de Chepoy', *Le Moyen Age*, vol. 10 (1897)

Pickford, C. E., 'Miscellaneous French Prose Romances' in *Arthurian Literature in the Middle Ages*, ed. R. S. Loomis (Oxford, 1959)

Phillipe de Mézières, *Le songe du vieil pélerin*, ed. G. W. Coopland (Cambridge, 1969)

Phillips, J. R. S., *The Medieval Expansion of Europe* (Oxford, 1988)

Piccolomini, E. S., see Pius II

Pierre d'Ailly, *Ymago Mundi*, ed. E. Buron (Paris, 1930)

Pius II, *I Commentarii*, ed. L. Totaro (Milan, 1984)

———. *Historia Rerum ubique Gestarum cum locorum descriptione non finita* (Venice, John of Cologne, 1477)

———. *Asiae Europaeque elegantis descriptio* (Cologne, 1531)

Prester John, the Mongols and the Ten Lost Tribes, ed. C. F. Beckingham and B. Hamilton (Aldershot, 1996)

Poggio Bracciolini, *Opera Omnia*, vol. 2 (Lutetiae Parisiorum, 1723; reprinted Turin, 1968)

———. *Historia de varietate de Fortunae*, ed. O. Merisalo (Helsinki, 1993)

———. 'The travels of Nicolò Conti in the East' in *India in the Fifteenth Century*, ed. R. H. Major (London, 1857)

Poggio Bracciolini and Ludovico de Varthema, *Narratives of Eastern Travel by Poggio Bracciolini and Ludovico de Varthema*, trans. J. Winter Jones, revised L. D. Hammond (Cambridge, Mass., 1963)

Porcher, J., *French Miniatures from Illuminated Manuscripts* (London, 1960)

Portugaliae Monumenta Cartographica, ed. A. Cortesão and A. Teixeira da Mota (Lisbon, 1960)

Prati, E. V. L., 'Nuove ricerche su Cristoforo Colombo nella Venezia del tardo Cinquecento: Le historie di Don Fernando', in *L'epopea delle scoperte*, ed. R. Zorzi (Florence, 1994)

Prestwich, M., *Edward I* (London, 1988)

Purchas, S., *Hakluytus Posthumus or Purchas his Pilgrimes* (London, 1906)

Quinn, D. B., 'Columbus and the North: England, Iceland, and Ireland', *William and Mary Quarterly*, vol. 59 (1992)

———. *England and the Discovery of America, 1481–1620* (London, 1973)

———. 'The Italian Renaissance and Columbus', *Renaissance Studies*, 6 (1992)

———. 'John Day and Columbus', *Geographical Journal*, 133 (1967)

Rabelais, F., *Complete Works*, trans. Sir Thomas Urquhart, vol. 2 (London, 1927)

Rabelais, F. *Oeuvres Complètes*, ed. G. Demerson (Paris, 1973)

Raccolta di documenti e studi pubblicati dalla R. Commissione Colombiana pel quarto centenario della scoperta dell'America (Rome, 1892–4)

Rachelwiltz, I. de, *Papal Envoys to the Great Khan* (London, 1971)

———. 'Yeh-lü Ch'u-ts'ai (1189–1243). Buddhist idealist and Confucian Statesmen' in *Confucian Personalities*, ed. A. F. Wright and D. Twitchett (Stanford, 1962)

Ramusio, G. B., *Navigazioni e riaggi*, ed. M. Milanesi (Turin, 1978–85)

Randles, W. G. L., *De la terre plate au globe terrestre* (Paris, 1980)

Ravenstein, E. G., *Martin Behaim: His Life and Globe* (London, 1908)

Reames, S. L., *The Legenda Aurea: A Reexamination of its Paradoxical History* (London, 1985)

Réau, L., *Iconographie de l'Art chrétien*, 3 vols (Paris, 1955–9)

Reichert, F. E., *Begegnungen mit China: Die Entdeckung Ostasiens im Mittelalter* (Sigmaringen, 1992)

———. 'Columbus und Marco Polo – Asien in America zur Literaturgeschichte der Entdeckungen', *Zeitschrift für Historische Forschung*, vol. 15 (1988)

Renzi, L., 'Il francese come lingua letteraria e il franco-lombardo', in *Storia della cultura veneta*

Reynolds, S., 'Social mentalities and the case of medieval scepticism', *Transactions of the Royal Historical Society*, series 6, vol. 1 (1991)

Ricci, M., and N. Trigault, *Histoire de l'expédition chrétienne au royaume de la Chine 1582–1610,* ed. J. Shis, G. Bessiere, J. Dehergne (n.p., 1978)

Richard, J., 'La conversion de Berke et les débuts de l'Islamisation de la Horde d'Or', *Revue des études islamiques* (1967)

———. *Croisés, missionnaires et voyageurs* (London, 1983)

———. 'Le début des relations entre la papauté et les Mongols de Perse', *Journal Asiatique*, 237 (1949)

———. 'Essor et déclin de l'Eglise catholique de Chine au XIVe siècle' in his *Orient et Occident*

———. 'L'extrême-orient légendaire au Moyen Age: Roi David et Prêtre Jean', *Annales d'Ethiopie*, vol. 2 (1957)

———. 'La mission en Europe de Rabbau Çauma et l'union des églises', in his *Orient et Occident au Moyen Age:*

———. 'Les missionaires latins dans l' Inde au XIVe siècle', *Studi Veneziani*, vol. 12 (1970)

———. 'Les Mongols et l'Occident: deux siècles de contacts' in *1274, Anné charnière*

———. 'Les navigations des occidentaux sur l'Océan Indien et la Mer caspienne (XIIe–XIVe siècles), in *Orient et Occident*

———. 'Isol le Pisan: Un aventurier franc gouverneur d'une province mongole?', in *Orient et Occident*

———. *Orient et Occident au Moyen Age: contacts et relations (XIIe–XVe siècles),* (London, 1976)

———. *La Papauté et les missions d'Orient au Moyen Age (XIIIe–XVe siècles)* (Rome, 1977)

———. 'Les premiers missionaires latins en Ethiopie (XIIe–XIVe siècles)' in his *Orient et Occident*, XXIV

———. *Les récits des voyages et des pèlerinages* (Brepols, 1981)

———. *Les relations entre l'Orient et l'Occident du Moyen Age* (London, 1977)

Richard, J., 'La vogue de l'Orient dans la littérature occidentale du Moyen Age', in his *Les relations entre l'Orient et l'Occident*

Richter, M., *Geraldus Cambrensis: The Growth of the Welsh Nation* (Aberystwyth, 1976)

Rieger, D., 'Marco Polo und Rustichello da Pisa. Der Reisende und sein Erzähler', *Reise und Reiseliteratur in der Frühen Neuzeit*, ed. X. von Ertzdorff and D. Neukirch (Amsterdam, 1992)

Ristoro d'Arezzo, *La composizione del Mondo colle sue cascioni*, ed. A. Morino (Florence, 1976)

Rockhill, W. W., 'Notes on the relations and trade of China with the Eastern Archipelago and the Coast of the Indian Ocean during the Fourteenth Century. Pt.i.', *T'oung Pao*, 15 (1914)

Roger, B., *Brief Summe of Geographie*, ed. E. G. R. Taylor (London, 1932)

Roger Bacon: Essays, ed. A. G. Little (Oxford, 1914)

Roger Bacon, *The Opus Majus*, ed. J. H. Bridges (Oxford, 1897)

Rogers, F. M., *The Travels of the Infante Dom Pedro of Portugal* (Cambridge, Mass., 1961)

Romana Camaroto, F., 'Odorico da Pordenone', *La Rassegna della letteratura italiana* (1991)

Roncaglia, R., 'La Letteratura franco-veneta' in *Storia di letteratura italiana*, ed. E. Cecchi and N. Sapegno, vol. 2, *Il Trecento* (Milan, 1965)

Roncière, M. de la, and Mollat du Jourdin, M., *Les Portulans Cartes marines du XIIIᵉ au XVIIᵉ siècle* (Fribourg, 1984)

Ross, D. J. A., *Alexander historiatus: A Guide to Medieval Illustrated Alexander Literature* (London, 1963)

———. 'Methods of Book Production in a XIVth Century French Miscellany, London B.M. Ms. Royal 19 D.1', *Scriptorium*, 6 (1952)

Rossabi, M 'The Muslims in the Early Yüan Dynasty' in *China under Mongol Rule*, ed. J. D. Langlois (Princeton, 1981)

———. *Khubilai Khan: His Life and Times* (London, 1988)

———. 'The reign of Khubilai Khan' in *The Cambridge History of China*, vol. 6: *Alien Regimes and Border States 907–1368*, ed. H. Franke and D. Twitchett (Cambridge, 1994)

———. *Voyager from Xanadu: Rabban Sauma and the First Journey from China to the West* (London, 1992)

Rouleau, F. A., 'The Yangchow Latin tombstone as a landmark of medieval Christianity', *Harvard Journal of Asiatic Studies*, 17 (1954)

Rubin, P., 'What men saw: Vasari's Life of Leonardo da Vinci and the Image of the Renaissance Artist', *Art History*, 13 (1990)

Ruy González de Clavijo, *Embajada a Tamorlan*, ed. F. Lopes Estra (Madrid, 1943)

———. *Embassy to Tamberlane*, ed. and trans. G. Le Strange (London, 1925)

Ryan, J. D., 'European travelers before Columbus: The fourteenth-century's discovery of India', *Catholic Historical Review*, 79 (1993)

Said, E. W., *Orientalism* (Harmondsworth, 1995)

Salimbene de Adam, *Cronica*, ed. G. Scalia (Bari, 1966)

Salzmann, L. F., *Medieval Byways* (London, 1913)

Sanz, C., *El Libro de Marco Polo: Notas historicas y biblograficas*, (Madrid, 1959)

Saunders, J. J., *The History of the Mongol Conquests* (London, 1971)

Saunders, J. J. 'Matthew Paris and the Mongols', *Essays in Medieval History Presented to Bertie Wilkinson*, ed. T. A. Sandquist and M. R. Powicke (Toronto, 1969)

Schein, S., 'Gesta Dei per Mongolos 1300: the Genesis of a non-event', *English Historical Review*, 94 (1979)

Schmidt, T. C., 'Die Entdeckung des Ostens und der Humanismus: Niccolò de' Conti und Poggio Bracciolinis "Historia de Varietate Fortunae"', *Mitteilungen des Instituts für Österreichische Geschichtsforschung*, 103 (1995)

Segre, C., 'Marco Polo, Filologia e industria culturale' in C. Segre, G. Ronchi, M. Milanesi, *Avventure del 'Milione'* (Parma, 1983)

Semans, S. E., 'Mapping the Unknown: Jesuit Cartography in China 1583–1773', Ph. D. diss., University of California, Berkeley, 1987

Serrano y Sanz, M., 'El Archivo Colombino de la Cartuja de las Cuevas', *Bóletin de la R. Academia de la Historia*, 96 (1930)

Seymour, M. C., *Sir John Mandeville* (Aldershot, 1993)

Shinobu Iwamura, *Manuscripts and Printed Editions of Marco Polo's Travels* (Tokyo, 1949)

Shirley, R. W., *The Mapping of the World: Early Printed World Maps 1472–1700* (London, 1984)

Simon de Saint Quentin, *Histoire des Tartares*, ed. J. Richard (Paris, 1965)

Sinica Franciscana, ed. A. van den Wyngaert (Quaracchi, 1929)

Sinor, D., *Inner Asia and its Contacts with Medieval Europe* (London, 1977)

——. 'The Mongols and Western Europe' in *A History of the Crusades*, ed. K. M. Setton, vol. 3: *The Fourteenth and Fifteenth Centuries*, ed. H. W. Hazard (London, 1975)

——. 'Un voyageur du treizième siècle: le Dominicain Julien de Hongrie', *Bulletin of the School of Oriental and African Studies*, 14 (1952)

Skelton, R. A., *Explorers' Maps: Chapters in the Cartographic Record of Geographical Discovery* (London, 1970)

Skelton, R. A., Marston, T. E., and Painter, G. D., *The Vinland Map and the Tartar Relation* (London, 1965)

Slessarev, V., *Prester John, the Letter and the Legend* (Minneapolis, 1959)

Smith, R. J., *Chinese Maps* (Hong Kong, 1996)

Sociétés et compagnies de commerce en Orient et dans l'Océan indien, ed. M. Mollat (Paris, 1970)

Southern, R., *Western Views of Islam in the Middle Ages* (Cambridge, Mass., 1962)

Spuler, B., 'Le Christianisme chez les Mongols aux XIIIe et XIVe siècles' in *1274: Année charnière*

Starn, R., *Contrary Commonwealth: The Theme of Exile in Medieval and Renaissance Italy* (London, 1982)

Stevenson, E. L., *Genoese World Map 1457. Facsimile and Critical Text* (New York, 1912)

Stinger, C. L., *Humanism and the Church Fathers: Ambrogio Traversari (1386–1439) and Christian Antiquity in the Italian Renaissance* (Albany, 1977)

Storia della cultura veneta, ed. G. Arnaldi, 2 vols (Vicenza, 1976)

Streicher, F., 'Die Kolumbus-Originale. Eine paläographische Studie', *Gesammelte Aufsätze zur Kulturgeschichte Spaniens: Spanische Forschungen der Görresgesellschaft*, 1 (1928)

Stussi, A., 'Un testamento volgare scritto in Persia nel 1263', *L'Italia dialettale*, n.s., vol. 11 (1962)

————. *Zibaldone manoscritto mercantile del sec. XIV* (Venice, 1967)

Surdich, F., 'Gli esploratori genovesi del period medievale', *Studi di Storia delle esplorazioni*, vol. 1 (1978)

————. 'Conti, Niccolò de', *Dizionario Biografico Italiano*, vol. 25 (1983)

Terrarossa, V., *Riflessioni geografiche circa le terre incognite* (Padua, 1686)

Testa, G. C., 'Bozza per un censimento dei manoscritti odoricioni' in *Odorico da Pordenone e la Cina; atti del convegno storico internazionale. Pordenone 28–29 maggio 1982*, ed. G. Melis (Pordenone, 1983)

Thiriet, F., *La Roumanie vénetienne au Moyen Age* (Paris, 1959)

Thomas, A. (ed.) *Entrée d'Espagne* (Paris, 1913)

Thomas, E., *Chronicles of the Pathán Kings of Delhi* (London, 1871)

Thorau, P., *The Lion of Egypt: Sultan Baybars I and the Near East in the Thirteenth Century*, trans. P. M. Holt (London, 1992)

Thorndike, L., *A History of Magic and Experimental Science* (New York, 1923–41)

————. 'Sanitation, baths, and street-cleaning in the Renaissance', *Speculum*, 3 (1928)

Throop, P. A., *Criticism of the Crusade* (Amsterdam, 1940)

Times Atlas of World Exploration, ed. F. Fernández-Armesto (London, 1991)

Tolan, J., 'Anti-hagiography: Embrico of Mainz's *Vita Mahumeti*', *Journal of Medieval History*, 22 (1996)

Traselli, C., 'Un italiano in Etiopa nel XV secolo: Pietro Rombulo da Messina', *Rassegna di Studi Etiopici*, vol. 1 (1941)

Trauzettel, R., 'Die Yüan-Dynastie' in *Die Mongolen*, ed. M. Weiers (Darmstadt, 1986)

Tucci, U., 'I primi viaggiatori e l'opera di Marco Polo' in *Storia della cultura veneta*, ed. G. Folena, vol. 1 (Vicenza, 1976)

Uzielli, G., *Paolo dal Pozzo Toscanelli: Iniziatore della scoperta d'America* (Florence, 1892)

————. *La vita e i tempi di Paolo dal Pozzo Toscanelli (Raccolta di Documenti e Studi pubblicati dalla R. Commissione Colombiniana*, vol. 5, pt 1, Rome, 1894)

Vansteenberghe, E., *Le cardinal Nicholas de Cues 1401–1464* (Paris 1920; reprinted Frankfurt am Main, 1965)

Vasoli, V., 'Profilo di un papa umanista: Tommaso Parentucelli', in his *Studi sulla cultura del Rinascimento* (Manduria, 1968)

Vaughan, R., *Chronicles of Matthew Paris* (Cambridge, 1958)

Viaggi in Persia, India e Giava. Di Niccolò Conti, Girolamo Adorno, e Girolamo da Santo Stefano, ed. M. Longhena (Milan, 1929)

Vicentini, E., 'Il Milione di Marco Polo come portolano', *Italica*, 71:2 (1994)

Vietor, A. O., 'A pre-Columbian map of the world, circa 1489', *Yale University Library Gazette*, 37 (1963) (reprinted in *Imago Mundi*, vol. 17 [1963])

Vignaud, H., *Toscanelli and Columbus* (London, 1902)

Vigneras, L.-A., 'New Light on the 1497 Cabot Voyage to America', *Hispanic American Historical Review*, 36 (1956)

Geoffroy de Villehardouin, Memoirs of the Crusades by Villehardouin and de Joinville, trans. F. Marzialis (London, 1908)

Vinaver E., *The Rise of Romance* (Oxford, 1971)

The Vinland Map and the Tartar Relation, ed. R. A. Skelton, T. E. Marston, G. D. Painter (London, 1965)

Viscardi, A., 'Arthurian influences in Italian Literature 1200–1500' in *Arthurian Literature in the Middle Ages*, ed. R. S. Loomis (Oxford, 1959)

———. *Letteratura Franco-Italiana* (Modena, 1941)

Waldron, A. N., 'The problem of the Great Wall', *Harvard Journal of Asiatic Studies*, 42 (1983)

Waley, A., *The Travels of an Alchemist. The Journey of the Taoist Ch'ang-ch'un* (London, 1931)

Wallis, H. G., 'The strange case of the Vinland Map; a symposium', *Geographical Journal*, 140 (1974)

Washburn, W. F., 'Japan on early European maps', *Pacific Historical Review*, 21 (1952)

Watts, P. M., *Nicholas Cusanus: A Fifteenth-Century Vision of Man* (Leiden, 1982)

Wehr, B., 'A propos de la genèse du "Devisement dou Monde" de Marco Polo', *Le passage à l'écrit des langues romanes*, ed. M. Selig, B. Frank, J. Hartmann, *Scripta Oralia*, vol. 46 (Tübingen, 1993)

Weiers, M., *Die Mongolen* (Darmstadt, 1986)

Whitfield, P., *New Found Lands: Maps in the History of Exploration* (London, 1998)

Wieser, F. V., *Die Weltkarte des Albertin de Virga* (Innsbruck, 1912)

William of Rubruck, see Guillaume de Rubruck

William of Tripoli, *De statu Saracenorum et Mahomete pseudopropheta eorum et eorum lege et fide*, in H. Prutz, *Kulturgeschichte der Kreuzzüge* (Berlin, 1883)

Williamson, J. A., *The Cabot Voyages and Bristol Discovery under Henry VII* (Cambridge, 1962)

Winter, H., 'A circular map in a Ptolemaic MS', *Imago Mundi*, vol. 10 (1953)

Wittkower R., 'Marco Polo and the pictorial tradition of the marvels of the East', in *Oriente Poliano*

———. 'Marvels of the East: A Study in the History of Monsters', *Journal of the Warburg and Courtauld Institutes*, 5 (1942)

Wood, F., *Did Marco Polo go to China?* (London, 1995)

Woodhouse, C. M., *George Gemistos Plethon: The Last of the Hellenes* (Oxford, 1986)

Wright, J. K., *The Geographical Lore of the Time of the Crusades* (New York, 1925; reprinted London, 1965)

———. *Leardo Map of the World* (New York, 1928)

Yee, C. D. K., 'Cartography in China' in *The History of Cartography*, vol, 2, pt 2, *Cartography in the Traditional East and Southeast Asian Societies*, ed. J. B. Harley and D. Woodward (London, 1994)

Yoeli, P., 'Abraham and Yehuda Cresques and the Catalan Atlas', *Cartographic Journal*, 7 (1970)

Yule, H., *Cathay and the Way Thither*, 2nd edn revised by H. Cordier, 3 vols (London, Hakluyt, 1915; photo-reproduction, New York, 1967)

Zaccagnini, G., 'Francesco Pipino, traduttore del "Milione", cronista e viaggiatore in Oriente nel secolo XIV', *Atti e memorie della R. Deputazione di storia patria per l'Emilia e la Romagna*, vol. 1 (1935–6)

Zarncke, F., 'Der Priester Johannes', *Abhandlungen der philologisch-historischen Classe der Königlich Sächsischen Gesellschaft der Wissenschaft*, vol. 7 (1879)

Zelzer, K. (ed.) *Die ältesten lateinischen Thomasakten* (Berlin, 1977)

Zurla, P., *Di Marco Polo e degli altri viaggiatori veneziani più illustri* (Venice, 1818–9)

Index

Persons born before 1500 are listed under their first names.

HOMI=
NES HAC LEGE
SVNT GENERATI,
QVI TVERENTVR
ILLVM GLOBVM,
QVEM IN HOC TEM=
PLO MEDIVM VI=
DES, QVAE TER=
RA DICITVR.
Cicero.

HOC
EST PVNCTVM,
QVOD INTER TOT
GENTES FERRO
ET IGNI DIVIDI=
TVR, O QVAM RIDI=
CVLI SVNT MOR=
TALIVM TER=
MINI?
Seneca.

QVID EI POTEST VIDERI MAGN
NITAS OMNIS, TOTIVSQVE MVN

TERRA SEPT

CIRCVLVS ARCTICVS.

AMERICA SIVE IN-
DIA NOVA. Ao 1492. a Christophoro
Colombo nomine regis Castellæ primum detecta.

ANIAN
regnum.

Noua
Franç-
cia.

Chilaga

Tolm

Totronte ac

Calicuas

Marata

Jagil.

Flori-
da.

QVIVIRA regnum.

TROPICVS CANCRI

Archipelago di

S. Lazaro

CIRCVLVS AEQVINOCTIALIS

Caribana

Quito

Peru.

Amazones.

Brasil.

Noua Guinea
que sit insula
nec ne certum.

Islas de Salomon.

MAR DEL ZVR.

Insulæ
incognitæ.

TROPICVS CAPRICORNI

MAR
PACIFICO.

Chica.

Hanc continentem
Australem nonnulli
Magellanicam regionem ab
eius inventore nuncupant.

Archipelago
de las islas.

CIRCVLVS ANTARCTICVS.

Terra del Fuego.

TERRA AVSTRA